SOCIETY OF SOUTHWEST ARCHIVISTS GUIDE TO ARCHIVAL AND MANUSCRIPT REPOSITORIES

Kathryn E. Stallard, General Editor
Southwestern University
Georgetown, Texas

Jesús F. de la Teja, Technical Editor
Southwest Texas State University
San Marcos, Texas

State Editors

Arizona
Jean Nudd
Department of Library, Archives and Public Records
Phoenix, Arizona

Arkansas
Wendy Richter
Ouachita Baptist University
Arkadelphia, Arkansas

Louisiana
Alfred E. Lemmon
Historic New Orleans Collection
New Orleans, Louisiana

New Mexico
Kathlene Ferris
University of New Mexico
Albuquerque, New Mexico

Oklahoma
John Caldwell
University of Oklahoma
Norman, Oklahoma

Texas (A-G)
Casey Greene
Rosenberg Library
Galveston, Texas

Texas (H-Z, El Paso)
Ann Massmann
University of Texas at El Paso
El Paso, Texas

©1993 SOCIETY OF SOUTHWEST ARCHIVISTS
ISBN: 0-9640169-0-7

PREFACE

On May 5, 1972, seven archivists from various institutions in the Southwestern United States met in Arlington, Texas to discuss the needs of archives, manuscript repositories, and records centers throughout the Southwest region. They concluded that the Southwest needed its own professional organization for people and institutions concerned with preserving our documentary heritage. Through their efforts, the Society of Southwest Archvists was formed.

Today, the Society of Southwest Archivists is an effective and dynamic organization. It encourages sound principles and standards for preserving records and other historical documents; promotes continuing education for archivists, records managers, and custodians of personal papers; maintains and strengthens relations with colleagues in allied disciplines; and provides a forum for discussing common interests.

In 1990, SSA's Executive Board along with President Robert S. Martin approved an ambitious proposal by Frank de la Teja to compile and publish a regional directory. As a Society, we gratefully acknowledge the leadership provided by Frank de la Teja and Kathryn Stallard, General Editor, and especially the State Editors who accomplished the real gathering of information. Over the next four years and with the support of succeeding Presidents, Toby Murray (University of Tulsa), Ed Oetting (Arizona State University) and Robert Tissing (Lyndon Baines Johnson Library), the project became a reality.

In publishing the *Society of Southwest Archivists Guide to Archival and Manuscript Repositories*, the Society has broadened its efforts to educate both archivists and non-archivists regarding the rich and sometimes incredible archival resources in the Southwest.

Dawn Letson
Texas Woman's University
President, The Society of Southwest Archivists

ACKNOWLEDGEMENTS

The editors would like to thank their respective institutions for their support during the project. The guide would not have been possible without this assistance, which ranged from allowing use of photocopying machines and telephones to release time and staff assistance.

CONTENTS

Preface iii
Acknowledgements iv
Introduction vi

States
   Arizona 1
   Arkansas 49
   Louisiana 71
   New Mexico 112
   Oklahoma 140
   Texas 162

Special Indexes
   Facilities/Equipment/Preservation 249
   Software, OPACs, Bibliographic Utilities 249
   Special Services/Programs 249
   Specialized Collection Formats 250
   Specialized Staff. 250

Subject Index 251
Questionnaire 257

INTRODUCTION

This guide is the Society of Southwest Archivists' first directory to archives, libraries, museums, and other institutions holding archival materials and manuscripts in the six state region that comprises the Society's membership. Although canvassing was limited to Arizona, Arkansas, Louisiana, New Mexico, Oklahoma, and Texas, membership in the Society was not a prerequisite for inclusion in the directory.

Entries for institutions include the following information: name of institution, address, telephone and fax numbers, name of contact person, type of institution, hours of operation, access and service information, and collection information (primary focus, main topics, inclusive dates, formats, description). In addition, the directory is designed to give archivists and those entrusted with the care of historical materials access to professional information that may be useful for institutional planning and professional development. To this end, users will also find information concerning the following: computerized finding aids, software, special services and programs (e.g. exhibits, newsletters, tours), facilities and equipment (e.g. temperature and humidity controls, disaster preparedness plans, preservation facilities), acquisitions reporting, staffing, institutional support for professional development, and patron use statistics. While this information is generally useful for institutional planning and professional development, it should also have specific practical value since it will enable archivists and others to identify and consult experienced colleagues, whether designing a disaster preparedness plan or solving a software problem.

PROJECT HISTORY AND METHODOLOGY

The directory project, initiated by the Society's publications chairman at the time, Frank de la Teja, began in October 1990 with the appointment of a general editor and 7 state editors. By June of 1991 a questionnaire had been designed, and state editors had almost completed their task of constructing comprehensive (excluding local government entities) mailing lists for institutions that might have relevant holdings. At the same time, the Society's board of directors met and requested that the project scale back in order to reduce mailing/printing costs. Consequently, the mailing list was reduced from approximately 2500 addresses to approximately 1500. Many smaller public libraries, many art centers, most military base libraries, some newspaper and medical libraries, some business libraries, some museums and historical sites, all zoos, and all of the Texas County Historical Commissioners were dropped from the mailing list. Except for zoos and the Texas County Historical Commissioners, decisions were generally made on a case by case basis, based on the probability that the institution had relevant materials. New Mexico and Arizona editors, because of their states' particular demographics, were able to canvas public libraries in cities with smaller populations than other states.

Questionnaires were mailed to the final 1500 institutions in early 1992. The appropriate state editor entered the information gathered from each institution into a 57 field Word Perfect document or an ASCII text, depending on available software/hardware. Throughout 1992 and early 1993 data entry and follow-up continued. Financial considerations generally limited second mailings only to institutions known to have archival or manuscript holdings.

The 57 field versions of the entries were edited into paragraph format, paragraph headings inserted, and index terms were edited for uniformity. In mid-summer 1993, state editors received drafts of the near-final versions for comparison to the original data. Final editorial revisions were completed during the fall of 1993.

state editors received drafts of the near-final versions for comparison to the original data. Final editorial revisions were completed during the fall of 1993.

The number of final entries totaled 451, excluding "see" references to institutions that did not respond to the Society's questionnaire but did to the National Historical Publications and Records Commission's (NHPRC) *Directory of Archives and Manuscript Repositories in the United States*, (National Historical Publications and Records Commission. 2nd edition. Phoenix: Oryx Press, 1988). The entries for the Society's directory often cover institutions different from the 303 institutions included in NHPRC's reporting for the same six states. For example, the Society's directory has 51 entries for New Mexico compared to NHPRC's 35. Of NHPRC's New Mexico 35 entries, 22 are in the NHPRC directory but not in the Society's, except for a "see" reference directing users to NHPRC's guide. Consequently, users will have the most complete coverage for a state if they consult both directories.

ORGANIZATION AND INDEXES

Entries are arranged alphabetically, first by state, then by city, and finally by name of institution within each city. A separate index at the back of the directory provides an alphabetical list of entries by name of institutions. Other indexes furnish access to subjects, collection formats (e.g. photographs, maps, oral histories, etc.), computerized finding aids/software, special services/programs (e.g. exhibits, tours, newsletter, etc.), and facilities/equipment/preservation (e.g. temperature and humidity controls, disaster preparedness plans, etc.).

The subject index was created by applying WordPerfect's indexing feature to the questionnaire category "main topic(s) of holdings." While most terms were used as received, some were edited for uniformity. For example, entries for "oil industry" were changed to "petroleum industry."

When an institution is also covered by the NHPRC *Directory of Archives and Manuscript Repositories in the United States*, the NHPRC number (e.g. NHPRC AZ500-88) will be listed at the end of the entry. The directory provides "see" references consisting of the institution's name and the NHPRC number for collections that responded to NHPRC but not to the Society. "See" references were added even for institutions where NHPRC notes "questionnaire not returned" because useful bibliographic references are sometimes given even though there is no other information.

SOURCES

All state editors, with noted exceptions, consulted the following sources in constructing their respective survey lists:

National Historical Publications and Records Commission. *Directory of Archives and Manuscript Repositories in the United States*. 2nd edition. Phoenix: Oryx Press, 1988.

Society of Southwest Archivists. *Membership Directory*. 1990/91.

American Library Directory, 1989-90. New York: R.R. Bowker, 1989. (Louisiana entries based on 1986 edition; Arkansas on 1990; Arizona and New Mexico entries based on library directories specifically relevant to their states--see below.))

American Association of Museums. *The Official Museum Directory, 1991.* New York: Macmillan Directory Division, 1991. (Texas entries for cities A-G are based on the 1989 edition; Louisiana entries are based on the 1990 edition; Arizona, Arkansas, New Mexico and Oklahoma editors used museum directories specifically relevant to their states--see below.)

Wheeler, Mary Bray, editor. *Directory of Historical Associations in the United States and Canada.* Nashville: AASLH Press, 1990. Texas entries for cities A-G are based on the 1986 edition; Louisiana, New Mexico, and Arkansas editors used directories relevant to their respective states--see below.)

Society of American Archivists. *Directory of Business Archives in the United States and Canada.* 1990.

In addition, state editors consulted the following more specific guides and directories for their respective states.

Arizona

Arizona Library Directory. Phoenix: Department of Library, Archives, and Public Records. State of Arizona, 1991.

Arizona Museum Association. Mailing List. 1991.

Official Directory Arizona Historical Museums and Related Cultural Organizations. Tucson: Arizona Historical Society, 1990-91.

Arkansas

Arkansas Department of Parks and Tourism. "Museums." [1991].

Arkansas Department of Parks and Tourism. "Museums and Historical Sites." [1991].

Arkansas Historical Association. "List of County and Local Historical Societies." [1991].

Louisiana

Directory of Louisiana Archives. Friends of the Archives of Louisiana, 1987.

Directory of Louisiana Museum and Historic Sites. Baton Rouge: Louisiana Association of Museums, n.d.

Tucker, Susan. *The New Orleans Guide to Collections on Women.* New Orleans: Newcomb College of Tulane University, 1989.

New Mexico

Directory of Special Libraries and Collections in New Mexico. Albuquerque: Special Libraries Association, Rio Grande Chapter, 1990.

New Mexico Directory of Hispanic Culture. Albuquerque: Hispanic Culture Foundation, 1990.

New Mexico Library Directory. Santa Fe: New Mexico State Library, 1991.

Oklahoma

Blessing, Patrick J. *Oklahoma Records and Archives.* Tulsa: University of Tulsa, 1978.

Directory of Oklahoma. Oklahoma City: Oklahoma State Election Board, University of Oklahoma Department of Libraries, (1973) 1985.

Hunt, David C. *Guide to Oklahoma Museums.* Norman: University of Oklahoma Press, 1981.

Texas (Cities A-G)

Directory of Special Libraries and Information Centers in Texas, 1985. Austin: Texas State Library, Library Development Division, 1987.

Filby, P. William, comp. *Directory of American Libraries with Genealogy of Local History Collections.* Wilmington, Delaware: Scholarly Resources, Inc., 1988.

Texas (El Paso, H-Z)

Directory of Special Libraries and Information Centers in Texas, 1985. Austin: Texas State Library, Library Development Division, 1987.

Tyler, Paula Eyrich, and Ronnie C. Tyler. *Texas Museums: A Guidebook.* Austin: University of Texas Press, 1983.

FUTURE EDITIONS OF THE GUIDE

The volunteer nature of the project and the limited financial resources of the Society dictated both the form and content of the Directory, but it is hoped that this is only the first edition of the Society's *Guide to Archival and Manuscript Holdings*. Future editions should be able to improve and expand the present edition, adding e-mail addresses and electronic records data, expanding subject indexes, including more institutions, and perhaps adding information concerning the history of states' records. If readers' institutions are not included in this edition or if they know of an institution that was not included, please remove and complete the questionnaire at the very end of the guide and mail or fax it to:

> Kathryn E. Stallard
> Senior Archivist
> John Tower Library and Archives
> Southwestern University
> Georgetown, TX 78628
> FAX: 512/863-1155

ARIZONA

Superstition Mountain Historical Society **TEL**: (602) 983-4888
P.O. Box 3845
Apache Junction, Arizona 85217

REPORTED BY: Gregory Davis, Director of Research, Acquisitions and Archives
TYPE OF INSTITUTION: archives, historical society, library, museum (private historical society)

HOURS: Tu-Su 10-4:30
ACCESS: public access by appointment only (Archives)
SERVICES: in-person, mail, phone, photocopies
RESTRICTIONS: limited personnel

PRIMARY COLLECTION FOCUS: Superstition Mountains
    Superstition Mountains, AZ (local history)
    Lost Dutchman's Mines
    military history
    mining
    ranching
    Native Americans
    Apache Trail
    folklore

COLLECTION FORMATS: manuscript collections, institution's records, books, pamphlets, films, government records, photographs, maps, oral histories, souvenirs, curios
COLLECTION ACCESS: some by card catalog, some by computer finding aids (used by staff), some not described
ACQUISITION REPORTED TO: Superstition Mountain Journal
STAFF (FTE): 1 administrative, 11 board members, 10 volunteers
SPECIAL SERVICES/PROGRAMS: exhibits, tours, newsletter, fund raising, lectures
FACILITIES/EQUIPMENT/PRESERVATION: fire detection controls, fire extinguishing system
PATRON USE STATISTICS: 25 in-house patrons, 30 telephone, 50 mail reference requests

---

St. David Arizona Family History Center **TEL**: (602) 586-2855
Stake Center, Pomerene Road
Box 2288
Benson, Arizona 85602

REPORTED BY: Joanne Kartchner, Director
TYPE OF INSTITUTION: Latter Day Saints Family History Center (religious)

HOURS: Tu 10am-7pm; W 6-8:30pm; Th 10am-8:30pm; Sa 10-4
ACCESS: open to general public
SERVICES: in-person, mail, phone, photocopies, microform copies, computer print-outs

PRIMARY COLLECTION FOCUS: genealogy
    genealogy
    St. David, AZ
    Pomerene, AZ
    Benson, AZ
    pioneers
    Latter Day Saints--membership records
    Mormons

COLLECTION FORMATS: manuscript collections, books, pamphlets, microforms, photographs
COLLECTION ACCESS: card catalog

STAFF FTE: 1 administrative, 20 volunteers

San Pedro Valley Arts and Historical Society
180 S. San Pedro
Box 1090
Benson, Arizona 85602

TEL: (602) 586-3070

REPORTED BY: [not listed]
TYPE OF INSTITUTION: museum, old fashioned store (private)

HOURS: Tu-F 10-4; Sa 10-2
ACCESS: open to general public
SERVICES: [not reported]

PRIMARY COLLECTION FOCUS: San Pedro Valley
    San Pedro Valley, AZ (local history)

COLLECTION FORMATS: institution's records, books, photographs, maps, oral histories, artifacts
COLLECTION ACCESS: some card catalog, some not described
STAFF FTE: volunteer
INSTITUTIONAL SUPPORT FOR PROFESSIONAL DEVELOPMENT: payment of dues
SPECIAL SERVICES/PROGRAMS: exhibits, newsletter, fund raising
FACILITIES/EQUIPMENT/PRESERVATION: fire extinguishing system

Bisbee Mining and Historical Museum, Lemuel Shattuck Memorial Library
5 Copper Queen Plaza
P.O. Box 14
Bisbee, Arizona 85603

TEL: (602) 432-7071

REPORTED BY: Boyd Nicholl, Curator of Archives
TYPE OF INSTITUTION: archives, historical society, library, museum (county, local, city, special)

HOURS: daily 10-4, except Christmas
ACCESS: open to general public
SERVICES: in-person, mail, phone, fee for reference, photocopies, photographs

PRIMARY COLLECTION FOCUS: Bisbee, Arizona, Cochise County, Arizona
    Bisbee, AZ (local history)
    Cochise County, AZ (local history)
    Mexico, Northern Sonora

INCLUSIVE DATES: 1877-1975
COLLECTION FORMATS: manuscript collections, institution's records, books, pamphlets, films, government
    records, photographs, maps, oral histories
COLLECTION ACCESS: card catalog, registers/inventories, computerized finding aids (used by staff)
SOFTWARE/SYSTEM: Apple Works
STAFF FTE: 1 administrative, 1 photo curator, volunteers, 1 clerical
INSTITUTIONAL SUPPORT FOR PROFESSIONAL DEVELOPMENT: reimbursement, use of facilities, use of
    clerical staff
SPECIAL SERVICES/PROGRAMS: exhibits, newsletter, lectures
FACILITIES/EQUIPMENT/PRESERVATION: fire detection controls, fire extinguishing system
PATRON USE STATISTICS: 200 in-house patrons, 100 telephone, 120 mail reference requests

Fort Verde State Historic Park
Holloman Street
P.O. Box 397
Camp Verde, Arizona 86322

TEL: (602) 567-3275
FAX: (602) 567-4036

REPORTED BY: Nora Graf, Park Ranger
TYPE OF INSTITUTION: historic park (state)

HOURS: M-Su 8-5, closed Christmas
ACCESS: public access by appointment only
SERVICES: in-person reference (limited), mail reference, phone reference, fee for reference and photocopies (large amount), photograph reproductions

PRIMARY COLLECTION FOCUS: military history
    Verde Valley
    military history
    Indian wars

INCLUSIVE DATES: 1865-1890, 1970-present
COLLECTION FORMATS: manuscript collections, books, institution's records, photographs, maps, photocopies from other institutions
COLLECTION ACCESS: computerized (used by staff)
STAFF FTE: 1 park manager, 3 park rangers
INSTITUTIONAL SUPPORT FOR PROFESSIONAL DEVELOPMENT: tuition, dues, reimbursement, workshops, mailings, telephone, facilities, use of clerical staff
FACILITIES/EQUIPMENT/PRESERVATION: temperature controls (limited), fire extinguishing system
PATRON USE STATISTICS: user statistics not kept

NHPRC AZ75-240

Casa Grande Valley Historical Society
110 W. Florence Blvd.
Casa Grande, Arizona 85222

TEL: (602) 836-2223

REPORTED BY: Tim Nimz, Director
TYPE OF INSTITUTION: historical society, museum (county/local)

HOURS: M-F 9-12
ACCESS: open to general public
SERVICES: in-person, mail, phone, photocopies, photographs

PRIMARY COLLECTION FOCUS: history and prehistory of Casa Grande Valley
    Casa Grande Valley, AZ (local history)
    business history
    Casa Grand Valley Historical Society (records)
    agriculture
    cotton
    irrigation
    historic preservation
    education

COLLECTION FORMATS: manuscript collections, institution's records, 1500 books, pamphlets, 1500 photographs, 100 maps, 100 oral histories
COLLECTION ACCESS: card catalog
STAFF FTE: .5 administrative, .5 volunteer
INSTITUTIONAL SUPPORT FOR PROFESSIONAL DEVELOPMENT: payment of dues, mailings, use of facilities, telephone, and clerical staff

SPECIAL SERVICES/PROGRAMS: exhibits
FACILITIES/EQUIPMENT/PRESERVATION: temperature controls

NHPRC AZ100-120

The Arizona Railway Museum **TEL**: (602) 821-1108
399 N. Delaware Street
P.O. Box 842
Chandler, Arizona 85224

REPORTED BY: Russell Lassuy, Secretary
TYPE OF INSTITUTION: museum (non-profit educational and historical organization)

HOURS: Sa & Su noon-4
ACCESS: open to general public
SERVICES: in-person, mail, phone

PRIMARY COLLECTION FOCUS: railways, especially memorabilia acquisition, preservation, restoration,
    display
    railway memorabilia
    railroads
    transportation--railroads
    railway equipment
    railway artifacts
    railroads--Arizona
    railroads--Southwest

COLLECTION FORMATS: 100 books, 500 pamphlets, 500 photographs, 50 maps
COLLECTION ACCESS: not described
STAFF FTE: all volunteer
INSTITUTIONAL SUPPORT FOR PROFESSIONAL DEVELOPMENT: payment of dues
SPECIAL SERVICES/PROGRAMS: exhibits, newsletter
PATRON USE STATISTICS: 2000 in-house patrons (museum)

Chandler Museum **TEL**: (602) 786-2842
178 E. Commonwealth
P.O. Box 926
Chandler, Arizona 85244

REPORTED BY: Al Wiatr, Curator
TYPE OF INSTITUTION: historical society, museum (city)

HOURS: daily, 12-4, except major holidays
ACCESS: open to general public
SERVICES: in-person, mail, phone

PRIMARY COLLECTION FOCUS: Chandler, Arizona
    Chandler, AZ (local history)
    business history
    schools
    personal papers

INCLUSIVE DATES: 1910-1970
COLLECTION FORMATS: personal papers and correspondence, maps, photographs, oral histories,
    pamphlets

COLLECTION ACCESS: repository guide
STAFF FTE: 1 curator, 30-40 volunteers
SPECIAL SERVICES/PROGRAMS: exhibits, tours, newsletter, lectures
FACILITIES/EQUIPMENT/PRESERVATION: temperature controls, fire detection controls
PATRON USE STATISTICS: user statistics not kept

Greenlee Historical Society Museum
317 Chase Creek
Box 787
Clifton, Arizona 85533

TEL: (602) 865-3115

REPORTED BY: Andres Paditen, President
TYPE OF INSTITUTION: archives, historical society, museum (county/local)

HOURS: [not reported]
ACCESS: open to general public
SERVICES: in person, mail, phone

PRIMARY COLLECTION FOCUS: Greenlee Co.
  mining
  ranching
  agriculture
  water

INCLUSIVE DATES: 1900-present
VOLUME: 22 cubic feet
COLLECTION FORMATS: 2 cubic feet manuscript collections, 2 cubic feet institution's records, 12 linear feet books/serials, few maps, 500 postcards, 24 films, 1 cubic feet slides, 1 cubic foot photographs, 6 tapes, 3 cubic feet newspapers
COLLECTION ACCESS: card catalog, container lists, registers/inventories
STAFF FTE: ca. 15 volunteers/docents, 1 temporary part-time clerk
INSTITUTIONAL SUPPORT FOR PROFESSIONAL DEVELOPMENT: in-house workshops, payment for mailings, use of facilities, payment for telephone use
SPECIAL SERVICES/PROGRAMS: exhibits, tours, fundraising/endowment, lectures/presentations
FACILITIES/EQUIPMENT/PRESERVATION: temperature controls, fire extinguishing system, fire detection controls
PATRON USE STATISTICS: user statistics not kept

Casa Grande Ruins National Monument
P.O. Box 518
Coolidge, Arizona 85228

TEL: (602) 723-3172
FAX: (602) 723-7209

REPORTED BY: Bill Grether, Supervisory Park Ranger
TYPE OF INSTITUTION: National Monument (federal)

HOURS: see below
ACCESS: by appointment only
SERVICES: in-person, phone, and mail reference photocopies
RESTRICTIONS: limited reference services and photocopies; some circulate

PRIMARY COLLECTION FOCUS: Hohokam culture, Casa Grande Ruins
  Casa Grande Ruins
  Hohokam culture
  National Park Service (records)

       Native Americans, prehistoric
       Native Americans, Southwestern
       parks and monuments, federal

INCLUSIVE DATES: prehistoric-present
COLLECTION FORMATS: manuscript collections, institution's records, books, pamphlets, films, videotapes, government records, photographs, maps
COLLECTION ACCESS: card catalog
STAFF FTE: 3.5 park rangers
INSTITUTIONAL SUPPORT FOR PROFESSIONAL DEVELOPMENT: tuition, dues, reimbursement, mailings, facilities, telephone, clerical
SPECIAL SERVICES/PROGRAMS: exhibits, tours, lectures, fund raising
FACILITIES/EQUIPMENT/PRESERVATION: humidity controls, fire extinguishing system, disaster preparedness plan
PATRON USE STATISTICS: user statistics not kept

NHPRC AZ175-120

Coolidge Historical Museum   **TEL**: (602) 723-7186
161 W. Harding
P.O. Box 1186
Coolidge, Arizona 85228

REPORTED BY: Ina R. Wilkerson, Conservator
TYPE OF INSTITUTION: historical society, library, museum (private, non-profit)

HOURS: Su 1-5, closed July-Aug
ACCESS: open to general public
SERVICES: mail

PRIMARY COLLECTION FOCUS: city of Coolidge
       Coolidge, AZ (local history)

INCLUSIVE DATES: 1900-1950
COLLECTION FORMATS: 100 books, 30 pamphlets, 100 photographs, 3 maps, 12 oral histories
COLLECTION ACCESS: registers/inventories
ACQUISITION REPORTED TO: membership via newsletter
STAFF FTE: 1 full-time volunteer, 10 part-time
INSTITUTIONAL SUPPORT FOR PROFESSIONAL DEVELOPMENT: payment for mailings
SPECIAL SERVICES/PROGRAMS: exhibits, tours, newsletter, fund raising
FACILITIES/EQUIPMENT/PRESERVATION: temperature controls
PATRON USE STATISTICS: 450 in-house patrons, 12 mail reference requests

---

Cochise County Historical and Archeological Society   **TEL**: (602) 364-5226
1116 G Avenue
Box 818
Douglas, Arizona 85608

REPORTED BY: Cindy Hayostek, President
TYPE OF INSTITUTION: archives, historical society, museum (county/local)

HOURS: weekdays 10-12 and 2-4
ACCESS: open to the general public
SEVICES: in-person, mail, phone, photocopies, photographs (fee for photo reproduction)

PRIMARY COLLECTION FOCUS: Cochise County, Arizona
   Cochise County, AZ (local history)
   Cochise County Historical and Archaeological Society (records)

INCLUSIVE DATES: 1900-present
COLLECTION FORMATS: institution's records, pamphlets, photographs, oral histories
COLLECTION ACCESS: card catalog (photographs), registers/inventories
STAFF FTE: .5 general archival, 6 volunteers, 1 clerical
INSTITUTIONAL SUPPORT FOR PROFESSIONAL DEVELOPMENT: tuition, reimbursement, mailings, telephone
SPECIAL SERVICES/PROGRAMS: exhibits, tours, newsletter, lectures, quarterly newsletter

---

The Amerind Foundation, Inc. **TEL**: (602) 586-3666
Dragoon Road
P.O. Box 248
Dragoon, Arizona 85609

REPORTED BY: Dr. Anne I. Woosley, Director
TYPE OF INSTITUTION: archaeological research foundation and museum (private, non-profit)

HOURS: M-Su 10-4 Sept-May; W-Su 10-4, June-Aug
ACCESS: open to scholarly researchers only
SERVICES: individual cases

PRIMARY COLLECTION FOCUS: prehistoric cultures of new world, especially Southwest and northern Mexico
   prehistoric cultures--new world
   Southwestern U.S.
   Mexico, Northern
   archaeology
   ethnology
   field records

INCLUSIVE DATES: 15,000 years ago to present
COLLECTION FORMATS: 100s manuscripts, 1000s books, 100s pamphlets, 1000s photographs, 100s maps, 100,000 others
COLLECTION ACCESS: variable: card catalog, registers, inventories, some not described
STAFF FTE: 20 volunteers, 1 clerical, 2 interns, on average
SPECIAL SERVICES/PROGRAMS: exhibits, tours, lectures
FACILITIES/EQUIPMENT/PRESERVATION: temperature controls, humidity controls, fire detection controls
PATRON USE STATISTICS: user statistics not kept

NHPRC AZ225-40

Arizona Historical Society **TEL**: (602) 774-6272
Pioneer Museum
2340 N. Fort Valley Road
Flagstaff, Arizona 86001

REPORTED BY: Bonnie Greer, Archivist
TYPE OF INSTITUTION: Historical Society, museum (state)

HOURS: M-F 8-5
ACCESS: open to general public by appointment only
SERVICES: in-person, mail, and phone reference, no fee, photocopies

PRIMARY COLLECTION FOCUS: Northern Arizona
   Northern Arizona (local history)

INCLUSIVE DATES: 1891-1960
COLLECTION FORMATS: 1000 linear feet manuscript collections, 18 linear feet institution's records, 500 books, 8 videos, 10,000 photographs, 100 maps, 20 oral histories
COLLECTION ACCESS: card catalog, registers
STAFF FTE: 1 administrative, .25 archivist, 1 curator, .10 volunteer
INSTITUTIONAL SUPPORT FOR PROFESSIONAL DEVELOPMENT: dues
SPECIAL SERVICES/PROGRAMS: exhibits
FACILITIES/EQUIPMENT/PRESERVATION: temperature controls, humidity controls, fire detection controls, fire extinguishing system, disaster preparedness plan
PATRON USE STATISTICS: not kept

Cross-Cultural Dance Resources, Inc.　　　　　　　　　　　　　　　　**TEL**: (602) 774-8108
518 S. Agassiz St.　　　　　　　　　　　　　　　　　　　　　　　　**FAX**: (602) 774-8108
Flagstaff, Arizona 86001

REPORTED BY: Kathleen Stemmler, Executive Director
TYPE OF INSTITUTION: non-profit organization, anthropology and art (academic)

HOURS: M W F 10-3
ACCESS: open to general public
SERVICES: mail, phone

PRIMARY COLLECTION FOCUS: anthropology of dance
   anthropology of dance
   performing arts
   dance
   music and graphic arts
   anthropology, cultural
   Native Americans, Southwestern U.S.
   Asia--dance
   Pacific--dance
   Africa--dance

VOLUME: 3000 items
COLLECTION FORMATS: 40 manuscript collections, 2500 books, 300 films, 100 photographs, 50 maps, 5 oral histories
COLLECTION ACCESS: not described, in process of computerizing
STAFF FTE: administrative, volunteer and student [numbers not specified]
FACILITIES/EQUIPMENT/PRESERVATION: fire detection controls, fire extinguishing system
PATRON USE STATISTICS: 20 in-house patrons, 100 telephone, 30 mail reference requests, all collections used

---

Flagstaff City-Coconino County Public Library　　　　　　　　　　　**TEL**: (602) 779-7670
300 W. Aspen Avenue　　　　　　　　　　　　　　　　　　　　　　**FAX**: (602) 774-9573
Flagstaff, Arizona 86001

REPORTED BY: John Irwin, Associate Director, Public Services
TYPE OF INSTITUTION: library (county/local)

HOURS: M-Th 10am-9pm; F-Sa 10-6; Su 1-4

ACCESS: public access by appointment only
SERVICES: in-person, mail, phone, photocopies

PRIMARY COLLECTION FOCUS: City of Flagstaff archives
    Flagstaff, AZ (municipal archives)
    Arizona, Coconino County

INCLUSIVE DATES: 1894-present
COLLECTION FORMATS: 300 cubic feet records, 500 maps
COLLECTION ACCESS: not described
STAFF FTE: [not reported]
FACILITIES/EQUIPMENT/PRESERVATION: temperature controls, humidity controls, fire detection controls, fire extinguishing system, disaster preparedness plan
PATRON USE STATISTICS: user statistics not kept

Lowell Observatory
1400 W. Mars Hill Road
Flagstaff, Arizona 86001

TEL: (602) 774-3358
FAX: (602) 774-6296

REPORTED BY: Antoinette Beiser, Librarian/Archivist
TYPE OF INSTITUTION: observatory (non-profit research institution)

HOURS: M 1-5; Tu 12-4, W-F 9-1
ACCESS: public access by appointment only
SERVICES: in-person, mail, phone, photocopies

PRIMARY COLLECTION FOCUS: files of staff members
    Lowell Observatory, AZ (records)
    scientific studies
    observatories--history
    government contracts
    Lowell, Percival--studies of Mars
    Sliphers, V. M.--redshift work
    Lampland, C. O.--radiometric work
    astronomy
    astrophysics
    astronomers

INCLUSIVE DATES: 1894-1980
VOLUME: 260 cubic feet
COLLECTION FORMATS: 110 cubic feet manuscript collections, 60 cubic feet institution's records, 10 cubic feet books, 60 cubic feet pamphlets, 3 cubic feet film, 5 cubic feet government records, 2 cubic feet photographs, 1 cubic foot oral histories
COLLECTION ACCESS: computerized finding aid (used by staff, patrons)
SOFTWARE/SYSTEM: Filemaker Pro/Claris Software database system
STAFF FTE: .5 administrative/photo curator, .5 archival, 2 clerical
INSTITUTIONAL SUPPORT FOR PROFESSIONAL DEVELOPMENT: tuition, dues, reimbursement, use of facilities, telephone, and clerical staff
SPECIAL SERVICES/PROGRAMS: exhibits, fund raising
FACILITIES/EQUIPMENT/PRESERVATION: temperature controls, humidity controls, fire detection controls, fire extinguishing system, disaster preparedness plan
PATRON USE STATISTICS: 10 in-house patrons, 10 telephone, other user statistics not kept

NHPRC AZ250-480

Museum of Northern Arizona
Harold S. Colton Memorial Library
Museum Archives and Manuscripts Collections
Route 4, Box 720
Flagstaff, Arizona 86001

TEL: (602) 774-5213
FAX: (602) 779-1527

REPORTED BY: Dorothy House, Head Librarian
TYPE OF INSTITUTION: museum, library (private)

HOURS: M-F 9-5
ACCESS: open to general public
SERVICES: in-person, phone, and mail reference, photocopies (fee for photocopies)

PRIMARY COLLECTION FOCUS: Northern Arizona, Southern Colorado Plateau
    archaeology, Southern Colorado Plateau
    ethnography, Southern Colorado Plateau
    natural history

COLLECTION FORMATS: manuscript collections, institution's records, pamphlets, ephemera, photographs, field notes, sand painting reproductions
COLLECTION ACCESS: inventories
STAFF FTE: 1 librarian, 1 library assistant
SPECIAL SERVICES/PROGRAMS: tours, lectures
FACILITIES/EQUIPMENT/PRESERVATION: temperature controls, fire detection controls, fire extinguishing system
PATRON USE STATISTICS: user statistics not kept

NHPRC AZ250-520

Riordan State Historic Park
Riordan Ranch Street
P.O. Box 217
Flagstaff, Arizona 86002

TEL: (602) 779-4395

REPORTED BY: Bill Och, Assistant Park Manager
TYPE OF INSTITUTION: historic park (state)

ACCESS: by appointment only
SERVICES: none except by appointment
RESTRICTIONS: none circulate

PRIMARY COLLECTION FOCUS: Riordan family
    Riordan family
    Arizona, Northern
    Chambers family
    Hillary, John

INCLUSIVE DATES: 1880s-1985
COLLECTION FORMATS: manuscript collections, institution's records, books, pamphlets, slides, photographs, maps, oral histories, artifacts (5000)
COLLECTION ACCESS: card catalog, inventories
STAFF FTE: 1 administrative, 1 park ranger
INSTITUTIONAL SUPPORT FOR PROFESSIONAL DEVELOPMENT: tuition, dues, reimbursement, facilities, mailings, clerical, telephone
SPECIAL SERVICES/PROGRAMS: exhibits, tours, lectures
FACILITIES/EQUIPMENT/PRESERVATION: temperature controls, fire extinguishing system
PATRON USE STATISTICS: user statistics kept but not available

SSA Institutional Directory

11

NHPRC AZ250-690

Special Collections and Archives
Cline Library
P.O. Box 6022
Northern Arizona University
Flagstaff, Arizona 86011-6022

TEL: (602) 523-5551
FAX: (602) 523-3770

REPORTED BY: Karen Underhill, Coordinator SC&A
TYPE OF INSTITUTION: archives, library (academic)

HOURS: M-F 8-5
ACCESS: open to the general public
SERVICES: in-person, mail, phone, photocopies, microfilm printer; fee for photos

PRIMARY COLLECTION FOCUS: Colorado Plateau history
- Arizona, Colorado Plateau--history and politics
- business history
- lumber industry
- banking
- merchants
- Native Americans--culture
- ranching--cattle and sheep
- water
- labor--AFL-CIO
- congressional papers
- Babbitt, Bruce
- Mormons
- Grand Canyon, AZ--pioneers, tourism, river guides

INCLUSIVE DATES: 1570s-present
VOLUME: 6000 linear feet
COLLECTION FORMATS: 276 manuscript collections, 1000 linear feet institution's records, 35,000 books, 100 linear feet pamphlets, 50 films, government records, 750,000 photographs (Emory Kolb Collection), 2000 maps, 552 oral histories
COLLECTION ACCESS: card catalog, repository guide, registers/inventories, computer finding aids
SOFTWARE/SYSTEM: Wordperfect, d-Base III and IV, Paradox
ACQUISITION REPORTED TO: OCLC, NAUCARL
STAFF FTE: 1 administrative, 2 archival, 1 map curator, 1 photo curator, 1 librarian
1 volunteer, 9 students, 1 intern, 1 clerical
INSTITUTIONAL SUPPORT FOR PROFESSIONAL DEVELOPMENT: tuition, reimbursement, in-house workshops, mailings, use of facilities, telephone, and clerical
SPECIAL SERVICES/PROGRAMS: exhibits, tours, classes, lectures
FACILITIES/EQUIPMENT/PRESERVATION: temperature, humidity, and fire detection controls, fire extinguishing system, preservation lab, disaster preparedness plan
PATRON USE STATISTICS: 2362 in-house patrons, 8000 telephone, 100 mail reference requests

NHPRC AZ250-575

McFarland Historical State Park, Library and Archives
Main Street and Ruggles Avenue
P.O. Box 109
Florence, Arizona 85232

TEL: (602) 868-5216

REPORTED BY: Kathryn C. Montano, Park Manager

TYPE OF INSTITUTION: archives, library, museum (state)

HOURS: Th-M 8-5, closed Tu and W
ACCESS: open to the general public
SERVICES: in-person, mail, phone, photocopies

PRIMARY COLLECTION FOCUS: life of Ernest McFarland (Arizona governor, Supreme Court justice, U.S. senator)
    McFarland, Ernest W.--Senator, Governor, Judge
    congressional papers
    gubernatorial records--Arizona
    Arizona Supreme Court--judicial records
    legal records
    Arizona, Central
    Arizona, Central Arizona Project
    military--G.I. Bill of Rights
    politics--Arizona and U.S.
    government--Arizona and U.S.

INCLUSIVE DATES: 1894-1985
VOLUME: 118 cubic feet, 125.5 linear feet
COLLECTION FORMATS: manuscript collections, books, pamphlets, films, government records, photographs, maps, other
COLLECTION ACCESS: repository guide, computerized finding aids (used by staff and patrons)
ACQUISITION REPORTED TO: professional journals
STAFF FTE: 1 administrative, 1 outreach, 5 volunteers
INSTITUTIONAL SUPPORT FOR PROFESSIONAL DEVELOPMENT: payment of dues, reimbursement, use of facilities, use of telephone
SPECIAL SERVICES/PROGRAMS: exhibits, fund raising
FACILITIES/EQUIPMENT/PRESERVATION: temperature controls, humidity controls, fire detection controls, fire extinguishing system
PATRON USE STATISTICS: 5 in-house patrons, 6 telephone, 3 mail reference requests, 12 reference photocopies

NHPRC AZ275-520

Fort Huachuca Historical Museum
Grierson and Boyd Avenues
ATZS-PTP-M
Fort Huachuca, Arizona 85613-6000

TEL: (602) 533-2474

REPORTED BY: Barbara N. Tuttle, Curator of Collections
TYPE OF INSTITUTION: museum (federal)

HOURS: M-F, 9-4; Sa-Su, 1-4
ACCESS: not open to general public
SERVICES: in-person, mail, phone
RESTRICTIONS: non-circulating

PRIMARY COLLECTION FOCUS: military/army
    military history
    army
    U.S.--War Department
    parks and monuments, federal

INCLUSIVE DATES: 1800-present
VOLUME: 5000 feet

COLLECTION ACCESS: registers/inventories
STAFF FTE: 1 administrative, 1 preservation, 1 clerical, 1 exhibit
INSTITUTIONAL SUPPORT FOR PROFESSIONAL DEVELOPMENT: tuition reimbursement for professional meetings, registration, and travel
SPECIAL SERVICES/PROGRAMS: exhibits, tours, lectures
FACILITIES/EQUIPMENT/PRESERVATION: temperature controls, fire detection controls, fire extinguishing system, disaster preparedness plan
PATRON USE STATISTICS: user statistics not kept

Hubbell Trading Post National Historic Site
P.O. Box 150
Ganado, Arizona 86505

TEL: (602) 755-3475
FAX: (602) 755-3405

REPORTED BY: Edward M. Chamberlin, Park Curator
TYPE OF INSTITUTION: National Park Service Historic Site (federal)

HOURS: Su-Sa 8-5, except Thanksgiving, Christmas and New Years (daylight saving time observed)
ACCESS: open to general public, appointments recommended
SERVICES: in-person, limited mail, phone, limited photocopies, some research assistance
RESTRICTIONS: limited staff

PRIMARY COLLECTION FOCUS: history of Hubbell family and business
- Hubbell family, Arizona
- Hubbell Trading Post, Arizona
- parks and monuments, federal

INCLUSIVE DATES: 1890-present
COLLECTION FORMATS: 1900 books, 10 pamphlets, 3600 photographs, 80 maps and architectural drawings, 100 oral histories (transcripts of oral histories circulate)
COLLECTION ACCESS: card catalog, container lists, computerized finding aid (used by staff)
SOFTWARE/SYSTEM: Automated National Catalog System, d-Base III+
STAFF FTE: 1 administrative, 1 archival
INSTITUTIONAL SUPPORT FOR PROFESSIONAL DEVELOPMENT: tuition, in-house workshops, use of facilities, telephone, clerical staff
SPECIAL SERVICES/PROGRAMS: exhibits, tours, classes
FACILITIES/EQUIPMENT/PRESERVATION: fire detection controls, fire extinguishing system
PATRON USE STATISTICS: 51 in-house patrons, 100 mail reference requests, 3750 microfiche copies

---

Gilbert Historical Museum
10 S. Gilbert Road
P.O. Box 1484
Gilbert, Arizona 85234

TEL: (602) 926-1577 or (602) 892-4097

REPORTED BY: Elizabeth Heagreu, Treasurer
TYPE OF INSTITUTION: museum, historical society (county, local, city)

HOURS: Tu-Sa 1-4 Oct-May; other times by appointment
ACCESS: open to the general public
SERVICES: in-person, mail, phone

PRIMARY COLLECTION FOCUS: Gilbert history
- Gilbert, AZ (local history)

INCLUSIVE DATES: 1890-present

COLLECTION FORMATS: institution's records, books, photographs, maps, oral histories
COLLECTION ACCESS: card catalog, registers
STAFF FTE: [not reported]
SPECIAL SERVICES/PROGRAMS: exhibits, tours, newsletter
PATRON USE STATISTICS: user statistics not kept

Grand Canyon National Park
P.O. Box 129
Grand Canyon, Arizona 86023

TEL: (602) 638-7769
FAX: (602) 638-7797

REPORTED BY: Carolyn Richard, Curator
TYPE OF INSTITUTION: archives, library, museum (federal)

HOURS: M-F 8-5
ACCESS: open to general public
SERVICES: in-person, mail, phone, fee for some reference, photocopies, photo loans

PRIMARY COLLECTION FOCUS: Grand Canyon cultural and natural history
      Grand Canyon, AZ--history
      archaeology
      ethnography
      biology
      paleontology
      geology
      parks and monuments, federal

INCLUSIVE DATES: 1800s-present
VOLUME: 50,000 items
COLLECTION FORMATS: 10,000 books, 200 pamphlets, 100 films, 30 cubic feet government records, 16,000 photographs, 100 maps, 100 oral histories
COLLECTION ACCESS: card catalog, computerized finding aid (in progress--used by staff)
SOFTWARE/SYSTEM: Automated National Catalog Systems and d-Base III
ACQUISITION REPORTED TO: National Catalog, National Park Service, Harpers Ferry, W.V.
STAFF FTE: 1 curator, 3 museum technicians, 1 volunteer
INSTITUTIONAL SUPPORT FOR PROFESSIONAL DEVELOPMENT: payment of dues, in-house workshops (NPS courses)
SPECIAL SERVICES/PROGRAMS: exhibits, tours, lectures
FACILITIES/EQUIPMENT/PRESERVATION: fire detection controls
PATRON USE STATISTICS: 350 in-house patrons, 100 telephone, 50 mail reference requests

NHPRC AZ350-290

Coronado National Memorial
Box 126, RR 1
Hereford, AZ 85615

TEL: (602) 366-5515
FAX: (602) 366-5705

REPORTED BY: Edward Lopez, Park Superintendent
TYPE OF INSTITUTION: National Parks Service (federal)

HOURS: M-F 8-5
ACCESS: by appointment only; not open to general public
SERVICES: very limited services

PRIMARY COLLECTION FOCUS: Spanish history

Southwest U.S.
natural resources, Southwest U.S.
Spanish history, Southwest U.S.
Spanish exploration, Southwest U.S.
Coronado expedition
parks and monuments, federal

INCLUSIVE DATES: various
COLLECTION FORMATS: manuscript collections, institution's records, books, pamphlets, videotapes, government records, photographs, maps, oral histories, natural resources reports
COLLECTION ACCESS: card catalog
STAFF FTE: 1 park ranger naturalist
INSTITUTIONAL SUPPORT FOR PROFESSIONAL DEVELOPMENT: tuition, dues, reimbursement, mailings, facilities, telephones
SPECIAL SERVICES/PROGRAMS: classes, lectures
FACILITIES/EQUIPMENT/PRESERVATION: fire detection controls, fire extinguishing system, disaster preparedness plan
PATRON USE STATISTICS: in-house patrons

NHPRC AZ375-120

Jerome Historical Society
315 Main Street
P.O. Box 156
Jerome, Arizona 86331

TEL: (602) 634-5477

REPORTED BY: Ellen Smith, Clerk
TYPE OF INSTITUTION: archives, historical society, museum (city)

HOURS: [not reported]
ACCESS: usually open to public, have no archivist at this time, so by appointment only
SERVICES: in-person, mail, phone, fee, photocopies

PRIMARY COLLECTION FOCUS: City of Jerome
Jerome, AZ (local history)
mining

INCLUSIVE DATES: 1880-present
COLLECTION FORMATS: records, government records, photographs, maps, oral histories, newspapers
COLLECTION ACCESS: computerized finding aids (used by staff)
SOFTWARE/SYSTEM: IBM First Choice
STAFF FTE: 1 archivist, 1 clerical
INSTITUTIONAL SUPPORT FOR PROFESSIONAL DEVELOPMENT: tuition, dues, professional meetings, registration and travel, mailings, use of facilities, telephone use
FACILITIES/EQUIPMENT/PRESERVATION: temperature controls, fire detection controls
PATRON USE STATISTICS: user statistics not kept

Mohave Museum of History and Arts
400 W. Beale
Kingman, Arizona 86401

TEL: (602) 753-3195

REPORTED BY: Ruth Simpson, Volunteer
TYPE OF INSTITUTION: historical society, museum (county/local)

HOURS: M-F 10-5, Sa-Su 1-5, closed major holidays

ACCESS: open to general public
SERVICES: in-person, mail, phone reference; photocopies
RESTRICTIONS: fragile holdings restricted to staff use; fee for reference; collections do not circulate

PRIMARY COLLECTION FOCUS: history of Mohave County
    Native Americans--culture
    military occupation
    ranching
    mining
    Andy Devine

INCLUSIVE DATES: pre-history to current
COLLECTION FORMATS: 2000 books, 2 cubic feet manuscripts, 5 cubic feet institution's records, 20 cubic feet pamphlets, 500 volumes government records, 45 videotapes, 8000 photographs, 4500 maps, memorabilia, newspapers, 200 oral histories
COLLECTION ACCESS: card catalog, container lists, registers/inventories, indexed
STAFF FTE: 2 administrative, 150 volunteer/docent
INSTITUTIONAL SUPPORT FOR PROFESSIONAL DEVELOPMENT: tuition and dues payment, reimbursement, payment for mailings, use of facilities, payment for telephone use
SPECIAL SERVICES/PROGRAMS: exhibits, newsletter, fund raising, lectures
FACILITIES/EQUIPMENT/PRESERVATION: temperature controls, fire detection controls, fire extinguishing system
PATRON USE STATISTICS: 28,000 in-house patrons (museum), other user statistics not kept

---

Lake Havasu City Historical Society   **TEL**: (602) 855-2178
P.O. Box 1043
Lake Havasu City, Arizona 86403

REPORTED BY: Elrose Dussault, President
TYPE OF INSTITUTION: historical society (city)

HOURS: [not reported]
ACCESS: [not reported]
SERVICES: [not reported]

PRIMARY COLLECTION FOCUS: Lake Havasu City
    Lake Havasu City, AZ (local history)
    London Bridge
    Native Americans
    newspapers

INCLUSIVE DATES: 1964-1992
COLLECTION FORMATS: manuscript collections, films, newspapers, oral histories
COLLECTION ACCESS: container lists
ACQUISITION REPORTED TO: monthly Historical Society meetings
STAFF FTE: volunteer
SPECIAL SERVICES/PROGRAMS: tours of Bridge, fund raising, lectures

---

Ak-Chin Him-Dak   **TEL**: (602) 568-9480
P.O. Box 897
Maricopa, Arizona 85239

REPORTED BY: Carol Lopez, Archivist
TYPE OF INSTITUTION: archives, museum (Native American)

HOURS: M-F 9-5, Sa 9-2
ACCESS: open to the general public
SERVICES: in-person, mail, and phone reference; photocopies
RESTRICTIONS: none circulate

PRIMARY COLLECTION FOCUS: Ak-Chin community and farms
- Ak-Chin
- Ak-Chin water settlement
- Native Americans, Southwest U.S.

INCLUSIVE DATES: 1912-present
COLLECTION FORMATS: manuscript collections, institution's records, books, pamphlets, films, photographs, maps, oral histories, newspapers
COLLECTION ACCESS: inventories
STAFF FTE: 1 archivist, 1 photo curator, 1 historian
INSTITUTIONAL SUPPORT FOR PROFESSIONAL DEVELOPMENT: tuition, dues, reimbursement, workshops, facilities, mailings, clerical, telephone
SPECIAL SERVICES/PROGRAMS: exhibits, tours, classes, fund raising, lectures
FACILITIES/EQUIPMENT/PRESERVATION: temperature controls, humidity controls, fire detection system, fire extinguishing system
PATRON USE STATISTICS: user statistics kept but not available

---

Mesa Southwest Museum
53 North MacDonald
Mesa, AZ 85201

TEL: (602) 644-2169
FAX: (602) 644-3424

REPORTED BY: Kathryn Edgar, Registrar
TYPE OF INSTITUTION: museum (city)

HOURS: Tu-F 10-5
ACCESS: by appointment only
SERVICES: limited reference services, photocopies (fee for copies)
RESTRICTIONS: none circulate

PRIMARY COLLECTION FOCUS: Mesa, Maricopa County
- Midvale, Frank
- Hale, John
- archaeology
- Mesa, AZ (local history)
- pioneers

COLLECTION FORMATS: manuscript collections, institution's records, books, pamphlets, government records, photographs, maps
COLLECTION ACCESS: inventories, computerized finding aids (used by staff)
SOFTWARE/SYSTEM: Dataease
STAFF FTE: 4
INSTITUTIONAL SUPPORT FOR PROFESSIONAL DEVELOPMENT: tuition, dues, mailings, telephones, facilities
SPECIAL SERVICES/PROGRAMS: newsletter, lectures
FACILITIES/EQUIPMENT/PRESERVATION: temperature controls, humidity controls, fire detection controls, fire extinguishing system
PATRON USE STATISTICS: user statistics not kept

NHPRC AZ435-520

Pipe Springs National Monument TEL: (602) 643-7105
Monument Library
Moccasin, Arizona 86022

REPORTED BY: Gary Hasty, Superintendent
TYPE OF INSTITUTION: National monument (federal)

HOURS: Daily 8-4:30 except Thanksgiving, Christmas and New Years
ACCESS: by appointment only
SERVICES: in-person, mail and telephone reference
RESTRICTIONS: limited reference, no photocopying; none circulate

PRIMARY COLLECTION FOCUS: Western expansion and settlement of Great Basin
    Western expansion
    Great Basin, settlement
    pioneers
    Arizona Strip
    parks and monuments, federal

INCLUSIVE DATES: 1870s-present (1870s-1880s focus)
VOLUME: 3 cubic feet
COLLECTION FORMATS: manuscript collections, institution's records, government records, photographs
COLLECTION ACCESS: card catalog, register
STAFF FTE: 1 park ranger
INSTITUTIONAL SUPPORT FOR PROFESSIONAL DEVELOPMENT: tuition, dues
FACILITIES/EQUIPMENT/PRESERVATION: fire extinguishing system, fire proof cabinets
PATRON USE STATISTICS: 10+ in-house patrons, 15 telephone, 15 mail

NHPRC AZ450-640

Pimeria Alta Historical Society TEL: (602) 287-4624
136 N. Grand Avenue
P.O. Box 2281
Nogales, Arizona 85628

REPORTED BY: Anne B. Wheeler, Registrar
TYPE OF INSTITUTION: historical society (other, 501-C-3, international)

HOURS: M-F 9-5; Sa 10-4; Su 1-4
ACCESS: open to general public
SERVICES: in-person, mail, phone, photocopies

PRIMARY COLLECTION FOCUS: Southern Arizona and Northern Sonora, Mexico
    Arizona, Southern
    Mexico, Northern Sonora
    ranching
    mining
    business history
    daily life
    water
    Nogales, AZ

INCLUSIVE DATES: early 1800s-present
VOLUME: 54 cubic feet
COLLECTION FORMATS: 9 cubic feet institution's records, 1000 books, 36 cubic feet pamphlets, 10 films, 9 cubic feet government records, 10,000 photographs, 250 maps, 125 oral histories
COLLECTION ACCESS: card catalog, repository guide

STAFF FTE: [not reported]
INSTITUTIONAL SUPPORT FOR PROFESSIONAL DEVELOPMENT: tuition, reimbursement
SPECIAL SERVICES/PROGRAMS: exhibits, tours, newsletter, lectures
FACILITIES/EQUIPMENT/PRESERVATION: temperature controls, disaster preparedness plan
PATRON USE STATISTICS: 250 in-house patrons, 75 telephone, 100 mail reference requests, 500 reference photocopies

NHPRC AZ475-640

Acadia Ranch Museum
Old Mt. Lemmon Highway
Box 10
Oracle, Arizona 85623

TEL: None

REPORTED BY: Evaline J. Auerback, President, Oracle Historical Society
TYPE OF INSTITUTION: archives, historical society, library, museum, art gallery (county, local)

HOURS: Sa 1-5 (occasionally closed)
ACCESS: public access by appointment only (except on Saturdays as noted)
SERVICES: [not reported]

PRIMARY COLLECTION FOCUS: Oracle, Mammoth history
    Oracle, AZ (local history)
    Mammoth, AZ (local history)
    mining--copper, gold, tungsten
    Buffalo Bill (William Cody)
    ranches--dude
    resorts--health (TB)
    Cody, William (Buffalo Bill)

INCLUSIVE DATES: 1875-present
COLLECTION ACCESS: registers/inventories, some not described
STAFF FTE: part-time volunteer
SPECIAL SERVICES/PROGRAMS: tours, newsletter, fund raising, lectures
PATRON USE STATISTICS: 2 mail reference requests

John Wesley Powell Memorial Museum
6 Lake Powell Boulevard
P.O. Box 547
Page, Arizona 86040

TEL: (602) 645-9496

REPORTED BY: Julia P. Betz, Executive Director
TYPE OF INSTITUTION: museum (private, non-profit)

HOURS: May-Sept. M-Sa 8-6, Su 10-6; Oct. M-Sa 8-6; Nov. M-F 8-5; March-April M-F 8-5; closed Dec.-Feb. except by appointment
ACCESS: by appointment only for library
SERVICES: in-person, mail and phone reference; photocopies (fee for photocopies)
RESTRICTIONS: none circulate

PRIMARY COLLECTION FOCUS: John Wesley Powell, Colorado River running
    Powell, John Wesley
    Colorado River running
    Page, AZ (local history)
    Lake Powell, AZ

Native Americans, Southwest U.S.

INCLUSIVE DATES: 1869-present
COLLECTION FORMATS: manuscript collections, institution's records, books, pamphlets, films, government records, photographs, maps, oral histories, slides
COLLECTION ACCESS: card catalog, computerized finding aids (used by staff)
STAFF FTE: 1 administrative, 1 general
INSTITUTIONAL SUPPORT FOR PROFESSIONAL DEVELOPMENT: tuition, dues, reimbursement
SPECIAL SERVICES/PROGRAMS: fund raising, lectures
FACILITIES/EQUIPMENT/PRESERVATION: temperature controls, fire detection controls, fire extinguishing system
PATRON USE STATISTICS: 3 in-house patrons, 10 telephone patrons, 50 mail requests, 1 collection used (John Wesley Powell), 50 photocopies

NHPRC AZ500-400

Colorado River Indian Tribes Library
Route 1, Box 23-B
Parker, Arizona 85344

TEL: (602) 669-9211
FAX: (602) 669-5675

REPORTED BY: Amelia Flores, Library Director
TYPE OF INSTITUTION: library (Indian Tribe)

HOURS: [see below]
ACCESS: public access by application only
SERVICES: in-person

PRIMARY COLLECTION FOCUS: Colorado River Indian Reservation
    Mohave Indians--culture
    Chemehuevi Indians--culture
    Hopi Indians--culture
    Navajo Indians--culture
    Colorado River Indian Reservation (records)
    Native Americans

COLLECTION FORMATS: institution's records, books, films, government records, photographs, maps, oral histories, other
COLLECTION ACCESS: card catalog
STAFF FTE: 1 administrative, 1 archivist, volunteers
INSTITUTIONAL SUPPORT FOR PROFESSIONAL DEVELOPMENT: tuition, reimbursement, mailings, use of facilities, phone, and clerical
SPECIAL SERVICES/PROGRAMS: tours, lectures
FACILITIES/EQUIPMENT/PRESERVATION: fire extinguishing system
PATRON USE STATISTICS: user statistics not kept

Northern Gila County Historical Society/Museum of the Forest
1001 W. Main St.
P.O. Box 2532
Payson, Arizona 85547

TEL: (602) 474-1541

REPORTED BY: Beth Counseller, Secretary
TYPE OF INSTITUTION: historical society, museum (county/local)

HOURS: Sa-Su 12-4
ACCESS: open to general public

PRIMARY COLLECTION FOCUS: Northern Gila County, Arizona
    Northern Gila County, AZ--prehistory
    Native Americans--civilizations
    Arizona--communities
    Native Americans--culture
    prehistory--Gila County, AZ

INCLUSIVE DATES: prehistory-present
COLLECTION FORMATS: books, pamphlets, films, government records, photographs, oral histories, artifacts
COLLECTION ACCESS: in process
STAFF FTE: volunteers [number not specified]
INSTITUTIONAL SUPPORT FOR PROFESSIONAL DEVELOPMENT: tuition, dues, reimbursement
SPECIAL SERVICES/PROGRAMS: exhibits, newsletter, fund raising, lectures
FACILITIES/EQUIPMENT/PRESERVATION: fire detection controls
PATRON USE STATISTICS: user statistics not kept

Arizona Jewish Historical Society
4143 N. 12th Avenue, Suite 100D
Phoenix, Arizona 85014

TEL: (602) 241-7870
FAX: (602) 265-0021

REPORTED BY: Beryl S. Morton, Curator/Archivist
TYPE OF INSTITUTION: archives, historical society, library (religious)

HOURS: M-F, no scheduled hours
ACCESS: public access by appointment only
SERVICES: mail, phone, photocopies, photo print service

PRIMARY COLLECTION FOCUS: Jewish experience in Arizona
    Southwestern U.S.--Jewish history
    Judaism--Arizona
    family history--Jewish
    business history--Jewish
    synagogues
    social agencies--Jewish

INCLUSIVE DATES: 1850-present
VOLUME: 10,000 items
COLLECTION FORMATS: 1000 institution's records, 100 books, 500 pamphlets, 5 films, 6000 photographs,
    10 maps, 50 oral histories, 2 exhibitions, 1 circulating exhibition
COLLECTION ACCESS: registers/inventories, just started computerized finding aids (used by staff)
STAFF FTE: no full-time staff; administrative, photo curator, oral history chair, computer specialist
INSTITUTIONAL SUPPORT FOR PROFESSIONAL DEVELOPMENT: payment of dues, reimbursement
SPECIAL SERVICES/PROGRAMS: exhibits, newsletter, fund raising, lectures
PATRON USE STATISTICS: user statistics not kept

Arizona Military Museum
5636 E. McDowell Road
Phoenix, Arizona 85008

TEL: (602) 267-2676
FAX: (602) 267-2688

REPORTED BY: John L. Johnson, COL, AUS Retired, Director
TYPE OF INSTITUTION: historical society, museum (federal)

HOURS: Tu, Th 9-2, Sa-Su, 1-4
ACCESS: open to general public

SERVICES: in-person, photocopies

PRIMARY COLLECTION FOCUS: Arizona, general military history
  Arizona
  military history
  Arizona Militia
  National Guard

INCLUSIVE DATES: 1865-present
VOLUME: 500 items
COLLECTION FORMATS: 125 institution's records, 300 books, 20 films, 25 government records, 25 maps, 25 oral histories
COLLECTION ACCESS: computerized finding aids (used by staff)
SOFTWARE/SYSTEM: d-Base
ACQUISITION REPORTED TO: Center for Military History
STAFF FTE: 4 administrative, 3 volunteers
SPECIAL SERVICES/PROGRAMS: exhibits, tours, newsletter, lectures
FACILITIES/EQUIPMENT/PRESERVATION: temperature controls, fire detection controls, disaster preparedness plan
PATRON USE STATISTICS: 5000 in-house patrons (museum), other user statistics not kept

---

Arizona Mining and Mineral Museum **TEL**: (602) 255-3791
Department of Mines
1502 W. Washington
Phoenix, Arizona 85007

REPORTED BY: Alice J. Rosenfeld, Tour guide
TYPE OF INSTITUTION: museum (state)

HOURS: M-F 8-5, Sa 1-5
ACCESS: open to general public
SERVICES: in-person, photocopies

PRIMARY COLLECTION FOCUS: minerals
  minerals
  mining
  fossils

COLLECTION FORMATS: films, oral histories
STAFF FTE: 1 administrative
SPECIAL SERVICES/PROGRAMS: exhibits, classes, lectures
PATRON USE STATISTICS: in-house and telephone (no statistics)

Arizona Southern Baptist Convention **TEL**: (602) 264-9421
4520 N. Central Avenue
Phoenix, Arizona 85012

REPORTED BY: Clarice Maben, Curator and Archivist
TYPE OF INSTITUTION: archives, historical society (religious)

HOURS: Tu,Th 1:30-4:30
ACCESS: [not reported]
SERVICES: [not reported]

PRIMARY COLLECTION FOCUS: Arizona Southern Baptist Convention
   Southern Baptist Convention, Arizona (records)
   Arizona Southern Baptist Convention--churches and associations
   Grand Canyon University Baptist Foundation of AZ
   Arizona Baptist Children's Service
   Baptist Church
   church history

INCLUSIVE DATES: 1928-present
COLLECTION FORMATS: institution's records, films, photographs, oral histories
COLLECTION ACCESS: card catalog
STAFF FTE: 1 archival, .2 other
INSTITUTIONAL SUPPORT FOR PROFESSIONAL DEVELOPMENT: pay dues, mailings, use of facilities
FACILITIES/EQUIPMENT/PRESERVATION: temperature controls, fire extinguishing system
PATRON USE STATISTICS: user statistics not kept

Arizona State Archives
Department of Library, Archives and Public Records
1700 W. Washington, Room 442
Phoenix, Arizona 85007

TEL: (602) 542-4159
FAX: (602) 542-4402

REPORTED BY: David H. Hoober, Division Director
TYPE OF INSTITUTION: archives (state)

HOURS: M-F 8-5, except state holidays
ACCESS: open to general public
SERVICES: in-person, mail, telephone, photocopies (fee for photocopies)
RESTRICTIONS: collections do not circulate

PRIMARY COLLECTION FOCUS: Arizona government
   Arizona--government, politics, and history
   Arizona--governors
   mining
   ranching
   cotton
   water
   Native Americans
   borderlands
   Hunt, George W. P., Governor (AZ)
   prisons--reform
   Arizona--county and local history
   Maxwell, George Hebard
   Colorado River

INCLUSIVE DATES: 1852-1991
VOLUME: 7,960 cubic feet
COLLECTION FORMATS: 20 cubic feet institution's records, 20 cubic feet films, 7,920 cubic feet government records
COLLECTION ACCESS: repository guide, registers/inventories, computerized finding aids (used by staff), some not described
SOFTWARE/SYSTEM: MicroMARC, Macintosh
STAFF FTE: 1 administrative, 3 general archival, 1 preservation, 1 clerical, 1 intern
INSTITUTIONAL SUPPORT FOR PROFESSIONAL DEVELOPMENT: tuition, reimbursement, mailings, in-house workshops, use of facilities, telephone, clerical staff
SPECIAL SERVICES/PROGRAMS: tours, lectures
FACILITIES/EQUIPMENT/PRESERVATION: temperature controls, fire detection controls
   disaster preparedness plan

PATRON USE STATISTICS: 458 in-house patrons, 1000 telephone, 250 mail reference requests, 454 collections used, 15,017 reference photocopies, 4108 microform copies
NHPRC AZ550-040

Atlatl
402 W. Roosevelt, Suite C
Phoenix, Arizona 85063

TEL: (602) 253-2731

REPORTED BY: Carla A. Roberts, Executive Director
TYPE OF INSTITUTION: Arts Service Organization (private, non-profit)

HOURS: M-F 9-5
ACCESS: public access by appointment only
SERVICES: in-person, mail, phone, fee for reference, photocopies, slides

PRIMARY COLLECTION FOCUS: Native American artists
  Native Americans--artists
  artists--Native Americans

COLLECTION FORMATS: institution's records, slide registry, artists' files
COLLECTION ACCESS: computerized finding aids (used by staff)
SOFTWARE/SYSTEM: MacIntosh, Microsoft Works
STAFF FTE: 1.5 administrative, 1 student
SPECIAL SERVICES/PROGRAMS: exhibits, newsletter, lectures
FACILITIES/EQUIPMENT/PRESERVATION: fire extinguishing system
PATRON USE STATISTICS: 20 in-house patrons, 780 telephone, 520 mail reference requests

---

Catholic Diocese of Phoenix
400 E. Monroe
Phoenix, Arizona 85004

TEL: (602) 257-0030
FAX: (602) 258-3425

REPORTED BY: Rev. Timothy R. Davern, Chancellor
TYPE OF INSTITUTION: archives (religious)

HOURS: M-F 8-4:30
ACCESS: not open to general public
SERVICES: no services

PRIMARY COLLECTION FOCUS: Catholic Diocese of Arizona
  Catholic Diocese of Arizona (records)
  Catholic Church
  church history

INCLUSIVE DATES: 1970-present
COLLECTION FORMATS: institution's records, photographs
COLLECTION ACCESS: not described
STAFF FTE: administration

Del Webb Corporation
Anchor Centre III, Suite 400
2231 E. Camelback Road
Phoenix, Arizona 85016

TEL: (602) 468-6862
FAX: (602) 468-6797

REPORTED BY: Diane H. Elliott, Records Administrator

TYPE OF INSTITUTION: Community Developer and Builder (business)

HOURS: M-F 7:30-4:30
ACCESS: not open to the general public
SERVICES: none
RESTRICTIONS: none circulate

PRIMARY COLLECTION FOCUS: business records, memorabilia, historical information on Webb projects
    Del Webb Corporation
    Del Webb subsidiaries
    business records
    Del Webb projects
    Sun City, AZ
    communities, master planned

INCLUSIVE DATES: 1929-present
COLLECTION FORMATS: institution's records, books, pamphlets, films, photographs, maps, oral histories, house organ
COLLECTION ACCESS: computerized finding aids (used by staff)
SOFTWARE/SYSTEM: Smart 3.1, Paradox
FACILITIES/EQUIPMENT/PRESERVATION: temperature controls, humidity controls, fire detection controls, fire extinguishing system, vaults off-site

---

Episcopal Church Diocese of Arizona
114 W. Roosevelt
P.O. Box 13647
Phoenix, Arizona 85002

TEL: (602) 254-0976
FAX: (602) 495-6603

REPORTED BY: Rev. Donald W. Monson, Diocesan Historiographer
TYPE OF INSTITUTION: Diocesan office (religious)

HOURS: see below
ACCESS: not open to general public
SERVICES: mail, phone

PRIMARY COLLECTION FOCUS: history of Episcopal Diocese of Arizona
    Episcopal Diocese of Arizona--history
    missions
    parishes--Episcopal
    Episcopal Bishops/Clergy--correspondence

INCLUSIVE DATES: 1869-present
VOLUME: 100 linear feet
COLLECTION FORMATS: 80% manuscript collections, 9% institution's records, 10% books, 1% photographs
COLLECTION ACCESS: container lists, registers/inventories, some not described
STAFF FTE: volunteer, no full-time positions
INSTITUTIONAL SUPPORT FOR PROFESSIONAL DEVELOPMENT: payment of dues, reimbursement
FACILITIES/EQUIPMENT/PRESERVATION: fire extinguishing system
PATRON USE STATISTICS: user statistics not kept

Hall of Flame Museum of Firefighting
6101 E. Van Buren St.
Phoenix, Arizona 85008

TEL: (602) 275-3473
FAX: (602) 945-1912

REPORTED BY: Peter M. Molloy, Director
TYPE OF INSTITUTION: library, museum (private)

HOURS: M-Sa 9-5
ACCESS: not open to general public
SERVICES: in-person, photocopies

PRIMARY COLLECTION FOCUS: history of firefighting
    firefighting--history
    firefighting--apparatus
    firefighting--methods

INCLUSIVE DATES: 1800-modern
COLLECTION FORMATS: books, pamphlets, photographs
COLLECTION ACCESS: card catalog
STAFF FTE: 1 part-time administrative
INSTITUTIONAL SUPPORT FOR PROFESSIONAL DEVELOPMENT: tuition, dues, reimbursement, use of facilities, telephone, clerical staff
SPECIAL SERVICES/PROGRAMS: exhibits, tours, newsletter, lectures
FACILITIES/EQUIPMENT/PRESERVATION: temperature controls, humidity controls, fire detection controls, fire extinguishing system, disaster preparedness plan
PATRON USE STATISTICS: 25,000 visitors (museum)

The Heard Museum Library and Archives
22 E. Monte Vista Road
Phoenix, Arizona 85004-1480

TEL: (602) 252-8840
FAX: (602) 252-9757

REPORTED BY: Mario Nick Klimiades, Librarian/Archivist
TYPE OF INSTITUTION: museum (private)

HOURS: see below
ACCESS: public access by appointment; with membership/admissions
SERVICES: in-person, mail, phone, photocopies, photographs

PRIMARY COLLECTION FOCUS: Native American history
    Native Americans--art
    Native Americans--culture
    ethnoarts--Southwestern U.S.
    Native Americans--writings
    anthropology
    Native Americans--artists
    music--Southwestern native
    technologies, indigenous
    ethnography

COLLECTION FORMATS: 40,000 books, 800 serials, 7000 biographies, 500 pamphlets, 1000s slides, oral histories, 10,000 photographs, manuscript collections, posters, institution's records, audio cassettes, albums, 300 videos
COLLECTION ACCESS: card catalog, registers/inventories, container lists, computerized finding aids (used by staff, patrons)
SOFTWARE/SYSTEM: Questor's Argus/Muse, wordprocessing
STAFF FTE: 1 administrative, 30 volunteers, 2 technicians
INSTITUTIONAL SUPPORT FOR PROFESSIONAL DEVELOPMENT: tuition, dues, reimbursement, in-

house workshops, mailings, use of facilities, telephone, and clerical staff
SPECIAL SERVICES/PROGRAMS: tours
FACILITIES/EQUIPMENT/PRESERVATION: temperature controls
PATRON USE STATISTICS: 1000 in-house patrons, 1000 telephone, other user statistics not kept

---

Historic First Presbyterian Church
402 W. Monroe
Phoenix, Arizona 85003

TEL: (602) 254-6356

REPORTED BY: Pamela McDonald, Secretary
TYPE OF INSTITUTION: church/school (religious)

ACCESS: by appointment only
SERVICES: reference requests will be answered; photocopies

PRIMARY COLLECTION FOCUS: First Presbyterian Church
　　　Presbyterians
　　　church history

INCLUSIVE DATES: 1927-present
VOLUME: 45 cubic feet
COLLECTION FORMATS: registers, institution's records, photographs, pamphlets, ephemera, blueprints
COLLECTION ACCESS: not described
STAFF FTE: 1 clerical
SPECIAL SERVICES/PROGRAMS: exhibit, tours, newsletter, fund raising
FACILITIES/EQUIPMENT/PRESERVATION: temperature controls, humidity controls, fire detection controls, fire extinguishing system, fire-proof vault

---

Phoenix Museum of History
1002 W. Van Buren
P.O. Box 926
Phoenix, Arizona 85001

TEL: (602) 253-2734

REPORTED BY: Cindy Myers, Executive Director
TYPE OF INSTITUTION: museum (private, non-profit)

HOURS: W-Su 11-4
ACCESS: open to general public
SERVICES: in-person, mail, phone

PRIMARY COLLECTION FOCUS: early Arizona
　　　Arizona--pioneer
　　　family history

INCLUSIVE DATES: 1850-1950
COLLECTION FORMATS: manuscript collections, books, institution's records, pamphlets, government records, photographs, maps, oral histories, personal papers
COLLECTION ACCESS: not described
STAFF FTE: 1 administrative, .5 museum aide, 30 volunteers
INSTITUTIONAL SUPPORT FOR PROFESSIONAL DEVELOPMENT: tuition, dues, reimbursement, mailings, use of facilities, telephone
SPECIAL SERVICES/PROGRAMS: exhibits, tours, classes, newsletter, fund raising, lectures, summer camp
FACILITIES/EQUIPMENT/PRESERVATION: temperature controls
PATRON USE STATISTICS: user statistics not kept

Phoenix Newspapers, Inc., Library
120 E. Van Buren
P.O. Box 1950
Phoenix, Arizona 85001

TEL: (602) 271-8115
FAX: (602) 271-8914

REPORTED BY: Paula Stevens, Library Manager
TYPE OF INSTITUTION: newspaper research library (business)

HOURS: M-F 7am-10pm; Sa 8:30am-5pm, Su 7am-7pm
ACCESS: not open to general public; limited services to other libraries w/fees
SERVICES: photo reprints for a fee
RESTRICTIONS: no public services

PRIMARY COLLECTION FOCUS: research library for Arizona Newspapers, Inc.
    newspapers--Arizona
    Arizona Republic
    Phoenix Gazette
    Arizona Business Gazette
    newspapers--photographs

INCLUSIVE DATES: 1948-present
VOLUME: 7 million clippings, 200,000 photographs
COLLECTION FORMATS: 200,000 photographs, 7 million clippings on microfiche
COLLECTION ACCESS: not described, computerized database
ACQUISITION REPORTED TO: full text of news stories since 1986 via Vu/Text, Dialog, DataTimes
STAFF FTE: 1 administrative, 1 photo librarian, 3 reference librarians, 8.5 clerical, 1 database supervisor, 4 online indexers
INSTITUTIONAL SUPPORT FOR PROFESSIONAL DEVELOPMENT: tuition, dues, reimbursement
FACILITIES/EQUIPMENT/PRESERVATION: fire extinguishing system, fire detection controls

Phoenix Public Library, Arizona Room
12 E. McDowell Road
Phoenix, Arizona 85004

TEL: (602) 262-4636

REPORTED BY: Fay Freed, Librarian II
TYPE OF INSTITUTION: library (city)

HOURS: M-Tu 9-9, W-Sa 9-5, closed Sundays and holidays
ACCESS: open to general public
SERVICES: in-person, phone, photocopies
RESTRICTIONS: very limited telephone reference, charge for photocopies

PRIMARY COLLECTION FOCUS: Phoenix and Arizona
    Arizona--history
    water
    biography
    Native Americans
    travel guides--Southwest
    McClintock, James H.
    Phoenix, AZ (local history)

VOLUME: 24,000 items
COLLECTION FORMATS: 16 drawers manuscripts, 2 drawers records, 22,000 books, 113 drawers pamphlets, 800 photographs, 1000 maps

ACCESS: card catalog, computerized finding aids (used by staff and patrons)
SOFTWARE/SYSTEM: CLSI
STAFF FTE: 1.5 librarians, part-time volunteer
INSTITUTIONAL SUPPORT FOR PROFESSIONAL DEVELOPMENT: tuition, payment of dues, reimbursement for meetings, use of telephone
PATRON USE STATISTICS: user statistics not kept
NHPRC AZ550-640

Research Library
Dept. of Library, Archives and Public Records
1700 W. Washington
Phoenix, Arizona 85007

TEL: (602) 542-3701
FAX: (602) 542-4400

REPORTED BY: Linda McCleary, Head, Reference/Document Services
TYPE OF INSTITUTION: library (state)

HOURS: M-F 8-5 except state holidays
ACCESS: open to general public
SERVICES: in-person, mail, phone, photocopies

PRIMARY COLLECTION FOCUS: Arizona History, federal documents, state documents, genealogy
    Arizona--history
    Southwestern U.S.--history
    Native Americans
    Arizona--government
    genealogy

INCLUSIVE DATES: 1863-present
VOLUME: 1.3 million items
COLLECTION FORMATS: 500,000 books, 10,000 photographs, maps, regional depository for government records; federal documents--2nd copies circulate
COLLECTION ACCESS: card catalog, computerized finding aids (used by staff and patrons)
SOFTWARE/SYSTEM: CD disk for Marcive
ACQUISITION REPORTED TO: OCLC
STAFF FTE: 6 reference librarians, 1 map curator, 8 clerical
INSTITUTIONAL SUPPORT FOR PROFESSIONAL DEVELOPMENT: tuition, reimbursement, in-house workshops, payment for mailings, use of facilities, use of clerical
SPECIAL SERVICES/PROGRAMS: tours
FACILITIES/EQUIPMENT/PRESERVATION: fire detection controls, disaster preparedness plan
PATRON USE STATISTICS: 7200 in-house patrons, 7200 telephone, 3600 mail reference requests, all collections used

NHPRC AZ550-040

Salt River Project Archives
Box 52025
Phoenix, Arizona 85072-2025

TEL: (602) 236-6618
FAX: (602) 236-6546

REPORTED BY: Fred Anderson, Historical Analyst
TYPE OF INSTITUTION: archives (business)

HOURS: M-F 8:30-5:00
ACCESS: public access by appointment only, not open to general public
SERVICES: in-person, photocopies

PRIMARY COLLECTION FOCUS: Salt River Reclamation Project
    Salt River Reclamation Project Dam, AZ
    canals
    power systems
    utilities
    irrigation--Salt River Valley, AZ

INCLUSIVE DATES: 1865-1985
COLLECTION FORMATS: books, photographs, maps, aerial photographs
COLLECTION ACCESS: computerized finding aids (used by staff)
SOFTWARE/SYSTEM: Documaster
STAFF FTE: 1 archival, 1 clerical
INSTITUTIONAL SUPPORT FOR PROFESSIONAL DEVELOPMENT: tuition and payment of dues reimbursement, use of facilities, payment for phone, use of clerical staff
FACILITIES/EQUIPMENT/PRESERVATION: temperature controls, humidity controls, fire detection controls, fire extinguishing system, disaster preparedness plan
PATRON USE STATISTICS: 200 in-house patrons, other user statistics not kept

---

Eastern Arizona Museum, Historical Society   **TEL**: (602) 485-2288
P.O. Box 274
Pima, Arizona 85543

REPORTED BY: Allen B. Weed
TYPE OF INSTITUTION: historical society, museum (county/local)

HOURS: W-F 2-4; Sa 1-5
ACCESS: open to the general public
SERVICES: [not reported]

PRIMARY COLLECTION FOCUS: Arizona Pioneers
    pioneers
    Pima, AZ (local history)
    Native Americans
    genealogy

COLLECTION FORMATS: manuscript collections, institution's records, books, photographs, maps, oral histories
COLLECTION ACCESS: not described
STAFF FTE: none
SPECIAL SERVICES/PROGRAMS: exhibits, tours
PATRON USE STATISTICS: over 1000 visitors (museum)

NHPRC AZ600-200

Southwestern Research Station   **TEL**: (602) 558-2396
American Museum of Natural History
P.O. Box G
Portal, Arizona 85632

REPORTED BY: Wade C. Sherbrooke, Director
TYPE OF INSTITUTION: museum (non-profit)

HOURS: year round
ACCESS: public access by appointment only
SERVICES: none

PRIMARY COLLECTION FOCUS: biological collections, history of Cave Creek Canyon, Stephen Reed
    biology--collections
    Cave Creek Canyon, AZ
    Reed, Stephen

VOLUME: 1 file drawer
COLLECTION FORMATS: photographs
COLLECTION ACCESS: not described
STAFF FTE: research station staff

Sharlot Hall Museum, Prescott Historical Society   **TEL**: (602) 445-3122
415 W. Gurley   **FAX**: (602) 776-9053
Prescott, Arizona 86301

REPORTED BY: Sue Abbey, Archivist
TYPE OF INSTITUTION: historical society (state and non-profit)

HOURS: Tu-Sa 10-5 April-October; 10-4 November-March; Su 1-5
ACCESS: open to general public
SERVICES: in-person, mail, phone, photocopies, photo reproductions

PRIMARY COLLECTION FOCUS: central and northern Arizona
    Prescott, AZ (local history)
    Arizona
    Arizona, Central and Northern
    Southwestern U.S.
    mining
    military history
    pioneers
    railroads
    ranching
    Yavapai County, AZ (local history and government)

INCLUSIVE DATES: 1860s-present
COLLECTION FORMATS: 90 cubic feet manuscript collections, 8 cubic feet institution's records, 12,000 books, 300 cubic feet pamphlets, 10 films, 92,000 photographs, 5600 maps, 500 oral histories
COLLECTION ACCESS: card catalog, container lists, computerized finding aids (used by staff)
SOFTWARE/SYSTEM: PC File
STAFF FTE: 2 archival, 6 volunteers
INSTITUTIONAL SUPPORT FOR PROFESSIONAL DEVELOPMENT: tuition, reimbursement
SPECIAL SERVICES/PROGRAMS: exhibits, tours, newsletter, lectures
FACILITIES/EQUIPMENT/PRESERVATION: temperature controls, humidity controls, fire detection controls, fire extinguishing system
PATRON USE STATISTICS: 1500 patrons

NHPRC AZ625-630

Quartzsite Historical Museum   **TEL**: [not reported]
Main Street, B-10   **FAX**: [not reported]
P.O. Box 270
Quartzsite, Arizona 85346

REPORTED BY: Meta J. Shepherd, President
TYPE OF INSTITUTION: historical society, museum (private)

HOURS: W-Su, 10 am-3 pm, November 15-April 15
ACCESS: open to general public
SERVICES: in-person, fee for copies, other

PRIMARY COLLECTION FOCUS: La Paz County, Arizona
  Quartzsite, AZ
  La Paz County, AZ (local history)

INCLUSIVE DATES: 1860-present
COLLECTION FORMATS: some manuscripts, some photographs
COLLECTION ACCESS: card catalog, registers/inventories
STAFF FTE: docent
SPECIAL SERVICES/PROGRAMS: tours

Tonto National Monument **TEL**: (602) 467-2241
P.O. Box 707
Roosevelt, Arizona 85545

REPORTED BY: Dessamae Lorrain, Park Ranger
TYPE OF INSTITUTION: National Monument (federal)

HOURS: daily 8-5, except Christmas
ACCESS: public access by appointment only (Archives)
SERVICES: in-person, mail, photocopies

PRIMARY COLLECTION FOCUS: Tonto National Monument
  Tonto National Monument, AZ (records)
  cliff dwellings
  Salado culture
  Native Americans--culture
  Sonora, Mexico--flora and fauna
  parks and monuments, federal

INCLUSIVE DATES: 1911-1991
VOLUME: very small
COLLECTION FORMATS: manuscript collections, institution's records, pamphlets, films, government records,
  photographs, maps
COLLECTION ACCESS: card catalog
STAFF FTE: 3 administrative, 1 archival, 1 outreach, 4 rangers, 2 volunteers, 1 student
INSTITUTIONAL SUPPORT FOR PROFESSIONAL DEVELOPMENT: tuition, reimbursement, mailings, use
  of facilities and telephone
FACILITIES/EQUIPMENT/PRESERVATION: limited temperature controls, fire extinguishing system
PATRON USE STATISTICS: user statistics not kept

Graham County Historical Society **TEL**: (602) 428-3633
Box 47
Safford, Arizona 85546

REPORTED BY: Spencer Brinkerhoff, President
TYPE OF INSTITUTION: historical society, museum (county/local)

HOURS: M-Tu 1-5
ACCESS: open to general public

PRIMARY COLLECTION FOCUS: Graham County
    Graham County, AZ (local history)
    furniture

COLLECTION FORMATS: 100 manuscript collections, 100 books, 5000 photographs, 25 oral histories
COLLECTION ACCESS: card catalog, registers/inventories
STAFF FTE: 1 volunteer, 1 employee
SPECIAL SERVICES/PROGRAMS: exhibits, tours, newsletter
PATRON USE STATISTICS: microform copies

Apache County Historical Society   **TEL**: (602) 337-2309
180 W. Cleveland
Box 146
St. Johns, Arizona 85936

REPORTED BY: Mrs. Nellie Olson, Director
TYPE OF INSTITUTION: archives, historical society, museum (county/local)

HOURS: [not reported]
ACCESS: open to general public, donations appreciated
SERVICES: photocopies

PRIMARY COLLECTION FOCUS: Apache County, museum exhibits

    Native Americans
    Apache County, AZ (local history)
    family history
    Arizona--history

COLLECTION FORMATS: institution's records, books, pamphlets, photographs, maps, oral histories, artifacts
    (prehistoric bones)
COLLECTION ACCESS: registers/inventories
STAFF FTE: 1 administrative
INSTITUTIONAL SUPPORT FOR PROFESSIONAL DEVELOPMENT: payment of dues
SPECIAL SERVICES/PROGRAMS: exhibits, tours
FACILITIES/EQUIPMENT/PRESERVATION: temperature controls, fire extinguishing system

---

Scottsdale Historical Society, Inc.   **TEL**: (602) 945-4499
7333 E. Scottsdale Mall
P.O. Box 143
Scottsdale, Arizona 85252

REPORTED BY: JoAnn Handley, Secretary
TYPE OF INSTITUTION: historical society, museum (non-profit, local)

HOURS: W-Sa 10-5; Su 12-4
ACCESS: public access by appointment only
SERVICES: in-person, telephone, and mail reference; photocopies (fee for photocopies)

PRIMARY COLLECTION FOCUS: history of Scottsdale
    Scottsdale, AZ (local history)
    agriculture
    Native Americans
    resorts--Scottsdale, AZ

INCLUSIVE DATES: 1888 - present
STAFF FTE: 60 volunteers
INSTITUTIONAL SUPPORT FOR PROFESSIONAL DEVELOPMENT: payment of dues, reimbursement for mailings, use of facilities
SPECIAL SERVICES/PROGRAMS: exhibits, tours, newsletter, fund raising, lectures
FACILITIES/EQUIPMENT/PRESERVATION: temperature controls, humidity controls, fire detection controls, fire extinguishing system
PATRON USE STATISTICS: user statistics not kept

Skull Valley Historical Society and Museum
Old Skull Valley Road
P.O. Box 143
Skull Valley, Arizona 86338

TEL: (602) 442-3469

REPORTED BY: Lou Ghering, Publicity Chairman
TYPE OF INSTITUTION: museum (non-profit corporation)

HOURS: Su 2-4, June-Sept or by appointment
ACCESS: open to general public
SERVICES: [not reported]

PRIMARY COLLECTION FOCUS: local history
    Skull Valley, AZ (local history)
    Native Americans--artifacts
    agriculture
    ranching
    railroads

COLLECTION FORMATS: photographs, oral histories, maps
STAFF FTE: volunteers [number not reported]

Apache-Sitgreaves National Forest
P.O. Box 640
Springerville, Arizona 85938

TEL: (602) 333-4301
FAX: (602) 333-6357

REPORTED BY: Bruce Donaldson
TYPE OF INSTITUTION: national forest (federal)

ACCESS: not open to general public
SERVICES: no public services
RESTRICTIONS: none circulate
PRIMARY COLLECTION FOCUS: prehistory of east central Arizona
    archaeology
    Native Americans--culture, prehistory
    Native Americans--culture, contemporary
    Euro-American culture, contemporary
    parks and monuments, records

INCLUSIVE DATES: prehistory-present
VOLUME: 120 cubic feet
COLLECTION FORMATS: manuscript collections, books, institution's records, pamphlets, films, government records, photographs, maps, oral histories, artifacts
COLLECTION ACCESS: some inventories; computerized finding aids
SOFTWARE/SYSTEM: BIB and Oracle

STAFF FTE: 1 administrative
INSTITUTIONAL SUPPORT FOR PROFESSIONAL DEVELOPMENT: tuition, reimbursement, mailing, facilities, telephone, clerical
SPECIAL SERVICES/PROGRAMS: exhibits, limited tours, lectures
FACILITIES/EQUIPMENT/PRESERVATION: fire detection, fire extinguishing
PATRON USE STATISTICS: user statistics not kept

NHPRC AZ700-40

Arizona Historical Society, Central Arizona Chapter
1300 N. College
Tempe, Arizona 85281

TEL: (602) 929-0292
FAX: (602) 967-5450

REPORTED BY: Janet Michaelieu, Librarian
TYPE OF INSTITUTION: historical society (state)

HOURS: M-F 8-5
ACCESS: public access by appointment only
SERVICES: in-person, mail, phone, photocopies

PRIMARY COLLECTION FOCUS: Arizona history
- architecture--drawings
- cemetery and burial records
- maps, Sanborn
- Arizona
- Arizona, Central
- Phoenix, AZ (local history)

INCLUSIVE DATES: 1850-1990
COLLECTION FORMATS: 280 linear feet manuscript collections, 3000 books, 500 pamphlets, 2000 films, 70,000 photographs, 100 maps, 800 oral histories, 2000 architectural drawings
COLLECTION ACCESS: card catalog, registers/inventories
STAFF FTE: 1 librarian, 12 volunteers, 1 student intern
INSTITUTIONAL SUPPORT FOR PROFESSIONAL DEVELOPMENT: tuition
FACILITIES/EQUIPMENT/PRESERVATION: temperature controls, humidity controls, fire detection controls, fire extinguishing system
PATRON USE STATISTICS: 900 in-house patrons, 1000 telephone, 260 mail reference requests, 100 collections used, 3000 reference photocopies

NHPRC AZ550-45 [note relocation and name change]

Arizona State University
School of Music, E-511
Southwest Tape Archives
Tempe, Arizona 85287

TEL: (602) 965-7568

REPORTED BY: Professor Richard Haefer
TYPE OF INSTITUTION: academic (state) [teaching archives]

ACCESS: by appointment only
SERVICES: very limited

PRIMARY COLLECTION FOCUS: ethnomusicology
- ethnomusicology
- Native Americans, Southwest U.S.
- Native Americans--musicology

COLLECTION FORMATS: audio tapes
COLLECTION ACCESS: not described
STAFF FTE: none
PATRON USE STATISTICS: user statistics not kept

NHPRC AZ750-32

Arizona Historical Foundation
Hayden Library, Arizona State University
Tempe, Arizona 85287

TEL: (602) 965-3283

REPORTED BY: Ed Oetting, Curator
TYPE OF INSTITUTION: library special collection (state, private foundation)

HOURS: M-F 8-5
ACCESS: open to general public
SERVICES: in-person, mail, phone, photocopies

PRIMARY COLLECTION FOCUS: history of Arizona and southwest
  Arizona
  Southwestern U.S.
  politics
  agriculture
  finance, Arizona Society of CPAs
  Goldwater, Barry, Senator
  Fannin, Paul
  cotton--Arizona Cotton Growers Association
  cattle--Arizona Cattle Growers Association
  bankers--Arizona Bankers Association

INCLUSIVE DATES: 1850-present
VOLUME: 4000 cubic feet
COLLECTION FORMATS: 2500 linear feet manuscript collections, 10,000 books, 40 cubic feet pamphlets, 20 cubic feet films, 300 microfilm rolls government records, 50,000 photographs, 3000 maps, 10 cubic feet oral histories, newspapers
COLLECTION ACCESS: card catalog, container lists, registers/inventories, computerized finding aids (used by staff)
SOFTWARE/SYSTEM: WordPerfect
ACQUISITION REPORTED TO: NUCMC, OCLC
STAFF FTE: 1 administrative, 2 archival/librarians, 1 volunteer, 1 intern
INSTITUTIONAL SUPPORT FOR PROFESSIONAL DEVELOPMENT: tuition, reimbursement, mailings, use of facilities, telephone
SPECIAL SERVICES/PROGRAMS: exhibits, tours, lectures
FACILITIES/EQUIPMENT/PRESERVATION: temperature controls, humidity controls, fire extinguishing system, preservation lab
PATRON USE STATISTICS: 1300 in-house patrons, 250 telephone, 90 mail reference requests, 9100 retrievals of collections

NHPRC AZ750-10

Department of Archives and Manuscripts
Hayden Library, Arizona State University
Tempe, Arizona 85287-1006

TEL: (602) 965-3145
FAX: (602) 965-9169

REPORTED BY: Edward C. Oetting, Head, Archives and Manuscripts

TYPE OF INSTITUTION: manuscript and archival, department (state/academic)

HOURS: Luhrs Reading Room, M 11-7, T-W 8-7, T-F 8-5, Sa 1-5; Archives M-F 1-5
ACCESS: Open to the general public
SERVICES: in-person, mail, and phone reference, photocopies, photographic reproductions

PRIMARY COLLECTION FOCUS: Arizona and Southwest United States, Chicano/Mexican American, Arizona State University, visual literacy

Arizona	Luhrs family
water	Chicanos
politics	Native Americans
Hayden, Carl T.	Montezuma, Carlos
Rhodes, John J.	Mexican Americans
mining	Arizona State University
McLaughlin, Herb and Dorothy	visual literacy
Hunt, George W.P.	Gammage, Grady
Southwestern U.S.	architectural records

INCLUSIVE DATES: 18th century-present
COLLECTION FORMATS: 3500 linear feet manuscript collections, 3000 linear feet institution's records, 30,000 books, 9937 pamphlets, 40 films, 650,000 photographs, 1500 maps, 175 oral histories
COLLECTION ACCESS: card catalog, repository guide, registers/inventories, computerized finding aids (used by staff and patrons)
SOFTWARE/SYSTEM: CARL, Q&A, MARCON
ACQUISITIONS REPORTED TO: OCLC, specialized/regional guide
STAFF FTE: 1 administrative, 3 general archival, 1 photo curator, 7.5 clerical, 1.5 student, 1 intern
INSTITUTIONAL SUPPORT FOR PROFESSIONAL DEVELOPMENT: tuition, reimbursement, mailings, use of facilities and clerical staff, payment for telephone
SPECIAL SERVICES/PROGRAMS: exhibits, tours, lectures/presentations
FACILITIES/EQUIPMENT/PRESERVATION: fire detection controls, disaster preparedness plan
PATRON USE STATISTICS: 8784 in-house patrons, 546 telephone, 37 mail, 26,500 reference photocopies
NHPRC AZ750-45

Tempe Historical Museum
809 E. Southern Avenue
Tempe, Arizona 85282

TEL: (602) 350-5100

REPORTED BY: Richard Bauer, Curator of Photographs and Archives
TYPE OF INSTITUTION: museum (city)

HOURS: M-Th 10-5; Sa 10-5, Su 1-5, closed Fridays and major holidays
ACCESS: research library and archives by appointment only
SERVICES: in-person, mail, phone, photocopies, other

PRIMARY COLLECTION FOCUS: history of Tempe
    Tempe, AZ (local history)
COLLECTION FORMATS: 20 manuscript collections, 1000 records, 1000 books, 1000 pamphlets, 100 films, 200 government records, 10,000 photographs, 100 maps, 100 oral histories
COLLECTION ACCESS: registers/inventories, catalog sheets
STAFF FTE: administrative, photo curator, 3 curators, 1 volunteer coordinator, 1 exhibit coordinator
INSTITUTIONAL SUPPORT FOR PROFESSIONAL DEVELOPMENT: payment of dues
SPECIAL SERVICES/PROGRAMS: exhibits, tours, classes, fund raising, lectures
FACILITIES/EQUIPMENT/PRESERVATION: temperature controls, humidity controls, fire detection controls, fire extinguishing system, preservation lab
PATRON USE STATISTICS: 150 in-house patrons, 400 collections used

Tombstone Courthouse State Historical Park **TEL**: (602) 457-3311
3rd and Toughnut Streets
P.O. Box 216
Tombstone, Arizona 85638

REPORTED BY: Hollis Cook, Park Manager
TYPE OF INSTITUTION: historic park, museum (state)

HOURS: Su-Sa 8-5, closed Christmas
ACCESS: open to general public
SERVICES: in-person, mail, and phone reference; photocopies
RESTRICTIONS: none circulate

PRIMARY COLLECTION FOCUS: 19th Century Western America
    Tombstone, AZ (local history)
    Cochise County, AZ
    Arizona, Southeast

INCLUSIVE DATES: 1877-1929
COLLECTION FORMATS: manuscript collections, books, pamphlets, government records, photographs, maps
COLLECTION ACCESS: card catalog
STAFF FTE: 4 park rangers
SPECIAL SERVICES/PROGRAMS: exhibits, tours, lectures
INSTITUTIONAL SUPPORT FOR PROFESSIONAL DEVELOPMENT: tuition, dues, reimbursement
FACILITIES/EQUIPMENT/PRESERVATION: fire extinguishing system
PATRON USE STATISTICS: user statistics not kept

NHPRC AZ760-760

Tubac Presidio State Historic Park **TEL**: (602) 398-2252
Broadway and River Road **FAX**: (602) 398-2252
P.O. Box 1296
Tubac, Arizona 85646

REPORTED BY: Robert Barnacastle, Park Manager
TYPE OF INSTITUTION: historic park (state) [The Tubac Historical Society operates the research room.]

HOURS: varies
ACCESS: by appointment only
SERVICES: in-person and mail reference, photocopies (fee for copies)
RESTRICTIONS: limited services

PRIMARY COLLECTION FOCUS: Tubac (local history)
    Tubac, AZ local history
    Arizona, territorial period

INCLUSIVE DATES: 1880 - present
COLLECTION FORMATS: manuscript collections, books, government records, photographs, maps, oral histories
COLLECTION ACCESS: card catalog
STAFF FTE: volunteers
SPECIAL SERVICES/PROGRAMS: exhibits, tours, classes, newsletter, fund raising
FACILITIES/EQUIPMENT/PRESERVATION: fire extinguishing system
PATRON USE STATISTICS: user statistics kept but not available

NHPRC AZ775-790

Arizona Historical Society
949 E. Second Street
Tucson, Arizona 85719

TEL: (602) 628-5774
FAX: (602) 628-5695

REPORTED BY: Rose Byrne, Acting Head, Archives Department
TYPE OF INSTITUTION: historical society (state)

HOURS: M-F 10-4, Sa 10-1
ACCESS: open to general public
SERVICES: in-person, mail, phone, photocopies
RESTRICTIONS: none circulate
PRIMARY COLLECTION FOCUS: Arizona history, Southwest US, Sonora, Mexico
    Arizona, early
    Native Americans
    mining
    ranching
    Southwestern U.S.
    Sonora, Mexico

INCLUSIVE DATES: 1540-present
COLLECTION FORMATS: 3000 linear feet manuscript collections, institution's records, 40,000 books, pamphlets, 150,000 photographs, 2000 maps, 500 oral histories
COLLECTION ACCESS: card catalog, container lists
STAFF FTE: 2 administrative, 2 archivists, 1 preservation, 1.5 photo, 1 outreach, 3 library, volunteers, clerical, students, interns
NHPRC AZ800-30

Arizona State Museum
Park Avenue and University Blvd.
University of Arizona
Tucson, Arizona 85721

TEL: (602) 621-4609
FAX: (602) 621-2976

REPORTED BY: Jan Bell, Curator of Collections
TYPE OF INSTITUTION: museum (state, part of Univ. of Arizona)

HOURS: M-F 8-5
ACCESS: public access by appointment
SERVICES: in-person, mail, phone, photocopies
RESTRICTIONS: some materials restricted, limits on photocopies

PRIMARY COLLECTION FOCUS: Southwestern anthropology
    Southwestern U.S.--anthropology
    anthropology
    anthropologists
    Arizona State Museum--archaeological projects documentation
    Arizona State Museum (records)
    Native Americans
    municipal agencies
    archaeology--Southwestern U.S.
    ethnography
    federal agencies

INCLUSIVE DATES: 1920-1992

VOLUME: 1000 linear feet
COLLECTION FORMATS: manuscript collections, institution's records, books, pamphlets, 30 films, archaeological project records, 250,000 photographs, 11,000 maps, oral histories
COLLECTION ACCESS: registers/inventories, container lists, computerized finding aids [used by staff, patrons (printouts only)]
STAFF FTE: 2 photo curators, 3/4 person archives
INSTITUTIONAL SUPPORT FOR PROFESSIONAL DEVELOPMENT: tuition, reimbursement, mailings, use of facilities, telephone, clerical staff
SPECIAL SERVICES/PROGRAMS: tours, lectures
FACILITIES/EQUIPMENT/PRESERVATION: temperature controls, fire detection controls, fire extinguishing system, conservation lab, disaster preparedness plan
PATRON USE STATISTICS: 96 in-house patrons, 173 collections used, 2500 reference photocopies

NHPRC AZ800-800

Bloom Southwest Jewish Archives   **TEL**: (602) 621-5774
1052 N. Highland Avenue
University of Arizona
Tucson, Arizona 85721

REPORTED BY: Prof. Abraham S. Chonin, Director and Research Professor
TYPE OF INSTITUTION: archives (state, academic)

HOURS: 7am-1pm
ACCESS: open to general public
SERVICES: in-person, mail, phone, photocopies (fee for copies)

PRIMARY COLLECTION FOCUS: pioneer Jewish history in Southwest (Arizona, New Mexico, West Texas)
  Southwestern U.S.--Jewish history
  Arizona--Jews
  New Mexico--Jews
  West Texas--Jews
  family history--Jewish
  biography
  Judaism--Southwestern U.S.

INCLUSIVE DATES: 1850s-present
VOLUME: 10,000 items
COLLECTION FORMATS: 500 manuscript collections, 100 institution's records, 300 books, 100 pamphlets, 50 films, 200 government records, 300 photographs, 100 maps, 100 oral histories
COLLECTION ACCESS: computerized finding aid (used by staff)
SOFTWARE/SYSTEM: WordPerfect 5.0 and 5.1, Lotus Magellan
ACQUISITION REPORTED TO: Jewish historical journals
STAFF FTE: 1 administrative, 3 volunteer, 2 intern
INSTITUTIONAL SUPPORT FOR PROFESSIONAL DEVELOPMENT: tuition, payment of dues, reimbursement, payment for mailings
SPECIAL SERVICES/PROGRAMS: tours, classes, lectures
FACILITIES/EQUIPMENT/PRESERVATION: fire detection controls, disaster preparedness plan
PATRON USE STATISTICS: user statistics not kept

Central Arizona Project Repository   **TEL**: (602) 670-6576
Federal Building
300 W. Congress St.
Tucson, Arizona 85701

REPORTED BY: Chris Cleary, Archivist
TYPE OF INSTITUTION: repository (federal)

HOURS: M-F 8-5
ACCESS: public access by appointment only
SERVICES: in-person, mail, phone, photocopies

PRIMARY COLLECTION FOCUS: archaeological materials from projects along the Central AZ Project Canal
    Central Arizona Project
    archaeology
    Arizona
    Native Americans
    water
    canals
    irrigation

INCLUSIVE DATES: 1965-present
COLLECTION FORMATS: institution's records, pamphlets, films, government records, photographs, maps, oral histories
COLLECTION ACCESS: Computerized finding aids (used by staff, patrons)
SOFTWARE/SYSTEM: d-Base IV
STAFF FTE: 4 administrative, 4 student
INSTITUTIONAL SUPPORT FOR PROFESSIONAL DEVELOPMENT: some reimbursement, telephone use
SPECIAL SERVICES/PROGRAMS: tours
FACILITIES/EQUIPMENT/PRESERVATION: fire detection controls, fire extinguishing system
PATRON USE STATISTICS: 6 in-house patrons, 6 telephone, 6 mail reference requests, 2 reference photocopies

---

Postal History Foundation   **TEL**: (602) 623-6652
920 N. 1st Avenue
P.O. Box 40725
Tucson, Arizona 85717

REPORTED BY: [not listed]
TYPE OF INSTITUTION: archives, library (non-profit)

HOURS: M-F 8-3
ACCESS: open to general public
SERVICES: in-person, mail, photocopies

PRIMARY COLLECTION FOCUS: philatelic and postal history
    philately
    postal history

INCLUSIVE DATES: 1776-present
COLLECTION FORMATS: manuscripts, films, government records, photographs, maps
COLLECTION ACCESS: card catalog
STAFF FTE: administrative, volunteer [numbers not specified]
INSTITUTIONAL SUPPORT FOR PROFESSIONAL DEVELOPMENT: reimbursement
SPECIAL SERVICES/PROGRAMS: exhibits, tours, classes, lectures, quarterly journal
FACILITIES/EQUIPMENT/PRESERVATION: fire detection controls
PATRON USE STATISTICS: 100 in-house patrons, 200 telephone

Saguaro National Monument
3693 S. Old Spanish Trail
Tucson, Arizona 85730

TEL: (602) 670-6680
FAX: (602) 670-6681

REPORTED BY: Margaret W. Weesner, Chief, Division of Science and Resource Mngt
TYPE OF INSTITUTION: National Monument (federal)

HOURS: M-F 8-5 (Archives)
ACCESS: public access by appointment only
SERVICES: no services

PRIMARY COLLECTION FOCUS: Saguaro National Monument
  Saguaro National Monument, AZ
  mining
  deeds
  Saguaro population
  cattle, feral
  natural resources

INCLUSIVE DATES: 1929-1950
VOLUME: 120
COLLECTION FORMATS: 50 manuscript collections, 50 photographs, 20 maps
COLLECTION ACCESS: not described, computerized finding aids (used by staff)
SOFTWARE/SYSTEM: Automated National Cataloging System, d-Base III
ACQUISITION REPORTED TO: National Park Service, Automated National Catalog System
STAFF FTE: Property Custodial Officer
SPECIAL SERVICES/PROGRAMS: exhibits, tours, lectures
FACILITIES/EQUIPMENT/PRESERVATION: temperature controls, fire detection controls,
    disaster preparedness plan
PATRON USE STATISTICS: user statistics not kept

University of Arizona
Arizona State Museum
Photographic Collections
Tucson, Arizona 85721

TEL: (602) 621-2445
FAX: (602) 621-2976

REPORTED BY: Kathy Hubenschmidt, Photo Collections Curator
TYPE OF INSTITUTION: museum (state)

HOURS: M-F 8-5
ACCESS: open to general public by appointment
SERVICES: in-person, mail, and telephone reference, fax reference, photocopies, photograph reproductions;
    fee for copies

PRIMARY COLLECTION FOCUS: anthropology, Southwest native cultures
    Native Americans--Southwest U.S.
    prehistoric cultures--Southwest U.S.
    anthropology

INCLUSIVE DATES: 1890-present
VOLUME: 250,000 images
COLLECTION FORMATS: photographs, videos, films, slides
COLLECTION ACCESS: card catalog, inventories, computerized finding aids (used by staff)
SOFTWARE/SYSTEM: INFO
STAFF FTE: 2 photo curators
INSTITUTIONAL SUPPORT FOR PROFESSIONAL DEVELOPMENT: tuition, reimbursement, mailings,

facilities, telephone, clerical
SPECIAL SERVICES/PROGRAMS: lectures
FACILITIES/EQUIPMENT/PRESERVATION: temperature controls, fire detection controls, fire extinguishing system, preservation lab, disaster preparedness plan
PATRON USE STATISTICS: 500 in-house patrons, 200 telephone, 200 mail

NHPRC AZ800-803

Arizona State Museum, Documentary Relations of the Southwest
University of Arizona
Tucson, Arizona 85721

TEL: (602) 621-6278
FAX: (602) 621-2976

REPORTED BY: Charles W. Polzer, Curator of Ethnohistory
TYPE OF INSTITUTION: museum (state, religious)

HOURS: M-F 8-5
ACCESS: open to general public (qualified researchers)
SERVICES: in-person, mail, phone
RESTRICTIONS: depends on archives of origin and time available

PRIMARY COLLECTION FOCUS: Spanish Colonial Southwestern U.S. and northern Mexico
    Spanish Colonial Southwestern U.S./northern Mexico
    Northern New Spain
    Jesuitica
    missionaries
    Southwestern U.S.--Spanish Colonial
    Mexico, northern
    ethnohistory--Southwestern U.S. and northern Mexico
    Catholic Church

INCLUSIVE DATES: 1538-1821
VOLUME: 1000 rolls of microfilm of foreign archival holdings
COLLECTION ACCESS: computerized finding aid (used by staff and some patrons)
SOFTWARE/SYSTEM: Infoware
STAFF FTE: 4 other
FACILITIES/EQUIPMENT/PRESERVATION: temperature controls, fire extinguishing system
PATRON USE STATISTICS: 300 in-house patrons, 200 telephone, 250 mail reference requests, 1000 collections used, 2500 reference photocopies

NHPRC AZ800-790

Center for Creative Photography
University of Arizona
Tucson, Arizona 85721

TEL: (602) 621-7968
FAX: (602) 621-9444

REPORTED BY: [not listed]
TYPE OF INSTITUTION: archives, library, museum (academic)

HOURS: M-F 10-5; Su 12-5 (hours vary)
ACCESS: open to general public
SERVICES: in-person, mail, phone, photocopies, photographic reproductions

PRIMARY COLLECTION FOCUS: history of photography as an art form
    photography, history of
    Adams, Ansel

Weston, Edward
Wolcott, Marion Post
Strand, Paul
Bullock, Wynn
Winogrand, Garry
Palfi, Marion
Newhall, Beaumont and Nancy
Callahan, Harry

INCLUSIVE DATES: 1839-1992
VOLUME: 50,000 photographs, 12,000 books, 3 million archival items
COLLECTION FORMATS: 2500 linear feet manuscript collections, 100 linear feet institution's records, 12,000 books, many pamphlets, 300 videos, 50,000 photographs, oral histories on video, negatives, camera equipment
COLLECTION ACCESS: card catalog, guide, registers/inventories, container lists, computerized finding aids (used by staff)
SOFTWARE/SYSTEM: books in OCLC, manuscripts in RLIN, photographs in INMAGIC (in-house only)
ACQUISITION REPORTED TO: OCLC, RLIN
STAFF FTE: 2 administrative, 1.75 archival, 1 photo curator, 1 outreach, 1 librarian, 2 clerical, 40 students and interns, 6 other
INSTITUTIONAL SUPPORT FOR PROFESSIONAL DEVELOPMENT: tuition, reimbursement, use of facilities
SPECIAL SERVICES/PROGRAMS: exhibits, tours, fund raising, lectures, journals and books, traveling exhibits
FACILITIES/EQUIPMENT/PRESERVATION: temperature controls, humidity controls, fire detection controls, fire extinguishing system
PATRON USE STATISTICS: 35,000 library patrons, 26,000 gallery, 2000 photo viewing appointments, 75 archival in-house patrons

NHPRC AZ800-820

Special Collections **TEL**: (602) 621-6423University of Arizona Library
University of Arizona
Tucson, Arizona 85721

REPORTED BY: Louis A. Hieb, Head Librarian, Special Collections
TYPE OF INSTITUTION: academic (academic, state)

HOURS: M-F 10-5; Sa 12-4
ACCESS: open to the general public
SERVICES: in-person, mail, phone, photocopies, photo reproductions
RESTRICTIONS: preservation concerns may prevent photocopy

PRIMARY COLLECTION FOCUS: Southwest including W. Texas, S. Colorado, New Mexico, Arizona,
Borderlands
Southwestern U.S.
Texas, West
Colorado, South
Arizona--history
Mexico, Sonora
Baja
Borderlands
Hispanics
Archaeology
New Mexico
Native Americans
literary manuscripts

INCLUSIVE DATES: prehistoric-present
VOLUME: 100,000+
COLLECTION FORMATS: 850 manuscript collections, institution's archives, 100,000+ books, 10,000 pamphlets, 100 films, pre-1985 Arizona government records, 40,000 photographs, 100 maps, 500 oral histories, 30,000 postcards
COLLECTION ACCESS: card catalog, registers/inventories, on-line catalog, computerized finding aids (used by staff and patrons)
SOFTWARE/SYSTEM: WordPerfect 5.1, d-Base
ACQUISITION REPORTED TO: NUCMC and OCLC
STAFF FTE: 1 administrative, 2 archival, 1 photo curator, 3 clerical, 6 student, 1 intern
INSTITUTIONAL SUPPORT FOR PROFESSIONAL DEVELOPMENT: tuition, reimbursement, in-house workshops, mailings, use of facilities, telephone
SPECIAL SERVICES/PROGRAMS: exhibits, tours, classes, fund raising, lectures, exhibit brochures
FACILITIES/EQUIPMENT/PRESERVATION: temperature controls, fire detection controls, fire extinguishing system, compact shelving
PATRON USE STATISTICS: 7000 in-house patrons, 1000 telephone, 250 mail reference requests, 20,000 collections used, 5000 reference photocopies

NHPRC AZ800-830

Arizona Historical Society, Yuma Chapter **TEL**: (602) 782-1841
240 Madison Avenue
Yuma, Arizona 85364

REPORTED BY: Carol Brooks, Curator
TYPE OF INSTITUTION: historical society (state)

HOURS: Tu-Sa 10-4
ACCESS: open to general public, access by appointment only
SERVICES: in-person, mail, phone, photocopies, photo reproduction
RESTRICTIONS: limited staff, limited phone and mail research

PRIMARY COLLECTION FOCUS: Lower Colorado River, Yuma and Imperial Counties, and Sonora
Lower Colorado River
Yuma County, AZ (local history)
Imperial County, CA
mining
steamboats
business history
military history
Mexico, Sonora

INCLUSIVE DATES: 1860-1920
COLLECTION ACCESS: card catalog
STAFF FTE: 1 administrative, 1 general, 50 volunteers, 1 clerical
INSTITUTIONAL SUPPORT FOR PROFESSIONAL DEVELOPMENT: tuition, reimbursement, use of facilities, use of clerical staff
SPECIAL SERVICES/PROGRAMS: exhibits, tours, classes, newsletter, fund raising, lectures, 4 annual trips to historic sites in area
FACILITIES/EQUIPMENT/PRESERVATION: temperature controls, humidity controls, fire detection controls, disaster preparedness plan

NHPRC AZ950-40

Yuma Territorial Prison State Historic Park
One Prison Hill Road
P.O. Box 10976
Yuma, Arizona 85366-8976

TEL: (602) 343-2500
FAX: (602) 783-7442

REPORTED BY: Richard Libengood
TYPE OF INSTITUTION: historic site, museum (state)

HOURS: Su-Sa 8-5, except Christmas day
ACCESS: open to general public
SERVICES: in-person, mail, phone, fee for reference, photocopies
RESTRICTIONS: non-circulating

PRIMARY COLLECTION FOCUS: Yuma Territorial Prison
    Yuma Territorial Prison, AZ--history
    prisons and prisoners
    prisons--artifacts
    Native Americans--arts and crafts
    diaries and journals--prisons and prisoners
    glasswork crafts
    firearms

INCLUSIVE DATES: 1875-1920
COLLECTION FORMATS: 50 books, 20 films, 10 maps, 10 oral histories, photographs
COLLECTION ACCESS: some registers/container lists, computerized finding aids (used by staff), some not described
SOFTWARE/SYSTEM: MacIntosh Custom
STAFF FTE: 1 administrative, .2 archival, .2 photo, .2 outreach, .1 A/V, 5.2 other, 1 volunteer, 1 student
INSTITUTIONAL SUPPORT FOR PROFESSIONAL DEVELOPMENT: some tuition, payment of dues, reimbursement, use of facilities, use of clerical staff
SPECIAL SERVICES/PROGRAMS: exhibits, tours, lectures
FACILITIES/EQUIPMENT/PRESERVATION: temperature controls
PATRON USE STATISTICS: 16 in-house patrons, 100 telephone, 200 mail reference requests

NHPRC AZ950-950

Desert Caballeros Western Museum/Maricopa County Historical Society
21 N. Frontier Street
P.O. Box 1446
Wickenburg, Arizona 85358

TEL: (602) 684-2272
FAX: (602) 684-2272

REPORTED BY: Sheila Kollasch, Curator
TYPE OF INSTITUTION: historical society, museum (private)

HOURS: M-Sa 10-4; Su 1-4
ACCESS: public access by appointment only
SERVICES: in-person, mail, photocopies

PRIMARY COLLECTION FOCUS: Wickenburg area history
    Wickenburg, AZ (local history)
    tourism--guest ranches
    mining
    ranching--Remuda Ranch, AZ
    mines--Vulture Mine
    Wickenburg, Henry
    mines--Stanton group

STAFF FTE: 1 administrative, 1 curator, 2 volunteers, 1 clerical
INSTITUTIONAL SUPPORT FOR PROFESSIONAL DEVELOPMENT: tuition, dues, reimbursement
FACILITIES/EQUIPMENT/PRESERVATION: temperature controls, humidity controls, fire detection controls, disaster preparedness plan
PATRON USE STATISTICS: user statistics not kept

Chiricahua National Monument
Dos Cabezas Route Box 6500
Willcox, Arizona 85643

TEL: (602) 824-3560
FAX: (602) 824-3421

REPORTED BY: Walt Sanger, Chief Interpreter
TYPE OF INSTITUTION: National monument (federal)

HOURS: M-F 8-5
ACCESS: by appointment only
SERVICES: limited in-person, mail and phone reference and photocopies

PRIMARY COLLECTION FOCUS: Far Away Ranch
    Far Away Ranch
    Chiricahua history
    parks and monuments, federal

COLLECTION FORMATS: manuscript collections, 2 feet of institution's records, 1000 books, pamphlets, films, government records, photographs, maps, oral histories
COLLECTION ACCESS: card catalog, computerized finding aids (used by staff and patrons)
SOFTWARE/SYSTEM: Clipper based database
STAFF FTE: 1 park ranger/curator
INSTITUTIONAL SUPPORT FOR PROFESSIONAL DEVELOPMENT: tuition, reimbursement, mailings, facilities, telephone, clerical
SPECIAL SERVICES/PROGRAMS: lectures
FACILITIES/EQUIPMENT/PRESERVATION: temperature controls, humidity controls, fire detection controls, fire extinguishing system, preservation lab, disaster preparedness plan
PATRON USE STATISTICS: user statistics not kept

NHPRC AZ850-120

Museum of the Southwest
1500 N. Circle I Road
c/o Willcox Chamber of Commerce and Agriculture
Willcox Cowboy Hall of Fame
Willcox, Arizona 85643

TEL: 602) 384-2272

REPORTED BY: Ellen Clark, Executive Director, CofC
TYPE OF INSTITUTION: museum (city)

HOURS: M-Sa 9-5; Su 1-5
ACCESS: open to the general public
SERVICES: in-person

PRIMARY COLLECTION FOCUS: Willcox area
    Willcox, AZ (local history)
    Native Americans
    cavalry
    pioneers
    cowboys--Cowboy Hall of Fame portraits

textiles

COLLECTION FORMATS: photographs, maps
COLLECTION ACCESS: card catalog, registers/inventories
STAFF FTE: 2 clerical
SPECIAL SERVICES/PROGRAMS: tours
FACILITIES/EQUIPMENT/PRESERVATION: fire extinguishing system

Navajo Nation Library System
Drawer K
Window Rock, Arizona 86515

TEL: (602) 871-6673
FAX: (602) 871-7304

REPORTED BY: Irving Nelson, Director
TYPE OF INSTITUTION: library (Navajo Nation)

HOURS: M-F 8-5
ACCESS: open to the public
SERVICES: in-person, mail, and telephone reference, photocopies (fee for photocopies)

PRIMARY COLLECTION FOCUS: Navajo Nation
    Navajo Nation
    Native Americans
    Correll, J. Lee
    Native Americans--ethnomusicology
    Navajo Times

INCLUSIVE DATES: 1600s-present
COLLECTION FORMATS: institution's records, books, pamphlets, films and videos, government records, photographs, maps, oral histories (Oneo Oral History Collection)
COLLECTION ACCESS: indexes, computerized finding aids (in process; used by staff)
SOFTWARE/SYSTEM: Macintosh ClarisWorks, Foxbase, Filepro
STAFF FTE: 1 administrator, 5 librarian technicians, volunteers, students
INSTITUTIONAL SUPPORT FOR PROFESSIONAL DEVELOPMENT: dues, reimbursement, workshops, mailings, telephone, facilities
SPECIAL SERVICES/PROGRAMS: tours, fund raising, lectures
FACILITIES/EQUIPMENT/PRESERVATION: temperature controls, fire detection controls, fire extinguishing system, disaster preparedness plan
PATRON USE STATISTICS: Overall 25,000 patrons

NHPRC AZ900-560

ARKANSAS

Clark County Historical Association
Riley-Hickingbotham Library, Ouachita Baptist University
P. O. Box 516
Arkadelphia, Arkansas 71923

TEL: (501) 245-5332

REPORTED BY: Wendy Richter, Archivist
TYPE OF INSTITUTION: archives, historical society (county/local)

HOURS: 8-4 M-F, other times by appointment
ACCESS: open to general public
SERVICES: in-person reference, copies, mail reference, phone reference

PRIMARY COLLECTION FOCUS: Clark County, Arkansas
    Clark County, AR (local history)
    Arkansas--history
    genealogy

INCLUSIVE DATES: 1818-present
COLLECTION FORMATS: manuscript collections, institution's records, books/serials, maps, pamphlets/ephemera, films/videotapes, photographs, oral histories, government records
COLLECTION ACCESS: card catalog, container lists, registers/inventories
ACQUISITION REPORTED TO: professional journals
STAFF (FTE): 1 general archival, 1 student
SPECIAL SERVICES/PROGRAMS: exhibits, tours, newsletter, lectures/presentations, publication of annual journal
FACILITIES/EQUIPMENT/PRESERVATION: temperature controls, humidity controls
PATRON USE STATISTICS: 425 in-house patrons, 250 mail reference requests

NHPRC AR60-600

Henderson State University
1100 Henderson Street
P. O. Box 7641
Arkadelphia, Arkansas 71999

TEL: (501) 246-5511, ext. 3296
FAX: (501) 246-3199

REPORTED BY: J. Robert Greene, Archivist
TYPE OF INSTITUTION: archives (academic)

HOURS: 9-4 M-F
ACCESS: open to the general public
SERVICES: in-person reference, photocopies, phone reference

PRIMARY COLLECTION FOCUS: Henderson State University papers
    Henderson State University (records)

INCLUSIVE DATES: 1850-present
VOLUME: 300 feet
COLLECTION FORMATS: manuscript collections, institution's records, pamphlets/ephemera, films/videotapes, photographs, other
COLLECTION ACCESS: repository guide, computerized finding aids (used by staff)
SOFTWARE/SYSTEM: dBase 4 program created for HSU
STAFF (FTE): .5 general archival, 1 student
INSTITUTIONAL SUPPORT FOR PROFESSIONAL DEVELOPMENT: payment for mailings, payment for telephone use
FACILITIES/EQUIPMENT/PRESERVATION: fire extinguishing system, humidity controls, preservation lab,

Arkansas

disaster preparedness plan

Ouachita Baptist University Library Special Collections **TEL**: (501) 245-5332
410 Ouachita
P. O. Box 3742
Arkadelphia, Arkansas 71998

REPORTED BY: Wendy Richter, Archivist
TYPE OF INSTITUTION: library (religious, academic)

HOURS: 8-4 M-F; other times by appointment
ACCESS: open to general public
SERVICES: in-person reference, copies, mail reference, phone reference

PRIMARY COLLECTION FOCUS: university records; Arkansas Baptist State Convention Archives; local
    history
    religion
    Baptists
    Arkansas--history
    Ouachita Baptist University (records)

INCLUSIVE DATES: 1830-present
VOLUME: 500 cubic feet (University); 200 cubic feet (Baptist State Convention Archives)
COLLECTION FORMATS: manuscripts, institutional records, books/serials, pamphlets/ephemera,
    films/videotapes, photographs, maps, oral histories
COLLECTION ACCESS: card catalog, container lists, registers/inventories
ACQUISITION REPORTED TO: professional journals
STAFF (FTE): 1 general archival, 1 student
INSTITUTIONAL SUPPORT FOR PROFESSIONAL DEVELOPMENT: course tuition
SPECIAL SERVICES/PROGRAMS: exhibits, tours, classes, lectures/presentations
FACILITIES/EQUIPMENT/PRESERVATION: temperature controls, humidity controls
PATRON USE STATISTICS: 90 (University), 40 (Baptist State Convention Archives) in-house patrons; 50
    (University), 140 (Baptist State Convention Archives) mail reference requests

NHPRC AR60-600

Arkadelphia: Clark County Library: NHPRC AR60-120

Sharp County Historical Society **TEL**: [not reported]
P. O. Box 185
Ash Flat, Arkansas 72513

REPORTED BY: Olivia R. Thompson, secretary-treasurer
TYPE OF INSTITUTION: historical society (county/local)

HOURS: see below
ACCESS: not open to the general public
SERVICES: mail reference

PRIMARY COLLECTION FOCUS: Sharp County
    Sharp County, AR (local history)
    genealogy

COLLECTION FORMATS: books/serials

STAFF (FTE): [not reported]
SPECIAL SERVICES/PROGRAMS: newsletter
PATRON USE STATISTICS: 100 mail reference requests

Arkansas College - Regional Studies Center   **TEL**: [not reported]
Arkansas College
Batesville, Arkansas 72501

REPORTED BY: Nancy Griffith
TYPE OF INSTITUTION: archives, library (academic)

HOURS: varies, usually 8-1 M-F
ACCESS: open to the general public
SERVICES: in-person reference, photocopies, mail reference
RESTRICTIONS: no time for extensive research

PRIMARY COLLECTION FOCUS: Arkansas history; Ozark folk music; Arkansas College
    Arkansas--history
    folklore
    Ozarks--folk music
    Arkansas College (records)
    music

COLLECTION FORMATS: manuscript collections, institution's records, books/serials, photographs, maps, pamphlets/ephemera, oral histories
COLLECTION ACCESS: card catalog, registers/inventories, computerized finding aids
ACQUISITION REPORTED TO: OCLC
STAFF (FTE): .5 professional
FACILITIES/EQUIPMENT/PRESERVATION: temperature controls, humidity controls

---

Saline County History & Heritage Society   **TEL**: (501) 778-5513
218 Market Street, Benton, Arkansas 72015
P. O. Box 221
Bryant, Arkansas 72022-0221

REPORTED BY: Carolyn Earle Billingsley
TYPE OF INSTITUTION: historical society, archives, library, museum (county/local)

HOURS: Tu, W, Th, 10-2; Su 1:30-4:00
ACCESS: open to general public
SERVICES: in-person reference

PRIMARY COLLECTION FOCUS: Saline County, Arkansas
    Saline County, AR (local history)

COLLECTION FORMATS: manuscript collections, books/serials, pamphlets/ephemera
COLLECTION ACCESS: card catalog, not described
STAFF (FTE): 1 volunteer/docent

Southern Arkansas University Tech   **TEL**: (501) 574-4518
Tech Station   **FAX**: (501) 574-4520
Camden, Arkansas 71701

52   Arkansas

REPORTED BY: Juanita Cook
TYPE OF INSTITUTION: library (academic)

HOURS: 8-9 M-Th; 8-4 F; 2-6 Su
ACCESS: not open to the general public
SERVICES: photocopies, phone reference

PRIMARY COLLECTION FOCUS: technology, humanities
    African Americans

COLLECTION FORMATS: oral histories
COLLECTION ACCESS: card catalog, computerized finding aids
ACQUISITION REPORTED TO: Other - NCA
STAFF (FTE): 1 administrative, 2 clerical
PATRON USE STATISTICS: 1000 in-house patrons

Faulkner County Library
Courthouse Square
Conway, Arkansas 72032

TEL: (501) 327-7482
FAX: (501) 327-9098

REPORTED BY: Ruth Voss, Library Director
TYPE OF INSTITUTION: library (county/local)

HOURS: 8-5 m-f; 7pm-9pm Tu & Th, 8-3 Sa
ACCESS: open to general public
SERVICES: in-person reference, photocopies, mail reference, phone reference, other
RESTRICTIONS: $10 non-resident fee

PRIMARY COLLECTION FOCUS: Faulkner County
    Faulkner Co., AR (local history)
    genealogy
    cemetery and burial records

COLLECTION FORMATS: institution's records; few documents; government records
COLLECTION ACCESS: card catalog, computerized finding aids (used by staff, patrons)
SOFTWARE/SYSTEM: Macintosh Filemaker Pro
ACQUISITION REPORTED TO: specialized/regional guide
STAFF (FTE): 1 administrative, 11 support staff
INSTITUTIONAL SUPPORT FOR PROFESSIONAL DEVELOPMENT: meeting reimbursement, payment for mailings, use of facilities, payment for phone use, use of clerical staff, tuition, dues
SPECIAL SERVICES/PROGRAMS: exhibits, tours, classes, newsletter, fundraising/endowment, lectures/presentations
FACILITIES/EQUIPMENT/PRESERVATION: fire extinguishing system

Hendrix College, O. C. Bailey Library
1601 Harkrider
Conway, Arkansas 72032

TEL: (501) 450-1302
FAX: (501) 450-3800

REPORTED BY: Robert Frizzell, Director
TYPE OF INSTITUTION: library (academic)

HOURS: 8:30-4:30 M-F
ACCESS: open to the general public
SERVICES: in-person reference, photocopies

PRIMARY COLLECTION FOCUS: Hendrix College, United Methodist Church in Arkansas
    Hendrix College, (records)
    Methodists
    Arkansas

INCLUSIVE DATES: 1820s-present
VOLUME: 100 linear feet
COLLECTION FORMATS: manuscript collections, institution's records, books/serials, maps, pamphlets/ephemera, photographs
COLLECTION ACCESS: container lists, registers/inventories
STAFF (FTE): .1 general archival, .1 student
PATRON USE STATISTICS: 25 in-house patrons, 25 mail reference requests, other user statistics not kept

NHPRC AR340-320

University of Central Arkansas Archives & Special Collections
Torreyson Library
Conway, Arkansas 72032

TEL: (501) 450-3418
FAX: (501) 450-5208

REPORTED BY: Tom W. Dillard, Director of Archives
TYPE OF INSTITUTION: archives (academic, state)

HOURS: 8-5 M-F
ACCESS: open to general public
SERVICES: in-person reference, photocopies, mail reference

PRIMARY COLLECTION FOCUS: Arkansas and local history
    Arkansas--government and politics
    environment
    women
    minorities
    arts and artists
    ecology
    Arkansas

INCLUSIVE DATES: 1800 - present
VOLUME: 20,000
COLLECTION FORMATS: manuscript collections, books/serials, pamphlets/ephemera, films/videotapes, government records, photographs, maps, oral histories
COLLECTION ACCESS: card catalog, container lists, computerized finding aids (used by staff, patrons)
SOFTWARE/SYSTEM: CLSI
ACQUISITION REPORTED TO: NUCMC, OCLC, professional journals
STAFF (FTE): 1 administrative, .5 clerical, .5 volunteer, 5 students
INSTITUTIONAL SUPPORT FOR PROFESSIONAL DEVELOPMENT: tuition, dues, meetings, travel, mailings, telephone, use of facilities, use of clerical staff
SPECIAL SERVICES/PROGRAMS: exhibits, tours, newsletters, lectures/presentations
FACILITIES/EQUIPMENT/PRESERVATION: temperature controls, humidity controls, fire detection controls, disaster preparedness plan
PATRON USE STATISTICS: 1200 in-house patrons, 50 telephone, 25 mail reference requests, 50 collections used, 1000 reference photocopies

NHPRC AR240-810

Fort Lincoln Center
City Hall
P. O. Box 297
DeValls Bluff, Arkansas 72041

TEL: (501) 998-2301

REPORTED BY: Sam A. Weems
TYPE OF INSTITUTION: historical society (county/local)

HOURS: 8-5 M-F
ACCESS: public access by appointment only
SERVICES: in-person reference, copies, mail reference, phone reference

PRIMARY COLLECTION FOCUS: Trans-Mississippi Civil War
  Civil War
  trans-Mississippi

COLLECTION FORMATS: manuscript collections, institution's records, books/serials, pamphlets/ephemera, government records, photographs, maps, oral histories
COLLECTION ACCESS: not described
STAFF (FTE): 1 volunteer/docent
INSTITUTIONAL SUPPORT FOR PROFESSIONAL DEVELOPMENT: dues payment, meeting reimbursement, in-house workshops, payments for mail, use of facilities, telephone usage, clerical staff usage
SPECIAL SERVICES/PROGRAMS: exhibits, tours, classes, fund-raising/endowment, lectures/presentations

---

Dolph: Izard County Historical Society: NHPRC AR270-360

Crittenden County Museum
1112 Main
P. O. Box 644
Earle, Arkansas 72331

TEL: (501) 792-7374

REPORTED BY: [not listed]
TYPE OF INSTITUTION: museum (county/local)

HOURS: [operating hours not given]
ACCESS: open to the general public
SERVICES: in-person reference

PRIMARY COLLECTION FOCUS: Crittenden County
  Crittenden County, AR (local history)

COLLECTION FORMATS: photographs, newspapers
COLLECTION ACCESS: container lists
STAFF (FTE): .5 administrative, 7 volunteer/docent

Center on War & the Child
35 Benton Street
P. O. Box 487
Eureka Springs, Arkansas 72632

TEL: (501) 253-8900

REPORTED BY: [not listed]
TYPE OF INSTITUTION: other - peace research (non-profit educational)

HOURS: 10-5 M-F
ACCESS: open to the general public
SERVICES: in-person reference, photocopies, phone reference, fee for reference

PRIMARY COLLECTION FOCUS: socialization of children to violence and war issues
    violence--school and community
    violence--television/movie
    violence--toys/play
    militarization of education
    children--the child soldier
    education--peace
    parenting for peace
    peace
    nonviolence

INCLUSIVE DATES: 1985 - present
VOLUME: 900
COLLECTION FORMATS: books/serials, pamphlets/ephemera, films/videotapes,
    photographs, news clippings
COLLECTION ACCESS: repository guide
ACQUISITION REPORTED TO: specialized/regional guide
STAFF (FTE): 1 administrative, 1 preservation
INSTITUTIONAL SUPPORT FOR PROFESSIONAL DEVELOPMENT: use of facilities and equipment
SPECIAL SERVICES/PROGRAMS: exhibits, newsletter, lectures/presentations
PATRON USE STATISTICS: user statistics not kept

Arkansas Air Museum
P. O. Box 1911
Fayetteville, Arkansas 72702

TEL: (501) 521-4947

REPORTED BY: John Kalagias, Museum Director
TYPE OF INSTITUTION: museum (non-profit)

HOURS: 9:30-4:30 daily
ACCESS: open to the general public
SERVICES: in-person reference

PRIMARY COLLECTION FOCUS: vintage aircraft; aviation books, manuals, & videos
    aircraft
    aviation

COLLECTION FORMATS: manuscript collections, books/serials, films/videotapes, photographs, oral histories
COLLECTION ACCESS: card catalog, computerized finding aids (used by staff), registers/inventories
SOFTWARE/SYSTEM: integrated
STAFF (FTE): administrative (no number given), volunteer/docent (no number given)
INSTITUTIONAL SUPPORT FOR PROFESSIONAL DEVELOPMENT: payment of dues, payment for
    mailings, use of facilities, travel reimbursement, payment for phone use
SPECIAL SERVICES/PROGRAMS: exhibits, tours, newsletter, fundraising/endowment,
    lectures/presentations
FACILITIES/EQUIPMENT/PRESERVATION: temperature controls, fire extinguishing system, fire detection
    controls, disaster preparedness plan

Arkansas

University of Arkansas Libraries Special Collections
MULN 130
Fayetteville, Arkansas 72701-1201

TEL: (501) 575-5577
FAX: (501) 575-5577

REPORTED BY: Andrea Cantrell, Head, Research Services
TYPE OF INSTITUTION: library (state/academic)

HOURS: 8-5 M-F, 9-1 Sa
ACCESS: open to general public
SERVICES: in-person reference, copies, mail reference, phone reference, photo duplication
RESTRICTIONS: cannot conduct in-depth research for mail or phone requests

PRIMARY COLLECTION FOCUS: Arkansas history, Arkansans
    Arkansas--politics
    literary manuscripts
    architects
    musicians
    folklore
    Arkansas--local history
    educators
    civic clubs
    Arkansas

INCLUSIVE DATES: 1800-present
VOLUME: 1200 collections, 8500 linear feet, 50,000 print titles
COLLECTION FORMATS: manuscript collections, institutional records, books/serials, pamphlets/ephemera, films/videotapes, government records, photographs, maps, oral histories
COLLECTION ACCESS: card catalog, container lists, repository guide, registers/inventories
ACQUISITION REPORTED TO: Chadwyck-Healey National Inventory of Documentary Sources
STAFF (FTE): 3 administrative, 1 photo curator, 1.5 general archival, .5 map, 1 field archivist, 1 public service, 5 non professional
INSTITUTIONAL SUPPORT FOR PROFESSIONAL DEVELOPMENT: course tuition
SPECIAL SERVICES/PROGRAMS: exhibits, newsletter, fund-raising/endowment, lectures/presentations
FACILITIES/EQUIPMENT/PRESERVATION: temperature controls, humidity controls, fire detection controls
PATRON USE STATISTICS: 2294 in-house patrons, 363 mail reference requests, 20,915 reference photocopies
NHPRC AR330-830

Fayetteville: Washington County Historical Society: NHPRC AR330-880

Gillett: Arkansas Post County Museum: NHPRC AR360-40

Gravette: Benton County Historical Society: NHRPC AR200-322

North Arkansas Regional Library
221 W. Stephenson Avenue
Harrison, Arkansas 72601

TEL: (501) 741-3665
FAX: (501) 741-3674

REPORTED BY: [not listed]
TYPE OF INSTITUTION: library (county/local)

HOURS: [not reported]
ACCESS: open to the general public
SERVICES: in-person reference, mail reference, photocopies

PRIMARY COLLECTION FOCUS: farming

farming
organic farming
agriculture

COLLECTION FORMATS: books/serials, pamphlets/ephemera, films/videotapes
COLLECTION ACCESS: card catalog
ACQUISITION REPORTED TO: OCLC
STAFF (FTE): shared support from other library functions (for both professional and non-professional staff)
FACILITIES/EQUIPMENT/PRESERVATION: temperature controls
PATRON USE STATISTICS: user statistics not kept

Delta Cultural Center
95 Missouri Street
Helena, Arkansas 72342

TEL: (501) 338-8919
FAX: (501) 338-8949

REPORTED BY: Ronnie Nichols, Director
TYPE OF INSTITUTION: archives, cultural center (state)

HOURS: 10-5 M-Sa, 12-5 Su; except holidays
ACCESS: open to the general public
SERVICES: in-person reference, mail reference

PRIMARY COLLECTION FOCUS: Delta culture, folklife, agriculture, civil history
Delta culture
folklife
ethnic groups
music
agriculture
civil history
Mississippi River
railroads

COLLECTION FORMATS: manuscript collections, pamphlets/ephemera, films/videotapes, photographs, maps
COLLECTION ACCESS: container lists, registers/inventories
STAFF (FTE): 2 administrative, 1 outreach officer
INSTITUTIONAL SUPPORT FOR PROFESSIONAL DEVELOPMENT: payment for mailings
SPECIAL SERVICES/PROGRAMS: exhibits, tours, classes, lectures/presentations
FACILITIES/EQUIPMENT/PRESERVATION: temperature controls, fire extinguishing system, humidity
controls, fire detection controls, disaster preparedness plan
PATRON USE STATISTICS: 30,000 in-house patrons, 50 mail reference requests

---

Garland County Historical Society
210 Woodbine
914 Summer Street
Hot Springs, Arkansas 71913

TEL: (501) 623-5875

REPORTED BY: Wendy Richter, President
TYPE OF INSTITUTION: archives, historical society (county/local)

HOURS: 9-12 Tu, other times by appointment
ACCESS: open to the general public
SERVICES: in-person reference, photocopies, mail reference

PRIMARY COLLECTION FOCUS: Garland County
Garland County, AR (local history)

Hot Springs, AR (local history)
tourism
bathing industry
genealogy
resorts--health

INCLUSIVE DATES: 1830 - present
VOLUME: 250 cubic feet
COLLECTION FORMATS: manuscript collections, books/serials, pamphlets/ephemera, maps, films/videotapes, government records, photographs, oral histories
COLLECTION ACCESS: card catalog, container lists, registers/inventories
ACQUISITION REPORTED TO: professional journals
STAFF (FTE): .5 administrative
SPECIAL SERVICES/PROGRAMS: exhibits, lectures/presentations, publication of annual journal
FACILITIES/EQUIPMENT/PRESERVATION: temperature controls
PATRON USE STATISTICS: user statistics not kept

NHPRC AR390-280

Hot Springs National Park
369 Central
P. O. Box 1860
Hot Springs, Arkansas 71901

TEL: (501) 623-1433
FAX: (501) 624-1705

REPORTED BY: Paul F. Sullivan, Ranger (Curator)
TYPE OF INSTITUTION: other - national park (federal)

HOURS: 9-5 daily (museum); 8-4:30 M-F (administration)
ACCESS: public access to library/archives by appointment only
SERVICES: in-person reference, photocopies, mail reference, phone reference

PRIMARY COLLECTION FOCUS: bathing/spa business in Hot Springs
  bathing industry
  spas
  Hot Springs, AR (local history)
  tourism
  resorts--health
  parks and monuments, federal

INCLUSIVE DATES: 1832-present
VOLUME: 100 cubic feet
COLLECTION FORMATS: institution's records, pamphlets/ephemera, photographs, government records
COLLECTION ACCESS: card catalog, container lists, repository guide, computerized aids (used by staff)
SOFTWARE/SYSTEM: Automated National Catalog System
ACQUISITION REPORTED TO: other - National Park Service
STAFF (FTE): [not reported]
FACILITIES/EQUIPMENT/PRESERVATION: temperature controls, fire extinguishing system, humidity controls, fire detection controls, disaster preparedness plan
PATRON USE STATISTICS: user statistics not kept

Hot Springs: Tri-Lakes Regional Library: NHPRC AR390-760

Jacksonport State Park Museum TEL: (501) 523-2143
P. O. Box 8
Jacksonport, Arkansas 72075

REPORTED BY: museum guide
TYPE OF INSTITUTION: museum (state)

HOURS: 8-5 W-Sa, 1-5 Su
ACCESS: open to the general public
SERVICES: [not reported]

PRIMARY COLLECTION FOCUS: Native Americans, military
    Native Americans
    military

Jonesboro: Crowley Ridge Regional Library: NHPRC AR480=130

Jonesboro: Holy Angels Convent: NHRPC AR480-320

Arkansas Geological Commission TEL: (501) 324-9165
3815 W. Roosevelt FAX: (501) 663-7360
Little Rock, Arkansas 72204

REPORTED BY: Norman Williams, State Geologist/Director
TYPE OF INSTITUTION: library, museum (state)

HOURS: 8-4:30 M-F
ACCESS: open to the general public
SERVICES: in-person reference, photocopies, mail reference, phone reference

PRIMARY COLLECTION FOCUS: geology
    geology

COLLECTION FORMATS: maps, photographs, institution's records
STAFF (FTE): .5 administrative
INSTITUTIONAL SUPPORT FOR PROFESSIONAL DEVELOPMENT: payment of dues, reimbursement for
    meetings and travel
SPECIAL SERVICES/PROGRAMS: exhibits, tours, lectures/presentations

---

Arkansas History Commission TEL: (501) 682-6900
One Capitol Mall
Little Rock, Arkansas 72201

REPORTED BY: John L. Ferguson, State Historian
TYPE OF INSTITUTION: archives (state)

HOURS: 8-5 M-F, 8-4:30 Sa
ACCESS: open to general public
SERVICES: in-person reference, photocopies, mail reference, phone reference

PRIMARY COLLECTION FOCUS: Arkansas history and genealogy
    Arkansas
    genealogy
    Arkansas--politics and government
    folklore

agriculture
business history
Arkansas--local history
religion
government records

COLLECTION ACCESS: card catalog, computerized finding aids, registers/inventories
STAFF (FTE): 2 administrative, 1 photo curator, 4 general archival, 1 preservation, 5 other professional, 26 volunteer/docent, 5 clerical
FACILITIES/EQUIPMENT/PRESERVATION: temperature controls, humidity controls, preservation lab
PATRON USE STATISTICS: 14,000

NHPRC AR510-25

Arkansas Historic Preservation Program
225 E. Markham, Suite 200
Little Rock, Arkansas 72201

TEL: (501) 324-9346
FAX: (501) 324-9345

REPORTED BY: Cathryn H. Buford, Director
TYPE OF INSTITUTION: state historic preservation office (state)

HOURS: 8-4:30 M-F
ACCESS: open to the general public
SERVICES: in-person reference, photocopies, mail reference, phone reference, reference fee

PRIMARY COLLECTION FOCUS: historic buildings
historic preservation
National Register of Historic Places
architecture
restoration--architectural
architecture--history
Arkansas--historic preservation

INCLUSIVE DATES: 1969-present
VOLUME: over 20,000 structure records
COLLECTION FORMATS: manuscript collections, institution's records, books/serials, photographs, pamphlets/ephemera, films/videotapes, government records, maps
COLLECTION ACCESS: card catalog, computerized finding aids (used by staff), registers/inventories
SOFTWARE/SYSTEM: dBase IV
ACQUISITION REPORTED TO: specialized/regional guide
STAFF (FTE): 6 administrative, 14 "preservation"
INSTITUTIONAL SUPPORT FOR PROFESSIONAL DEVELOPMENT: tuition, dues, meetings, travel, in-house workshops, use of facilities
SPECIAL SERVICES/PROGRAMS: exhibits, classes, newsletter, lectures/presentations
PATRON USE STATISTICS: user statistics not kept

Arkansas Territorial Restoration
200 East Third Street
Little Rock, Arkansas 72201

TEL: (501) 324-9351
FAX: (501) 324-9345

REPORTED BY: Ellen Korenblat, Registrar
TYPE OF INSTITUTION: museum and historic site (state)

HOURS: 9-5 M-Sa, 1-5 Su

ACCESS: open to the general public
SERVICES: [not reported]

PRIMARY COLLECTION FOCUS: Arkansas-made decorative, mechanical & fine arts, 1819-1870
  Arkansas--nineteenth century
  arts--mechanical
  arts--fine
  trans-Mississippi South region
  Arkansas territory

INCLUSIVE DATES: 1801-1900
VOLUME: 7000+
COLLECTION FORMATS: manuscript collections; books/serials; photographs; maps; decorative, mechanical, and fine arts objects
COLLECTION ACCESS: card catalog, computerized finding aids (used by staff), registers/inventories
SOFTWARE/SYSTEM: Willoughby's MIMSY
STAFF (FTE): 7 administrative, 4 general archival, 1 preservation, 3 guides, 2 education, 30 volunteer, 2 research, 2 actors
INSTITUTIONAL SUPPORT FOR PROFESSIONAL DEVELOPMENT: tuition, meetings, in-house workshops
SPECIAL SERVICES/PROGRAMS: exhibits, tours, newsletter, lectures/presentations
FACILITIES/EQUIPMENT/PRESERVATION: temperature controls, fire extinguishing system, humidity controls, fire detection controls, preservation lab, disaster preparedness plan

NHPRC AR510-13

Central Arkansas Library System
700 Louisiana Street
Little Rock, Arkansas 72201

TEL: (501) 370-5952
FAX: (501) 375-7451

REPORTED BY: Philip Jones, Head, Reference Services Department
TYPE OF INSTITUTION: library (county/local)

HOURS: 8:30-8 M,Tu,Th; 8:30-6 W,F,Sa; 1-5 Su (Sept.-May)
ACCESS: open to the general public
SERVICES: in-person reference, photocopies, mail reference, phone reference, reference fee

PRIMARY COLLECTION FOCUS: Pulaski County, Arkansas
  Arkansas
  Little Rock, AR
  Pulaski County, AR (local history)
  genealogy

COLLECTION FORMATS: books/serials, pamphlets/ephemera, photographs, maps
COLLECTION ACCESS: card catalog
ACQUISITION REPORTED TO: OCLC
STAFF (FTE): .5 intern
INSTITUTIONAL SUPPORT FOR PROFESSIONAL DEVELOPMENT: reimbursement for professional meetings
FACILITIES/EQUIPMENT/PRESERVATION: temperature controls
PATRON USE STATISTICS: user statistics not kept

Diocese of Little Rock
2415 N. Tyler Avenue
P. O. Box 7239
Little Rock, Arkansas 72217

TEL: (501) 664-0340

REPORTED BY: Sr. Catherine Markey, OSB, Archivist
TYPE OF INSTITUTION: archives (religious)

HOURS: by appointment only
ACCESS: public access by appointment only; serious researchers
SERVICES: photocopies, mail reference
RESTRICTIONS: written request required

PRIMARY COLLECTION FOCUS: Diocese of Little Rock
    Diocese of Little Rock
    religion
    Catholic Church
    genealogy

INCLUSIVE DATES: 1843 - present
VOLUME: 140 linear feet
COLLECTION FORMATS: institution's records, books/serials, pamphlets/ephemera, films/videotapes, photographs, oral histories
COLLECTION ACCESS: card catalog, container lists, registers/inventories
STAFF (FTE): 1 archivist
INSTITUTIONAL SUPPORT FOR PROFESSIONAL DEVELOPMENT: tuition, dues, reimbursement for meetings, travel, mailings, use of facilities, telephone use
FACILITIES/EQUIPMENT/PRESERVATION: temperature controls, fire extinguishing system, humidity controls, disaster preparedness plan
PATRON USE STATISTICS: user statistics not kept

NHPRC AR10-145

Old State House Museum
300 West Markham
Little Rock, Arkansas 72201

TEL: (501) 324-9685
FAX: (501) 324-9688

REPORTED BY: [not listed]
TYPE OF INSTITUTION: museum (state)

HOURS: 9-5 M-Sa, 1-5 Su
ACCESS: open to general public
SERVICES: graphic reproductions of architectural renderings

PRIMARY COLLECTION FOCUS: architecture; early 20th century Arkansas
    Arkansas
    architecture--twentieth century
    Arkansas--architecture
    architecture--drawings

INCLUSIVE DATES: 1900-1950
VOLUME: 3000
COLLECTION ACCESS: registers/inventories
STAFF (FTE): [not reported]
SPECIAL SERVICES/PROGRAMS: exhibits, tours, classes, newsletter, fundraising/endowment, lectures/presentations
FACILITIES/EQUIPMENT/PRESERVATION: temperature controls, fire extinguishing system, humidity controls, fire detection controls, preservation lab

University of Arkansas for Medical Sciences
4301 West Markham
UAMS Library, Slot 586
Little Rock, Arkansas 72205-7186

TEL: (501) 686-6733
FAX: (501) 686-6745

REPORTED BY: Edwina Walls, Head, Special Collections
TYPE OF INSTITUTION: library (academic)

HOURS: 8-5 M-F
ACCESS: open to general public
SERVICES: in-person reference, photocopies, mail reference, phone reference

PRIMARY COLLECTION FOCUS: history of the health sciences in Arkansas
    health sciences--Arkansas
    medicine, history of
    Arkansas--health care
    hospitals

INCLUSIVE DATES: 1654 - present
COLLECTION FORMATS: manuscript collections, institution's records, books/serials, pamphlets/ephemera, photographs
COLLECTION ACCESS: container lists, computerized finding aids (used by staff)
SOFTWARE/SYSTEM: MicroMARC
STAFF (FTE): 1 administrative, .5 clerical
INSTITUTIONAL SUPPORT FOR PROFESSIONAL DEVELOPMENT: tuition, meeting registration and travel, payment for mailings, use of facilities, telephone use, use of clerical staff
SPECIAL SERVICES/PROGRAMS: exhibits, classes, newsletter, fundraising/endowment (in connection with friends group only), lectures/presentations
FACILITIES/EQUIPMENT/PRESERVATION: temperature controls, fire extinguishing system, humidity controls, fire detection controls, disaster preparedness plan

NHPRC AR10-824

Little Rock: Missionary Baptist Seminary: NHPRC AR510-520

Little Rock: Quapaw Quarter Association: NHPRC AR510-680

Little Rock: University of Arkansas at Little Rock, Library, Archives and Special Collections: NHPRC AR510-810

Woodruff County Historical Society
P. O. Box 332
McCrory, Arkansas 72101

TEL: (501) 731-2846

REPORTED BY: Lela Knight Ashburn, editor
TYPE OF INSTITUTION: historical society (county/local)

HOURS: by appointment
ACCESS: no office space
SERVICES: mail reference, phone reference, will check court house records and library materials

PRIMARY COLLECTION FOCUS: Woodruff County
    Woodruff County, AR (local history)
    folklore
    genealogy

STAFF (FTE): 1 volunteer/docent
SPECIAL SERVICES/PROGRAMS: annual book

Marianna - Lee County Museum   **TEL**: (501) 295-2469
67 West Main Street
Marianna, Arkansas 72360

REPORTED BY: Suzanne Keasler
TYPE OF INSTITUTION: museum (county/local)

HOURS: 10-12am and 2-4pm Wednesdays, other days by appointment
ACCESS: open to the general public, public access by appointment
SERVICES: [not reported]

PRIMARY COLLECTION FOCUS: Lee County
      Lee County, AR (local history)

COLLECTION FORMATS: photographs
COLLECTION ACCESS: card catalog
STAFF (FTE): 2 volunteer/docent
SPECIAL SERVICES/PROGRAMS: tours
PATRON USE STATISTICS: user statistics not kept

Monticello: Drew County Historical Museum, Southeast Research Archives Center: NHPRC AR600-160

Montgomery County Historical Society   **TEL**: (501) 867-3121
Highway 270
P. O. Box 520
Mount Ida, Arkansas 71957

REPORTED BY: Debbie Baldwin, President
TYPE OF INSTITUTION: historical society (county/local)

HOURS: 8-5 M-F
ACCESS: open to general public
SERVICES: in-person reference, copies, mail reference, phone reference
RESTRICTIONS: research assistance given as staff time permits

PRIMARY COLLECTION FOCUS: Montgomery County records
      Montgomery County, AR (local history)
      genealogy

COLLECTION ACCESS: not described
STAFF (FTE): 1 volunteer/docent
SPECIAL SERVICES/PROGRAMS: exhibits, newsletter
PATRON USE STATISTICS: 100 in-house patrons, 50 telephone, 250 mail reference requests

---

Pike County Archives and History Society   **TEL**: [not reported]
Court House Square
Box 238
Murfreesboro, Arkansas 71958

REPORTED BY: Dorothy Partain, member
TYPE OF INSTITUTION: archives, historical society (county/local)

HOURS: by appointment
ACCESS: public access by appointment only
SERVICES: mail reference

PRIMARY COLLECTION FOCUS: Pike County
    Pike County, AR (local history)
    genealogy

INCLUSIVE DATES: 1895-present
COLLECTION FORMATS: manuscript collections, institution's records, books/serials, photographs, maps, pamphlets/ephemera, films/videotapes, government records, oral histories
COLLECTION ACCESS: card catalog
STAFF (FTE): 1 volunteer/docent
INSTITUTIONAL SUPPORT FOR PROFESSIONAL DEVELOPMENT: use of facilities and equipment
SPECIAL SERVICES/PROGRAMS: newsletter

Jackson County Library
213 Walnut Street
P. O. Box 190
Newport, Arkansas 72112

TEL: (501) 523-2952
FAX: (501) 523-4283

REPORTED BY: Ila B. Lacy, Librarian/Director
TYPE OF INSTITUTION: library (county/local)

HOURS: 9:30-6 M-F; 9:20-Noon Sa
ACCESS: open to the general public
SERVICES: in-person reference, photocopies

PRIMARY COLLECTION FOCUS: Jackson County history and genealogy
    Jackson County, AR (local history)
    genealogy
    Civil War
    Revolutionary War

VOLUME: 2017
COLLECTION FORMATS: books/serials, films/videotapes, photographs, maps, oral histories
COLLECTION ACCESS: card catalog, computerized finding aids (used by staff)
SOFTWARE/SYSTEM: Follett Circulation Plus
ACQUISITION REPORTED TO: OCLC
STAFF (FTE): 1 administrative, 1 archival, 1 clerical
FACILITIES/EQUIPMENT/PRESERVATION: fire detection controls, disaster preparedness plan
PATRON USE STATISTICS: 87-100 (monthly) in-house patrons, 5 (monthly) mail reference requests, 50-75 (monthly) reference photocopies, 30-40 (monthly) microfilm/fiche copies

---

Mississippi County Historical & Genealogical Society
P. O. Box 483
Osceola, Arkansas 72370

TEL: (501) 763-2827

REPORTED BY: Richard Hartness, President
TYPE OF INSTITUTION: historical society (county/local)

HOURS: by appointment
ACCESS: public access by appointment only
SERVICES: [not listed]

PRIMARY COLLECTION FOCUS: Mississippi County
    Mississippi County, AR (local history)
    genealogy

COLLECTION ACCESS: not described
STAFF (FTE): [not reported]
SPECIAL SERVICES/PROGRAMS: lectures/presentations, publication of quarterly journal

---

Randolph County Historical Society   **TEL**: (501) 892-9545 or (501) 892-8329
202 E. Church at No. Bettis
Pocahontas, Arkansas 72455-2899

REPORTED BY: Donald L. Waterworth, Sr., President
TYPE OF INSTITUTION: historical society, museum (non-profit, tax-exempt)

HOURS: open daily, weather permitting, May through first Sat. in November
ACCESS: open to general public, public access by appointment
SERVICES: photocopies, mail reference, fee for reference

PRIMARY COLLECTION FOCUS: farm history of Randolph Co. and northeast Arkansas
    farm history
    Randolph County, AR (local history)
    Arkansas, Northeast
    agriculture
    barns

COLLECTION FORMATS: books/serials, photographs, farm equipment and parts
COLLECTION ACCESS: not described
STAFF (FTE): 1 administrative
SPECIAL SERVICES/PROGRAMS: exhibits, tours, newsletter
PATRON USE STATISTICS: 50 telephone patrons, 200 mail reference requests

---

Depot Museum   **TEL**: (501) 887-5821
Highway 67 South
P. O. Box 10
Prescott, Arkansas 71857

REPORTED BY: J. W. Teeter, museum board
TYPE OF INSTITUTION: historical society, museum (county/local, city)

HOURS: 10-12 and 2-5 M-Sa
ACCESS: open to the general public
SERVICES: in-person reference

PRIMARY COLLECTION FOCUS: Nevada County people and events
    Nevada County, AR (local history)
    cemetery and burial records

INCLUSIVE DATES: 1880 - present
COLLECTION FORMATS: films/videotapes, photographs, maps, oral histories

COLLECTION ACCESS: card catalog
STAFF (FTE): volunteer/docent (number not given)
SPECIAL SERVICES/PROGRAMS: newsletter
FACILITIES/EQUIPMENT/PRESERVATION: temperature controls, humidity controls
PATRON USE STATISTICS: 1050 in-house patrons, other user statistics not kept

---

Plantation Agriculture Museum
4815 Highway 161
P. O. Box 62
Scott, Arkansas 72142

TEL: (501) 961-1409

REPORTED BY: Ben H. Swadley, Director
TYPE OF INSTITUTION: museum (state)

HOURS: 8-5 T-Sa, 1-5 Su, closed Mondays except Monday holidays
ACCESS: open to general public
SERVICES: in-person reference, photocopies, mail reference
RESTRICTIONS: time and staff limitations may apply

PRIMARY COLLECTION FOCUS: cotton agriculture, plantation-related
    cotton
    agriculture
    plantation life and culture

INCLUSIVE DATES: 1900-1955
VOLUME: 1500
COLLECTION FORMATS: books/serials, pamphlets/ephemera, films/videotapes, government records,
    photographs, maps, oral histories
COLLECTION ACCESS: collections undergoing registration
ACQUISITION REPORTED TO: internal only
STAFF (FTE): 3 administrative, 1 volunteer/docent
INSTITUTIONAL SUPPORT FOR PROFESSIONAL DEVELOPMENT: tuition, dues payment, meeting
    registration, travel, payment for mailings
SPECIAL SERVICES/PROGRAMS: exhibits, tours, newsletter, lectures/presentations, special events
FACILITIES/EQUIPMENT/PRESERVATION: temperature controls, humidity controls, fire detection controls,
    preservation lab
PATRON USE STATISTICS: user statistics not kept

White County Public Library
113 E. Pleasure
Searcy, Arkansas 72143

TEL: (501) 268-2449
FAX: (501) 268-5682

REPORTED BY: Sue Ann Schlosser, Director
TYPE OF INSTITUTION: library (county/local)

HOURS: 9-8 M, 9-6 Tu-Th, 9-5 F, 10-5 Sa
ACCESS: open to the general public
SERVICES: in-person reference, photocopies, mail reference, phone reference (research assistance available
    Thursday afternoons)

PRIMARY COLLECTION FOCUS: White County
    White County, AR (local history)
    genealogy
    schools

organizations

VOLUME: 300
COLLECTION FORMATS: institution's records, books/serials, microfilm
COLLECTION ACCESS: not described
ACQUISITION REPORTED TO: County board of trustees for library
STAFF (FTE): 1 reference librarian, 1 volunteer/docent
PATRON USE STATISTICS: user statistics not kept

Arkansas Oil & Brine Museum
3853 Smackover Highway
Smackover, Arkansas 71762

TEL: (501) 725-2877
FAX: (501) 725-3818

REPORTED BY: Don Lambert, Director
TYPE OF INSTITUTION: museum (state)

HOURS: [operating hours not given]
ACCESS: open to general public
SERVICES: in-person reference, photocopies, mail reference, phone reference

PRIMARY COLLECTION FOCUS: South Arkansas oil boom era of the 1920s to today
    Arkansas, South
    oil boom
    geology
    petroleum industry

COLLECTION ACCESS: card catalog, computerized finding aids (used by staff)
STAFF (FTE): 1 general archival, 1 photo curator
INSTITUTIONAL SUPPORT FOR PROFESSIONAL DEVELOPMENT: tuition, dues, reimbursement, mailings, facilities, telephone
SPECIAL SERVICES/PROGRAMS: exhibits, tours, newsletter, fundraising/endowment, lectures/presentations
FACILITIES/EQUIPMENT/PRESERVATION: temperature controls, fire extinguishing system, humidity controls, fire detection controls, preservation lab, disaster preparedness plan

---

Ethnic Minority Memorabilia Association
P. O. Box 55
Washington, Arkansas 71862

TEL: (501) 983-2482 or (501) 983-2340

REPORTED BY: Mildred L. Smith, Founder/Director
TYPE OF INSTITUTION: historical society, museum (academic, state, county/local, religious)

HOURS: during all park festivals; other times by appointment
ACCESS: public access by appointment
SERVICES: [not reported]

PRIMARY COLLECTION FOCUS: black history
    black history and heritage
    minorities
    African Americans
    Arkansas--African Americans

COLLECTION ACCESS: container lists, registers/inventories

ACQUISITION REPORTED TO: newspaper
STAFF (FTE): 1 administrative, 1 volunteer/docent

Southwest Arkansas Regional Archives   **TEL**: (501) 983-2633
Highway 195
P. O. Box 136
Washington, Arkansas 71862

REPORTED BY: Donna K. Matteson, Volunteer
TYPE OF INSTITUTION: archives (independent, non-profit, tax-exempt)

HOURS: 9-4, 7 days a week
ACCESS: open to the general public
SERVICES: in-person reference, photocopies, mail reference, phone reference, photo reproduction, fees

PRIMARY COLLECTION FOCUS: 12-county area in southwest Arkansas
    Arkansas, Southwest
    Arkansas, Southwest--politics
    Arkansas, Southwest--daily life
    civic records

INCLUSIVE DATES: 1818-present
COLLECTION FORMATS: manuscript collections, ephemera
COLLECTION ACCESS: card catalog
STAFF (FTE): 1 administrative, 1 general archival, 5 volunteer/docent
SPECIAL SERVICES/PROGRAMS: classes, fundraising/endowment, workshops
FACILITIES/EQUIPMENT/PRESERVATION: fire detection controls
PATRON USE STATISTICS: 2000 in-house patrons, 500 telephone, 1500 mail reference requests

---

Washington: Old Washington State Park: NHPRC AR950-600

Cross County Historical Society   **TEL**: (501) 238-8248
Cross County Court House
P. O. Box 943
Wynne, Arkansas 72396

REPORTED BY: Jimmie S. James, Secretary
TYPE OF INSTITUTION: archives, historical society (county/local)

HOURS: 11-4 M-F
ACCESS: open to general public
SERVICES: in-person reference, mail reference, phone reference

PRIMARY COLLECTION FOCUS: Cross County, Arkansas
    Cross County, AR (local history)
    genealogy

COLLECTION FORMATS: books/serials, pamphlets/ephemera, government records, photographs, maps
COLLECTION ACCESS: not described
STAFF (FTE): 1 secretary
PATRON USE STATISTICS: user statistics not kept

State University: Arkansas State University, Dean B. Ellis Library, Arkansas Room: NHPRC AR890-20

State University: Arkansas State University, Museum Library: NHPRC AR890-30

LOUISIANA

Louisiana State University at Alexandria   **TEL**: (318) 473-6437
James C. Bolton Library
8100 Highway 71 South
Alexandria, LA 71302-9121

REPORTED BY: Dr. Anna Burn
TYPE OF INSTITUTION: library (academic)

HOURS: M-Th 7:30-6:30, F 7:30-4:30
ACCESS: open to the general public
SERVICES: in-person reference, mail reference, phone reference, photocopies
PRIMARY COLLECTION FOCUS: local history, university records
    Alexandria, LA
    Louisiana, central
    Louisiana State University, Alexandria (records)

COLLECTION FORMATS: manuscript collections, institution's records, books/serials, pamphlets/ephemera, photographs
COLLECTION ACCESS: card catalog, registers/inventories
STAFF (FTE): operated by library personnel
INSTITUTIONAL SUPPORT FOR PROFESSIONAL DEVELOPMENT: tuition/registration reimbursement for courses, workshops, etc., use of facilities and equipment permitted
SPECIAL SERVICES/PROGRAMS: exhibits
FACILITIES/EQUIPMENT/PRESERVATION: fire extinguishing system, disaster preparedness plan
PATRON USE STATISTICS: information not available
NHPRC LA 26-480

Rapides Parish Library   **TEL**: (318) 442-1840
411 Washington St.   **FAX**: (318) 445-6478
Alexandria, Louisiana 70301

REPORTED BY: Wesby M. Saunders, Reference Coordinator
TYPE OF INSTITUTION: library (country/local)

HOURS: M-Sa 9-6
ACCESS: open to the general public
SERVICES: in-person reference, mail and phone reference, photocopies

PRIMARY COLLECTION FOCUS: Louisiana, Central Louisiana
    Louisiana, Central
    Louisiana

COLLECTION FORMATS: 200 maps, films/videotapes
COLLECTION ACCESS: card catalog
STAFF (FTE): 2 professional, 2 non-professional
FACILITIES/EQUIPMENT/PRESERVATION: temperature controls; fire detection controls, fire extinguishing system
PATRON USE STATISTICS: 2,500 contacts

Bienville Parish Library   **TEL**: (318) 263-7410
604 South Maple Street
Arcadia, Louisiana 71001-3699

REPORTED BY: Mrs. Joyce Lilly, Director
TYPE OF INSTITUTION: library (county/local)

HOURS: M,F 8:30-5; Tu 8:30-6; W, Th 8:30-6; S 8:30-12
ACCESS: open to general public
SERVICES: in-person reference, photocopies

PRIMARY COLLECTION FOCUS: Louisiana materials and genealogy
    Louisiana--history
    genealogy

COLLECTION ACCESS: card catalog
ACQUISITION REPORTED TO: other
STAFF (FTE): 1 administrative, 8 staff-general for parish library
FACILITIES/EQUIPMENT/PRESERVATION: temperature controls, fire extinguishing system, disaster
    preparedness plan

Diocese of Baton Rouge, Archives
1800 South Acadian Thruway
P. O. Box 2028
Baton Rouge, Louisiana 70821

TEL: (504) 387-0561
FAX: (504) 336-8789

REPORTED BY: Mrs. Una F. Daigre, Acting Archivist
TYPE OF INSTITUTION: archives (religious)

HOURS: M-F 9-2
ACCESS: public access by appointment only
SERVICES: in-person/mail reference, fee for reference, photocopies

PRIMARY COLLECTION FOCUS: sacramental registers from parish churches, Baton Rouge diocese
    Catholic Church
    Baton Rouge, LA (diocese records and history)
    genealogy

INCLUSIVE DATES: 1728-1990
COLLECTION FORMATS: institution's records, book/serials, pamphlets/ephemera, photographs
COLLECTION ACCESS: card catalog, repository guide, registers/inventories
STAFF (FTE): 1 general archival, 5 volunteer/docent
FACILITIES/EQUIPMENT/PRESERVATION: temperature controls, humidity controls, fire detection controls
PATRON USE STATISTICS: user statistics not kept

East Baton Rouge Parish Library, Centroplex Branch
120 St. Louis St.
P. O. Box 1471
Baton Rouge, Louisiana 70821

TEL: (504) 389-4960

REPORTED BY: Sylvia Walker, Asst, Head of Branch Division
TYPE OF INSTITUTION: library (county/local)

HOURS: M-Th 8-7, F-Sa 9-6, Su 2-6
ACCESS: call for specific hours for archival area

SERVICES: in-person, mail, and phone reference; photocopies

PRIMARY COLLECTION FOCUS: history of East Baton Rouge Parish
  East Baton Rouge, LA (parish history)

COLLECTION FORMATS: 100 manuscript collections; 75 institution's records; 50 books/serials; 100 pamphlets/ephemera; 200 films/videotapes; 1000 government records; 2600 photographs; 100 maps; 80 oral histories
COLLECTION ACCESS: card catalog, registers/inventories
STAFF (FTE): branch librarian, 4 hrs. per week; library technician, 15 hrs. per week
INSTITUTIONAL SUPPORT FOR PROFESSIONAL DEVELOPMENT: tuition/registration reimbursement for courses, workshops, etc.
SPECIAL SERVICES/PROGRAMS: exhibits
FACILITIES/EQUIPMENT/PRESERVATION: fire extinguishing system
PATRON USE STATISTICS: user statistics not kept

Louisiana and Lower Mississippi Valley Collections
Hill Memorial Library
Louisiana State University
Baton Rouge, Louisiana 70803

TEL: (504) 388-6568
FAX: (504) 388-6992

REPORTED BY: Faye Phillips, Head, Louisiana & Lower Mississippi Valley Collections
TYPE OF INSTITUTION: library (academic)

HOURS: M-F 9-5, Sa 9-1pm, except holidays
ACCESS: open to the general public
SERVICES: in-person, mail, phone reference, photocopies, other reproduction services
RESTRICTIONS: some collections restricted by condition or donor request

PRIMARY COLLECTION FOCUS: Louisiana and the lower Mississippi Valley region
  Louisiana
  Mississippi River Valley, lower
  Civil War
  Louisiana--politics
  Louisiana--social/economic history
  Louisiana State University (records)
  slavery
  plantation life and culture
  newspapers on microfilm project

INCLUSIVE DATES: 1650's-present
VOLUME: 25,000 linear feet
COLLECTION FORMATS: manuscript collections, institution's records, books/serials, pamphlets/ephemera, films/videotapes, government records, photographs, maps, oral histories, other
COLLECTION ACCESS: card catalog, container lists, computerized finding aids (used by staff)
SOFTWARE/SYSTEM: NOTIS, RLIN, and OCLC
ACQUISITION REPORTED TO: NUCMC, RLIN, OCLC
STAFF (FTE): 1 administrative, 5 general archival, 1 book technical services, 3 public service
  1 volunteer/docent, 20 student
INSTITUTIONAL SUPPORT FOR PROFESSIONAL DEVELOPMENT: reimbursement for professional meetings, registration, use of facilities and equipment, payment for phone use, use of clerical staff permitted
SPECIAL SERVICES/PROGRAMS: exhibits, tours, classes, fund raising/endowment, lectures/presentations
FACILITIES/EQUIPMENT/PRESERVATION: temperature controls, humidity controls, fire detection controls, fire extinguishing system, preservation lab
PATRON USE STATISTICS: 16,000 in-house patrons, 400 telephone patrons, 300 mail reference requests, 9000 collections used, 2000 microfilm/fiche copies

NHPRC LA62-500

Louisiana Division of Historic Preservation - Baton Rouge
1051 North 3rd Street
P.O. Box 44247
Baton Rouge LA 70804

TEL: (504) 342-8160
FAX: (504) 342-8173

REPORTED BY: Betty Chauvin
TYPE OF INSTITUTION: federal and state agency
HOURS: M-F 8-4:30
ACCESS: open to the general public
SERVICES: in-person reference, mail reference, phone reference
PRIMARY COLLECTION FOCUS: National Register of Historic Places
    architecture
    historic buildings

INCLUSIVE DATES: information not available
VOLUME: information not available
COLLECTION FORMATS: nomination forms for national register
COLLECTION ACCESS: registers/inventories
STAFF (FTE): 6 administrative, 1 clerical
INSTITUTIONAL SUPPORT FOR PROFESSIONAL DEVELOPMENT: tuition/registration reimbursement for
    courses, workshops, etc.
SPECIAL SERVICES/PROGRAMS: lectures/presentations, newsletter
FACILITIES/EQUIPMENT/PRESERVATION: fire extinguishing system
PATRON USE STATISTICS: information not available

NHPRC-LA62-430

Louisiana Secretary of State
Archives and Records Division
3851 Essen Lane
P.O. Box 94125
Baton Rouge LA 70804-9125

TEL: (504) 922-1206
FAX: (504) 922-0002

REPORTED BY: Doug Harrison
TYPE OF INSTITUTION: archives (state)

HOURS: M-F 8-4:30, Sa 9-5, Su 1-5
ACCESS: open to the general public
SERVICES: in person reference, mail reference, phone reference, photocopies
PRIMARY COLLECTION FOCUS: Louisiana State Administrative Documents
    Louisiana--government
    Louisiana--legislative records

INCLUSIVE DATES: 1760-present
VOLUME: 23,500 cubic feet
COLLECTION FORMATS: manuscript collections, institution's records, books/serials, pamphlets/ephemera,
    films/videotapes, government records, photographs, maps, oral histories
ACCESS: card catalog, repository guide, registers/inventories, container lists,
    computerized finding aids
STAFF (FTE): 20 administrative, 12 clerical
INSTITUTIONAL SUPPORT FOR PROFESSIONAL DEVELOPMENT: payment for mailings, payment for
    telephone use, use of facilities and equipment permitted, use of clerical staff permitted

SPECIAL SERVICES/PROGRAMS: exhibits, tours, classes, newsletter, fund
 raising/endowment, lectures/presentations
FACILITIES/EQUIPMENT/PRESERVATION: temperature controls, humidity controls, fire detection controls,
 fire extinguishing system, preservation lab, disaster preparedness plan
PATRON USE STATISTICS: information not available

NHPRC LA 62-470

Louisiana State University Museum [previously called Anglo-American Art Museum] **TEL**: (504) 388-4003
Tower Drive, LSU, Baton Rouge, LA **FAX**: (504) 388-6400
Memorial Tower, LSU
Baton Rouge, Louisiana 70803

REPORTED BY: H. Parrott Bacot and Mabel N. Bartkiewiz
TYPE OF INSTITUTION: museum (state)

HOURS: M-F 9-4, Sa 10-12 and 1-4, Su 1-4
ACCESS: public access by appointment only
SERVICES: in-person, mail, phone reference, photocopies

PRIMARY COLLECTION FOCUS: British and American, emphasis on Louisiana; institution's records
 Anglo-American Art Museum (records)

INCLUSIVE DATES: 1450-present
VOLUME: approx. 2000 linear feet
COLLECTION FORMATS: 1650 institution's records, 5 series books/serials
 2000 photographs
COLLECTION ACCESS: computerized finding aids (used by staff), registers/inventories
SOFTWARE/SYSTEM: d-Base II
ACQUISITION REPORTED TO: university authorities
STAFF (FTE): 1 administrative, 1 clerical, 6 student
INSTITUTIONAL SUPPORT FOR PROFESSIONAL DEVELOPMENT: dues for professional organization
 membership, reimbursement for professional meetings, payment for mailings & phone, use of
 facilities, clerical staff
SPECIAL SERVICES/PROGRAMS: exhibits, tours, classes, newsletters, fund raising/endowment,
 lectures/presentations
FACILITIES/EQUIPMENT/PRESERVATION: temperature controls, humidity controls
PATRON USE STATISTICS: user statistics not kept

John B. Cade Library **TEL**: (504) 771-2854
Southern University **FAX**: (504) 771-4113
Baton Rouge, Louisiana 70813

REPORTED BY: Mrs. Ledell B. Smith, Archivist
TYPE OF INSTITUTION: archives (academic)

HOURS: [operating hours not given]
ACCESS: open to the general public
SERVICES: in-person, mail, phone reference, photocopies
RESTRICTIONS: non-circulating

PRIMARY COLLECTION FOCUS: institutional records
 Southern University, LA (administrative/faculty records)
 African Americans

INCLUSIVE DATES: 1880-present
COLLECTION FORMATS: 20,000 files manuscript collections, 40,000 files institution's records, 3332 books/serials, 2000 pamphlets/ephemera, 1800 photographs
COLLECTION ACCESS: card catalog
STAFF (FTE): 1 administrative, 1 general archival, 1 preservation, 2 student
INSTITUTIONAL SUPPORT FOR PROFESSIONAL DEVELOPMENT: payment for mailings, payment for telephone use
SPECIAL SERVICES/PROGRAMS: exhibits, tours, classes
FACILITIES/EQUIPMENT/PRESERVATION: temperature controls, fire detection controls, fire extinguishing system, preservation lab
PATRON USE STATISTICS: 1543 in-house patrons, 400 telephone patrons, 30 mail reference requests, 9073 collections used, 491 reference photocopies

NHPRC LA62-710

State Library of Louisiana
700 N. Third St.
P. O. Box 131
Baton Rouge, Louisiana 70821

TEL: (504) 342-4914
FAX: (504) 342-3547

REPORTED BY: Virginia R. Smith, Head Louisiana Section
TYPE OF INSTITUTION: library (state)

HOURS: M-F 8-4:30
ACCESS: open to the general public
SERVICES: in-person, mail, phone reference, photocopies, photographs, data-bases

PRIMARY COLLECTION FOCUS: Louisiana
  Louisiana
  slavery
  WPA

INCLUSIVE DATES: beginning to present
COLLECTION FORMATS: 65,000 pamphlets/ephemera, 260 feet films/video, government records, photographs, maps, oral histories
COLLECTION ACCESS: card catalog, computerized finding aids (used by staff, patrons)
SOFTWARE/SYSTEM: Galaxy
ACQUISITION REPORTED TO: OCLC
STAFF (FTE): 2 librarians, 1 clerical, 1 student
INSTITUTIONAL SUPPORT FOR PROFESSIONAL DEVELOPMENT: tuition/registration reimbursement for courses, workshops, etc., reimbursement for professional meetings registration and travel
PATRON USE STATISTICS: 1700 mail reference requests

NHPRC LA62-490

Bossier Parish Central Library
2206 Beckett St.
Bossier City, Louisiana 71111

TEL: (318) 746-1693

REPORTED BY: Beverly K. Barkley, Central Librarian
TYPE OF INSTITUTION: library (county/local)

HOURS: M-F 9-6, Sa 9-5
ACCESS: open to the general public

SERVICES: in-person reference

PRIMARY COLLECTION FOCUS: Bossier Parish materials
    Bossier Parish, LA (local history)

COLLECTION FORMATS: government records, photographs, maps, oral histories
COLLECTION ACCESS: card catalog
STAFF (FTE): [not reported]
INSTITUTIONAL SUPPORT FOR PROFESSIONAL DEVELOPMENT: use of facilities and equipment permitted
FACILITIES/EQUIPMENT/PRESERVATION: fire detection controls, fire extinguishing system
PATRON USE STATISTICS: user statistics not kept.

Chalmette National Park
8606 W. St. Bernard Highway
Chalmette, Louisiana 70043

TEL: (504) 589-4428

REPORTED BY: Ron Merril, Park Ranger
TYPE OF INSTITUTION: museum (federal)

HOURS: M-F 8-5
ACCESS: open to the general public
SERVICES: mail reference, photocopies

PRIMARY COLLECTION FOCUS: War of 1812, Battle of New Orleans
    military history
    burial records
    War of 1812
    Battle of New Orleans
    parks and monuments, federal

INCLUSIVE DATES: 1815 - 1865.
COLLECTION FORMATS: manuscript collections, books/serials, government records
COLLECTION ACCESS: container lists
STAFF (FTE): 1 professional
FACILITIES/EQUIPMENT/PRESERVATION: temperature controls, humidity controls, fire detection controls, fire extinguishing system

---

Lumcon Library
8124 Highway 56
Chauvin, Louisiana 70344

TEL: 851-2800

REPORTED BY: library staff
TYPE OF INSTITUTION: library (academic)

HOURS: M-F 8-4:30
ACCESS: not open to the general public
SERVICES: [not reported]

PRIMARY COLLECTION FOCUS: marine sciences and geology
    marine sciences
    geology

COLLECTION FORMATS: 30,000 books/serials, 200 maps, 10,000 microfiches

COLLECTION ACCESS: card catalog, computerized finding aids (used by staff, patrons)
SOFTWARE/SYSTEM : Pro-Cite
ACQUISITION REPORTED TO: OCLC
STAFF (FTE): 1 administrative, 2 volunteer/docent, 1 clerical, 1 student
INSTITUTIONAL SUPPORT FOR PROFESSIONAL DEVELOPMENT: reimbursement professional dues, meetings, travel; pay mailings, telephone, use of clerical staff, facilities & equipment
FACILITIES/EQUIPMENT/PRESERVATION: temperature controls, humidity controls, disaster preparedness plan
PATRON USE STATISTICS: user statistics not kept

Grant Parish Library
300 Main Street
Colfax, Louisiana 71417

TEL: (318) 627-9920

REPORTED BY: Helen Sorrell, Library Director
TYPE OF INSTITUTION: library (county/local)

HOURS: M-F 8-5, Sa 9-1
ACCESS: open to the general public
SERVICES: in-person, mail, phone references; photocopies

PRIMARY COLLECTION FOCUS: Grant Parish history (vertical file), family histories
  Grant Parish, LA (local history)
  genealogy

COLLECTION ACCESS: card catalog
STAFF (FTE): 1 administrative, 2 clerical
INSTITUTIONAL SUPPORT FOR PROFESSIONAL DEVELOPMENT: dues for professional organization memberships, reimbursement for professional meetings, in-house workshops on regular basis
SPECIAL SERVICES/PROGRAMS: exhibits
FACILITIES/EQUIPMENT/PRESERVATION: temperature controls, fire extinguishing system
PATRON USE STATISTICS: 10,000 in-house patrons, 1000 telephone patrons, 100 mail reference requests, 500 reference photocopies, 50 microfilm/fiche copies

---

Rice Museum Inc.
P. O. Box 1176
Crowley, Louisiana 70527

TEL: (318) 783-5745
FAX: (318) 783-0724

REPORTED BY: Diane Hoffpauer
TYPE OF INSTITUTION: museum (county/local)

HOURS: W-F 9-4
ACCESS: public access by appointment only
SERVICES: mail reference

PRIMARY COLLECTION FOCUS: farm equipment and displays related to rice industry
  rice industry
  agriculture--rice

INCLUSIVE DATES: 1750-1960
COLLECTION FORMATS: pamphlets/ ephemera, photographs, maps, oral histories
COLLECTION ACCESS: not described
STAFF (FTE): volunteer/docent, student
INSTITUTIONAL SUPPORT FOR PROFESSIONAL DEVELOPMENT: payment of dues for professional

organization memberships, payment for mailings
SPECIAL SERVICES/PROGRAMS: exhibits, tours, lectures/presentations
FACILITIES/EQUIPMENT/PRESERVATION: temperature controls, fire extinguishing system
PATRON USE STATISTICS: user statistics not kept

Arnold LeDoux Library
Louisiana State University at Eunice
LSU-E Drive
P. O. Box 1129
Eunice, Louisiana 70535

TEL: (318) 456-7311
FAX: (318) 546-6620

REPORTED BY: Kenneth P. Neal, General Librarian Sciences/Social Sciences/Humanities
TYPE OF INSTITUTION: library (academic)

HOURS: M-Th 8-8, F 8-4:30, Sa 9-12, Su 1-5
ACCESS: open to the general public
SERVICES: in-person, mail, phone reference, photocopies
PRIMARY COLLECTION FOCUS: Louisiana History, Acadian Genealogy, Community College Collections
    Louisiana--history
    genealogy--Acadian
    Acadia

COLLECTION FORMATS: books/serials, oral histories
COLLECTION ACCESS: card catalog, computerized findings aids (used by staff, patrons)
SOFTWARE/SYSTEM CD-ROM Intelligent Catalog (Bibliophile)
STAFF (FTE): 1 administrative, 3 librarians, 4 clerical, 4 student
INSTITUTIONAL SUPPORT FOR PROFESSIONAL DEVELOPMENT: reimbursement for professional meetings
SPECIAL SERVICES/PROGRAMS: exhibits, tours
FACILITIES/EQUIPMENT/PRESERVATION: temperature controls, fire detection controls, disaster preparedness plan
PATRON USE STATISTICS: 12 in-house patrons, 24 telephone patrons, 6 mail reference requests, 24 reference photocopies

---

Southeastern Louisiana University
SLU, University Station
Center for Regional Studies, Box 730
Hammond, Louisiana 70402

TEL: (504) 549-2151

REPORTED BY: Joy J. Jackson, Director of Center for Regional Studies
TYPE OF INSTITUTION: other (state)

HOURS: M-F 8-4:30
ACCESS: open to the general public
SERVICES: in-person, mail, phone reference, photocopies
RESTRICTIONS: limited mail and phone reference

PRIMARY COLLECTION FOCUS: Florida Parishes of Louisiana
    Florida Parishes, LA (local history)
    business history
    lumber industry
    strawberry industry
    shipping industry--Lake Pontchartrain, LA, local rivers
    Morrison, James H.--congressional papers
    Davis, Jimmie--gubernatorial papers

Kennedy Assassination (FBI files)

INCLUSIVE DATES: 1860-1980's
COLLECTION ACCESS: card catalog, container lists, registers/inventories
STAFF (FTE): 1 administrative, 1 clerical, 3 student
INSTITUTIONAL SUPPORT FOR PROFESSIONAL DEVELOPMENT: tuition/registration reimbursement for courses, workshops, etc., reimbursement for professional meeting registration and travel, use of facilities and equipment permitted
SPECIAL SERVICES/PROGRAMS: exhibits, classes, newsletter, lectures/presentations
FACILITIES/EQUIPMENT/PRESERVATION: temperature controls, humidity controls, fire extinguishing system
PATRON USE STATISTICS: user statistics not kept

NHPRC LA286-720

La Salle Parish Library
221 N. First
P. O. Drawer 1387
Jena, Louisiana 71342

TEL: (318) 992-5675

REPORTED BY: Glenn Rambo, Director
TYPE OF INSTITUTION: library (county/local)

HOURS: M-F 8-5, Sa 9-1
ACCESS: open to the general public
SERVICES: [not reported]

PRIMARY COLLECTION FOCUS: Louisiana and local history
    Louisiana
    LaSalle Parish, LA (local history)

COLLECTION FORMATS: books, pamphlet, ephemera, microfilm
COLLECTION ACCESS: card catalog, container lists
ACQUISITION REPORTED TO: state library database
STAFF (FTE): 1 professional

Diocese of Lafayette
1408 Carmel Ave.
Lafayette, Louisiana 70501-4298

TEL: (318) 261-5639

REPORTED BY: Regina Arnaud, Ph.B, M.L.S., Archivist
TYPE OF INSTITUTION: archives (religious)

HOURS: M-F 8-4
ACCESS: public access by appointment only
SERVICES: in-person, mail, phone references, fee for reference, photocopies
RESTRICTIONS: restricted to non-confidential matters

PRIMARY COLLECTION FOCUS: Diocese records/administration (including Bishop/Papal correspondence)
    Lafayette, LA (diocese records and history)
    Catholic Church
    Louisiana, Southwest

INCLUSIVE DATES: 1766-; bulk, 1917-present
COLLECTION FORMATS: 2000 manuscript collections; 233 institution's records; 400 books/serials; 1000 pamphlets/ephemera; 50 films/videotapes; 1000 photographs; 15 oral histories; 200 blueprints; few

government records
COLLECTION ACCESS: card catalog, computerized findings aids (used by staff), computer index
SOFTWARE/SYSTEM Red Ball
ACQUISITION REPORTED TO: specialized/regional guide
STAFF (FTE): 1 administrative, 1 clerical
INSTITUTIONAL SUPPORT FOR PROFESSIONAL DEVELOPMENT: dues for professional organization membership; payment for mailings, telephone use; use of clerical staff
SPECIAL SERVICES/PROGRAMS: tours
FACILITIES/EQUIPMENT/PRESERVATION: temperature controls, humidity controls, fire detection controls
PATRON USE STATISTICS: user statistics not kept

NHPRC LA358-160

New Orleans - Santa Fe Archives of the Christian Brothers
1522 Breaux Bridge Rd.
1522 Carmel Dr.
Lafayette, Louisiana 71501

TEL: (318) 234-1973

REPORTED BY: Br. Leo M. Harvey, FSC.
TYPE OF INSTITUTION: archives (religious)

HOURS: not open to general public
ACCESS: permission of Provincial required for access
SERVICES: [not reported]

PRIMARY COLLECTION FOCUS: Christian Brothers and the Apostolate in the Southwest U.S.
    Christian Brothers
    Catholic Church
    religious communities

COLLECTION FORMATS: manuscript collections, books, photographs
COLLECTION ACCESS: computerized finding aids (used by staff)
SOFTWARE/SYSTEM: Archives Maintenance Software
ACQUISITION REPORTED TO: Regional Association of Christian Brothers Archivists
STAFF (FTE): 1 professional

University of Southwestern Louisiana
302 E. St. Mary Blvd.
USL P. O. Box 40199
Lafayette, Louisiana 70504

TEL: (318) 231-5702
FAX: (318) 231-5841

REPORTED BY: Bruce Turner, Head of Archives and Special Collections
TYPE OF INSTITUTION: archives, Library (academic)

HOURS: M, T 7:30am-9pm, W-F 7:30-4:30, Sa 10-2
ACCESS: open to the general public
SERVICES: in-person, mail, phone reference, photocopies, microfilm (fee)

PRIMARY COLLECTION FOCUS: Acadiana
    agriculture
    architecture
    literature
    politics
    education

Acadiana
Louisiana, Southwest
University of Southwestern Louisiana (records)
petroleum industry
Louisiana--colonial

INCLUSIVE DATES: 1730's-present
VOLUME: 2250 linear feet
COLLECTION FORMATS: 1350 feet manuscript collections; 600 feet institution's records; 30,000 books/serials; 500 maps, 50 feet pamphlets/ephemera; 50 film/videotapes; 60,000 photographs; 100 oral histories; government records
COLLECTION ACCESS: card catalog, computerized finding aids (used by staff), registers/inventories, not described
SOFTWARE/SYSTEM: MSWord, WordPerfect, DOBIS
ACQUISITION REPORTED TO: OCLC, LAMA
STAFF (FTE): 1 administrative, 1 clerical, 4 student
INSTITUTIONAL SUPPORT FOR PROFESSIONAL DEVELOPMENT: tuition/registration reimbursement for courses, workshops, etc., reimbursement for professional meeting registration and travel, use of facilities and equipment permitted
SPECIAL SERVICES/PROGRAMS: exhibits, tours, classes, lectures/presentations
FACILITIES/EQUIPMENT/PRESERVATION: fire extinguishing system, disaster preparedness plan
PATRON USE STATISTICS: 400 in-house patrons, 70 telephone patrons, 40 mail reference patrons, 45 collections used, 697 microfilm/fiche

NHPRC LA358-800

Diocese of Lake Charles, Archives
414 Iris St.
P. O. Box 3223
Lake Charles, Louisiana 70602

TEL: (318) 429-7412

REPORTED BY: [not reported]
TYPE OF INSTITUTION: archives (religious/diocesan)

HOURS: [not reported]
ACCESS: [not reported]
SERVICES: [not reported]

PRIMARY COLLECTION FOCUS: Catholic history, institutional records
Lake Charles, LA (diocese records and history)
Louisiana, Southwest
Catholic Church

NHPRC LA358-165

Frazar Memorial Library
McNeese State University
P. O. Box 91445
Lake Charles, LA 70609

TEL: (318) 475-5734

REPORTED BY: Kathie Bordelon, Archivist/Special Collections Librarian
TYPE OF INSTITUTION: archives, library (academic)

HOURS: M-F 8-4 or by appointment
ACCESS: open to the general public

SERVICES: in-person, mail, phone reference, photocopies

PRIMARY COLLECTION FOCUS: Southwest Louisiana, McNeese State University, Lake Charles, John McNeese
business history
theater
Lake Charles, LA (local history)
church history
McNeese State University (records)
Louisiana, Southwest
McNeese, John

INCLUSIVE DATES: 1867-present
VOLUME: 1008.78 linear feet
COLLECTION FORMATS: 65 processed manuscript collections; institution's records; 2169 books/serials; 1500 photographs; 104 oral histories; 450 pamphlets/ephemera
COLLECTION ACCESS: repository guide, register/inventories, other
ACQUISITION REPORTED TO: specialized/regional guide
STAFF (FTE): 1 administrative, 2 volunteer/docent, 2 student
INSTITUTIONAL SUPPORT FOR PROFESSIONAL DEVELOPMENT: reimbursement tuition/registration courses, professional meetings, travel; pay mailings, telephone; use of facilities/equipment
SPECIAL SERVICES/PROGRAMS: exhibits, tours, newsletter, fund raising/endowment, lectures/presentations
FACILITIES/EQUIPMENT/PRESERVATION: temperature controls, preservation lab
disaster preparedness plan
PATRON USE STATISTICS: 60 in-house patrons, 35 telephone patrons, 20 mail reference patrons, 20 collections used, 250 reference photocopies

NHPRC LA395-520

Vernon Parish Library
301 E. Courthouse St.
Leeville, Louisiana 71446

TEL: (318) 239-2027, 1-800-737-2231
FAX: (318) 239-0666

REPORTED BY: Howard L. Coy, Jr., Director
TYPE OF INSTITUTION: library (county/local)

HOURS: M-Sa 8-5:30; T, Th until 7:30pm
ACCESS: open to the general public
SERVICES: in-person, mail, phone reference, photocopies
RESTRICTIONS: limited mail reference

PRIMARY COLLECTION FOCUS: Vernon Parish
Vernon Parish, LA (local history, limited archival materials)
Vernon Parish, LA--tax rolls
genealogy

COLLECTION FORMATS: books/serials, government records, newspaper (Leesville Leader)
COLLECTION ACCESS: card catalog
ACQUISITION REPORTED TO: Lasernet
STAFF (FTE): [not reported]
INSTITUTIONAL SUPPORT FOR PROFESSIONAL DEVELOPMENT: reimbursement for professional meetings
PATRON USE STATISTICS: user statistics not kept

Desoto Parish Library TEL: (318) 872-6100
109 Crosby
Mansfield, Louisiana 71052

REPORTED BY: Wanda A. Berry, Director
TYPE OF INSTITUTION: library (local)

HOURS: M 9-6; Tu-F 9-5; Sa 9-1
ACCESS: open to the general public
SERVICES: in-person reference, limited mail/phone reference, photocopies

PRIMARY COLLECTION FOCUS: local genealogy
Desoto Parish, LA--genealogy

Mansfield State Commemorative Area TEL: (318) 872-1474
Rt. 3 Box 459
Mansfield LA 71052

REPORTED BY: John House
TYPE OF INSTITUTION: museum (state)

HOURS: 9-5 seven days a week
ACCESS: open to the general public
PRIMARY COLLECTION FOCUS: Civil War
Battle of Mansfield, LA
Civil War

INCLUSIVE DATES: 1860-1865
COLLECTION FORMATS: manuscript collections, institution's records, books/serials, pamphlets/ephemera, photographs, maps
COLLECTION ACCESS: registers/inventories
STAFF (FTE): 5 administrative
INSTITUTIONAL SUPPORT FOR PROFESSIONAL DEVELOPMENT: use of facilities and equipment permitted
SPECIAL SERVICES/PROGRAMS: exhibits, tours, lectures/presentations
FACILITIES/EQUIPMENT/PRESERVATION: temperature controls, humidity controls, fire detection controls, fire extinguishing system, disaster preparedness plan
PATRON USE STATISTICS: information not available
NHPRC LA 465-480

Sabine Parish Library TEL: (318) 256-4150
750 East Main
Many, Louisiana 71449-3199

REPORTED BY: Jeanne H. Pickett
TYPE OF INSTITUTION: library (county/local)

HOURS: M,Tu 8-6, W-F 8-5, Sa 8-12 noon
ACCESS: open to the general public
SERVICES: in-person, mail, phone reference, photocopies

PRIMARY COLLECTION FOCUS: Sabine Parish History and Sabine Parish Genealogy
Sabine Parish, LA (local history)
genealogy

INCLUSIVE DATES: 1843-Present
COLLECTION FORMATS: manuscripts collections, books/serials, films/videotapes, government records, photographs
COLLECTION ACCESS: card catalog, register/inventories
STAFF (FTE): [not reported]
INSTITUTIONAL SUPPORT FOR PROFESSIONAL DEVELOPMENT: reimbursement for professional meetings registration and travel
FACILITIES/EQUIPMENT/PRESERVATION: fire extinguishing system
PATRON USE STATISTICS: user statistics not kept.

Marksville State Commemorative Area
700 Martin Luther King Drive
Marksville, Louisiana 71360

TEL: (318) 253-8954

REPORTED BY: Ward E. Zischke, Curator
TYPE OF INSTITUTION: museum (state)

HOURS: Su-Sa 9-5
ACCESS: open to the general public
SERVICES: in-person reference, mail reference

PRIMARY COLLECTION FOCUS: Marksville Indian culture tradition, 1-400 AD
  Native Americans
  Marksville Indians

COLLECTION ACCESS: registers/inventories, computerized finding aids (used by staff)
SOFTWARE/SYSTEM Deskmate
ACQUISITION REPORTED TO: professional journal(s)
STAFF (FTE): 1 administrative, 1 other
INSTITUTIONAL SUPPORT FOR PROFESSIONAL DEVELOPMENT: use of facilities and equipment permitted
SPECIAL SERVICES/PROGRAMS: exhibits, tours, lectures/presentations
FACILITIES/EQUIPMENT/PRESERVATION: temperature controls, fire extinguishing system
PATRON USE STATISTICS: 3,240 in-house patrons

Northeast Louisiana University
Sandel Library
Archives and Special Collections
700 University Ave.
Monroe LA 711209-0720

TEL: (318) 342-1050

REPORTED BY: Glenn Jodan
TYPE OF INSTITUTION: library (academic)

HOURS: M-F 7:30-4:30
ACCESS: open to the general public
SERVICES: in-person reference, photocopies
PRIMARY COLLECTION FOCUS: Northeast Louisiana
  Louisiana--politics
  Louisiana--economics
  Louisiana--social and cultural life

INCLUSIVE DATES: 1860-present
COLLECTION FORMATS: manuscript collections, institution's records, books/serials,

pamphlets/ephemera, films/videotapes, photographs, maps, oral histories
COLLECTION ACCESS: card catalog, registers/inventories
STAFF (FTE): 2 administrative
INSTITUTIONAL SUPPORT FOR PROFESSIONAL DEVELOPMENT: use of facilities and equipment permitted
SPECIAL SERVICES/PROGRAMS: exhibits, tours, classes
FACILITIES/EQUIPMENT/PRESERVATION: temperature controls, humidity controls, fire detection controls, fire extinguishing system, disaster preparedness plan
PATRON USE STATISTICS: information not available
NHPRC LA 535-560

Ouachita Parish Public Library
1800 Stubbs Ave.
Monroe, Louisiana 71201

TEL: (318) 387-1950
FAX: (318) 388-4874

REPORTED BY: Hermione M. Driskell, Special Collections
TYPE OF INSTITUTION: library (parish)

HOURS: Special Collections M-F 9:30-4:30
ACCESS: open to the general public
SERVICES: in-person, mail, phone reference, fee for reference, photocopies

PRIMARY COLLECTION FOCUS: general public; Northeast Louisiana University
  genealogy
  Louisiana, Northeast (local history)

COLLECTION FORMATS: institution's records, books/serials, pamphlets/ephemera films/video, government records, photographs, maps, oral histories
COLLECTION ACCESS: computerized findings aids (used by staff, patrons)
STAFF (FTE): [not reported]
INSTITUTIONAL SUPPORT FOR PROFESSIONAL DEVELOPMENT: reimbursement tuition/registration courses, professional dues, meetings, travel; pay mailings; use of facilities/equip; in house workshops
SPECIAL SERVICES/PROGRAMS: exhibits, tours, classes-genealogy
FACILITIES/EQUIPMENT/PRESERVATION: temperature controls, fire detection controls, fire extinguishing system
PATRON USE STATISTICS: user statistics not kept

NHPRC LA535-600

Morgan City Archives
200 Everett St.
P. O. Box 430
Morgan City, Louisiana 70381

TEL: (504) 380-4621

REPORTED BY: Catherine Dilsaver, Curator
TYPE OF INSTITUTION: archives (city)

HOURS: M-F 9-12 and 1-5
ACCESS: open to the general public
SERVICES: mail, phone reference, fee for reference, photocopies

PRIMARY COLLECTION FOCUS: Atchafalaya Basin, Morgan City, St. Mary Parish history
  Louisiana, Atchafalaya Basin
  Morgan City, LA (local history)

St. Mary Parish, LA (records, council meeting films)

INCLUSIVE DATES: 1800-1992
COLLECTION FORMATS: manuscript collections, maps, newspapers, vertical files
COLLECTION ACCESS: card catalog, repository guide, registers/inventories
STAFF (FTE): 1 administrative, 1 general archival, 1 clerical, 5 member Board of Commissioners
SPECIAL SERVICES/PROGRAMS: exhibits, tours, lectures/presentations
FACILITIES/EQUIPMENT/PRESERVATION: temperature controls, humidity controls, fire extinguishing system
PATRON USE STATISTICS: 900 in-house patrons, 104 telephone patrons, 100 mail reference requests, 85 collections used, 1050 microfilm/fiche copies

---

Cammie G. Henry Research Center
Archives and Manuscripts Collections
Watson Library
Northwestern State University of Louisiana
Natchitoches, LA 71457

TEL: (318) 357-4585 or 357-4468
FAX: (318) 357-4470

REPORTED BY: Mary Lind Wernet
TYPE OF INSTITUTION: archives/special collections (academic)

HOURS: M-F 8-12 & 1-5 (generally)
ACCESS: open to public, but best to call before traveling to archives
SERVICES: in person, mail, & phone reference, photocopies, photo & microfilm reproduction, oral history tape reproduction (user provides blank tape--fees for reference & copies
RESTRICTIONS: some collections/items restricted

PRIMARY COLLECTION FOCUS: colonial Natchitoches and history of North Louisiana, especially 1812 to statehood

Louisiana--Cane River Region
Natchitoches, LA (local history)
Louisiana--Spanish Colonial
Louisiana--French Colonial
Louisiana--American Territory
horticulture--Southern United States
anthropology

archaeology
Federal Writers Project
women's clubs
artists
literary manuscripts
plantation life and culture
genealogy

INCLUSIVE DATES: 1725 - 1970
VOLUME: 1,100+ cubic feet
COLLECTION FORMATS: 1000 linear feet manuscript collections, 100 linear feet institution's records, 8400 (titles) books/serials, 58 linear feet pamphlets/ephemera, 42 VHS oral history videotapes, 35 linear feet government records, ca. 46 linear feet photographs, 3007 maps, 1147 oral histories
COLLECTION ACCESS: card catalog, container lists, registers/inventories, repository subject guide, computerized finding aids (used by staff)
SOFTWARE/SYSTEM First Choice, WordPerfect
ACQUISITION REPORTED TO: NUCMC, specialized/regional guide, professional journals
STAFF (FTE): 1 general archivist, volunteer/docent, 3 students
INSTITUTIONAL SUPPORT FOR PROFESSIONAL DEVELOPMENT: tuition/registration/professional meeting reimbursement ($200 limit), in house workshops, use of facilities and equipment, payment for mailings and telephone
SPECIAL SERVICES/PROGRAMS: exhibits, tours, lectures/presentations, assist with History Department archives internship program
FACILITIES/EQUIPMENT/PRESERVATION: fire detection controls, fire extinguishing system, preservation lab (ca. $200 preservation budget)
PATRON USE STATISTICS: 50 telephone patrons, 120 mail reference, other statistics not kept
NHPRC LA570-540

Academy of the Sacred Heart
4521 St. Charles Ave.
New Orleans, Louisiana 70115

TEL: (504) 891-1943
FAX: (504) 891-9939

REPORTED BY: [not listed]
TYPE OF INSTITUTION: archives (academic, religious)

HOURS: N/A
ACCESS: not open to the general public
SERVICES: N/A

PRIMARY COLLECTION FOCUS: Sacred Heart Academy
    Academy of the Sacred Heart, LA (records)

COLLECTION FORMATS: institution's records, films/videos, photographs, oral histories
COLLECTION ACCESS: container lists
STAFF (FTE): [not reported]

Archives of the Archdiocese of New Orleans
1100 Chartres Street
New Orleans, Louisiana 70116

TEL: (504) 529-2651
FAX: (504) 529-2001

REPORTED BY: Charles E. Nolan, Archivist
TYPE OF INSTITUTION: archives (religious)

HOURS: M-F 9-5
ACCESS: public access by appointment only
SERVICES: in-person, mail, and phone reference; photocopies; fee for reference
RESTRICTIONS: fees, genealogical requests answered by mail only

PRIMARY COLLECTION FOCUS: Louisiana Catholic history
    Catholic Church
    New Orleans, Archdiocese of (records)
    genealogy--Louisiana
    New Orleans--education and social history
    religious communities

INCLUSIVE DATES: 1718-present
VOLUME: ca. 850 linear feet
COLLECTION FORMATS: 40 linear feet manuscript collections, 680 linear feet institution's records, 100 linear feet books/serials, 10 linear feet pamphlets/ephemera, 3 linear feet photographs, 2 linear feet oral histories, 15 linear feet other
COLLECTION ACCESS: card catalog, container lists, registers/inventories, computerized finding aids (used by staff)
SOFTWARE/SYSTEM: DataPerfect, WordPerfect, Alpha 4
STAFF (FTE): 2 administrative, 1 volunteer/docent, 1 clerical
INSTITUTIONAL SUPPORT FOR PROFESSIONAL DEVELOPMENT: dues for professional memberships, reimbursement for professional meetings
SPECIAL SERVICES/PROGRAMS: tours, classes, lectures/presentations, archivist teaches graduate archives course at local university
FACILITIES/EQUIPMENT/PRESERVATION: temperature controls, humidity controls, fire detection controls, fire extinguishing system, disaster preparedness plan
PATRON USE STATISTICS: user statistics not kept

NHPRC LA600-40

Achives of the Dominican Congregation of Saint Mary
580 Broadway
New Orleans LA 70118

TEL: (504) 861-8183
FAX: (504) 861-8718

REPORTED BY: Sister Dorothy Dawes
TYPE OF INSTITUTION: archives (religious)
HOURS: M-F 9-5
ACCESS: public access by appointment only
SERVICES: phone reference, fee for reference, photocopies

PRIMARY COLLECTION FOCUS: Dominican Congregation of St. Mary
   religious communities
   Catholic Church

INCLUSIVE DATES: 1860-present
COLLECTION FORMATS: manuscript collections, institution's records, books/serials,
   pamphlets/ephemera, films/videotapes, photographs, oral histories
STAFF (FTE): 1 administrative
INSTITUTIONAL SUPPORT FOR PROFESSIONAL DEVELOPMENT: tuition/registration, reimbursement for courses, workshops, etc., reimbursement for professional meetings, use of facilities and equipment permitted
SPECIAL SERVICES/PROGRAMS: exhibits
FACILITIES/EQUIPMENT/PRESERVATION: temperature controls, fire detection controls, fire extinguishing system
PATRON USE STATISTICS: information not available

Historic New Orleans Collection
Manuscripts Division
533 Royal St.
New Orleans, Louisiana 70130

TEL: (504) 523-4662
FAX: (504) 522-5108

REPORTED BY: Alfred E. Lemmon, Curator of Manuscripts
TYPE OF INSTITUTION: museum/research center (private: Kemper and Leila Williams Foundation)

HOURS: Tu-Sa 10-4:30
ACCESS: open to the general public
SERVICES: in-person reference, mail and phone reference, photocopies

PRIMARY COLLECTION FOCUS: New Orleans, Louisiana, and Gulf Coast
   New Orleans
   Louisiana
   Louisiana--antebellum
   Battle of New Orleans
   Civil War
   New Orleans, German Community
   arts--visual and performing
   land tenure records
   Louisiana--colonial
   family papers
   Louisiana--social/economic history

INCLUSIVE DATES: 1718 - present
VOLUME: 5000 linear feet
COLLECTION FORMATS: 500 manuscript collections, institution's records,
   books, photographs, visual material in curatorial division
COLLECTION ACCESS: registers/inventories, container lists, computerized finding aids (used by staff, patrons)

SOFTWARE/SYSTEM Quixis
ACQUISITION REPORTED TO: NUCMC, professional journals, specialized guides
STAFF (FTE): 5 (manuscripts division only)
INSTITUTIONAL SUPPORT FOR PROFESSIONAL DEVELOPMENT: reimbursement tuition/registration, professional meetings, travel
SPECIAL SERVICES/PROGRAMS: exhibits, tours, Historic New Orleans Collection Quarterly, MSS Division Update, lectures/presentations
FACILITIES/EQUIPMENT/PRESERVATION: temperature controls, humidity controls, fire detection controls, fire extinguishing system, disaster preparedness plan
PATRON USE STATISTICS: 1,500 patrons (manuscript division only)

NHPRC LA600-310

Hotel Dieu Hospital
2021 Perdido St.
P. O. Box 61262
New Orleans, Louisiana 70161

TEL: (504) 588-3000
FAX: (504) 524-7584

REPORTED BY: Sister Benedicta Burkart, D.C., Archivist

RECORDS TRANSFERRED TO: **Marillac Archives**
                              7800 Natural Bridge
                              St. Louis, MO 63112
                              (314) 382-2800

NHPRC LA600-320 [note relocation]

Jackson Barracks Military Library
Office of the Adjutant General, Building 51
New Orleans, Louisiana 70146

TEL: (504) 278-6241

REPORTED BY: Lionel J. Bienvenu
TYPE OF INSTITUTION: archives, library (state)

HOURS: M-F 8-4
ACCESS: open to the general public
SERVICES: in-person, mail, phone reference, photocopies, microfilm

PRIMARY COLLECTION FOCUS: Louisiana state military history
   Confederate States of America
   Adjutant General Archives
   Louisiana--military history
   military history
   Civil War

INCLUSIVE DATES: 1697-1991
COLLECTION FORMATS: 20 linear feet manuscript collections; 10 linear feet institution's records; 8100 books/serials; 2 cases maps; 2 feet photographs; 2 feet government records; 1000 pamphlets/ephemera
COLLECTION ACCESS: card catalog
STAFF (FTE): 1 administrative, 2 volunteer/docent

NHPRC LA600-455

Longue Vue House and Gardens
7 Bamboo Road
New Orleans, Louisiana 70124

TEL: (504) 488-5488
FAX: (504) 486-7015

REPORTED BY: Lydia Schmalz
TYPE OF INSTITUTION: museum (private decorative arts museum)

HOURS: M-Sa 10-4:30, Su 1-5
ACCESS: open to the general public
SERVICES: [not reported]

PRIMARY COLLECTION FOCUS: decorative arts/architecture, small family/business archives
    personal papers
    business history
    architecture

INCLUSIVE DATES: decorative arts late 17th-20th century
VOLUME: 3000 linear feet
STAFF (FTE): [not reported]
SPECIAL SERVICES/PROGRAMS: exhibits, tours, classes, newsletter, fund raising/endowment, lectures/presentations
FACILITIES/EQUIPMENT/PRESERVATION: temperature controls, humidity controls, fire detection controls, fire extinguishing system
PATRON USE STATISTICS: user statistics not kept

Louisiana State Museum Historical Center
400 Esplanade
P. O. Box 2448
New Orleans, Louisiana 70176-2440

TEL: (504) 568-6968
FAX: (504) 568-6969

REPORTED BY: Kathryn Page, Curator of Maps and Manuscripts
TYPE OF INSTITUTION: archives, library, museum (state)

HOURS: W-F 10-4
ACCESS: public access by appointment only
SERVICES: in-person, mail, phone reference, photocopies
RESTRICTIONS: copyright

PRIMARY COLLECTION FOCUS: Louisiana
    Louisiana
    Louisiana--colonial
    Louisiana--cultural history
    Louisiana--politics
    social history--Louisiana
    Civil War
    Reconstruction

INCLUSIVE DATES: c. 1500-present
COLLECTION FORMATS: ca. 500 linear feet manuscript collections; ca. 200 linear feet institution's records; 50,000 books/serials; 500 audiovisual; 500 linear feet photographs; 3000 maps; 1000 oral histories 2000 pamphlets/ephemera
COLLECTION ACCESS: card catalog, repository guide, registers/inventories, container lists
STAFF (FTE): 1 administrative, 4 volunteer/docents, 2 intern
INSTITUTIONAL SUPPORT FOR PROFESSIONAL DEVELOPMENT: reimbursement for professional meetings, payment for mailings, use of facilities and equipment permitted
SPECIAL SERVICES/PROGRAMS: exhibits, tours, classes, newsletter, fund raising/endowment,

lectures/presentations
FACILITIES/EQUIPMENT/PRESERVATION: temperature controls, humidity controls, fire detection controls, fire extinguishing system, preservation lab
PATRON USE STATISTICS: 500 in-house patrons, 1000 telephone patrons, 200 mail reference patrons, 100 collections used

NHPRC LA600-465

Louisiana State University
Medical Center
433 Bolivar St.
New Orleans LA 70112

TEL: (504) 568-6100

REPORTED BY: Judith Caruthers
TYPE OF INSTITUTION: library (academic)
HOURS: M-F 8:30-4:30
ACCESS: public access by appointment only
SERVICES: in-person, mail, and phone reference
PRIMARY COLLECTION FOCUS: health sciences
    medicine, history of
    nursing

INCLUSIVE DATES: 1930-present
COLLECTION FORMATS: manuscript collections, institution's records, books/serials, pamphlets/ephemera, government records, photographs
STAFF (FTE): maintained by library personnel
INSTITUTIONAL SUPPORT FOR PROFESSIONAL DEVELOPMENT: tuition/registration reimbursement for courses, workshops, etc., use of facilities and equipment permitted
FACILITIES/EQUIPMENT/PRESERVATION: temperature controls, humidity controls, fire detection controls, fire extinguishing system, disaster preparedness plan
PATRON USE STATISTICS: information not available

NHPRC LA 600-490

Loyola University Library, Special Collection & Archives
6363 St. Charles Avenue
New Orleans, Louisiana 70118

TEL: (504) 865-3186

REPORTED BY: Art Carpenter, Archivist
TYPE OF INSTITUTION: library (academic)

HOURS: M-F 8:30-4:45
ACCESS: open to the general public
SERVICES: in-person, mail, phone reference, photocopies

PRIMARY COLLECTION FOCUS: influence of the Society of Jesus and Loyola University on history of New Orleans
    Society of Jesus, New Orleans Province
    Loyola University (records)
    New Orleans--history
    social reform
    Catholic Church
    Louisiana--colonial
    missionaries

INCLUSIVE DATES: 1830-present
VOLUME: ca. 1000 linear feet
COLLECTION FORMATS: ca. 600 linear feet manuscript collections, ca. 350 linear feet institution's records, 20,000 books
COLLECTION ACCESS: registers/inventories
ACQUISITION REPORTED TO: NUCMC, OCLC
STAFF (FTE): 1 general archival
INSTITUTIONAL SUPPORT FOR PROFESSIONAL DEVELOPMENT: tuition/registration reimbursement for courses, reimbursement for professional meetings (registration & travel), payment for phone use, use of facilities and equipment
SPECIAL SERVICES/PROGRAMS: exhibits
FACILITIES/EQUIPMENT/PRESERVATION: temperature controls, fire detection controls
PATRON USE STATISTICS: 200 in-house patrons, 100 telephone patrons, 20 mail reference requests

NHPRC LA600-505

John T. Christian Library
New Orleans Baptist Theological Seminary
4110 Seminary Place
New Orleans, Louisiana 70126

TEL: (504) 282-4455 ext. 3288

REPORTED BY: Mr. Ken Taylor, Director
TYPE OF INSTITUTION: library (religious)

HOURS: M-Th 8am-10pm, F 8am-9:30pm, Sa 9-2, during regular term
ACCESS: public access by appointment only
SERVICES: in-person reference, photocopies

PRIMARY COLLECTION FOCUS: religion and theology, Baptist Church
    Baptist Church
    New Orleans Baptist Theological Seminary (records)

COLLECTION FORMATS: 200,000 books/serials, 4000 pamphlets/ephemera, 2000 films/videotapes, photographs
COLLECTION ACCESS: card catalog
ACQUISITION REPORTED TO: OCLC
STAFF (FTE): 4 administrative, 1 preservation, 1 audiovisual officer, 5 clerical, 3 student
INSTITUTIONAL SUPPORT FOR PROFESSIONAL DEVELOPMENT: reimbursement tuition/registration courses, professional dues and meetings, pay mailings and telephone, use of clerical staff, facilities/equipment
SPECIAL SERVICES/PROGRAMS: classes
FACILITIES/EQUIPMENT/PRESERVATION: fire detection controls
PATRON USE STATISTICS: user statistics not kept.

NHPRC LA600-540

New Orleans Notarial Archives
Civil District Court Building
421 Loyola Ave.
New Orleans, Louisiana 70112

TEL: (504) 568-8577
FAX: (504) 568-8599

REPORTED BY: Sally K. Reeves, Archivist
TYPE OF INSTITUTION: archives (state)

HOURS: M-F 9-4; extended Reading Room hours to 6pm M-Th
ACCESS: open to the general public
SERVICES: in-person, mail, phone reference fee for reference(mail), photocopies
RESTRICTIONS: Dreyfous Reading Room volumes restricted

PRIMARY COLLECTION FOCUS: New Orleans contracts
    New Orleans, LA--notarial records
    contracts, sales, mortgages
    architecture--drawings
    surveys and plans
    wills
    business history
    African Americans

INCLUSIVE DATES: 1731-present
VOLUME: 38,000 notarial volumes, 5015 civil engineers' drawings (detailing property boundaries, buildings & features on property, landscaping, architectural details, etc.)
COLLECTION FORMATS: manuscript collections, plans, notarial acts and attachments
COLLECTION ACCESS: computerized finding aids (used by staff), not described, shelf list
SOFTWARE/SYSTEM: d-Base 4.1
STAFF (FTE): 2 administrative, 2 general archival, 1 preservation, 2 clerical, 4 book clerks, 2 microfilm technicians, 1 registration clerk
INSTITUTIONAL SUPPORT FOR PROFESSIONAL DEVELOPMENT: reimbursement tuition/registration for courses, professional meetings, travel; pay for mailings, telephone; use of clerical staff, facilities/equipment
SPECIAL SERVICES/PROGRAMS: exhibits, tours, lectures/presentations
FACILITIES/EQUIPMENT/PRESERVATION: temperature controls, fire detection controls, Halon extinguishing, preservation lab, disaster preparedness plan
PATRON USE STATISTICS: user statistics not kept

New Orleans Opera Association **TEL**: (504) 529-2278, 524-1018
333 St. Charles Ave., Suite 907 **FAX**: (504) 529-7668
New Orleans. Louisiana 70130

REPORTED BY: Dean M. Shapiro, Marketing Assistant
TYPE OF INSTITUTION: Performing Arts Association for Opera (non-profit organization)

HOURS: M-F 9-5
ACCESS: public access by appointment only
SERVICES: [not reported]

PRIMARY COLLECTION FOCUS: opera
    opera

COLLECTION FORMATS: books/serials, pamphlets/ephemera, photographs, files/clippings
STAFF (FTE): volunteer/docent
SPECIAL SERVICES/PROGRAMS: newsletter, fund raising/endowment, lectures/presentations, community outreach program
PATRON USE STATISTICS: user statistics not kept

New Orleans Public Library - Louisiana Division **TEL**: (504)596-2610
219 Loyola Ave. **FAX**: (504) 596-2609
New Orleans, Louisiana 70112

REPORTED BY: Wayne Everard, Archivist
TYPE OF INSTITUTION: library (city)

HOURS: M-Th 10-6, F-Sa 10-5
ACCESS: open to the general public
SERVICES: in-person, mail, phone reference, fee for reference, photocopies

PRIMARY COLLECTION FOCUS: New Orleans Municipal and other local government records
    New Orleans, LA--politics and government
    New Orleans, LA--legal records

INCLUSIVE DATES: 1769-1992
COLLECTION FORMATS: 180 cubic feet manuscript collections; 142 feet institution's records; 7100 books/serials; 425 feet audiovisual, 39,000 photographs; 1500 maps; 12,000 feet government records; 35 feet pamphlets/ephemera
COLLECTION ACCESS: card catalog, registers/inventories, container lists, computerized finding aids (used by staff, patrons)
SOFTWARE/SYSTEM USMARC format, entered into OCLC, downloaded into local DYNIX
ACQUISITION REPORTED TO: OCLC, professional journal(s)
STAFF (FTE): 1 administrative, 2 general archival, 1 photo curator, 2 volunteer/docent, 1 clerical, 2 microfilming technicians
INSTITUTIONAL SUPPORT FOR PROFESSIONAL DEVELOPMENT: reimbursement tuition/registration for courses, professional dues, meetings, travel; in-house workshops, pay for mailings, telephone; use of facilities/staff
SPECIAL SERVICES/PROGRAMS: exhibits, fund raising/endowment, lectures/presentations
FACILITIES/EQUIPMENT/PRESERVATION: fire detection controls, preservation lab
PATRON USE STATISTICS: user statistics not kept
NHPRC LA600-555

Preservation Resource Center
604 Julia St.
New Orleans, Louisiana 70130

TEL: (504) 581-7032
FAX: (504) 522-9275

REPORTED BY: Stephanie Musser, Josephine B. See, PhD
TYPE OF INSTITUTION: preservation society

HOURS: M-F 9-5
ACCESS: open to the general public
SERVICES: in-person reference

PRIMARY COLLECTION FOCUS: New Orleans, LA & national articles of interest to preservation
    real estate
    preservation
    New Orleans, LA
    historic preservation

INCLUSIVE DATES: August 1975-present
COLLECTION FORMATS: newspaper tear sheets, other
COLLECTION ACCESS: card catalog
STAFF (FTE): 1 administrative, 1 general archival
SPECIAL SERVICES/PROGRAMS: tours, newsletter, fund raising/endowment, lectures/presentations, other
FACILITIES/EQUIPMENT/PRESERVATION: temperature controls, fire detection controls, fire extinguishing system
PATRON USE STATISTICS: user statistics not kept

Archives of the Sisters of Mercy
301 N. Jefferson Davis Parkway
P. O. Box 19024
New Orleans, Louisiana 70179

TEL: (504)483-5000

REPORTED BY: Sister Mary Hermenia Muldrey, RSM
TYPE OF INSTITUTION: archives, library (religious)

HOURS: by appointment, usually between 1-4 M-F
ACCESS: public access by appointment only
SERVICES: in-person/mail references, photocopies (fee for postage or copies)

PRIMARY COLLECTION FOCUS: records of the Order and Southern branch convents
    Sisters of Mercy
    Catholic Church
    religious communities

INCLUSIVE DATES: 1869 to present
COLLECTION FORMATS: 45 linear feet institution's records, 36 feet books/serials
COLLECTION ACCESS: card catalog, container lists
STAFF (FTE): 1 administrative
INSTITUTIONAL SUPPORT FOR PROFESSIONAL DEVELOPMENT: reimbursement tuition/registration for
    courses, professional meetings, travel; pay mailings; use of facilities/equipment
FACILITIES/EQUIPMENT/PRESERVATION: fire detection controls

NHPRC LA600-690

Sisters of the Holy Family Collection
6901 Chef Menteur Highway
New Orleans, Louisiana 70126-5290

TEL: (504) 241-5400

REPORTED BY: Sr. M. Boniface Adams
TYPE OF INSTITUTION: convent archives (religious)

HOURS: M-F 9-12; 1-4
ACCESS: not open to the general public
SERVICES: mail and phone reference, photocopies

PRIMARY COLLECTION FOCUS: Sisters of the Holy Family and their apostolate
    Sisters of the Holy Family (records)
    education, religious
    elderly, care of
    religious communities
    Catholic Church

INCLUSIVE DATES: 1842 - present
COLLECTION ACCESS: not catalogued
STAFF (FTE): 1 professional

Southern University at New Orleans
6400 Press Dr.
New Orleans, Louisiana 70126

TEL: (504) 286-5384
FAX: (504) 286-5131

REPORTED BY: Florence E. Borders, Archivist
TYPE OF INSTITUTION: archives, library, museum (state)

HOURS: M-F 9-5; other times by appointment
ACCESS: open to the general public
SERVICES: in-person, mail, phone reference, photocopies.

PRIMARY COLLECTION FOCUS: humanities, humanities enrichment component under Title III
  Africa
  Africans
  African Americans
  art--African

INCLUSIVE DATES: 20th Century
COLLECTION FORMATS: 500 pieces African art, ca. 20 feet manuscript collections, ca. 1000 books/serials, ca. 100 films/videotapes, ca. 10 maps
COLLECTION ACCESS: card catalog, repository guide
ACQUISITION REPORTED TO: NUCMC
STAFF (FTE): 2 administrative, 1 general archival, 3 student
INSTITUTIONAL SUPPORT FOR PROFESSIONAL DEVELOPMENT: reimbursement for professional meetings, registration & travel, payment mailings, payment for phone use, use of facilities & equipment use of clerical staff
SPECIAL SERVICES/PROGRAMS: exhibits, newsletter, lectures/presentations, other
FACILITIES/EQUIPMENT/PRESERVATION: temperature controls, humidity controls, fire extinguishing system
PATRON USE STATISTICS: 150 in-house patrons, 25 telephone patrons, 30 mail reference requests, 10 collections used, 200 reference photocopies

---

Touro Infirmary Archives **TEL**: (504) 897-8090
1401 Foucher St. **FAX**: (504) 897-8322
New Orleans, Louisiana 70125

REPORTED BY: Catherine C. Kahn, Archivist
TYPE OF INSTITUTION: archives (hospital)

HOURS: T, W, Th 9-4
ACCESS: open to the general public
SERVICES: in-person, mail, phone reference, photocopies
RESTRICTIONS: patient records restricted

PRIMARY COLLECTION FOCUS: historic records of Touro Hospital, founded by Judah Touro in 1852
  Touro Hospital, Louisana
  hospitals
  medicine, history of
  physicians

INCLUSIVE DATES: 1852-present
COLLECTION FORMATS: institution's records (minutes, annual reports of trustees, 1854-present, admission books, 1855-1900), films/videotapes, photographs, oral histories
COLLECTION ACCESS: computerized finding aids (used by staff)
SOFTWARE/SYSTEM MicroMARC-AMC
STAFF (FTE): 1 general archival, 2 volunteer/docent
INSTITUTIONAL SUPPORT FOR PROFESSIONAL DEVELOPMENT: tuition/registration reimbursement for courses, workshops, reimbursement for professional meetings-travel, payment for mailings
SPECIAL SERVICES/PROGRAMS: exhibits, newsletter, fund raising/endowment
FACILITIES/EQUIPMENT/PRESERVATION: temperature controls, humidity controls, fire detection controls, fire extinguishing system, preservation lab
PATRON USE STATISTICS: user statistics not kept

Louisiana

Amistad Research Center
6823 St. Charles Ave.
Tilton Hall, Tulane University
New Orleans, Louisiana 70118

TEL: (504) 865-5535
FAX: (504) 865-6740

REPORTED BY: Frederick Steilow, Executive Director
TYPE OF INSTITUTION: archives, library (special)

HOURS: M-Sa 8:30-5
ACCESS: open to the general public
SERVICES: in-person, mail, phone references, photocopies, microfilm

PRIMARY COLLECTION FOCUS: ethnic history and civil rights
- African Americans
- Appalachian whites
- Native Americans
- Asian Americans
- race relations
- gay rights
- United Church of Christ (Congregationalist)
- American Missionary Association (records)
- missionaries

INCLUSIVE DATES: ca. 1790 to the present
COLLECTION FORMATS: 7000 linear feet manuscript collections, 21,000 books, 30,000 pamphlets/ephemera, 30,000 photographs, 400 oral histories
COLLECTION ACCESS: card catalog, repository guide, registers/inventories
ACQUISITION REPORTED TO: NUCMC, OCLC
STAFF (FTE): 2 administrative, 9 general archival, 2 clerical, 12 student
INSTITUTIONAL SUPPORT FOR PROFESSIONAL DEVELOPMENT: tuition/registration reimbursement of courses, workshops, etc., reimbursement for professional meeting(s), registration, travel
SPECIAL SERVICES/PROGRAMS: exhibits, tours, newsletter, lectures/presentations
FACILITIES/EQUIPMENT/PRESERVATION: temperature controls, humidity controls, fire detection controls, fire extinguishing system
PATRON USE STATISTICS: 525 in-house patrons, 463 telephone patrons, 164 mail reference requests

NHPRC LA600-20 [Note address change.]

Latin American Library, Tulane University
Howard-Tilton Memorial Library
New Orleans, Louisiana 70118

TEL: (504) 865-5681
FAX: (504) 865-6773

REPORTED BY: Ruth R. Olivera, Curator of Manuscripts
TYPE OF INSTITUTION: library (academic)

HOURS: M-F 8:30-5, Sa 9-5 (during regular school session)
ACCESS: open to the general public
SERVICES: in-person, mail, phone reference, photocopies, other reproduction services
RESTRICTIONS: researchers are advised of copyright restrictions

PRIMARY COLLECTION FOCUS: Latin America, especially Mexico/Central America, photographs
- Catholic Church
- personal papers
- Latin America
- Native Americans
- Mexico

INCLUSIVE DATES: 1500-present
VOLUME: 498 linear feet of manuscripts collections, 1700 historical photographs
COLLECTION FORMATS: 100 manuscripts collections, 70 photograph collections, government records
COLLECTION ACCESS: card catalog
ACQUISITION REPORTED TO: NUCMC
STAFF (FTE): 1 administrative, .6 curator of manuscripts
INSTITUTIONAL SUPPORT FOR PROFESSIONAL DEVELOPMENT: tuition/registration reimbursement for courses, workshops, etc., payment for mailings, payment for phone use, use of facilities/equipment
SPECIAL SERVICES/PROGRAMS: exhibits
FACILITIES/EQUIPMENT/PRESERVATION: temperature controls, humidity controls, fire detection controls

NHPRC LA600-760

Manuscripts Department, Tulane University
Howard-Tilton Memorial Library
7001 Freret St.
New Orleans, Louisiana 70118-5682

TEL: (504) 865-5685
FAX: (504) 865-6773

REPORTED BY: Leon C. Miller, Manuscripts Librarian
TYPE OF INSTITUTION: manuscripts repository (academic)

HOURS: M-F 8:30-5, Sa 9-1, (summer Sa 10-1)
ACCESS: open to the general public
SERVICES: in-person, mail, phone reference, photocopies, photographs

PRIMARY COLLECTION FOCUS: Tulane University; New Orleans; Louisiana

Louisiana	women's history
agriculture	Civil War
business history	medicine, history of
education	steamboats
art	literary manuscripts--Southern authors
religion	plantation life and culture
philanthropy	politics
Judaism	waterways

INCLUSIVE DATES: 1682-present
VOLUME: 1,000,000 plus items
COLLECTION FORMATS: ca. 900 manuscript collections (17,000 linear feet); 400+ linear feet books/pamphlets; ca. 2500 films/videotapes; 200,000 photographs
COLLECTION ACCESS: card catalog, registers/inventories, container lists, computerized finding aids (used by staff, patrons)
SOFTWARE/SYSTEM OCLC, NOTIS
ACQUISITION REPORTED TO: NUCMC, OCLC
STAFF (FTE): 2.5 general archival, 1 volunteer/docent, 2 student, 3 interns
INSTITUTIONAL SUPPORT FOR PROFESSIONAL DEVELOPMENT: reimbursement tuition/registration for courses, professional meetings, and travel; pay mailings and telephone; use of clerical staff, facilities/equipment
SPECIAL SERVICES/PROGRAMS: exhibits, tours, classes, newsletter, lectures/presentations, internship program
FACILITIES/EQUIPMENT/PRESERVATION: temperature controls, humidity controls, fire detection controls, disaster preparedness plan
PATRON USE STATISTICS: 662 in-house patrons, 434 mail reference requests

NHPRC LA600-755

Middle American Research Institute
Dinwiddie Hall, 4th Floor
Tulane University
6823 St. Charles Ave.
New Orleans, Louisiana 70118

TEL: (504) 865-5110
FAX: (504) 862-8778

REPORTED BY: Kathe Tujillo, Asst. to the Director
TYPE OF INSTITUTION: archives, museum, research institute (academic)

HOURS: M-F 8:30-4
ACCESS: open to the general public
SERVICES: in-person reference (please call before coming)

PRIMARY COLLECTION FOCUS: Mexico and Central America
    archaeology--pre-Columbian
    anthropology
    Mexico
    Central America

INCLUSIVE DATES: pre-Columbian to present
COLLECTION FORMATS: 61 volumes books/serials, 10,000 photographs, 100 maps, pre-Columbian artifacts
COLLECTION ACCESS: card catalog, repository guide, computerized finding aids (used by staff)
SOFTWARE/SYSTEM: Paradox (photo and slides only)
STAFF (FTE): 1 director, 1 assistant director, 1 volunteer/docent, 4 student
INSTITUTIONAL SUPPORT FOR PROFESSIONAL DEVELOPMENT: reimbursement for professional
    meeting, use of facilities and equipment permitted
SPECIAL SERVICES/PROGRAMS: exhibits, tours, lectures/presentations
FACILITIES/EQUIPMENT/PRESERVATION: fire detection controls, disaster preparedness plan
PATRON USE STATISTICS: user statistics not kept

Southeastern Architectural Archive
Special Collections Division
Howard-Tilton Memorial Library
Tulane University
70001 Freret Street
New Orleans LA 70118-5682

TEL: (504) 865-5699
FAX: (504) 865-6773

REPORTED BY: Kelvin Williams, Assistant Curator
TYPE OF INSTITUTION: archives (academic)

HOURS: M-F 8:30-5
ACCESS: open to the general public
SERVICES: in-person, mail, and phone reference, photocopies, photographs
PRIMARY COLLECTION FOCUS: gulf south architectural record focusing on New Orleans and Louisiana
    architecture
    plantation life and culture
    urban life
    engineering
    art

INCLUSIVE DATES: founding of Louisiana - present
VOLUME: 500,000 drawings, 30,000 photos
COLLECTION FORMATS: photographs, maps, drawings
COLLECTION ACCESS: card catalog, container lists, registers/inventories
STAFF (FTE): 2 administrative

INSTITUTIONAL SUPPORT FOR PROFESSIONAL DEVELOPMENT: tuition/registration reimbursement for courses, workshops, reimbursement for professional meetings, payment for mailings
SPECIAL SERVICES/PROGRAMS: exhibits
FACILITIES/EQUIPMENT/PRESERVATION: temperature controls, humidity controls, fire detection controls, fire extinguishing system, preservation lab
PATRON USE STATISTICS: 500 in-house patrons, 300 telephone patrons

NHPRC LA 600-761

Tulane University Archives
Howard-Tilton Memorial Library
Tulane University
7001 Freret St.
New Orleans, Louisiana 70118

TEL: (504) 865-5691
FAX: (504) 865-6773

REPORTED BY: Robert G. Sherer, University Archivist
TYPE OF INSTITUTION: archives (academic)

HOURS: M-F 8:30-5; Sa 9-1
ACCESS: open to general public
SERVICES: in-person, mail, and phone reference, photocopies, photographs

PRIMARY COLLECTION FOCUS: Tulane University
  Tulane University (records)

INCLUSIVE DATES: 1834 - present
COLLECTION FORMATS: 2500 linear feet institution's records, 735 dissertations and theses, 245 films and videos, 55,000 photographs, 8 maps
COLLECTION ACCESS: container lists, computerized finding aids (used by staff)
SOFTWARE/SYSTEM WordPerfect 5.1
STAFF (FTE): 1.5 professional staff, 1 non professional
INSTITUTIONAL SUPPORT FOR PROFESSIONAL DEVELOPMENT: reimbursement for professional meetings, registration, and partial travel
SPECIAL SERVICES/PROGRAMS: exhibits
FACILITIES/EQUIPMENT/PRESERVATION: temperature controls, humidity controls, fire detection controls, fire extinguishing system

---

Rudolph Matas Medical Library
Tulane Medical Center
1430 Tulane Ave.
New Orleans, Louisiana 70112

TEL: (504) 588-5155
FAX: (504) 587-7417

REPORTED BY: Patricia Copeland, Chief of Information Services
TYPE OF INSTITUTION: library (academic)

HOURS: M-F 9:30-4:30
ACCESS: not open to the general public (except by special permission)
SERVICES: in-person, mail, phone reference, photocopies

PRIMARY COLLECTION FOCUS: medicine & surgery; especially women in medicine; physicians in Louisiana
  medicine and surgery, history of
  women in medicine
  physicians

INCLUSIVE DATES: 1471-1871
COLLECTION FORMATS: 4881 books/serials, 1800 pamphlets/ephemera, 3400 photographs
COLLECTION ACCESS: card catalog, computerized finding aids (used by staff, patrons)
SOFTWARE/SYSTEM Pro-Cite; NOTIS
ACQUISITION REPORTED TO: OCLC
STAFF (FTE): 3 reference librarians, 1 cataloger
INSTITUTIONAL SUPPORT FOR PROFESSIONAL DEVELOPMENT: tuition/registration reimbursement for courses, workshops, etc.
SPECIAL SERVICES/PROGRAMS: History of Medicine Society Meeting lecture
FACILITIES/EQUIPMENT/PRESERVATION: fire extinguishing system
PATRON USE STATISTICS: 31 in-house patrons, 60 mail reference requests, 150 collections used, 500 reference photocopies
NHPRC LA600-765

William Ransom Hogan Jazz Archive
Howard-Tilton Memorial Library
Tulane University
7001 Freret St.
New Orleans, Louisiana 70118

TEL: (504) 865-5688
FAX: (504) 865-6773

REPORTED BY: Bruce Boyd Raeburn, Ph.D., Curator
TYPE OF INSTITUTION: archives (academic)

HOURS: M-F 8:30-5, Sa 9-1
ACCESS: open to the general public
SERVICES: in-person, mail, phone reference, copies, photographic & audio dup.
RESTRICTIONS: reproduction subject to discretion of curator

PRIMARY COLLECTION FOCUS: New Orleans Jazz with related music and its practitioners
  music--U.S.
  New Orleans--social history
  jazz discography
  music history
  labor unions--musicians

INCLUSIVE DATES: 1880-present
COLLECTION FORMATS: 12 linear feet manuscript collections; 2000/450 books/serials; 55 linear feet pamphlets/ephemera; 251 films/videotapes; 42,000 sheet music/orchestral; 2000 oral histories; 50,000 sound recordings
COLLECTION ACCESS: card catalog, repository guide, registers/inventories, computerized finding aids (used by staff)
SOFTWARE/SYSTEM ASK SAM
ACQUISITION REPORTED TO: OCLC
STAFF (FTE): 1 administrative, 2 volunteer/docents; 2 student
INSTITUTIONAL SUPPORT FOR PROFESSIONAL DEVELOPMENT: reimbursement tuition/registration courses, professional meetings, travel; pay telephone; use of facilities/equipment
SPECIAL SERVICES/PROGRAMS: exhibits, tours, newsletter, lectures/presentations
FACILITIES/EQUIPMENT/PRESERVATION: temperature controls, humidity controls, fire detection controls, fire extinguishing system
PATRON USE STATISTICS: 1243 in-house patrons, 164 telephone patrons, 254 mail reference patrons, 10,802 collections used, 6,753 reference photocopies

NHPRC LA600-764

Archives & Manuscripts/Special Collections Department
Earl K. Long Library
University of New Orleans
New Orleans, Louisiana 70148

TEL: (504) 286-6543
FAX: (504) 286-7277

REPORTED BY: D. Clive Hardy, Archivist and Department Head
TYPE OF INSTITUTION: archives, library (state, academic)

HOURS: M-F 8-4:30, Sa 9-1, closed University holidays
ACCESS: open to the general public
SERVICES: in-person, mail, phone reference, photocopies
RESTRICTIONS: all services restricted by limited staff

PRIMARY COLLECTION FOCUS: materials concerning New Orleans area from late 19th century-present,
 archives Louisiana Supreme Court, 1813-1879
 New Orleans, LA--history
 labor unions
 business history
 preservation organizations
 New Orleans--civic groups
 legal records
 ethnic groups
 church history

INCLUSIVE DATES: 1813-present
VOLUME: 7,500 linear feet
COLLECTION FORMATS: 4498 linear feet manuscript collections; 980 linear feet institution's records; 670 linear feet books/serials; 116 linear feet audiovisual; 35 linear feet oral histories government records; pamphlets/ephemera; photographs; maps
COLLECTION ACCESS: card catalog, register/inventories
ACQUISITION REPORTED TO: NUCMC, OCLC, specialized/regional guide, professional journals
STAFF (FTE): 2 general archival, 1 clerical, 4 student, 2 senior citizen under Fed. Government Program
INSTITUTIONAL SUPPORT FOR PROFESSIONAL DEVELOPMENT: reimbursement for tuition/registration for courses (% depends on funds), professional meetings, travel; pay for mailings, telephone; use of facilities, staff
SPECIAL SERVICES/PROGRAMS: exhibits, tours
FACILITIES/EQUIPMENT/PRESERVATION: temperature controls, fire detection controls, fire extinguishing system
PATRON USE STATISTICS: 519 in-house patrons

NHPRC LA600-775

Ursuline Convent Museum and Archives
2734 Nashville Ave.
New Orleans, Louisiana 70115

TEL: (504) 866-1742

REPORTED BY: Sister Joan Marie Aycock, O.S.U., Archivist
TYPE OF INSTITUTION: archives (religious)

HOURS: by appointment
ACCESS: public access by appointment only
SERVICES: fee for reference

PRIMARY COLLECTION FOCUS: history of the Ursulines in New Orleans
 Ursilines

religious communities
Catholic Church

INCLUSIVE DATES: 1727-present
STAFF (FTE): 1
PATRON USE STATISTICS: user statistics not kept

Xavier University of Louisiana **TEL**: (504) 486-7411
Archives and Special Collections
7325 Palmetto Street
New Orleans LA 70125

REPORTED BY: Lester Sullivan
TYPE OF INSTITUTION: library (academic)

HOURS: M-F 8:30-5
ACCESS: open to the general public
SERVICES: in-person, mail, and phone reference, photocopies

PRIMARY COLLECTION FOCUS: Xavier University of Louisiana
   Xavier University of Louisiana (records)
   African Americans--culture
   Catholic Church
   Southern U.S.
   Gulf of Mexico
   Caribbean

INCLUSIVE DATES: 1760-present
VOLUME: 600 linear feet
COLLECTION FORMATS: manuscript collections, institution's records, books/serials, pamphlets/ephemera, films/videotapes, photographs, maps, oral histories
COLLECTION ACCESS: card catalog, repository guide, registers/inventories, container lists
STAFF (FTE): 2.5 administrative
INSTITUTIONAL SUPPORT FOR PROFESSIONAL DEVELOPMENT: tuition/registration reimbursement for courses, workshops, etc., reimbursement for professional meetings, payment of mailings, payment for telephone use, use of facilities and equipment permitted, use of clerical staff permitted
SPECIAL SERVICES/PROGRAMS: exhibits, tours, newsletter, lectures/presentations
FACILITIES/EQUIPMENT/PRESERVATION: temperature controls, humidity controls, fire detection controls, fire extinguishing system, preservation lab, disaster preparedness plan
PATRON USE STATISTICS: 500 in-house patrons, 600 telephone patrons, 200 mail reference requests (does not include undergraduate students)
NHPRC LA 600-920

New Orleans: St. Mary's Dominican College, closed. Direct correspondence to 7300 St. Charles Ave., 70118: NHPRC LA600-710

New Orleans: Dillard University, Will W. Alexander Library: NHPRC LA600-160

Louisiana College, Norton Memorial Library **TEL**: (318) 487-7201
Louisiana College **FAX**: (318) 487-7191
Pineville, Louisiana 71359

REPORTED BY: Landrum Salley, Director
TYPE OF INSTITUTION: library (academic)

HOURS: M-Th 7:45am-10pm, F 7:45-5, Sa 10-5:30
ACCESS: open to the general public
SERVICES: in-person reference, photocopies

PRIMARY COLLECTION FOCUS: Central Louisiana material and Baptist material
    Louisiana, Central
    Baptist Church
    Louisiana College (records)

COLLECTION FORMATS: institution's records, books/serials, pamphlets/ephemera, photographs, oral histories
COLLECTION ACCESS: card catalog
STAFF (FTE): 1 administrative
PATRON USE STATISTICS: user statistics not kept
NHPRC LA670-480

Iberville Parish Library
24605 J. Gerald Berret Blvd.
P. O. Box 736
Plaquemine, Louisiana 70764

TEL: (504) 687-4439

REPORTED BY: Virginia Borron, Adult Services
TYPE OF INSTITUTION: library (local/county)

HOURS: M 8:30-6, T-Th 8:30-5:30, F 8:30-5, Sa 9-4
ACCESS: open to the general public.
SERVICES: in-person, phone reference, photocopies
PRIMARY COLLECTION FOCUS: Louisiana collection, genealogy
    genealogy
    Louisiana--history

VOLUME: 2,500
COLLECTION FORMATS: 2500 books/serials, 150 photographs, 12 oral histories
COLLECTION ACCESS: card catalog
ACQUISITION REPORTED TO: specialized/regional guide
STAFF (FTE): 2 administrative, 21 clerical
INSTITUTIONAL SUPPORT FOR PROFESSIONAL DEVELOPMENT: payment of dues for professional organization memberships, reimbursement for professional meetings
SPECIAL SERVICES/PROGRAMS: exhibits, tours
FACILITIES/EQUIPMENT/PRESERVATION: temperature controls, fire detection controls

---

Louisiana Tech University, Prescott Memorial Library
300 Everett St.
Louisiana Tech University
Ruston, Louisiana 71272

TEL: (318) 257-2935
FAX: (318) 257-2447

REPORTED BY: Michael A. DiCarlo, Assistant Director of Public Services
TYPE OF INSTITUTION: library (academic)

HOURS: archives M-F 8-5
ACCESS: open to the general public
SERVICES: in-person, mail, phone reference, photocopies (fee for copies)

PRIMARY COLLECTION FOCUS: private & corporate records for N. Louisiana; institution's records

Louisiana, North
Louisiana Tech University (records)
business history

COLLECTION ACCESS: card catalog, repository guide, registers/inventories
ACQUISITION REPORTED TO: OCLC
STAFF (FTE): 1 administrative, 4 student
INSTITUTIONAL SUPPORT FOR PROFESSIONAL DEVELOPMENT: reimbursement for professional meetings, registration & travel; payment for mailings & phone, use of facilities and equipment
SPECIAL SERVICES/PROGRAMS: exhibits, classes
PATRON USE STATISTICS: user statistics not kept

NHPRC LA780-490

Lincoln Parish Library
509 West Alabama
Ruston, Louisiana 71270

TEL: (318) 255-1920

REPORTED BY: Julia K. Avant, Librarian, Marsha K. Clinton, Asst. Librarian
TYPE OF INSTITUTION: library (county/local)

HOURS: M-Sa 9-6
ACCESS: open to general public
SERVICES: in-person, mail, phone reference, photocopies

PRIMARY COLLECTION FOCUS: genealogy and local history
   Lincoln Parish, LA (local history)
   genealogy

COLLECTION FORMATS: 1800 books/serials, 100 photographs, 6 maps, 600 microfilm
COLLECTION ACCESS: card catalog, computerized finding aids (used by staff, patrons)
SOFTWARE/SYSTEM SIRSI software
ACQUISITION REPORTED TO: specialized/regional guide
STAFF (FTE): [not reported]
SPECIAL SERVICES/PROGRAMS: lectures/presentations
FACILITIES/EQUIPMENT/PRESERVATION: temperature controls
PATRON USE STATISTICS: user statistics not kept

St. Joseph Abbey and Seminary College
Pere Rouquette Library
St. Benedict, Louisiana 70457

TEL: (504) 892-1800
FAX: (504) 892-3723

REPORTED BY: Fr. Timothy J. Burnett, O.S.B., Director of Library
TYPE OF INSTITUTION: archives (religious)

HOURS: M-F 8-5
ACCESS: public access by appointment only
SERVICES: in-person reference, photocopies
RESTRICTIONS: no circulation to non-affiliated members of the community

PRIMARY COLLECTION FOCUS: institutional history
   Louisiana--religious life
   Florida Parishes, LA (local history)
   New Orleans (local history)

St. Josephs Abbey and Seminary College (records)

INCLUSIVE DATES: 1889-present
COLLECTION FORMATS: manuscript collections, institution's records, books/serials, pamphlets/ephemera, photographs
COLLECTION ACCESS: not described (archives), card catalog(library)
STAFF (FTE): 1 non-specialist curator,
INSTITUTIONAL SUPPORT FOR PROFESSIONAL DEVELOPMENT: dues for professional organization memberships, payment of dues for professional meeting registration and travel, payment for mailings
FACILITIES/EQUIPMENT/PRESERVATION: temperature controls
PATRON USE STATISTICS: user statistics not kept.

St. Joseph Abbey Archives
St. Joseph Abbey
St. Benedict, Louisiana 70457

TEL: (504) 892-1800

REPORTED BY: Rev. Jonathan DeFrange, O.S.B., Archivist
TYPE OF INSTITUTION: archives (religious)

HOURS: by appointment
ACCESS: public access by appointment only
SERVICES: in-person, mail, phone reference, photocopies

PRIMARY COLLECTION FOCUS: history of St. Joseph Abbey
  Catholic Church--history
  Benedictine Order
  Florida Parishes, LA (local history)
  Germans--Louisiana
  St. Joseph Abbey (records)
  church history

INCLUSIVE DATES: 1889-present
COLLECTION FORMATS: 200 manuscripts collections, 1000 institution's records, 100 books/serials, 100 pamphlets/ephemera, 20 films/videotapes, 2000 photographs, 30 oral histories
COLLECTION ACCESS: container lists
STAFF (FTE): 1 administrative, 1 photo curator
INSTITUTIONAL SUPPORT FOR PROFESSIONAL DEVELOPMENT: payment of dues for professional organization memberships, payment for mailings, payment for telephone use
FACILITIES/EQUIPMENT/PRESERVATION: temperature controls, humidity controls, fire detection controls, fire extinguishing system, preservation lab
PATRON USE STATISTICS: 50 in-house patrons, 3 telephone patrons, 10 mail reference requests, 20 collections used, 10 reference photocopies

---

Centenary College of Louisiana
Magale Library
2911 Centenary Blvd.
Shreveport LA 71104

TEL: (318) 869-5462

REPORTED BY: Ella C. Edward
TYPE OF INSTITUTION: library (academic)

HOURS: no set hours
ACCESS: open to the general public
SERVICES: in-person, mail reference, phone reference, photocopies

PRIMARY COLLECTION FOCUS: Centenary College, Louisiana Methodist Conference
    Centenary College
    Louisiana Methodist Conference
    London, Jack
    Corrington, William

INCLUSIVE DATES: 1825-present
VOLUME: 565 linear feet
COLLECTION FORMATS: manuscript collections, institution's records, books/serials, pamphlets/ephemera, films/videotapes, photographs, maps, oral histories
COLLECTION ACCESS: card catalog, computerized finding aids, registers/inventories
SOFTWARE/SYSTEM: MicroMARC
STAFF (FTE): 1 part time administrative
INSTITUTIONAL SUPPORT FOR PROFESSIONAL DEVELOPMENT: payment for mailings, payment for telephone use, use of facilities and equipment permitted, payment for telephone use, use of clerical staff permitted
SPECIAL SERVICES/PROGRAMS: exhibits
FACILITIES/EQUIPMENT/PRESERVATION: temperature controls, fire extinguishing system, humidity controls, fire detection controls
PATRON USE STATISTICS: information not available

NHPRC LA885-120

Louisiana State University in Shreveport
1 University Place
Shreveport, Louisiana 71115

TEL: (318) 797-5226
FAX: (318) 797-5156

REPORTED BY: Stephen J. Hussman, Archivist
TYPE OF INSTITUTION: archives, library (academic)

HOURS: M-F 8-4:30, hours subject to change
ACCESS: open to the general public
SERVICES: in-person, mail, phone reference, photocopies, other reproduction services

PRIMARY COLLECTION FOCUS: history of Shreveport, Northwest Louisiana & Red River Region
    Louisiana, Northwest
    Louisiana--social/economic history
    plantation life and culture
    Civil War
    petroleum industry
    Red River, LA

architecture
women's history
transportation
agriculture

INCLUSIVE DATES: 1832-Present
VOLUME: 5,000 linear feet
COLLECTION FORMATS: 5,000 linear feet manuscript collections, 93 linear feet institution's records, 293 feet books/serials, 9700 rolls films, 600 videotapes, 10,000 photographs, 90 linear feet maps, 112 oral histories, 400 linear feet architectural records
COLLECTION ACCESS: card catalog, repository guide, registers/inventories, container lists, computerized finding aids (for inventory only--used by staff)
SOFTWARE/SYSTEM Volkswriter
ACQUISITION REPORTED TO: specialized/regional guide, professional journal(s)
STAFF (FTE): 2 general archival, 2 volunteer/docent, 2 student, 1 visiting scholar/archivist
INSTITUTIONAL SUPPORT FOR PROFESSIONAL DEVELOPMENT: tuition for continued education only 50%, use of facilities and equipment permitted
SPECIAL SERVICES/PROGRAMS: lectures/presentations
FACILITIES/EQUIPMENT/PRESERVATION: disaster preparedness plan
PATRON USE STATISTICS: 567 in-house patrons, 71 telephone patrons, 24 mail reference requests, 211 collections used, 3 microfilm/fiche copies

NHPRC LA885-480

Pioneer Heritage Center
Campus of LSU-SHREVEPORT
One University Place
Shreveport, Louisiana 71115

TEL: (318) 797-5332
FAX: (318) 797-5180

REPORTED BY: [not listed]

ALL ARCHIVAL MATERIALS MOVED TO LSU-SHREVEPORT ARCHIVES MUSEUM

Shreveport: R. W. Norton Art Gallery, Reference Library: NHPRC LA885-690

Historical Research Center
205 Audubon Ave.
Thibodaux, Louisiana 70301

TEL: (504) 446-2383

REPORTED BY: Msgr. Roland J. Bourdreaux, Archivist
TYPE OF INSTITUTION: archives (religious)

HOURS: M, T, Th 8-4
ACCESS: open to general public
SERVICES: in-person, mail, phone reference; fee for reference

PRIMARY COLLECTION FOCUS: sacramental records
    Catholic Church
    genealogy

INCLUSIVE DATES: 1817-1910
COLLECTION ACCESS: repository guide, register/inventories, computerized finding aids (used by staff)
SOFTWARE/SYSTEM word processing, check requisitions, filing, data base
STAFF (FTE): 1 administrative, 1 general archival, 8 volunteer/docent, 2 clerical
FACILITIES/EQUIPMENT/PRESERVATION: temperature controls, humidity controls, fire detection controls, fire extinguishing system
PATRON USE STATISTICS: 240 in-house patrons, 130 telephone patrons, 350 mail reference patrons

---

Allen J. Ellender Archives
Nicholls State University
Allen J. Ellender Library
P. O. Box 2028
Thibodaux, Louisiana 70310

TEL: (504) 448-4621
FAX: (504) 448-4925

REPORTED BY: Carol A. Mathias, Head Archives and Special Collections
TYPE OF INSTITUTION: library (academic)

HOURS: M, W-F 8-4:30, T 8am-9pm, first Saturday of month 12-4
ACCESS: open to the general public
SERVICES: in-person, mail, phone reference, photocopies

PRIMARY COLLECTION FOCUS: history and culture of South Central Louisiana.
    Louisiana, South Central
    Ellender, Allen J., Senate papers
    congressional papers
    Nicholls State University (records)
    genealogy
    plantation life and culture
    business history

INCLUSIVE DATES: 1651-present
VOLUME: 4500 linear feet
COLLECTION FORMATS: 1524 linear feet manuscript collections, 850 linear feet institution's records, 8500 books/serials, 1850 films/videotapes
COLLECTION ACCESS: card catalog, register/inventories, computerized finding aids (used by staff)
SOFTWARE/SYSTEM: MicroMARC
STAFF (FTE): 2 administrative
INSTITUTIONAL SUPPORT FOR PROFESSIONAL DEVELOPMENT: reimbursement for professional meetings(s) registration and travel (50%)

SPECIAL SERVICES/PROGRAMS: exhibits, tours, lectures/presentations
FACILITIES/EQUIPMENT/PRESERVATION: temperature controls
PATRON USE STATISTICS: 1120 in-house patrons, 88 telephone patrons, 12 mail reference requests

NHPRC LA920-560

NEW MEXICO

Ghost Ranch
Route 84
Abiquiu, New Mexico 87510

TEL: (505) 685-4333
FAX: (505) 685-4519

REPORTED BY: Lidie Miller, Librarian
TYPE OF INSTITUTION: library (religious)

HOURS: 24 hrs/day everyday
ACCESS: not open to general public, open only to guests of ranch
SERVICES: in-person, mail, and phone reference

PRIMARY COLLECTION FOCUS: religion, Southwest history
    religion
    Southwestern U.S.--history
    archaeology

VOLUME: ca. 20,000 items
COLLECTION FORMATS: institution's records, pamphlets/ephemera, maps
COLLECTION ACCESS: card catalog, container lists
STAFF (FTE): 0.5 professional, volunteers and clerical
INSTITUTIONAL SUPPORT FOR PROFESSIONAL DEVELOPMENT: travel, use of facilities, clerical staff
FACILITIES/EQUIPMENT/PRESERVATION: temperature controls, fire detection controls
PATRON USE STATISTICS: user statistics not kept

Space Center
Top of New Mexico Highway 2001
P.O. Box 533
Alamogordo, New Mexico 88311-0533

TEL: (505) 437-2840
FAX: (505) 437-7722

REPORTED BY: George M. House, Curator
TYPE OF INSTITUTION: museum (state)

HOURS: 9-6 daily (Summer), 9-5 daily (Winter)
ACCESS: open to the general public, and by appointment
SERVICES: in-person, mail, phone, photocopies, and archival photographs

PRIMARY COLLECTION FOCUS: aerospace industries
    space sciences
    aerospace industries
    science and technology

INCLUSIVE DATES: early 20th Century-present
COLLECTION FORMATS: 300 manuscript collections, 3500 books/serials, 264 films/videotapes, 3000 photographs, 21 oral histories, biographies, and subject vertical files
COLLECTION ACCESS: card catalog, registers/inventories, computerized finding aids (used by staff)
SOFTWARE/SYSTEM: MacCards, Microsoft Works Database, Hypercard
STAFF (FTE): 10 administrative, 2 general archivist, 5 preservation, 2 outreach, 1 audio/visual, 10 other professional, 44 volunteer
INSTITUTIONAL SUPPORT FOR PROFESSIONAL DEVELOPMENT: tuition/registration reimbursement, professional dues, meeting registration and travel, in-house workshops, mailings, telephone, use of facilities
SPECIAL SERVICES/PROGRAMS: exhibits, tours, classes, newsletter, fund raising/endowment, lectures/presentations, outreach
FACILITIES/EQUIPMENT/PRESERVATION: temperature controls, humidity controls, fire detection control, fire extinguishing system, disaster preparedness plan

PATRON USE STATISTICS: 60 in-house patrons, 800 telephone, 60 mail reference requests, 10,000 reference photocopies

---

Albuquerque Museum of Art, History, and Science
2000 Mountain Rd. NW
P.O. Box 1293
Albuquerque, New Mexico 87103

TEL: (505) 243-7255
FAX: (505) 764-6546

REPORTED BY: Byron A. Johnson, Curator of History
TYPE OF INSTITUTION: museum (city)

HOURS: Tu-Su 9-5, closed holidays
ACCESS: public access by appointment only
SERVICES: in-person, mail, phone, reproduce photographs
RESTRICTIONS: all duplication requests evaluated for appropriateness

PRIMARY COLLECTION FOCUS: historical/documentary local history photographs
    photography, history of
    architecture
    Albuquerque, NM (local history)
    business history
    portraiture
    Native Americans
    New Mexico

INCLUSIVE DATES: 1868-ca. 1970
VOLUME: ca. 65,000 still photographs
COLLECTION FORMATS: ca. 65,000 still photographs
COLLECTION ACCESS: computerized finding aids (used by staff, patrons)
SOFTWARE/SYSTEM: The Photoarchivist, database with analog videodisc
STAFF (FTE): 1 administrative, 2 volunteer
INSTITUTIONAL SUPPORT FOR PROFESSIONAL DEVELOPMENT: tuition/registration reimbursement, membership dues, reimbursement for meeting registration and travel
SPECIAL SERVICES/PROGRAMS: exhibits, lectures
FACILITIES/EQUIPMENT/PRESERVATION: temperature controls, fire detection controls, fire extinguishing system
PATRON USE STATISTICS: 150 in-house patrons, 250 telephone, 10 collections used

NHPRC NM114-35

Albuquerque Public Library, Special Collections
423 Central Ave. NE
Albuquerque, New Mexico 87102

TEL: (505) 848-1376
FAX: (505) 764-1574

REPORTED BY: [not listed]
TYPE OF INSTITUTION: library (city)

HOURS: Tu, Th 12:30-8; W, F, Sa 9-5:30
ACCESS: open to the general public
SERVICES: in-person, phone reference, photocopies
RESTRICTIONS: nothing copied that is copyrighted

PRIMARY COLLECTION FOCUS: city government
    Albuquerque--library history

Albuquerque, NM--city archives
civic organizations--history

INCLUSIVE DATES: 1883-1984
COLLECTION FORMATS: manuscript collections, institution's records, pamphlets/ephemera, videotapes, government records, photographs, maps
COLLECTION ACCESS: card catalog
STAFF (FTE): 1 administrative
SPECIAL SERVICES/PROGRAMS: exhibits, tours, lectures
PATRON USE STATISTICS: user statistics not kept

Center for Southwest Research
General Library, University of New Mexico
Albuquerque, New Mexico 87131

TEL: (505) 277-6451
FAX: (505) 277-6019

REPORTED BY: Kathlene Ferris, Curator of Manuscripts
TYPE OF INSTITUTION: library (academic)

HOURS: M-F 8-4:30
ACCESS: open to the general public
SERVICES: in-person, mail, and phone reference, photocopies, photograph reproduction
RESTRICTIONS: duplication requests evaluated for appropriateness

PRIMARY COLLECTION FOCUS: New Mexico, Southwest and Latin American history & culture
- Southwestern U.S.--history
- social life and customs
- politics and government--New Mexico
- Native Americans
- ethnic communities
- African Americans
- New Mexico--local history
- business history
- borderlands
- Latin America

INCLUSIVE DATES: 1565-1992
COLLECTION FORMATS: manuscript collections, institution's records, books/serials, pamphlets, films/videotapes, photographs, maps, oral histories
COLLECTION ACCESS: card catalog, repository guide, inventories, computerized finding aids (used by staff, patrons)
SOFTWARE/SYSTEM: dBase III plus, Innopac, Prism
ACQUISITION REPORTED TO: OCLC
STAFF (FTE): 1 administrative, 6 general archival, 0 .5 preservation 1 photo archivist, 1 outreach, 1 oral historian, 2 clerical, 20 students, 3 interns
INSTITUTIONAL SUPPORT FOR PROFESSIONAL DEVELOPMENT: tuition/registration reimbursement, professional meeting registration & travel, payment for mailings, use of facilities and equipment
SPECIAL SERVICES/PROGRAMS: exhibits, tours, fundraising/endowment, lectures/presentations
FACILITIES/EQUIPMENT/PRESERVATION: preservation lab
PATRON USE STATISTICS: 5296 in-house patrons, 224 collections used
NHPRC NM114-900 [note name change]

Chaco Culture National Historical Park
c/o Department of Anthropology, University of New Mexico
Albuquerque, New Mexico 87131

TEL: (505) 766-3780
FAX: (505) 277-0874

REPORTED BY: Philip Lopiccolo, Museum Technician
TYPE OF INSTITUTION: National Park Service (federal)

HOURS: M-F 8-4:30
ACCESS: public access by appointment only
SERVICES: in-person reference, mail reference
RESTRICTIONS: some restrictions on maps, photos, copyright

PRIMARY COLLECTION FOCUS: Chaco Canyon, Southwestern archaeology
    Chacoan archaeology
    archaeology--field notes
    archaeology--site reports
    archaeology--photographs
    archaeology--maps
    New Mexico--archaeology
    parks and monuments, federal

INCLUSIVE DATES: 1930s-1992
COLLECTION FORMATS: 2000 manuscript collections, 60 linear feet government records, 20,000 photographs, 2000 maps
COLLECTION ACCESS: card catalog, repository guide
ACQUISITION REPORTED TO: National Park Service
STAFF (FTE): 1 archaeological curator, 1 volunteer/docent, 2 interns
INSTITUTIONAL SUPPORT FOR PROFESSIONAL DEVELOPMENT: tuition/registration reimbursed, professional meeting registration & travel reimbursed, mailings, telephone use
FACILITIES/EQUIPMENT/PRESERVATION: fire detection controls
PATRON USE STATISTICS: 100 in-house patrons, 100 collections used

---

Indian Pueblo Cultural Center, Pueblo Archives and Library   **TEL**: (505) 843-7270
2401 12th St.
Albuquerque, New Mexico 87107

REPORTED BY: Fred Gillette Sturm, Associate Director
TYPE OF INSTITUTION: Cultural Center (All Indian Pueblo Council)

HOURS: M 8-12 noon, Tu 9-12 & 1-4, W 8-4, F 10-2
ACCESS: open to the general public
SERVICES: in-person, mail, phone, photocopies, and microfilm

PRIMARY COLLECTION FOCUS: Pueblo Indian history and culture
    Pueblo Indians
    archaeology
    anthropology
    sociology
    economic history
    politics
    art history
    ethnohistory
    Native Americans

COLLECTION FORMATS: 150 manuscript collections, 1000 books/serials, 500 pamphlets/ephemera, 200 maps, 50 films/videotapes, 500 government records, 1000 photographs, 500 oral histories
COLLECTION ACCESS: card catalog, registers/inventories, computerized finding aids (used by staff, patrons)
STAFF (FTE): 2 general archival, 6 volunteer, 2 clerical
INSTITUTIONAL SUPPORT FOR PROFESSIONAL DEVELOPMENT: payment for mailings, telephone use, use of facilities, use of clerical staff
SPECIAL SERVICES/PROGRAMS: exhibits, classes, fund raising/endowments, lectures/presentations

FACILITIES/EQUIPMENT/PRESERVATION: fire detection controls, fire extinguishing system
PATRON USE STATISTICS: user statistics not kept

Maxwell Museum of Anthropology
University of New Mexico
Albuquerque, New Mexico 87131

TEL: (505) 277-4405
FAX: (505) 277-0874

REPORTED BY: Katherine Pomonis, Administrative Coordinator
TYPE OF INSTITUTION: archives, museum (academic)

HOURS: 10 hours/week
ACCESS: open to the general public
SERVICES: in person reference, photocopies

PRIMARY COLLECTION FOCUS: Southwestern U.S., international anthropology
  Southwestern U.S.
  ethnology--early 20th century
  ethnography
  anthropology
  archaeology
  Native Americans

COLLECTION FORMATS: photographs (ca. 200.000), films (16mm) and videotapes, field notes
COLLECTION ACCESS: card catalog, registers/inventories, computerized finding aids (used by staff)
SOFTWARE/SYSTEM: Argus/Questor Systems Ltd.
STAFF (FTE): administrative (number not specified), volunteer/docent (number not specified)
INSTITUTIONAL SUPPORT FOR PROFESSIONAL DEVELOPMENT: reimbursement for tuition/registration,
  professional meetings & travel, payment for mailings, telephone use
SPECIAL SERVICES/PROGRAMS: exhibits
FACILITIES/EQUIPMENT/PRESERVATION: temperature controls, humidity controls

NHPRC NM114-880

Medical Center Library
University of New Mexico
Albuquerque, New Mexico 87131-5686

TEL: (505) 277-0656
FAX: (505) 277-5350

REPORTED BY: Janet H. Johnson, Archives Manager
TYPE OF INSTITUTION: library (state university, academic, medical school)

HOURS: M-F 8-12 and by appointment
ACCESS: open to the general public
SERVICES: in-person, mail, phone, photocopies, and photographs

PRIMARY COLLECTION FOCUS: history of public health and medicine in the Southwest
  physicians
  hospitals
  health facilities
  tuberculosis sanatoria
  medicine, history of
  public health
  folk medicine

INCLUSIVE DATES: 1880-present
VOLUME: 386 linear feet

COLLECTION FORMATS: 38 linear feet manuscript collections, 324 linear feet records, 48 books/serials, 12.6 feet pamphlets, 20 films/videotapes, 2500 photographs, 160 oral histories
COLLECTION ACCESS: card catalog, container lists, computerized finding aids (used by staff, patrons)
SOFTWARE/SYSTEM: Innopac
STAFF (FTE): 1 general archival
INSTITUTIONAL SUPPORT FOR PROFESSIONAL DEVELOPMENT: reimbursement for meeting registration and travel
SPECIAL SERVICES/PROGRAMS: exhibits
FACILITIES/EQUIPMENT/PRESERVATION: temperature controls, humidity controls, fire detection controls
PATRON USE STATISTICS: user statistics not kept

Menaul Historical Library of the Southwest   **TEL**: (505) 345-7727
301 Menaul Blvd. NE
Albuquerque, New Mexico 87107

REPORTED BY: Barbara Evans, Acting Director
TYPE OF INSTITUTION: archives, library, museum (academic, religious)

HOURS: M-F 8:30-5
ACCESS: open to the general public
SERVICES: in-person, mail, and phone reference; photocopies; photo archives; fee for reference

PRIMARY COLLECTION FOCUS: Presbyterian missions in the Southwest
  Presbyterian Church--history
  religion
  missionaries
  hospitals
  education
  Southwestern U.S.--missionaries

INCLUSIVE DATES: 1881-present
COLLECTION FORMATS: 5 cubic feet records, 133 feet books/serials, 90 feet pamphlets, 51 films/videotapes, 442 folders photographs, 204 oral histories, 59 microfilms
COLLECTION ACCESS: card catalog, registers/inventories, container lists
STAFF (FTE): 1 administrative, 3 volunteer
INSTITUTIONAL SUPPORT FOR PROFESSIONAL DEVELOPMENT: tuition/registration reimbursement, professional dues, meeting registration and travel, use of facilities and equipment
SPECIAL SERVICES/PROGRAMS: exhibits, tours, newsletter, lectures/presentations
FACILITIES/EQUIPMENT/PRESERVATION: temperature controls, humidity controls, fire detection controls, fire extinguishing system
PATRON USE STATISTICS: user statistics not kept

NHPRC NM114-525

Albuquerque: Archdiocese of Santa Fe, Archives: NHPRC NM114-50

Albuquerque: Telephone Pioneers of America, Zia Council, Telephone Pioneer Museum: NHPRC NM114-760

Albuquerque: University of Albuquerque, Center for Learning and Information Resources. No longer exists. Records transferred to the University of New Mexico, Center for Southwest Research.

Albuquerque: University of New Mexico, Dept. of Biology, Museum of Southwestern Biology/Herbarium and Museum of Botany: NHPRC NM114-825

Albuquerque: University of New Mexico, Jonson Gallery: NHPRC NM114-870

Artesia Historical Museum and Art Center
505 West Richardson Ave.
Artesia, New Mexico 88210

TEL: (505) 748-2390

REPORTED BY: Nancy Klawans, Director
TYPE OF INSTITUTION: museum (city)

HOURS: Tu-Sa 10-12 & 1-5, closed holidays
ACCESS: open to the general public
SERVICES: in-person, mail reference, photocopies
RESTRICTIONS: research access by appointment

PRIMARY COLLECTION FOCUS: local and Southeastern New Mexico history
    Artesia, NM (local history)

INCLUSIVE DATES: 1870s-1960s
COLLECTION FORMATS: manuscript collections, books/serials, films/videos, government records,
    photographs, oral histories
COLLECTION ACCESS: container lists, registers/inventories, computerized finding aids (used by staff)
SOFTWARE/SYSTEM: Minaret
ACQUISITION REPORTED TO: specialized/regional guide
STAFF (FTE): 1 administrative, 1 general archival, 1 registrar
INSTITUTIONAL SUPPORT FOR PROFESSIONAL DEVELOPMENT: tuition reimbursement, professional
    dues, meeting reimbursement, payment for mailings, telephone use, use of facilities
SPECIAL SERVICES/PROGRAMS: exhibits, tours by appointment, art shows
FACILITIES/EQUIPMENT/PRESERVATION: temperature controls, humidity controls, fire detection controls,
    fire extinguishing system
PATRON USE STATISTICS: 1500 in-house patrons, 25-50 mail reference requests, all collections used, 300
    reference photocopies

Sandoval County Historical Society
Edmond Road
P.O. Box 692
Bernalillo, New Mexico 87004

TEL: (505) 867-5671

REPORTED BY: Martha Liebert, Archivist
TYPE OF INSTITUTION: archives, historical society, museum (county/local)

HOURS: on request
ACCESS: public access by appointment only
SERVICES: [not reported]

PRIMARY COLLECTION FOCUS: local history - Sandoval County, N.M.
    Sandoval County, NM (local history)
    genealogy
    Pueblo Indians

INCLUSIVE DATES: 1540-1990
VOLUME: 1500+ items
COLLECTION FORMATS: 50 manuscript collections, 350 books/serials, 50 pamphlets/ephemera, 2
    films/videotapes, 1000 photographs, 75 maps, 10 oral histories
COLLECTION ACCESS: card catalog

STAFF (FTE): 6 volunteers
SPECIAL SERVICES/PROGRAMS: exhibits, tours, newsletter, fund raising/endowment, lectures/presentations
PATRON USE STATISTICS: user statistics not kept

San Juan County Archaeological Research Center and Library **TEL**: (505) 632-2013
6131 U.S. Highway 64 **FAX**: (505) 632-2013
P.O. Box 125
Bloomfield, New Mexico 87413

REPORTED BY: Penny Whitten, Librarian
TYPE OF INSTITUTION: library, museum (private non-profit with some county support)

HOURS: 9-5 daily
ACCESS: open to the general public
SERVICES: in-person, mail, phone, and photocopies (charge for photocopies)

PRIMARY COLLECTION FOCUS: archaeology, anthropology and local history
  archaeology
  anthropology
  Farmington, NM (local history)
  Navajo Indians--religion and mythology
  San Juan County, NM (local history)
  botany--native plants--Southwestern US

INCLUSIVE DATES: late 1800s-present
COLLECTION FORMATS: manuscript collections, 55 linear feet records, 5000 books/serials, pamphlets/ephemera, films/videotapes, photographs, maps, oral histories, technical reports
COLLECTION ACCESS: card catalog, registers/inventories
STAFF (FTE): 1 librarian, volunteers
INSTITUTIONAL SUPPORT FOR PROFESSIONAL DEVELOPMENT: partial reimbursement for tuition/registration, professional memberships, meeting registration and travel, use of facilities, clerical staff
SPECIAL SERVICES/PROGRAMS: newsletter
PATRON USE STATISTICS: user statistics not kept

Carlsbad Public Library **TEL**: (505) 885-6776
101 S. Halagueno
Carlsbad, New Mexico 88220

REPORTED BY: Mary E. Elms, Director
TYPE OF INSTITUTION: library (municipal)

HOURS: M-Th 10-8, F & Sa 10-6, Su 2-6
ACCESS: open to the general public
SERVICES: in-person reference, phone reference, photocopies

PRIMARY COLLECTION FOCUS: New Mexico, Southwest, Waste Isolation Pilot Project (WIPP)
  Carlsbad, NM (local history)
  Carlsbad Caverns, NM
  Waste Isolation Pilot Project (WIPP)
  nuclear waste--depositories

COLLECTION FORMATS: manuscript collections, books/serials, pamphlets/ephemera, government records
COLLECTION ACCESS: card catalog, repository guide

STAFF (FTE): 2 administrative, reference librarian, 6 clerical, 3 students
INSTITUTIONAL SUPPORT FOR PROFESSIONAL DEVELOPMENT: tuition/registration reimbursement,
    meeting registration and/or travel reimbursement
PATRON USE STATISTICS: user statistics not kept

Carlsbad: United Methodist Church, New Mexico Annual Conference Archives: NHPRC NM200-800

Philmont Museum/Seton Memorial Library   **TEL**: (505) 376-2281
Philmont Scout Ranch
Cimarron, New Mexico 87714

REPORTED BY: Annette Carlisle, Librarian
TYPE OF INSTITUTION: library, museum (private: Boy Scouts of America)

HOURS: M-F 8-12, 1-5
ACCESS: open to the general public
SERVICES: in-person, mail, and phone reference; photocopies

PRIMARY COLLECTION FOCUS: Northeastern NM, Philmont Ranch, Ernest Thompson Seton
    New Mexico, Northeastern
    Southwestern U.S.--history
    Seton, Ernest Thompson
    Philmont Ranch and Philmont Scout Ranch

COLLECTION FORMATS: 15 linear feet institution's records, 25,000 photos, 200 maps, 5000
    books/serials, 75 film/video
COLLECTION ACCESS: card catalog, computerized finding aids (used by staff)
SOFTWARE/SYSTEM: Paradox
STAFF (FTE): 1 administrative, 1 general archival
INSTITUTIONAL SUPPORT FOR PROFESSIONAL DEVELOPMENT: reimbursement for course
        tuition/registration and professional meetings, payment for telephone use, use of facilities/equipment
SPECIAL SERVICES/PROGRAMS: exhibits, tours, lectures/presentations
FACILITIES/EQUIPMENT/PRESERVATION: fire extinguishing system, fire detection controls
PATRON USE STATISTICS: 200 in-house patrons, 40 mail reference requests, 100 reference photocopies
NHPRC NM266-720

Sacramento Mountains Historical Society, Inc.   **TEL**: (505) 682-2932
U.S. Highway 82
P.O. Box 435
Cloudcroft, New Mexico 88317

REPORTED BY: Marie Wuersching, Museum Curator
TYPE OF INSTITUTION: archives, historical society, library, museum (county/local)

HOURS: [not reported]
ACCESS: open to the general public
SERVICES: in-person, mail, photocopies, and a fee for reference

PRIMARY COLLECTION FOCUS: local history - Otero County, N.M.
    Otero County, NM (local history)
    Sacramento Mountains, NM

INCLUSIVE DATES: 1880s-present

COLLECTION FORMATS: manuscript collections, records, books/serials, pamphlets/ephemera, microfilms, films/videotapes, government records, photographs, maps, oral histories
COLLECTION ACCESS: card catalog
STAFF (FTE): administrative, general archival, map curator, photo curator, volunteers, clerical
SPECIAL SERVICES/PROGRAMS: exhibits, tours, newsletter, fund raising/endowment, lectures/presentations
FACILITIES/EQUIPMENT/PRESERVATION: temperature controls

Clovis: High Plains Historical Foundation, Inc.: NHPRC NM3-4-320

Columbus Historical Society **TEL**: [not reported]
Highway 11
Box 562
Columbus, New Mexico 88029

REPORTED BY: Curator
TYPE OF INSTITUTION: historical society (county/local)

HOURS: M-F 10-4
ACCESS: open to the general public
SERVICES: [not reported]

PRIMARY COLLECTION FOCUS: local history
  Columbus, NM (local history)

COLLECTION FORMATS: historical artifacts and data
STAFF (FTE): volunteers
SPECIAL SERVICES/PROGRAMS: newsletter

Deming Luna Mimbres Museum **TEL**: (505) 546-2382
301 S. Silver
Deming, New Mexico 88030

REPORTED BY: Dolly Shannon, Acting Archivist
TYPE OF INSTITUTION: historical society (county/local)

HOURS: museum: M-S 9-4, archives by appointment
ACCESS: open to the general public
SERVICES: in-person reference, mail reference, photocopies, photo reproductions

PRIMARY COLLECTION FOCUS: New Mexico, Southwestern New Mexico
  personal papers
  military records
  Bataan-Corregidor
  Villa Raid
  Camp Cody
  Native Americans
  New Mexico--Southwestern
  Mimbres Indians

INCLUSIVE DATES: Pre-Columbian-present
COLLECTION FORMATS: 420 manuscript collections, 120 books/serials, 300 pamphlets/ephemera, 4 films, government records, photographs, posters, 25 maps, 20 oral histories, scrap books
COLLECTION ACCESS: card catalog

STAFF (FTE): 69 volunteers
INSTITUTIONAL SUPPORT FOR PROFESSIONAL DEVELOPMENT: tuition/registration reimbursed, professional meetings reimbursed, payment for mailings
PATRON USE STATISTICS: user statistics not kept

Farmington Museum
302 N. Orchard
Farmington, New Mexico 87401

TEL: (505) 599-1174 or 599-1179
FAX: (505) 599-1185

REPORTED BY: Julie Platt, Curator
TYPE OF INSTITUTION: museum (city)

HOURS: Tu-F 12-5, Sa 10-5, Su-M closed
ACCESS: open to the general public
SERVICES: in-person, mail, phone, photocopies, and photographs
RESTRICTIONS: photo policy

PRIMARY COLLECTION FOCUS: local history, natural history, Native Americans
  Native Americans
  trading posts
  Farmington, NM (local history)
  natural history
  geology
  natural gas industry
  petroleum industry

INCLUSIVE DATES: 1876-
VOLUME: over 2000
COLLECTION FORMATS: 100 manuscript collections, 200 volumes, 100 pamphlets/ephemera, 12 films, 100 government records, 1959 photographs, 163 maps, 40 oral histories
COLLECTION ACCESS: card catalog
SOFTWARE/SYSTEM: R:Base by Microrim (used by staff)
ACQUISITION REPORTED TO: specialized/regional guide
STAFF (FTE): 1 administrative, 2 museum specialists, 25 volunteer, 3 clerical, 20 board members
INSTITUTIONAL SUPPORT FOR PROFESSIONAL DEVELOPMENT: tuition/registration, membership dues, meeting registration/travel, mailings, use of facilities, telephone, clerical staff
SPECIAL SERVICES/PROGRAMS: exhibits, tours, newsletter, fund raising/endowment, lectures/presentations, children's program
FACILITIES/EQUIPMENT/PRESERVATION: temperature control, fire detection controls, fire extinguishing system
PATRON USE STATISTICS: 18000 in-house patrons, 500 telephone, 100+ mail reference requests, 200 collections used, 200 reference photocopies

---

Southwest Oral History Institute
3151 West Main
P.O. Box 3411
Farmington, New Mexico 87499

TEL: (505) 325-8219

REPORTED BY: Diana Ohlson, Director
TYPE OF INSTITUTION: oral history (county/local)

HOURS: 3-7pm Mon.-Fri.
ACCESS: not open to the general public
SERVICES: fee for reference

PRIMARY COLLECTION FOCUS: oral history
    Southwestern U.S.--history
    biography

INCLUSIVE DATES: 1981-present
VOLUME: 60 tapes
COLLECTION FORMATS: oral histories
COLLECTION ACCESS: holdings not described
STAFF (FTE): 1 administrative

Farmington: San Juan County Museum Association, San Juan Co. Archaeological Research Center and Library at Salmon Ruin: NHPRC NM398-720

Folsom Museum
Main Street
Folsom, New Mexico 88419

TEL: (505) 278-2122, Fall/Winter 278-3616

REPORTED BY: [not listed]
TYPE OF INSTITUTION: museum (county/local)

HOURS: Sa & Su 10-5; May - Sept. 10-5 every day
ACCESS: open to the general public
SERVICES: in-person, mail, photocopies, books, and a fee for reference

PRIMARY COLLECTION FOCUS: local history
    anthropology
    Folsom, NM (local history)

INCLUSIVE DATES: 1888-1988
COLLECTION FORMATS: manuscript collections, books, pamphlets, photographs, maps
COLLECTION ACCESS: card catalog, registers/inventories
STAFF (FTE): 3 volunteers
FACILITIES/EQUIPMENT/PRESERVATION: fire extinguishing system
PATRON USE STATISTICS: user statistics not kept

Thomas Branigan Memorial Library
200 E. Picacho Ave.
Las Cruces, New Mexico 88005

TEL: (505) 526-1045

REPORTED BY: Gene D. Atkins, Head, Technical Services
TYPE OF INSTITUTION: library (county/local, city)

HOURS: M-Th 10-9, F-Sa 10-6, Su 1-5 (winter)
ACCESS: open to the general public
SERVICES: in-person, mail, phone, photocopies, and a fee for reference

PRIMARY COLLECTION FOCUS: New Mexico history, geology, archaeology
    New Mexico--history
    geology
    archaeology
    genealogy
    Las Cruces, NM (local history)
    New Mexico--statutes

INCLUSIVE DATES: 1592-present
COLLECTION FORMATS: institution's records, 6000+ books/serials, 30 file drawers pamphlets/ephemera, 200 films/videotapes, 500 government records, 300 photographs, 100 maps, oral histories
COLLECTION ACCESS: card catalog, container lists
ACQUISITION REPORTED TO: OCLC
STAFF (FTE): 0.5 administrative, 1 volunteer
INSTITUTIONAL SUPPORT FOR PROFESSIONAL DEVELOPMENT: meeting registration and travel, use of facilities
SPECIAL SERVICES/PROGRAMS: tours, fund raising/endowment
FACILITIES/EQUIPMENT/PRESERVATION: fire detection controls, fire extinguishing system
PATRON USE STATISTICS: user statistics not kept

Las Cruces: New Mexico State University, Library, Rio Grande Historical Collections/Hobson-Huntsinger Univ. Archives: NHPRC NM494-570

Carnegie Public Library
500 National Ave.
Las Vegas, New Mexico 87701

TEL: (505) 454-1401 ex. 272

REPORTED BY: Ann Kaiser, Library Director
TYPE OF INSTITUTION: library (county/local)

HOURS: T, Th, Sa 10-5:30; W, F 10-6, Su 2-5:30
ACCESS: open to the general public
SERVICES: in-person reference, phone reference, photocopies

PRIMARY COLLECTION FOCUS: Southwest and local history
    Las Vegas, NM (local history)

COLLECTION FORMATS: 100 books/serials, 50 pamphlets/ephemera, 130 oral histories
COLLECTION ACCESS: card catalog
ACQUISITION REPORTED TO: OCLC
STAFF (FTE): 2 administrative, 1 volunteer, 5 clerical
INSTITUTIONAL SUPPORT FOR PROFESSIONAL DEVELOPMENT: use of facilities and equipment, use of clerical staff
PATRON USE STATISTICS: 500 in-house patrons, 100 telephone, 1,000 reference photocopies

---

New Mexico Highlands University
National Avenue
Donnelly Library, New Mexico Highlands University
Las Vegas, New Mexico 87701

TEL: (505) 454-3332
FAX: (505) 454-0026

REPORTED BY: Irisha Corral and Laura Baser
TYPE OF INSTITUTION: library (academic)

HOURS: M-Th 7:30am-10pm, F 7:30am-5pm, Sa 1-5pm, Su 2-10pm
ACCESS: open to the general public
SERVICES: in-person, mail, phone, photocopies, fee according to level of service

PRIMARY COLLECTION FOCUS: Southwest history
    Southwestern U.S.--history
    Fort Union, NM (local history)
    New Mexico--history

education
Spanish government--documents
Mexican government--documents

INCLUSIVE DATES: 1900s-present
VOLUME: ca. 700
COLLECTION FORMATS: 166,391 books, 77,258 serials, 76,406 government records, 2000 photographs, 9,240 maps, microfiche
COLLECTION ACCESS: card catalog, computerized finding aids (used by staff, patrons)
SOFTWARE/SYSTEM: OPAC
ACQUISITION REPORTED TO: OCLC
STAFF (FTE): 3 administrative, 3 clerical, 9 technical/para-professional
SPECIAL SERVICES/PROGRAMS: exhibits, tours
FACILITIES/EQUIPMENT/PRESERVATION: temperature controls, fire extinguishing system
PATRON USE STATISTICS: 1002 telephone patrons, 23 mail reference, 550 collections used

NHPRC NM513-560

T.R. Rough Riders' Memorial & City Museum
725 Grand Ave.
City Box 179
Las Vegas, New Mexico 87701

TEL: (505) 425-8726

REPORTED BY: Harold F. Thatcher, Director/Curator
TYPE OF INSTITUTION: historical society, museum (city)

HOURS: M-Sa 1-12, 1-4
ACCESS: open to general public
SERVICES: in person reference

PRIMARY COLLECTION FOCUS: [not reported]
military history
Spanish American War (Cuban liberation)
Las Vegas, NM (local history)

INCLUSIVE DATES: 1821-32, 1846
COLLECTION FORMATS: 3 manuscript collections, numerous oral histories, other
COLLECTION ACCESS: printed pamphlet and papers
ACQUISITION REPORTED TO: City of Las Vegas, Museum Board
STAFF (FTE): 2 general professional staff
INSTITUTIONAL SUPPORT FOR PROFESSIONAL DEVELOPMENT: payment for dues, mailings, telephone; use of facilities, use of clerical staff
SPECIAL SERVICES/PROGRAMS: exhibits, tours, lectures/presentations, radio program
FACILITIES/EQUIPMENT/PRESERVATION: city fire detection
PATRON USE STATISTICS: daily in-house patrons, occasional mail requests

---

Lincoln County Heritage Trust
Main Street
P.O. Box 98
Lincoln, New Mexico 88338

TEL: (505) 653-4025

REPORTED BY: Robert L. Hart, Director
TYPE OF INSTITUTION: museum (private, non-profit)

HOURS: winter: 9-5 daily, closed M; summer: 9-6 daily
ACCESS: public access by appointment only
SERVICES: in-person, mail, and photocopies

PRIMARY COLLECTION FOCUS: local history
    Lincoln County, NM (local history)
    Lincoln County (NM) War, 1878-1879
    Billy the Kid

INCLUSIVE DATES: 1847-1912
VOLUME: 50 cubic feet
COLLECTION FORMATS: 20 cubic feet manuscript collections, 21 cubic feet books/serials, 1 cubic foot pamphlets, 5 cubic feet films/videotapes, 3 cubic feet photographs
COLLECTION ACCESS: container lists, registers/inventories, computerized finding aids (used by staff)
SOFTWARE/SYSTEM: MacIntosh
STAFF (FTE): 1 administrative, 1 clerical, 1 intern, 2.4 interpreters
INSTITUTIONAL SUPPORT FOR PROFESSIONAL DEVELOPMENT: tuition/registration, membership dues, meeting registration and travel
SPECIAL SERVICES/PROGRAMS: exhibits, tours, lectures/presentations
FACILITIES/EQUIPMENT/PRESERVATION: fire detection controls
PATRON USE STATISTICS: user statistics not kept

Lincoln County Historical Society   **TEL**: (505) 653-4529
Dr. Woods' House Museum
P.O. Box 91
Lincoln, New Mexico 88338

REPORTED BY: Alice Blakestad, Historian
TYPE OF INSTITUTION: historical society (county/local)

HOURS: archives by appointment
ACCESS: open to general public
SERVICES: in-person, mail, phone, photocopies, fee for reference

PRIMARY COLLECTION FOCUS: Southeastern New Mexico history
    Lincoln County (NM) War, 1878-1879
    Billy the Kid
    Lincoln County, NM (local history)

COLLECTION FORMATS: books/serials, films/videotapes, government records, photographs, oral histories
COLLECTION ACCESS: card catalog, index
STAFF (FTE): 2 volunteer
SPECIAL SERVICES/PROGRAMS: tours, newsletter, lectures/presentations
PATRON USE STATISTICS: 14,000 in-house patrons (includes museum), 300-400 mail reference

---

Lincoln: Museum of New Mexico, Monument Division, Lincoln State Monument: NHPRC NM532-520

Los Alamos: Bandelier National Monument, Library and Photo File: NHPRC NM570-80

Los Alamos: Los Alamos County Historical Museum and Society: NHPRC NM570-480

Lovington Public Library
115 South Main Street
Lovington, New Mexico 88260

TEL: (505) 396-3144
FAX: (505) 396-7189

REPORTED BY: Mary Lee Smith, Director
TYPE OF INSTITUTION: library (city)

HOURS: M-F 9:30-5:30 (Winter M, Tu, Th 9:30-7:30) Sa 9:30-1:30
ACCESS: open to the general public
SERVICES: in-person, mail, phone, photocopies, and microfilm
RESTRICTIONS: no in-depth reference; single questions only

PRIMARY COLLECTION FOCUS: local history
    Lea County, NM (local history)
    genealogy

VOLUME: 3900 items
COLLECTION FORMATS: books/serials, maps, microfilm
COLLECTION ACCESS: card catalog, bibliography
STAFF (FTE): 1 administrative, 3 clerical, 1 student, 1 technician
INSTITUTIONAL SUPPORT FOR PROFESSIONAL DEVELOPMENT: tuition/registration reimbursement, meeting registration and travel
SPECIAL SERVICES/PROGRAMS: tours
FACILITIES/EQUIPMENT/PRESERVATION: temperature controls, disaster preparedness plan
PATRON USE STATISTICS: user statistics not kept

Mountainair: Gran Quivira National Monument, Library: NHPRC NM646-280

Eastern New Mexico University, Historical Services
Portales, New Mexico 88130

TEL: (505) 562-2636
FAX: (505) 562-2647

REPORTED BY: Mary J. Walker
TYPE OF INSTITUTION: library (state)

HOURS: 8-5 M-F, 7pm-9:30pm M, Th
ACCESS: open to the general public
SERVICES: in-person, mail, phone, photocopies, and photographs

PRIMARY COLLECTION FOCUS: local history, science fiction, in-house archives
    Roosevelt County, NM (local history)
    science fiction
    politics
    Southwestern U.S.--history
    Eastern New Mexico University, Historical Services (records)

INCLUSIVE DATES: 1900-
VOLUME: 1692.5 cubic feet, 22715 volumes, 1381 sound recordings
COLLECTION FORMATS: 853 cubic feet manuscript collections, 839.5 cubic feet records, 22715 volumes, 1381 films/videos, 1332 oral histories, 60 maps, 92 prints
COLLECTION ACCESS: on line catalog, container lists, registers/inventories, computerized finding aids (used by staff, patrons)
SOFTWARE/SYSTEM: Pro-Cite, Microsoft Works
STAFF (FTE): 1 administrative, 1 clerical, 7 students
INSTITUTIONAL SUPPORT FOR PROFESSIONAL DEVELOPMENT: tuition/registration reimbursed (50%), travel reimbursed (70%), mailings, use of facilities, telephone and clerical staff

SPECIAL SERVICES/PROGRAMS: exhibits
FACILITIES/EQUIPMENT/PRESERVATION: temperature controls, fire detection controls
PATRON USE STATISTICS: total patron count, 5130

NHPRC NM668-210 [note name change]

Eastern New Mexico University - Roswell
52 University Blvd.
P.O. Box 6000
Roswell, New Mexico 88202-6000

TEL: (505) 624-7281
FAX: (505) 624-7119

REPORTED BY: Rollah Aston - Director, Learning Resource Center
TYPE OF INSTITUTION: library (academic)

HOURS: M-Th 8-9:30pm, F 8-3pm, Sa 9-4, Su 2-5pm
ACCESS: open to the general public
SERVICES: in-person, phone, photocopies, and microfiche/film reproduction

PRIMARY COLLECTION FOCUS: local history, in-house archives
- Chaves County, NM (local history)
- nursing
- Roswell, NM (local history)
- University of New Mexico, Roswell (records)

INCLUSIVE DATES: 1867-
COLLECTION FORMATS: 20 cubic feet records, 230 volumes, 30 serials, 11 oral histories, 9 sound recordings
COLLECTION ACCESS: computerized finding aids: on-line catalog (used by staff, patrons)
SOFTWARE/SYSTEM: Bibliofile
ACQUISITION REPORTED TO: OCLC
STAFF (FTE): 1 administrative, 1 audio/video officer, 3 clerical, 15 students
INSTITUTIONAL SUPPORT FOR PROFESSIONAL DEVELOPMENT: tuition/registration reimbursement, membership dues travel reimbursement, mailings, use of facilities, telephone use
SPECIAL SERVICES/PROGRAMS: tours, classes
FACILITIES/EQUIPMENT/PRESERVATION: temperature controls, humidity controls, fire detection controls, fire extinguishing system
PATRON USE STATISTICS: 73,880 in-house patrons, 23,402 collections used, 121,991 photocopies, 7702 microform copies

---

Historical Center for Southeast New Mexico
200 North Lea Avenue
Roswell, New Mexico 88201

TEL: (505) 622-8333

REPORTED BY: Elvis E. Fleming, volunteer archivist
TYPE OF INSTITUTION: archives, historical society, and museum (state, county/local, city)
HOURS: archives F 1-4; historical society M-F 9-12 noon; museum F-Su 1-4
ACCESS: open to the general public
SERVICES: in-person, mail, phone, photocopies, photographs, and tapes

PRIMARY COLLECTION FOCUS: local history
- Roswell, NM (local history)
- Chaves County, NM (local history)
- Pecos Valley, NM (local history)
- Llano Estacado (Staked Plains)
- business history

INCLUSIVE DATES: 1890-1980
VOLUME: 300 cubic feet
COLLECTION FORMATS: 6 cubic feet manuscript collections, 5 cubic feet records, 100 books/serials, pamphlets, films/videotapes, government records, photographs, maps, oral histories
COLLECTION ACCESS: card catalog, registers/inventories
STAFF (FTE): 4 volunteers, 8 students
INSTITUTIONAL SUPPORT FOR PROFESSIONAL DEVELOPMENT: payment for mailings, telephone use, use of facilities
SPECIAL SERVICES/PROGRAMS: exhibits, tours, newsletter, fund raising/endowments, lectures/presentations
FACILITIES/EQUIPMENT/PRESERVATION: temperature controls, fire extinguishing system
PATRON USE STATISTICS: 25 in-house patrons, 15 telephone, 25 mail reference, 15 collections used, 10 reference photocopies

NHPRC NM684-120 [note name change]

New Mexico Military Institute
101 W. College Blvd.
Roswell, New Mexico 88201-5173

TEL: (505) 624-8384
FAX: (505) 624-8390

REPORTED BY: Kathy Flanary, Library Media Specialist
TYPE OF INSTITUTION: archives, library, museum (state, academic)

HOURS: 8-4 daily
ACCESS: rare books by appointment, archives not open to general public
SERVICES: [not reported]

PRIMARY COLLECTION FOCUS: military history of the Southwest
   military history
   literature

COLLECTION FORMATS: institution's records
COLLECTION ACCESS: computerized finding aids, registers/inventories
SOFTWARE/SYSTEM: CLSI, Gaylord Galaxy
STAFF (FTE): 2 administrative, 2 librarians, 1 cataloger
INSTITUTIONAL SUPPORT FOR PROFESSIONAL DEVELOPMENT: tuition/registration reimbursed, meeting registration and travel
SPECIAL SERVICES/PROGRAMS: exhibits, tours, classes, lectures/presentations
FACILITIES/EQUIPMENT/PRESERVATION: fire extinguishing system

Roswell Museum and Art Center
100 W. 11th St.
Roswell, New Mexico 88201

TEL: (505) 624-6744
FAX: (505) 624-6765

REPORTED BY: Kathy Sabin, Assistant Curator/Librarian
TYPE OF INSTITUTION: archives, library, museum (city)

HOURS: M-Sa 9-5, 1-5 Su
ACCESS: open to the general public
SERVICES: in-person, mail, phone, and photocopies
RESTRICTIONS: in-house use of books, publications, files only

PRIMARY COLLECTION FOCUS: Southwestern art and history
   art history

artists
Southwestern U.S.--history
Native Americans
space sciences
Goddard, Robert H.

INCLUSIVE DATES: 16th Century-present
COLLECTION FORMATS: institution's records, 5000 books, 3500 serials, 2000 pamphlets/ephemera, 55 films/videotapes, 200 photographs and slides
COLLECTION ACCESS: container lists, computerized finding aids (used by staff, patrons)
SOFTWARE/SYSTEM: Inmagic
ACQUISITION REPORTED TO: RLIN
STAFF (FTE): 8 administrative, 4 security, 50 volunteers, 3 clerical, 1 student
INSTITUTIONAL SUPPORT FOR PROFESSIONAL DEVELOPMENT: tuition/registration reimbursement, professional memberships, meeting registration & travel, in-house workshops, mailings, use of facilities
SPECIAL SERVICES/PROGRAMS: exhibits, tours, classes, fund raising/endowment, lectures/presentations
FACILITIES/EQUIPMENT/PRESERVATION: temperature controls, fire extinguishing system, disaster preparedness plan
PATRON USE STATISTICS: user statistics not kept
NHPRC NM684-690

Museum of Indian Arts and Culture, Laboratory of Anthropology   **TEL**: (505) 827-6344
708 Camino Lejo
P.O. Box 2087
Santa Fe, New Mexico 87504-2087

REPORTED BY: Willow Powers, Archivist
TYPE OF INSTITUTION: museum (state)

HOURS: M-F 8-5, Sa 9-2
ACCESS: public access by appointment only
SERVICES: in-person, phone, and photocopies

PRIMARY COLLECTION FOCUS: anthropology of the Southwest
    archaeology
    anthropology
    ethnology
    Native Americans--art
    anthropologists
    Southwestern U.S.--anthropology

INCLUSIVE DATES: 1915-present
VOLUME: 400 linear feet, 8000 photographs
COLLECTION FORMATS: 300 linear feet manuscript collections, 75 linear feet records, pamphlets, 8000 photographs, maps
COLLECTION ACCESS: repository guide, computerized finding aids (used by staff)
SOFTWARE/SYSTEM: Inmagic
ACQUISITION REPORTED TO: OCLC
STAFF (FTE): 1 administrative, volunteers, occasional students and interns
INSTITUTIONAL SUPPORT FOR PROFESSIONAL DEVELOPMENT: tuition/registration reimbursement, some travel, mailings, use of facilities, telephone calls
SPECIAL SERVICES/PROGRAMS: exhibits, tours, lectures/presentations
PATRON USE STATISTICS: 100 in-house patrons, 65 telephone, 30 mail reference, 30 collections used
NHPRC NM722-535 [note name change]

Museum of New Mexico, Photoarchives TEL: (505) 827-6472
110 Washington Ave.
P.O. Box 2087
Santa Fe, New Mexico 87504

REPORTED BY: Arthur L. Olivas, Photographic Archivist
TYPE OF INSTITUTION: archives, historical society, library, museum (state)

HOURS: M-F 1-5
ACCESS: open to the general public
SERVICES: in-person, mail, phone, and photocopies

PRIMARY COLLECTION FOCUS: New Mexico, West (U.S.), American Indians, history of photography
- New Mexico--history
- U.S.--Western
- Latin America
- Far East
- Middle East
- railroads
- agriculture
- mining
- Native Americans
- photography--history of

INCLUSIVE DATES: 1848-present
VOLUME: 450,000 items
COLLECTION FORMATS: 2500 books/serials, 447,500 photographs
COLLECTION ACCESS: repository guide, registers/inventories
STAFF (FTE): 2 photo curators, 1 photographer
FACILITIES/EQUIPMENT/PRESERVATION: fire detection controls
PATRON USE STATISTICS: user statistics not kept

National Park Service Southwest Region TEL: (505) 988-6832
1220 South St. Francis Drive
P.O. Box 728
Santa Fe, New Mexico 87501

REPORTED BY: Dr. Walter Wait
TYPE OF INSTITUTION: archives (federal)

HOURS: M-F 8-4:30
ACCESS: public access by appointment only
SERVICES: in-person reference

PRIMARY COLLECTION FOCUS: archaeology of the Southwest
- archaeology
- Southwestern U.S.--archaeology
- parks and monuments, federal

INCLUSIVE DATES: 1930s-present
VOLUME: 100 cubic feet
COLLECTION FORMATS: 15 manuscript collections, 85 government records, 30,000 photographs
COLLECTION ACCESS: container lists, registers/inventories, computerized finding aids (used by staff)
SOFTWARE/SYSTEM: WordPerfect
STAFF (FTE): 1 administrative, 1 general archival, 1 volunteer
FACILITIES/EQUIPMENT/PRESERVATION: humidity controls

New Mexico State Highway and Transportation Dept. Library
1120 Cerrillos Rd.
P.O. Box 1149
Santa Fe, New Mexico 87504-1149

TEL: (505) 827-5534
FAX: (505) 827-3214

REPORTED BY: Dinah Lea Jentgen, Librarian
TYPE OF INSTITUTION: library (state)

HOURS: M-F 7:45-11:30, 12:30-4:30
ACCESS: open to the general public
SERVICES: in-person, mail, phone
RESTRICTIONS: one person operation; excessive demands can not be met

PRIMARY COLLECTION FOCUS: transportation
- transportation--New Mexico
- transportation--planning
- highways--construction
- highways--history of

INCLUSIVE DATES: 1909-1992
COLLECTION FORMATS: 17,000 books/serials, pamphlets/ephemera, 30 volumes government records, 3 albums photographs
COLLECTION ACCESS: card catalog, computerized finding aids (used by staff)
SOFTWARE/SYSTEM: Data Trek, Databridge
ACQUISITION REPORTED TO: OCLC
STAFF (FTE): 1 librarian
INSTITUTIONAL SUPPORT FOR PROFESSIONAL DEVELOPMENT: tuition/registration reimbursement, meeting registration and some travel, use of facilities
SPECIAL SERVICES/PROGRAMS: newsletter, acquisitions list
FACILITIES/EQUIPMENT/PRESERVATION: temperature controls, humidity controls, disaster preparedness plan
PATRON USE STATISTICS: 561 in-house patrons, 277 telephone, 145 mail reference requests, 1754 collections used, 86 reference photocopies

---

New Mexico State Library, Southwest Collection
301 Don Gaspar
Santa Fe, New Mexico 87501

TEL: (505) 827-3805

REPORTED BY: Dr. Guillermo Lux
TYPE OF INSTITUTION: library (state)

HOURS: M-F 8-5
ACCESS: open to the general public
SERVICES: in-person, mail and phone reference; photocopies

PRIMARY COLLECTION FOCUS: Southwest history
- Southwestern U.S.--history

COLLECTION FORMATS: books/serials, government records, maps
COLLECTION ACCESS: card catalog
ACQUISITION REPORTED TO: OCLC
STAFF (FTE): 1 administrative, 2 general archival
INSTITUTIONAL SUPPORT FOR PROFESSIONAL DEVELOPMENT: use of facilities and equipment
SPECIAL SERVICES/PROGRAMS: exhibits, tours, newsletter, lectures/presentations

FACILITIES/EQUIPMENT/PRESERVATION: temperature controls, humidity controls, fire detection controls, fire extinguishing system

---

New Mexico State Records Center and Archives
404 Montezuma
Santa Fe, New Mexico 87503

TEL: (505) 827-7332
FAX: (505) 827-7331

REPORTED BY: J. Richard Salazar, Chief, Archival Services Division
TYPE OF INSTITUTION: archives (state, county)

HOURS: M-F 8-5
ACCESS: open to the general public
SERVICES: in-person, mail, phone, photocopies, and microfilm printouts

PRIMARY COLLECTION FOCUS: New Mexico state government and history
- Spanish government--records
- Mexican government--records
- Territorial government--records
- New Mexico state government--records
- New Mexico--history
- Southwestern U.S.--history

INCLUSIVE DATES: 1621-present
VOLUME: 15,000 cubic feet
COLLECTION FORMATS: 3000 cubic feet manuscript collections, 12,000 feet records, 4000 books/serials, 600 films/videotapes, 50,000+ photographs, 2000 maps
COLLECTION ACCESS: card catalog, registers/inventories, computerized finding aids (used by staff)
STAFF (FTE): 1 administrative, 4 general archival, 1 preservation, 1 map curator, 1 photo curator, 1 clerical
INSTITUTIONAL SUPPORT FOR PROFESSIONAL DEVELOPMENT: professional memberships
SPECIAL SERVICES/PROGRAMS: tours, classes, lectures/presentations
FACILITIES/EQUIPMENT/PRESERVATION: temperature controls, fire detection controls, fire extinguishing system, disaster preparedness plan
PATRON USE STATISTICS: 7000 in-house patrons, 2500 telephone, 1000 mail reference requests

NHPRC NM772-570

Palace of the Governors History Library
110 Washington Ave.
P.O. Box 2087
Santa Fe, New Mexico 87504-2087

TEL: (505) 827-6470

REPORTED BY: Orlando A. Romero, Research Librarian
TYPE OF INSTITUTION: library and museum (state)

HOURS: M-F 10-4:45
ACCESS: open to the general public
SERVICES: in-person, phone, photocopies, and microfilm
RESTRICTIONS: pencils only, identification required

PRIMARY COLLECTION FOCUS: Southwest history
- Southwestern U.S.--history
- ethnohistory
- New Mexico--history
- Spanish government--documents

INCLUSIVE DATES: 1681-present
COLLECTION FORMATS: 300 linear feet manuscript collections, 15,000 books, 500 linear feet pamphlets, 3000 maps, newspapers
COLLECTION ACCESS: card catalog, registers/inventories, indexes
ACQUISITION REPORTED TO: OCLC
STAFF (FTE): 1 librarian, 0.5 cataloger
INSTITUTIONAL SUPPORT FOR PROFESSIONAL DEVELOPMENT: tuition/registration reimbursement, meeting registration and travel, use of facilities
SPECIAL SERVICES/PROGRAMS: tours, lectures/presentations
FACILITIES/EQUIPMENT/PRESERVATION: fire detection controls
PATRON USE STATISTICS: 6000 in-house patrons, 3200 telephone, 500 mail reference
NHPRC NM772-530

School of American Research
660 Barcia
P.O. Box 2188
Santa Fe, New Mexico 87504-2188

TEL: (505) 982-3583
FAX: (505) 989-9809

REPORTED BY: Jane Gillentine, Librarian
TYPE OF INSTITUTION: research center (academic)

HOURS: general: M-F 9-12 & 1-5; library: M-F 9-12, 1-4
ACCESS: public access by appointment only
SERVICES: library: phone reference, photocopies

PRIMARY COLLECTION FOCUS: anthropology, ethnography
    White, Amelia Elizabeth
    anthropology
    ethnology

COLLECTION FORMATS: photographs (Art Dept.), books, serials, 1 manuscript collection
COLLECTION ACCESS: card catalog, registers/inventories, computerized finding aids (used by staff)
SOFTWARE/SYSTEM: Inmagic
STAFF (FTE): 1 administrative, 1 volunteer/docent, 1 clerical
INSTITUTIONAL SUPPORT FOR PROFESSIONAL DEVELOPMENT: reimbursement for course tuition/registration and professional meetings, payment of dues for professional memberships
STAFF (FTE): [not reported]
PATRON USE STATISTICS: 15 in-house patrons, 30 telephone patrons

---

Supreme Court Law Library
Supreme Court Bldg. 237 Don Gasper
P.O. Drawer L
Santa Fe, New Mexico 87504

TEL: (505) 827-4850
FAX: (505) 827-4853 (call first)

REPORTED BY: Kevin M. Lancaster, Associate Librarian
TYPE OF INSTITUTION: library (state, special)

HOURS: M-TH 8-8, F 8-5:30, Sa 10-4
ACCESS: open to the general public
SERVICES: in-person, mail, phone, photocopies, and fiche copies
RESTRICTIONS: no legal research or advice

PRIMARY COLLECTION FOCUS: law history
    law, history of

New Mexico--statutes
natural resources--law
Native Americans--law

INCLUSIVE DATES: 1600s-present
VOLUME: 160,000 items
COLLECTION FORMATS: 150 volumes records, 150,000 books/serials, 500 volumes government records, 10,000 microfiche
COLLECTION ACCESS: card catalog, repository guide, registers/inventories, computerized finding aids (used by staff)
SOFTWARE/SYSTEM: Reflex 2, Paradox
STAFF (FTE): 1 administrative, 2 librarians, 3 clerical, 1 financial
INSTITUTIONAL SUPPORT FOR PROFESSIONAL DEVELOPMENT: tuition/registration reimbursement, professional dues, meeting registration, use of facilities
SPECIAL SERVICES/PROGRAMS: tours, classes, lectures/presentations
FACILITIES/EQUIPMENT/PRESERVATION: fire detection controls, fire extinguishing system

---

Wheelwright Museum of American Indian Art
704 Camino Lejo
P.O. Box 5153
Santa Fe, New Mexico 87502

TEL: (505) 982-4636
FAX: (505) 989-7386

REPORTED BY: Lynette Miller, Curator
TYPE OF INSTITUTION: museum (private non-profit)

HOURS: Museum: M-Sa 10-5, Su 1-5; Library: M-F 9-5
ACCESS: public access by appointment only
SERVICES: give help only to serious researchers

PRIMARY COLLECTION FOCUS: Native American art and culture
Native Americans--art
Native Americans
Navajo Indians
Pueblo Indians
Apache Indians

INCLUSIVE DATES: 1500-present
COLLECTION FORMATS: 50 linear feet manuscript collections, 70 feet records, 3000 books/serials, 2000 pamphlets/ephemera, 40 films/videotapes, 6000 photographs, 200 recordings
COLLECTION ACCESS: card catalog, registers/inventories
STAFF (FTE): 1 curator, 1 assistant curator, 1 volunteer
INSTITUTIONAL SUPPORT FOR PROFESSIONAL DEVELOPMENT: professional dues, meeting registration and travel
SPECIAL SERVICES/PROGRAMS: exhibits, newsletter, lectures/presentations
FACILITIES/EQUIPMENT/PRESERVATION: temperature controls, humidity controls, fire detection controls, fire extinguishing system
PATRON USE STATISTICS: user statistics not kept

Santa Fe: Anthropology Film Center, Visual Anthropology Resource Collection: NHPRC NM722-30

Santa Fe: Institute of American Indian Arts, Museum: NHPRC NM722-360

Santa Fe: Southwest Foundation for Audio-Visual Resources, Anthropology Film Center: NHPRC NM722-730

Silver City Museum
312 W. Broadway
Silver City, New Mexico 88061

TEL: (505) 388-5721, 538-5921

REPORTED BY: Debra A. Swearingin, Curator of Collections and Registration
TYPE OF INSTITUTION: museum (city)

HOURS: Tu-F 9-4:30, Sa-Su 10-4, closed M
ACCESS: open to the general public
SERVICES: in-person, mail, phone, photocopies, and a fee for reference

PRIMARY COLLECTION FOCUS: local history
    Silver City, NM (local history)
    Grant County, NM (local history)

COLLECTION FORMATS: manuscript collections, pamphlets/ephemera, photographs, maps, oral histories
COLLECTION ACCESS: holdings not described
STAFF (FTE): 1 administrative, 2 curators
INSTITUTIONAL SUPPORT FOR PROFESSIONAL DEVELOPMENT: tuition/registration reimbursement
SPECIAL SERVICES/PROGRAMS: exhibits, newsletter, fund raising/endowment, lectures/presentations
FACILITIES/EQUIPMENT/PRESERVATION: temperature controls, humidity controls, fire detection controls,
    disaster preparedness plan
PATRON USE STATISTICS: user statistics not kept

NHPRC NM760-720

Western New Mexico University Museum
1000 West College
P.O. Box 680
Silver City, New Mexico 88061

TEL: (505) 538-6386
FAX: (505) 538-6178

REPORTED BY: Cynthia Ann Bettison, Museum Director
TYPE OF INSTITUTION: museum (state, academic)

HOURS: M-F 8-4:30, Su 1-4
ACCESS: open to the general public
SERVICES: in-person
RESTRICTIONS: no photographing or videotaping without permission

PRIMARY COLLECTION FOCUS: New Mexico and local history
    Southwestern U.S.--history
    archaeology
    education
    mining
    ethnic communities

VOLUME: 15,000 items
COLLECTION FORMATS: 100 manuscript collections, 300 records, 600 books/serials, 200
    pamphlets/ephemera, 20 films/videotapes, 10,000 photographs, 100 maps, 700 oral histories
COLLECTION ACCESS: repository guide, registers/inventories, container lists, computerized finding aids
    (used by staff)
SOFTWARE/SYSTEM: Nutplus II
STAFF (FTE): 1 administrative, 4 volunteers, 1 clerical, 10 students, 1 intern
INSTITUTIONAL SUPPORT FOR PROFESSIONAL DEVELOPMENT: tuition/registration reimbursement,
    professional dues, meeting registration & travel, mailings, telephone, use of facilities
SPECIAL SERVICES/PROGRAMS: exhibits, tours, classes, newsletter, lectures/presentations

FACILITIES/EQUIPMENT/PRESERVATION: fire detection controls, fire extinguishing system
PATRON USE STATISTICS: user statistics not kept

Silver City: Gila National Forest: NHPRC NM760-280

Silver City: Western New Mexico University, Museum: NHPRC NM760-900

New Mexico Institute of Mining and Technology Library
Campus Station
Socorro, New Mexico 87801

TEL: (505) 835-5766
FAX: (505) 835-5754

REPORTED BY: Kay Krehbiel, Public Services Librarian
TYPE OF INSTITUTION: library (academic)

HOURS: M-F 8-5
ACCESS: public access by individual request
SERVICES: [not reported]

PRIMARY COLLECTION FOCUS: in-house archives
    New Mexico Institute of Mining and Technology (records)
    mining

INCLUSIVE DATES: 1889-present
COLLECTION FORMATS: institution's records, books/serials, pamphlets/ephemera, photographs
COLLECTION ACCESS: container lists
STAFF (FTE): volunteer
FACILITIES/EQUIPMENT/PRESERVATION: fire extinguishing system
PATRON USE STATISTICS: user statistics not kept

Santa Fe Trail Museum
518 Maxwell
P.O. Box 323
Springer, New Mexico 87747

TEL: [not reported]

REPORTED BY: Ruth A. Kennedy, Secretary
TYPE OF INSTITUTION: museum (county/local, city)

HOURS: M-F 9-5, by appointment only in Winter months
ACCESS: open to the general public
SERVICES: in-person, mail, and phone reference

PRIMARY COLLECTION FOCUS: local history
    Springer, NM (local history)
    Colfax County, NM (local history)
    Santa Fe Trail

COLLECTION FORMATS: photographs
COLLECTION ACCESS: holdings not described
STAFF (FTE): 1 administrative, 2 volunteer, 1 student
PATRON USE STATISTICS: user statistics not kept

Harwood Foundation of the University of New Mexico **TEL**: (505) 758-9826
238 Ledoux Street
P.O. Box 4080
Taos, New Mexico 87571

REPORTED BY: David Witt, Director
TYPE OF INSTITUTION: museum (state)

HOURS: M-F 9-5
ACCESS: public access by appointment only
SERVICES: in-person reference

PRIMARY COLLECTION FOCUS: art and art history
    art history
    artists
    Taos, NM (local history)

INCLUSIVE DATES: 1898-present
COLLECTION FORMATS: institution's records, books/serials, pamphlets/ephemera,
    photographs, oral histories
COLLECTION ACCESS: registers/inventories
STAFF (FTE): 1 curator
SPECIAL SERVICES/PROGRAMS: exhibits
PATRON USE STATISTICS: user statistics not kept

Millicent Rogers Museum Library **TEL**: (505) 758-2462
Museum Road **FAX**: (505) 758-5157
P.O. Box A
Taos, New Mexico 87571

REPORTED BY: Ann L. McVicar, Librarian
TYPE OF INSTITUTION: library, museum (private)

HOURS: museum 9-5 daily, library open by appointment only
ACCESS: public access by appointment only
SERVICES: [not reported]

PRIMARY COLLECTION FOCUS: American Indian and Hispanic art, archaeology and anthropology
    Native Americans--art
    Hispanic Americans--art
    archaeology
    anthropology

VOLUME: 5000 items
COLLECTION FORMATS: 4000 books/serials, 1000 pamphlets/ephemera, 12 films/videotapes
COLLECTION ACCESS: card catalog
STAFF (FTE): 1 volunteer
INSTITUTIONAL SUPPORT FOR PROFESSIONAL DEVELOPMENT: professional organization dues

---

Taos: Kit Carson Memorial Foundation, Historical Research Library and Archives: NHPRC NM874-440

Geronimo Springs Museum **TEL**: (505) 894-6600
211 Main Street
Truth or Consequences, New Mexico 87901

REPORTED BY: Ann Welborn, Director
TYPE OF INSTITUTION: museum (historical society)

HOURS: M-Sa 9-5
ACCESS: open to the general public
SERVICES: [not reported]

PRIMARY COLLECTION FOCUS: local history
    Truth or Consequences, NM (local history)
    Sierra County, NM (local history)
    anthropology
    television--history
    Mimbreno Indians
    Native Americans

COLLECTION FORMATS: manuscript collections, photographs, films/videotapes, serials, oral histories
COLLECTION ACCESS: registers/inventories
STAFF (FTE): 1 administrative, volunteers
PATRON USE STATISTICS: 7000 museum visitors, 10 mail reference requests

NHPRC NM912-280

Tucumcari: Tucumcari Historical Research Institute, Museum: NPRRC NM950-270

Fort Union National Monument   **TEL**: [not reported]
Highway 161
P.O. Box 127
Watrous, New Mexico 87753

REPORTED BY: [not listed]
TYPE OF INSTITUTION: National Monument (federal)

HOURS: 8-5 daily
ACCESS: public access by appointment only
SERVICES: in-person, mail, and photocopies
RESTRICTIONS: degree of retrieval complexity/difficulty

PRIMARY COLLECTION FOCUS: history of Fort Union, N.M.
    Fort Union, NM (local history)
    military history
    forts
    parks and monuments, federal

INCLUSIVE DATES: 1851-1891
VOLUME: 23,000 items
COLLECTION FORMATS: 500 manuscript collections, 22300 government records, 100 photographs, 50
    maps, 10 oral histories
COLLECTION ACCESS: holdings not described
STAFF (FTE): 1 historian
INSTITUTIONAL SUPPORT FOR PROFESSIONAL DEVELOPMENT: tuition/registration reimbursement,
    membership dues, meeting registration, travel
SPECIAL SERVICES/PROGRAMS: exhibits, tours, lectures/presentations
FACILITIES/EQUIPMENT/PRESERVATION: fire detection controls, disaster preparedness plan
PATRON USE STATISTICS: user statistics not kept

OKLAHOMA

East Central University
Linscheid Library
Ada, OK 74820

TEL: (405) 332-8000
FAX: (405) 521-6517

REPORTED BY: John Jax, Social Sciences Librarian
TYPE OF INSTITUTION: library (academic)

HOURS: M-Th 8-10, F 8-5, Su 2-10
ACCESS: open to general public
SERVICES: in-person reference, mail reference, phone reference

PRIMARY COLLECTION FOCUS: Oklahoma, East Central University, Pontotoc County, Ada
- Oklahoma--history
- Oklahoma--literature
- Pontotoc County, OK (local history)
- East Central [OK] University (records)
- Ada, OK

INCLUSIVE DATES: late 1800's to present
VOLUME: 1800 feet
COLLECTION FORMATS: manuscript collections (175 feet), institution's records (50 feet), books/serials (1540), pamphlets/ephemera (10 feet), films (5 feet), government records (10 feet), photographs (5 feet), maps (2 feet)
COLLECTION ACCESS: card catalog, computerized finding aids (used by staff, patrons)
SOFTWARE/SYSTEM: Innovative Interfaces, Inc.
ACQUISITION REPORTED TO: OCLC
STAFF (FTE): 1 administrative, 1 general archival, 1 audio-visual officer, 1 clerical, 1 student
INSTITUTIONAL SUPPORT FOR PROFESSIONAL DEVELOPMENT: tuition/registration reimbursement, reimbursement for professional meetings registration/travel, payment for mailings
SPECIAL SERVICES/PROGRAMS: exhibits, tours, classes, lectures/presentations
FACILITIES/EQUIPMENT/PRESERVATION: temperature controls, humidity controls, fire detection controls, disaster preparedness plan
PATRON USE STATISTICS: 150 in-house patrons, 6 telephone, 5 collections used, 26 reference photocopies

---

Alva: Northwestern Oklahoma State University, Library: OK42-560

Confederate Memorial Museum
Highway 69 North
MAIL ADDRESS: P. O. Box 245
Atoka, OK 74525

TEL: (405) 889-7192

REPORTED BY: Gwen Walker, Site Manager
TYPE OF INSTITUTION: historical society, museum (state, county/local)

HOURS: M 9-1, T-Sa 9-4
ACCESS: open to the general public
SERVICES: in-person, mail, and phone reference; photocopies

PRIMARY COLLECTION FOCUS: Atoka, OK
- Atoka, OK (local history)

COLLECTION FORMATS: photographs, cemetery records
SPECIAL SERVICES/PROGRAMS: exhibits, tours, newsletter

FACILITIES/EQUIPMENT/PRESERVATION: temperature controls

Bartlesville Public Library and History Museum
600 S. Johnstone
Bartlesville, OK 74003

TEL: (918) 337-5353
FAX: (918) 337-5338

REPORTED BY: Joan Singleton, Public Services Librarian
TYPE OF INSTITUTION: library, museum (county/local, city)

HOURS: M-Th 9-9, F-Sa 9-5:30
ACCESS: open to the general public
SERVICES: in-person, mail, and phone reference, photocopies
RESTRICTIONS: will not do in-depth research

PRIMARY COLLECTION FOCUS: Bartlesville area
    Bartlesville, OK (local history)
    Native Americans, Washington Co., OK
    Five Civilized Tribes
    genealogy

INCLUSIVE DATES: 1895 to present
VOLUME: 5,000 in Local/Family History Collection
COLLECTION FORMATS: books/serials, pamphlets/ephemera, films/videotapes, state government records, photographs, maps, oral histories, microforms
COLLECTION ACCESS: registers/inventories, computerized finding aids (used by staff and patrons)
SOFTWARE/SYSTEM: Dynix System
ACQUISITION REPORTED TO: state-wide link-up
STAFF (FTE): 2 (local/family history)
INSTITUTIONAL SUPPORT FOR PROFESSIONAL DEVELOPMENT: tuition/registration, reimbursement for courses, use of facilities and equipment, payment for telephone use
SPECIAL SERVICES/PROGRAMS: exhibits, tours
FACILITIES/EQUIPMENT/PRESERVATION: temperature controls, humidity controls, fire detection controls, fire extinguishing system, disaster preparedness plan
PATRON USE: user statistics not kept

NHPRC OK118-70

Jones and Plummer Trail Museum
Beaver County Fairgrounds
P. O. Box 457
Beaver, OK 73932

TEL: (405) 625-4439

REPORTED BY: Fannie Judy, President
TYPE OF INSTITUTION: historical society, museum

HOURS: W-F 1-5:30, Sa 1-5, Su 2:30-5
ACCESS: open to the general public

PRIMARY COLLECTION FOCUS: artifacts relating to Beaver County history
    Beaver County, OK (local history)

COLLECTION FORMATS: manuscript collections, institution's records, books/serials, films/videotapes, government records, photographs, maps
COLLECTION ACCESS: card catalog

INSTITUTIONAL SUPPORT FOR PROFESSIONAL DEVELOPMENT: payment of dues for professional organization memberships
FACILITIES/EQUIPMENT/PRESERVATION: temperature controls

Top of Oklahoma Historical Society Cherokee Outlet Museum
303 S. Main
Blackwell, OK 74631

TEL: (405) 363-0209

REPORTED BY: Bret A. Carter, Board of Directors
TYPE OF INSTITUTION: historical society, museum (county/local)

HOURS: M-F 9-5
ACCESS: open to the general public
SERVICES: in-person reference, mail reference

PRIMARY COLLECTION FOCUS: Blackwell area of Kay County
    Kay County, OK (local history)
    Blackwell, OK
    legal records

INCLUSIVE DATES: 1893 to present
COLLECTION FORMATS: manuscript collections, institution's records, books/serials, pamphlets/ ephemera, government records, photographs, maps, oral histories
COLLECTION ACCESS: registers/inventories
STAFF (FTE): volunteer/docent
SPECIAL SERVICES/PROGRAMS: exhibits, tours, newsletter, fund raising/endowment
PATRON USE STATISTICS: 500 in-house patrons

Arkansas River Historical Society
5350 Cimarron Road
Catoosa, OK 74015

TEL: (918) 266-2291
FAX: (918) 266-7678

REPORTED BY: Jack Thisler, Vice-President for Oklahoma
TYPE OF INSTITUTION: historical society, museum (special)

HOURS: M-F 8-4:30
ACCESS: open to the general public

PRIMARY COLLECTION FOCUS: Arkansas River Navigation System
    Arkansas River (OK)
    Arkansas River (AR)
    Arkansas River (KS)
    Arkansas River (CO)
    Arkansas River Navigation System
    Kerr-McClellan Waterway

INCLUSIVE DATES: 1930s to present
COLLECTION FORMATS: manuscript collections, books, pamphlets, photographs, maps

---

Alfalfa County Museum
102 West Main
P. O. Box 201
Cherokee, OK 73728

TEL: none

REPORTED BY: Mildred Fisher
TYPE OF INSTITUTION: historical society, museum (county/local)

HOURS: Tu-F 1-5 and by appointment
ACCESS: open to the general public

PRIMARY COLLECTION FOCUS: Alfalfa County, OK
    Alfalfa County, OK (local history)

STAFF (FTE): 2 volunteer/docent

Chickasha: University of Science and Arts of Oklahoma, Nash Library: OK228-610

Claremore: Will Rogers Memorial Library: OK245-880

Talbot Library and Museum
South Colcord Avenue
Rt. 4, Box 6
Colcord, OK 74338

TEL: (918) 326-4532

REPORTED BY: Virgil Talbot, Librarian and Curator
TYPE OF INSTITUTION: library, museum (independent non-profit organization)

HOURS: Tu-Sa 9-5, Su 1-5
ACCESS: open to the general public
SERVICES: in-person, photocopies, mail reference, phone reference
RESTRICTIONS: restricted by number of staff available

PRIMARY COLLECTION FOCUS: Indian history, general history, genealogy
    Oklahoma, Colcord, OK (local history)
    Anti-Horse Thief Association
    Anti-Thief Association
    Arkansas, Northwest--history
    Cherokee Indians

COLLECTION FORMATS: manuscript collections; books/serials
COLLECTION ACCESS: varied
STAFF (FTE): 2 volunteer/docent
FACILITIES/EQUIPMENT/PRESERVATION: temperature controls

Cushing Public Library
215 North Steele
P. O. Box 551
Cushing, Oklahoma 74023

TEL: (918) 225-4188

REPORTED BY: Carolyn S. Clark, President, Cushing Genealogical Society
TYPE OF INSTITUTION: library (city)

HOURS: M-Th 9-8, F-Sa 9-6
ACCESS: open to the general public
SERVICES: in-person reference, mail reference, photocopies

PRIMARY COLLECTION FOCUS: Payne County, City of Cushing, genealogy
    Payne County, OK--cemetery lists/histories

Cushing, OK--funeral records
genealogy

COLLECTION FORMATS: books/serials, photographs, microfilm
COLLECTION ACCESS: card catalog

Arbuckle Historical Society
12 Main (Santa Fe Depot)
Davis, OK 73030

TEL: (405) 369-2518

REPORTED BY: Pat Norrell, President
TYPE OF INSTITUTION: historical society, library, museum (city)

HOURS: afternoons daily
ACCESS: open to the general public

PRIMARY COLLECTION FOCUS: local history
    Davis, OK (local history)

COLLECTION FORMATS: photographs, maps, oral histories
COLLECTION ACCESS: not described
STAFF (FTE): volunteer/docent

Stephens County Historical Museum
Fuqua Park
P. O. Box 1294
Duncan, OK 73533

TEL: (405) 252-0717

REPORTED BY: Don Stevens, Curator
TYPE OF INSTITUTION: archives, historical society, museum (county/local)

HOURS: Sa-Su, Tu, Th 1-4
ACCESS: open to the general public

PRIMARY COLLECTION FOCUS: local history
    Duncan, OK (local history)

COLLECTION FORMATS: pamphlets/ephemera, films/videotapes, photographs
COLLECTION ACCESS: card catalog
STAFF (FTE): 1 administrative; 4 volunteer/docent
SPECIAL SERVICES/PROGRAMS: exhibits, tours
FACILITIES/EQUIPMENT/PRESERVATION: fire extinguishing system

Edmond Historical Society
431 South Boulevard
Edmond, OK 73034

TEL: (405) 340-0078

REPORTED BY: Geneva Hudson, President
TYPE OF INSTITUTION: historical society, museum (membership)

HOURS: W-F 10-4, Sa 1-4
ACCESS: open to the general public

SERVICES: in-person, mail, phone reference, photocopies (copies made off-site)

PRIMARY COLLECTION FOCUS: city of Edmond and environs
    Edmond, OK (local history)
    medicine, history of
    business history
    farm history
    ranch history
    exploration
    transportation
    social history
    education

COLLECTION FORMATS: books/serials (747/145), videotapes (3), photographs (750), oral histories (16), church records (9), city directories (10)
COLLECTION ACCESS: card catalog, container lists, computerized finding aid (used by staff)
SOFTWARE/SYSTEM: IBM compatible
STAFF (FTE): 40 volunteer/docent, 5 clerical
SPECIAL SERVICES/PROGRAMS: exhibits, tours, newsletter, fund raising/endowment lectures/presentations, in-school visitation
FACILITIES/EQUIPMENT/PRESERVATION: temperature controls, fire extinguishing system, disaster preparedness plan
PATRON USE STATISTICS: 3200 in-house patrons, 150 telephone, 25 mail reference requests

---

Special Collections/University Archives/Oklahoma Collection
100 N. University Drive
Evans Hall, University of Central Oklahoma
Edmond, OK 73034-0132

TEL: (405) 341-2980, ext. 2882
FAX: (405) 341-4964

REPORTED BY: Mary Lou Bond, Archivist
TYPE OF INSTITUTION: archives, library (state, academic)

HOURS: M 8-8, Tu-F 8-5, Sa 8:30-12:30
ACCESS: open to the general public
SERVICES: in-person, mail, phone reference, photocopies, microforms, fee maybe
RESTRICTIONS: non-circulating

PRIMARY COLLECTION FOCUS: state and local history, University archives, Dust Bowl
    Oklahoma--history
    University of Central Oklahoma (records)
    Central State [OK] University (records)
    Edmond, OK (local history)
    Oklahoma--townsite case files
    Oklahoma--local history
    Oklahoma--Dept. of Health and Human Services
    Rader, Lloyd E.
    ranching (cattle industry)
    pioneers
    military history

INCLUSIVE DATES: 1865 to present
VOLUME: 7500 books/serials; 1300 linear feet
COLLECTION FORMATS:
COLLECTION ACCESS: card catalog, container lists, registers/inventories, computerized finding aids (used by staff, patrons)
SOFTWARE/SYSTEM: NOTIS, d-Base
ACQUISITION REPORTED TO: OCLC

STAFF (FTE): 1 administrative, 1 clerical, 5 student
INSTITUTIONAL SUPPORT FOR PROFESSIONAL DEVELOPMENT: payment for dues, professional
  memberships, travel reimbursement, in-house workshops, payment for mailings, use of facilities, use
  of clerical staff
SPECIAL SERVICES/PROGRAMS: exhibits, tours, lectures/presentations, submit articles to campus, area,
  and other publications
FACILITIES/EQUIPMENT/PRESERVATION: temperature controls, humidity controls, fire detection controls,
  fire extinguishing, disaster preparedness plan
PATRON USE STATISTICS: 1780 in house patrons, 140 telephone, 20 mail reference requests, 1960
  collections used, 1400 reference photocopies, 234 microfilm/fiche copies

---

El Reno: Canadian County Historical Museum: OK338-120

El Reno: El Reno Carnegie Library: OK338-200

Zollars Memorial Library, Phillips University   **TEL**: (405) 237-4433
P.O. Box 2400 University Station
Enid, OK 73702

REPORTED BY: Rick Sayre, Director
TYPE OF INSTITUTION: library (academic)

HOURS: access during library hours
ACCESS: open to the general public
SERVICES: in-person, mail, phone reference, photocopies, other reproduction
RESTRICTIONS: Living Legend audio cassettes require family permission

PRIMARY COLLECTION FOCUS: Phillips University
  Phillips University, OK (records)
  Enid, OK (local history)

INCLUSIVE DATES: 1926 to present
COLLECTION FORMATS: books/serials (4200), pamphlets/ephemera and photographs (20 linear feet),
  videotapes (85), oral histories (330 tapes), institution's records
COLLECTION ACCESS: card catalog
ACQUISITION REPORTED TO: OCLC
STAFF (FTE): volunteer/docent
INSTITUTIONAL SUPPORT FOR PROFESSIONAL DEVELOPMENT: use of clerical staff permitted

NHPRC OK355-640

Museum of the Cherokee Strip   **TEL**: (405) 237-1907
507 South Fourth
Enid, OK 73701

REPORTED BY: Rob Howell, Director
TYPE OF INSTITUTION: historical society, museum (state)

HOURS: Tu-F 9-5, Sa-Su 2-5
ACCESS: open to the general public
SERVICES: in person, mail, phone reference, photocopies
RESTRICTIONS: some photographs restricted

PRIMARY COLLECTION FOCUS: Northwest Oklahoma, Cherokee Strip
Museum of Cherokee Strip, history of
petroleum industry
aviation
Enid, OK (local history)
Oklahoma, Northwest

INCLUSIVE DATES: 1890-1970s
COLLECTION FORMATS: manuscript collections (1.5 cubic feet), institutions's records (6 cubic feet), books (500), films (15), government records (25 cubic feet), photos (10 cubic feet), maps (30), oral histories (100)
COLLECTION ACCESS: card catalog, registers/inventories, computerized finding aids (used by staff)
SOFTWARE/SYSTEM: WordPerfect 5.1
ACQUISITION REPORTED TO: state and local historical societies
STAFF (FTE): 2 administrative, 3 volunteer/docent
INSTITUTIONAL SUPPORT FOR PROFESSIONAL DEVELOPMENT: use of facilities and equipment
SPECIAL SERVICES/PROGRAMS: exhibits, newsletter, lectures/presentations
FACILITIES/EQUIPMENT/PRESERVATION: temperature controls, fire detection controls, fire extinguishing system, disaster preparedness plan

---

Fort Sill Museum
437 Quanah Road
Fort Sill, OK 73501-5100

TEL: (405) 351-5123

REPORTED BY: Towana Spivey, Director
TYPE OF INSTITUTION: archives, library, museum (federal)

HOURS: M-F 7:30-4
ACCESS: public access by appointment only
SERVICES: in-person, mail reference, photocopies

PRIMARY COLLECTION FOCUS: Fort Sill, Indian history, military history
Native Americans
Plains Indians
Apache Indians
military history
Fort Sill, OK
Indian Territory (OK)

COLLECTION FORMATS: books/serials (10,000), pamphlets/ephemera (200,000), films/videotapes (150), photographs (35,000), maps (600)
COLLECTION ACCESS: card catalog, registers/inventories
STAFF (FTE): 2 administrative, 1 photo curator, 1 general archival, 30 volunteer/docent
SPECIAL SERVICES/PROGRAMS: exhibits, tours, lectures/presentations
FACILITIES/EQUIPMENT/PRESERVATION: preservation lab, disaster preparedness plan, temperature controls, humidity controls, fire extinguishing system, fire detection controls
PATRON USE STATISTICS: 2000 in-house patrons, 3000 mail reference requests

NHPRC OK372-240

Canadian Rivers Historical Society and Museum
Main and Broadway
Rt 1, Box 139
Geary, OK 73040

TEL: (405) 884-5526

REPORTED BY: Merle Rinehart, President
TYPE OF INSTITUTION: historical society, museum (city)

HOURS: W, F 9-4, or by appointment
ACCESS: open to the general public

PRIMARY COLLECTION FOCUS: Geary, OK
    Geary, OK (local history)
    Blaine County, OK
    Canadian River Valley

INCLUSIVE DATES: 1892 to present
COLLECTION FORMATS: manuscript collections, institution's records, photographs
COLLECTION ACCESS: card catalog
STAFF (FTE): administrative, volunteer/docent
FACILITIES/EQUIPMENT/PRESERVATION: fire extinguishing system

No Man's Land Historical Museum   **TEL**: (405) 349-2670
Sewell Street
P. O. Box 278
Goodwell, OK 73939

REPORTED BY: Joan Kachel, Manager
TYPE OF INSTITUTION: historical society, museum (state)

HOURS: Tu-F 9-5, Sa-Su 1-5
ACCESS: public access by appointment only
SERVICES: limited service due to small staff

PRIMARY COLLECTION FOCUS: history of the Oklahoma Panhandle
    No Man's Land (OK)
    Oklahoma Panhandle
    Dust Bowl (OK)
    Santa Fe Trail

INCLUSIVE DATES: 1860-present
VOLUME: 5000
COLLECTION ACCESS: card catalog, registers/inventories
STAFF (FTE): 1 staff member
SPECIAL SERVICES/PROGRAMS: exhibits, tours, lectures/presentations
FACILITIES/EQUIPMENT/PRESERVATION: fire extinguishing system
PATRON USE STATISTICS: user statistics not kept

NHPRC OK389-560

Oklahoma Territorial Museum   **TEL**: (405) 282-1889
406 E. Oklahoma
Guthrie, OK 73044

REPORTED BY: Michael Bruce, Curator II
TYPE OF INSTITUTION: museum (state)

HOURS: Tu-F 9-5, Sa 10-4, Su 1-4
ACCESS: public access by appointment only, limited research hours

SERVICES: in-person reference, photocopies

PRIMARY COLLECTION FOCUS: Logan County, City of Guthrie
  Guthrie, OK (local history)
  Logan County, OK

INCLUSIVE DATES: 1889-1913
VOLUME: 4000 items, plus ledgers
COLLECTION FORMATS: manuscript collections (2000), government records (3000), photographs (1000), maps (20)
COLLECTION ACCESS: registers/inventories
STAFF (FTE): 1 administrative, 2 curators
SPECIAL SERVICES/PROGRAMS: exhibits, tours
FACILITIES/EQUIPMENT/PRESERVATION: fire detection controls, disaster preparedness plan
PATRON USE STATISTICS: 150 in-house patrons, 20 telephone, 20 mail reference requests, 30 collections used, 20 reference copies

NHPRC OK406-600

Kingfisher: Chisholm Trail Museum and Governor A. J. Seay Mansion: OK456-120

Museum of the Great Plains
601 Ferris Avenue
P. O. Box 68
Lawton, OK 73502

TEL: (405) 581-3460

REPORTED BY: Deborah Anna Baroff, Curator of Special Collections
TYPE OF INSTITUTION: museum, archives, library (city)

HOURS: M-F 8-5, Sa 10-5:30, Su 1-5:30
ACCESS: open to general public, museum collections by appointment only
SERVICES: in-person, mail, phone reference, photocopies, photographic reproductions (fee)

PRIMARY COLLECTION FOCUS: genealogy, Oklahoma history (archives), Great Plains (museum)
  pioneers
  photography, history of
  archaeology
  Native Americans
  Oklahoma--regional history
  agriculture
  genealogy

INCLUSIVE DATES: Mid-nineteenth century to present
VOLUME: 23,000 volumes, 300,000 documents, 30,000 photographs
COLLECTION FORMATS: manuscript collections (300,000 items), books (23,000), serials (10,000), photographs (30,000), maps
COLLECTION ACCESS: card catalog, repository guide, registers/inventories
ACQUISITION REPORTED TO: OCLC (research library)
STAFF (FTE): photo curator, general archival, preservation, map curator
INSTITUTIONAL SUPPORT FOR PROFESSIONAL DEVELOPMENT: reimbursement for courses, reimbursement for professional meetings, payment for mailings
SPECIAL SERVICES/PROGRAMS: exhibits, tours, newsletter, fund raising/endowment, lectures/presentations
FACILITIES/EQUIPMENT/PRESERVATION: temperature controls & humidity controls, fire detection controls, fire extinguishing system, preservation lab, disaster preparedness plan
PATRON USE STATISTICS: 10 in-house patrons, 6 telephone, 30 mail reference requests, 38 collections

used

NHPRC OK490-520

Pittsburg County Genealogical and Historical Society **TEL**: (918) 426-0388
113 East Carl Albert Parkway
McAlester, OK 74501

REPORTED BY: Lucille Beckham, Librarian
TYPE OF INSTITUTION: library, museum (county/local)

HOURS: M-F 9-3; first Monday night each month, 6-9
ACCESS: open to general public
SERVICES: in-person, mail, phone reference, photocopies

PRIMARY COLLECTION FOCUS: genealogy
    Pittsburg County, OK
    Indian Territory (OK)
    genealogy

VOLUME: 400 plus books, etc.
COLLECTION FORMATS: books/serials, pamphlets/ephemera, films/videotapes, photographs, maps
COLLECTION ACCESS: card catalog
STAFF (FTE): volunteers

Medford: Grant County Historical Society; Grant County Museum: OK524-280

Five Civilized Tribes Museum **TEL**: (918) 683-1701
Agency Hill on Honor Heights Drive
Muskogee, OK 74401

REPORTED BY: Cleathel Robinson, Administrative Assistant
TYPE OF INSTITUTION: library, museum (private)

HOURS: M-Sa 10-5, Su 1-5
ACCESS: public access by appointment only

PRIMARY COLLECTION FOCUS: Five Civilized Tribes
    Cherokee Indians
    Chickasaw Indians
    Choctaw Indians
    Creek Indians
    Seminole Indians
    Five Civilized Tribes
    Native Americans

COLLECTION FORMATS: books/serials, government records, photographs, maps
COLLECTION ACCESS: not described
STAFF (FTE): 3 administrative, 1 grant writer, 2 clerical
SPECIAL SERVICES/PROGRAMS: exhibits, tours, classes, newsletter
PATRON USE STATISTICS: 30,000 in-house patrons, 4,380 telephone, 900 mail reference requests

NHPRC OK541-240

Carl Albert Congressional Research and Studies Center
630 Parrington Oval
Monnet Hall, University of Oklahoma
Norman, OK 73019-0235

TEL: (405) 325-5401
FAX: (405) 325-6419

REPORTED BY: John Caldwell, Assistant Curator
TYPE OF INSTITUTION: archives, library (academic, state)

HOURS: M-F 8-5 (closed on University holidays)
ACCESS: open to the general public
SERVICES: in-person, mail, phone reference, photocopies

PRIMARY COLLECTION FOCUS: U. S. Congress and Members, Oklahoma Politics
- U. S. Congress
- politics
- Oklahoma--politics
- California--politics
- New Jersey--politics
- Kansas--politics
- Civil War
- Wisconsin--politics
- congressional papers

INCLUSIVE DATES: 1850s to present
VOLUME: 4000 cubic feet
COLLECTION FORMATS: manuscript collections (4000 cubic feet), pamphlets/ephemera (within collections), films/videotapes, photos (20,000), maps (500), oral histories (250)
COLLECTION ACCESS: card catalog, registers/inventories, container lists, computerized finding aids (used by staff)
SOFTWARE/SYSTEM: MicroMARC:amc, WordPerfect
STAFF (FTE): 2.5 general archival, 1.5 student
INSTITUTIONAL SUPPORT FOR PROFESSIONAL DEVELOPMENT: tuition reimbursement, reimbursement for professional meetings, payment for mailings, use of facilities/equipment
SPECIAL SERVICES/PROGRAMS: exhibits, tours, classes, newsletter, fund raising/endowment, lectures/presentations
FACILITIES/EQUIPMENT/PRESERVATION: temperature controls
PATRON USE STATISTICS: 70 in-house patrons, 60 telephone, 35 mail reference requests, 35 collections used

---

Oklahoma Museum of Natural History
1335 Asp Avenue
Norman, OK 73019

TEL: (405) 325-4712
FAX: (405) 325-7699

REPORTED BY: Julie Droke, Collections Manager
TYPE OF INSTITUTION: museum (state, academic)

HOURS: Tu-F 10-5, Sa-Su 2-5
ACCESS: open to the general public

PRIMARY COLLECTION FOCUS: natural history, anthropology
- social sciences
- earth sciences
- ethnology
- archaeology
- classics
- life science
- paleontology

paleobotany
anthropology

VOLUME: 3,709,700 specimens
COLLECTION FORMATS: institutional records, films/videotapes, photographs (7000), maps (1000), oral histories (5), artifacts/specimens (3,709,700)
COLLECTION ACCESS: catalog, registers/inventories
STAFF (FTE): 14 administrative/professional, 8 volunteer/docent, 6 student, 2 interns
INSTITUTIONAL SUPPORT FOR PROFESSIONAL DEVELOPMENT: tuition/registration, reimbursement for professional meetings, payment for mailings, use of facilities, use of clerical staff
SPECIAL SERVICES/PROGRAMS: exhibits, tours, classes, newsletter, fund raising/endowment, lectures/presentations
FACILITIES/EQUIPMENT/PRESERVATION: fire detection controls, disaster preparedness plan

---

Western History Collections, University of Oklahoma
630 Parrington Oval, Room 452
Norman, OK 73019

TEL: (405) 325-3641
FAX: (405) 325-2943

REPORTED BY: Donald L. DeWitt, Curator
TYPE OF INSTITUTION: library (academic)

HOURS: M-F 8-5, Sa 8-noon (September-May)
ACCESS: open to the general public
SERVICES: in-house/mail/phone reference, photocopies, photographic prints

PRIMARY COLLECTION FOCUS: history of the Trans-Mississippi West
  Native Americans
  Oklahoma
  American frontier
  West, the (United States)

INCLUSIVE DATES: 1800-1980s
VOLUME: 10,500 linear feet
COLLECTION FORMATS: manuscript collections (10,500), institution's records (2500), books/serials (60,000), films (500), photographs (125,000), maps (3500), oral histories (1500)
COLLECTION ACCESS: container lists, repository guide, computerized finding aids (used by staff, patrons), registers/inventories
SOFTWARE/SYSTEM: RLIN, AMC, SAS
ACQUISITIONS REPORTED TO: RLIN
STAFF: 1 administrative, 1 general archival, 1 librarian, 1 university archivist, 1 clerical
INSTITUTIONAL SUPPORT FOR PROFESSIONAL DEVELOPMENT: reimbursement for professional meetings registration/travel, payment for mailings, payment for telephone use, use of facilities/equipment, use of clerical staff
SPECIAL SERVICES/PROGRAMS: exhibits, tours, fund raising/endowment, lectures/presentations
FACILITIES/EQUIPMENT/PRESERVATION: temperature controls, preservation lab, disaster preparedness plan
PATRON USE STATISTICS: 4244 in-house patrons, 1208 telephone, 399 mail reference requests

NHPRC OK558-790 [includes Carl Albert Center, which has separate entry in this guide]

Episcopal Diocese of Oklahoma Archives
924 North Robinson
Oklahoma City, OK 73102

TEL: none reported

REPORTED BY: Rev. Stan Upchurch
TYPE OF INSTITUTION: Archives (religious)

HOURS: W 10-2 or by appointment
ACCESS: public access by appointment only
SERVICES: in-person reference, mail reference

PRIMARY COLLECTION FOCUS: church business, Bishops' papers
    Bishops' papers
    church history
    mission records
    Episcopal Church

INCLUSIVE DATES: 1871 to present
COLLECTION ACCESS: descriptive aids only begun, will have computerized finding aids (used by staff)
SOFTWARE/SYSTEM: Minaret
STAFF (FTE): 1 administrative, 2 volunteer/docent
INSTITUTIONAL SUPPORT FOR PROFESSIONAL DEVELOPMENT: tuition/registration reimbursement, dues payment, professional meetings reimbursement, payment for mailings, telephone use
SPECIAL SERVICES/PROGRAMS: exhibits, classes
FACILITIES/EQUIPMENT/PRESERVATION: temperature controls, fire extinguishing system, humidity controls, fire detection controls, disaster preparedness plan
PATRON USE STATISTICS: 20 in-house patrons, 10 telephone, 80 mail reference requests, 4 collections used, 20 reference photocopies

---

Forty-fifth Infantry Division Museum
2145 N.E. 36th
Oklahoma City, OK 73111

TEL: (405) 424-5313

REPORTED BY: Michael E. Gonzales, Curator
TYPE OF INSTITUTION: museum (state)

HOURS: M-F 9-5, Sa 10-5, Su 1-5
ACCESS: open to the general public
SERVICES: photocopies

PRIMARY COLLECTION FOCUS: military history, Oklahoma
    military history
    Oklahoma

INCLUSIVE DATES: 1830-present
COLLECTION FORMATS: manuscript collections (30 linear feet), books/serials (1000 linear feet), pamphlets/ephemera (1000 linear feet), films/videotapes, photographs (4000 linear feet), maps (800 linear feet), oral histories (600 hours)
COLLECTION ACCESS: registers/inventories
STAFF (FTE): 1 historian/curator, 68 volunteer/docent, 2 clerical
INSTITUTIONAL SUPPORT FOR PROFESSIONAL DEVELOPMENT: payment of dues for professional organization memberships, reimbursement for meetings, registration/travel, payment for telephone use
SPECIAL SERVICES/PROGRAMS: exhibits
FACILITIES/EQUIPMENT/PRESERVATION: temperature controls, fire detection controls, disaster preparedness plan
PATRON USE STATISTICS: 37,000 in-house

Oklahoma City University/Oklahoma United Methodist Archives **TEL**: (405) 521-5067
2501 N. Blackwelder
Oklahoma City, OK 73106

REPORTED BY: Joan McCullough, Archivist
TYPE OF INSTITUTION: archives, library (state, academic, religious)

HOURS: M-F 8:30-12:30, 1:30-4:30
ACCESS: open to the general public
SERVICES: in-person, mail, phone reference, photocopies

PRIMARY COLLECTION FOCUS: Oklahoma City University, Okla. Conference, United Methodist Church
    United Methodist Church (OK)
    Oklahoma City University (records)
    Methodist Church

INCLUSIVE DATES: 1840s to present
COLLECTION FORMATS: institution's records, books/serials, pamphlets, films/videotapes, photographs,
    maps, oral histories, other
COLLECTION ACCESS: card catalog, container lists, registers/inventories, not described
STAFF (FTE): 1 other
INSTITUTIONAL SUPPORT FOR PROFESSIONAL DEVELOPMENT: tuition/registration reimbursement,
    payment of dues for professional organizations, payment for mailings, use of facilities, payment for
    telephone use
FACILITIES/EQUIPMENT/PRESERVATION: fire detection controls
PATRON USE STATISTICS: 100 in-house patrons, 65 telephone, 25 mail reference requests, 2 collections
    used, 10-50 reference copies

NHPRC OK592-780

Oklahoma County Historical Society **TEL**: (405) 521-1889
4300 Sewell
Oklahoma City, OK 73118

REPORTED BY: Pendleton Woods, Museum Chairman
TYPE OF INSTITUTION: archives, historical society, library, museum (county/local)

HOURS: M, W, F 10-3
ACCESS: open to the general public
SERVICES: in-person reference

PRIMARY COLLECTION FOCUS: Oklahoma County
    Oklahoma County (local history)
    Oklahoma City
    historic preservation

COLLECTION FORMATS: books/serials, photographs
COLLECTION ACCESS: not described
STAFF (FTE): 0.3 administration
SPECIAL SERVICES/PROGRAMS: exhibits, tours

Oklahoma City: Oklahoma Heritage Association, Archives Division: OK592-630

Oklahoma Department of Libraries
200 N.E. 18th
Oklahoma City, OK 73105

TEL: (405) 521-2502
FAX: (405) 525-7804

REPORTED BY: Gary Harrington, Head, State Archives Division
TYPE OF INSTITUTION: archives, library (State)

HOURS: M-F 8-5
ACCESS: open to the general public
SERVICES: in-person, mail, phone reference, photocopies, microforms
RESTRICTIONS: maps/some registers not copied, other copies at discretion of Head

PRIMARY COLLECTION FOCUS: state agency permanent and non-permanent records
    Oklahoma--executive branch
    Oklahoma--legislative branch
    Oklahoma--judicial branch
    Oklahoma Territory

INCLUSIVE DATES: 1870s to present
VOLUME: 27,000 cubic feet (archives) and 22,000 cubic feet (records center)
COLLECTION FORMATS: manuscript collections (1000 cubic feet), government records (47,850 cubic feet), photographs (100 cubic feet), maps (50 cubic feet)
COLLECTION ACCESS: repository guide, registers/inventories, container lists, computerized finding aids (used by staff)
ACQUISITION REPORTED TO: OCLC, NOTIS

STAFF (FTE): 1 administrative, 3 general archival, 4 records managers, 3 micrographic technicians, 6 support staff
INSTITUTIONAL SUPPORT FOR PROFESSIONAL DEVELOPMENT: tuition/registration reimbursement for courses, reimbursement for professional meeting registration, use of facilities and equipment
SPECIAL SERVICES/PROGRAMS: tours, classes, newsletter, lectures/presentations
FACILITIES/EQUIPMENT/PRESERVATION: temperature controls & humidity controls, fire detection controls, fire extinguishing system, preservation lab, disaster preparedness plan
PATRON USE STATISTICS: 3,036 in-house patrons, 3,682 telephone, 955 mail reference requests, 20-30/month collections used, numerous reference copies, 31,070 microfiche, 24,515 feet of microfilm

NHPRC OK592-620

Oklahoma Historical Society
2100 North Lincoln Blvd.
Oklahoma City, OK 73105

TEL: (405) 521-2491
FAX: (405) 525-3272

REPORTED BY: William D. Welge, Director, Archives and Manuscripts Division
TYPE OF INSTITUTION: historical society (state)

HOURS: M-Sa 9-5
ACCESS: open to the general public
SERVICES: in-person, mail reference, photocopies

PRIMARY COLLECTION FOCUS: Native Americans, diaries, letters, journals, business records
    Native Americans
    historians
    Oklahoma--history
    WPA
    Federal Writers Project
    Oklahoma--government
    Oklahoma--politics

Indian Territory (OK)
business history
Five Civilized Tribes

INCLUSIVE DATES: 1840s-1930s
VOLUME: 2500 cubic feet

COLLECTION FORMATS: manuscript collections (2000 cubic feet), institution's records (50 cubic feet), books/serials (6100), films/videos (1,000,000 feet), photographs (165,000), maps (650), oral histories (62,000)
COLLECTION ACCESS: card catalog, registers/inventories
ACQUISITION REPORTED TO: NUCMC
STAFF (FTE): 1 administrative, 1 photo curator, 3 general archival, 5 preservation, 3 other (professional), 1 volunteer/docent, 1 clerical, 3 interns
INSTITUTIONAL SUPPORT FOR PROFESSIONAL DEVELOPMENT: tuition/registration reimbursement for courses, reimbursement for professional meetings registration/travel, use of facilities/equipment
SPECIAL SERVICES/PROGRAMS: exhibits, tours, classes, lectures/presentations
FACILITIES/EQUIPMENT/PRESERVATION: temperature controls, humidity controls, fire detection controls, fire extinguishing system
PATRON USE STATISTICS: 10,000 in-house patrons, 7,800 telephone, 2,500 mail reference requests

NHPRC OK592-640

Oklahoma City: The Ninety-Nines, Inc., Library and Archives: OK592-570

Oklahoma City: Oklahoma Christian College, Oklahoma Living Legends: OK592-580

Oklahoma City: Oklahoma Historical Society, Library Resources Division: OK592-650

Okmulgee: Creek Council House Museum, Archives: OK609-120

Ponca City: Ponca City Cultural Center Museum: OK634-640

Pawnee County Historical Society　　　　　　　　　　　　　　　　　　　　　　　　　　**TEL**: (918) 762-3881
P. O. Box 472
Pawnee, OK 74058

REPORTED BY: Dana Hicks, President
TYPE OF INSTITUTION: historical society (county/local)

HOURS: not given
ACCESS: by appointment only

PRIMARY COLLECTION FOCUS: Pawnee County
Pawnee County, OK (local history)
education

COLLECTION FORMATS: photographs (500), oral histories (10)
COLLECTION ACCESS: not described
SPECIAL SERVICES/PROGRAMS: exhibits

Eastern Oklahoma Historical Society　　　　　　　　　　　　　　　　　　　　　　　　　　**TEL**: (918) 647-8221
Rt. 1, Box 111
Poteau, OK 74953

REPORTED BY: Laird and Ruth King
TYPE OF INSTITUTION: historical society, museum (county/local)

HOURS: 1-4 daily
ACCESS: open to the general public
RESTRICTIONS: Kerr Home tours limited by occupancy at time of visit

PRIMARY COLLECTION FOCUS: Eastern Oklahoma
    Kerr, Robert S.
    Oklahoma, Eastern--history
    Choctaw Indians
    Spiro Mounds
    Runestone, Heavener
    Native Americans

COLLECTION ACCESS: not described
STAFF (FTE): volunteer/docent
INSTITUTIONAL SUPPORT FOR PROFESSIONAL DEVELOPMENT: use of facilities and equipment permitted, payment for telephone use
SPECIAL SERVICES/PROGRAMS: exhibits, tours

McClain County Historical Society and Museum
203 Washington Street
Purcell, OK 73080

TEL: (405) 527-5894

REPORTED BY: Joyce A. Rex, Historian
TYPE OF INSTITUTION: historical society, museum

HOURS: 12-4 weekdays, Su 2-4
ACCESS: open to the general public
SERVICES: in-person reference

PRIMARY COLLECTION FOCUS: McClain County
    McClain County, OK (local history)
    Blanchard, OK
    Purcell, OK

COLLECTION FORMATS: photographs (1000), oral histories (25), microfilmed territorial family records
COLLECTION ACCESS: registers/inventories, repository guide
STAFF (FTE): 12 volunteer/docent, 1 other
SPECIAL SERVICES/PROGRAMS: newsletter
FACILITIES/EQUIPMENT/PRESERVATION: temperature controls, humidity controls

---

Sapulpa: Sapulpa Historical Society, Inc.; Sapulpa Historical Museum: OK685-710

Sapulpa: Sapulpa Public Library: OK685-720

Historical Society of Pottawatomie County
614 East Main Street
P. O. Box 114
Shawnee, OK 74801

TEL: (405) 275-8412

REPORTED BY: Andrew P. Wilson, Curator
TYPE OF INSTITUTION: historical society, museum (private)

HOURS: Tu-F 10-4, Su 2-4
ACCESS: open to the general public
SERVICES: in-person, mail, phone reference

PRIMARY COLLECTION FOCUS: Pottawatomie County
    Pottawatomie County, OK
    railroads

COLLECTION FORMATS: manuscript collections (600), institution's records (3), books/serials (600), pamphlets/ephemera (500), films/videotapes (4), government records (100), photographs (4500), maps (25), oral histories (27)
COLLECTION ACCESS: card catalog
ACQUISITION REPORTED TO: Oklahoma Museums Association, Oklahoma Historical Society
STAFF (FTE): volunteer/docent
SPECIAL SERVICES/PROGRAMS: exhibits, tours
FACILITIES/EQUIPMENT/PRESERVATION: temperature controls

NHPRC OK763-640

Shawnee: Oklahoma Baptist University: OK736-600

Special Collections & University Archives, Oklahoma State University
Oklahoma State University Library
Stillwater, OK 74078

TEL: (405) 744-6311
FAX: (405) 744-5183

REPORTED BY: Heather M. Lloyd, Associate Professor & Head, Special Collections/Archives
TYPE OF INSTITUTION: library (academic)

HOURS: M-F 8-5
ACCESS: open to the general public
SERVICES: in-person/mail/phone reference; photocopies; photographs off-site

PRIMARY COLLECTION FOCUS: Oklahoma State University and surrounding area
    Oklahoma State University (records)
    Oklahoma--agriculture
    Oklahoma--politics
    water resources
    agriculture
    politics
    journalism

INCLUSIVE DATES: 1890 to present
VOLUME: 6072 linear feet
COLLECTION FORMATS: manuscript collections (1722 linear feet), institution's records (2946 linear feet), books/serials (723 linear feet), pamphlets (147 linear feet), films (372 linear feet), government records (9 linear feet), photographs (153), maps (350), oral histories (25)
COLLECTION ACCESS: card catalog, container lists, computerized finding aids (used by staff, patrons), registers
SOFTWARE/SYSTEM: NOTIS (for University Library and OCLC)
STAFF: 1 administrative, 2 general archival, .08 volunteer, 2 clerical, 2.5 student
INSTITUTIONAL SUPPORT FOR PROFESSIONAL DEVELOPMENT: tuition/registration reimbursement, reimbursement for professional meetings registration/travel, use of facilities/equipment permitted

SPECIAL SERVICES/PROGRAMS: exhibits, tours, lectures/presentations
FACILITIES/EQUIPMENT/PRESERVATION: temperature controls, humidity controls, fire detection controls, disaster preparedness plan
PATRON USE STATISTICS: user statistics not kept (will be next year)

NHPRC OK753-600

Tahlequah: Cherokee National Historical Society/Museum: OK778-120

Tahlequah: Northeastern Oklahoma State University, Library: OK778-560

Tonkawa: Northern Oklahoma College, Library: OK812-560

Thomas Gilcrease Institute of American History and Art
1400 Gilcrease Museum Road
Tulsa, OK 74127

TEL: (918) 582-3122
FAX: (918) 592-2248

REPORTED BY: Sarah Erwin, Curator of Archival Collections
TYPE OF INSTITUTION: museum (city)

HOURS: Library M-F 9-12, 1-4:45, Museum M-Sa 9-5, Su/holidays 1-5
ACCESS: public access to library by appointment only
SERVICES: in-person, mail, phone reference, photocopies
RESTRICTIONS: no photocopies of manuscripts, rare books, or historic photos

PRIMARY COLLECTION FOCUS: American History, 1492 through 19th century, Native Americans
    United States, Western--exploration
    history--U.S.
    Native Americans
    Five Civilized Tribes
    West, the (United States)

INCLUSIVE DATES: 1492-1900
VOLUME: 100,000
COLLECTION FORMATS: manuscript collections (40,000), books/serials (50,000), pamphlets/ephemera (1000), government records (500), photographs (10,000), maps (1000)
COLLECTION ACCESS: repository guide for manuscripts only
STAFF (FTE): 1 general archival, 3 volunteer/docent

NHPRC OK829-520

University of Tulsa
600 South College Ave
Tulsa, OK 74104-3189

TEL: (918) 631-2496
FAX: (918) 631-3791

REPORTED BY: Lori N. Curtis, Assistant Curator of Special Collections
TYPE OF INSTITUTION: archives, library (academic)

HOURS: M-F 8-5
ACCESS: public access by appointment only
SERVICES: in-person, mail, phone reference, photocopies, other reproduction

PRIMARY COLLECTION FOCUS: modern literature, oil industry, World War I, VietNam, Native Americans
    literature, world

American literature
British literature
Irish literature
petroleum industry
World War I
Vietnam War--literature
Native Americans
Native Americans--literature
Native Americans--law

INCLUSIVE DATES: 17th - 20th centuries
VOLUME: 125,000 books, 3000 linear feet of manuscripts
COLLECTION FORMATS: manuscript collections (2000 linear feet), institution's records (1000 linear feet), books/serials (125,000), pamphlets/ephemera, government records (500 linear feet), photographs, maps (100)
COLLECTION ACCESS: registers/inventories, computerized finding aids (used by staff, patrons)
SOFTWARE/SYSTEM: on-line catalog, Lias-TV, PC-File, WordPerfect
ACQUISITION REPORTED TO: OCLC
STAFF (FTE): 2 administrative/general archival, 2.5 clerical, .25 student
INSTITUTIONAL SUPPORT FOR PROFESSIONAL DEVELOPMENT: tuition/registration reimbursement for courses, reimbursement for professional meeting registration/travel, payment for mailings/telephone, use of facilities/clerical staff
SPECIAL SERVICES/PROGRAMS: exhibits, lectures/presentations, guides, exhibit catalogs, other publications
FACILITIES/EQUIPMENT/PRESERVATIONS: temperature controls & humidity controls, fire detection controls, preservation lab, disaster preparedness plan
PATRON USE STATISTICS: 800 in-house patrons, 175 collections used, 10,500 reference photocopies, other statistics not kept

NHPRC OK829-790

Tulsa: Tulsa County Historical Society: OK829-770

Vinita: Vintita Public Library: OK854-840

Wewoka: Seminole Nation Museum: OK922-720

Plains Indians and Pioneers Museum and Art Gallery
2009 Williams
P. O. Box 1167
Woodward, OK 73802

TEL: (405) 256-2002

REPORTED BY: Louise B. James, Curator
TYPE OF INSTITUTION: archives, museum (private foundation)

HOURS: Tu-Sa 10-5, Su 1-4
ACCESS: museum open to general public, archives by appointment
SERVICES: in-person and mail reference, photocopies
RESTRICTIONS: limited staffing precludes extensive research reference

PRIMARY COLLECTION FOCUS: Woodward, OK, and vicinity
Woodward, OK (local history)
Oklahoma--Northwest
Temple Houston
agriculture
ranching

INCLUSIVE DATES: 1893 to present
COLLECTION FORMATS: manuscript collections, books/series (1,000), films/videotapes (50), photographs (4,000), maps, oral histories (300)
COLLECTION ACCESS: card catalog in progress
STAFF (FTE): 1 administrative, 1 general archival, 20 volunteer/docent, 1 clerical
INSTITUTIONAL SUPPORT FOR PROFESSIONAL DEVELOPMENT: reimbursement for professional meeting registration and travel, payment for mailings
SPECIAL SERVICES/PROGRAMS: exhibits, tours, newsletter, fund raising/endowment, lectures/presentations
FACILITIES/EQUIPMENT/PRESERVATION: temperature controls, fire detection controls
PATRON USE STATISTICS: 12,000

NHPRC OK956-640

TEXAS

Abilene Christian University
1600 Campus Court
ACU Station, Box 8177
Abilene, TX 79699

TEL: (915) 674-2538
FAX: (915) 674-2202

REPORTED BY: Erma Jean Loveland, Special Services Librarian
TYPE OF INSTITUTION: library (academic)

HOURS: Callie Faye Milliken Special Collections/ACU Archives, weekdays, 1-5
ACCESS: open to the general public: 1-5; by appointment only: 8-12
SERVICES: in-person, mail, phone, copies, fees
RESTRICTIONS: Materials are not taken from the room. Photocopies may be made on request of most materials, depending on their condition. Some collections are closed.
PRIMARY COLLECTION FOCUS: ACU Institutional; Hon. Omar Burleson, U.S. Rep 1947-1979; Herald of Truth national radio and television program; Christian Chronicle archives; Restoration Studies of Church of Christ
- Abilene Christian University (records)
- Church of Christ
- Burleson, Omar
- railroads
- religion
- education

INCLUSIVE DATES: 1476-
COLLECTION FORMATS: 116 linear feet manuscript collections, 475 linear feet institution's records, 8935 books, 87.5 linear feet pamphlets, 1242 films, 3945 photographs, 154 oral histories, 5801 cassettes
COLLECTION ACCESS: card catalog, container lists, computerized finding aids (used by staff), registers, other: cataloged materials are accessible on Abilene Library consortium online catalog
SOFTWARE/SYSTEM: WordPerfect 5.1, DataPerfect 2.1
ACQUISITION REPORTED TO: OCLC
STAFF (FTE): 1 administrative, 6 volunteer/docent (.3 FTE), 1 clerical (1 FTE), 3 student (.75 FTE)
INSTITUTIONAL SUPPORT FOR PROFESSIONAL DEVELOPMENT: professional meetings registration/travel (up to $400), workshops, mailings, telephone, use of facilities
SPECIAL SERVICES/PROGRAMS: exhibits, classes, newsletter, fund raising, lectures
FACILITIES/EQUIPMENT/PRESERVATION: temperature controls, fire detection controls, fire extinguishing system
PATRON USE STATISTICS: user statistics not kept

Hardin-Simmons University
2400 Hickory
Box 1172, HSU
Abilene, TX 79698

TEL: (915) 670-1239

REPORTED BY: Dr B. W. Aston, Director, Rupert Richardson Research Center for the Southwest
TYPE OF INSTITUTION: archives, library (academic, religious)

HOURS: M-F 8-5
ACCESS: open, by appointment
SERVICES: in-person, mail, phone, photocopies

PRIMARY COLLECTION FOCUS: papers of local lawyers, businessmen, and representatives
- Crane, R. C.
- Latimer, Truett
- Simmons, James B.
- Wolfe, Thomas

Grubbs, Walter
lawyers
ranching
business history

VOLUME: "small"
COLLECTION FORMATS: manuscript collections, books (some circulate), 12,000 photographs, maps, oral histories
COLLECTION ACCESS: card catalog, guide, not described
STAFF (FTE): Dr. Aston is in the History Dept., other (non-professional--number not reported)
INSTITUTIONAL SUPPORT FOR PROFESSIONAL DEVELOPMENT: mailings, telephone, facilities, clerical
SPECIAL SERVICES/PROGRAMS: lectures, other
PATRON USE STATISTICS: 100 telephone patrons, 25 mail reference requests, other user statistics not kept

NHPRC TX7-320

Archives, NW Texas Conference of the United Methodist Church   **TEL**: none reported
McMurry University
Sayles Blvd. at S. 14th
Box 296, McMurry University
Abilene, TX 79697

REPORTED BY: Jewell Posey and Pat Williamson, Archivists
TYPE OF INSTITUTION: archives (religious)

HOURS: M-Th, 15 hours weekly (flexible schedule)
ACCESS: by appointment
SERVICES: in-person, copies

PRIMARY COLLECTION FOCUS: records of the NW Texas Conference of the United Methodist Church
United Methodist Church--Northwest Texas Conference
religion
Methodist Church
church history

INCLUSIVE DATES: 1866-
VOLUME: ca. 220 shelf feet
COLLECTION FORMATS: books, oral histories, clippings
COLLECTION ACCESS: guide, container lists
STAFF (FTE): two part-time archivists
INSTITUTIONAL SUPPORT FOR PROFESSIONAL DEVELOPMENT: dues, meetings registration
SPECIAL SERVICES/PROGRAMS: exhibits (occasional)
PATRON USE STATISTICS: user statistics not kept

NHPRC TX7-800

The Old Jail Art Center - Shackelford County Archives   **TEL**: (915) 762-2269
211 South Second
Route One, Box One
Albany, TX 76430

REPORTED BY: Joan Farmer, Archivist
TYPE OF INSTITUTION: archives, museum (non-profit art museum/depository for historical archives)

HOURS: T-Sa 10-5; Su 2-5; closed Mondays & major holidays

ACCESS: Open
SERVICES: in-person reference, mail, phone, fee, photocopies

PRIMARY COLLECTION FOCUS: history of Shackelford County and extended area
   Shackelford County, TX (local history)
   Fort Griffin, TX

INCLUSIVE DATES: 1874-1991
COLLECTION FORMATS: manuscript collections, institution's records, books, pamphlets, films, government records, over 3000 photographs, maps, other
COLLECTION ACCESS: by catalog number and description
STAFF (FTE): general archival [number not reported]
INSTITUTIONAL SUPPORT FOR PROFESSIONAL DEVELOPMENT: memberships, mailings, telephone, facilities, clerical
SPECIAL SERVICES/PROGRAMS: exhibits, tours, lectures
FACILITIES/EQUIPMENT/PRESERVATION: temperature controls, humidity controls, fire detection controls, fire extinguishing system, disaster preparedness plan
PATRON USE STATISTICS: ca. 100 in-house patrons, 50 telephone, all collections used, other user statistics not kept

---

Archives of the Big Bend
Bryan Wildenthal Library, Sul Ross State University
Box C-149, Sul Ross State University
Alpine, TX 79832

TEL: (915) 837-8127
FAX: (915) 837-8400

REPORTED BY: Melleta Bell, Archivist
TYPE OF INSTITUTION: archives, library (academic)

HOURS: M-F 8-12; 1-5 excepting school holiday periods
ACCESS: Open
SERVICES: in-person reference, photocopies
RESTRICTIONS: A few collections have reproduction restrictions. Reproductions of materials in collections limited to reasonable amount and compliance with copyright restrictions.

PRIMARY COLLECTION FOCUS: Big Bend/Trans Pecos region of Texas
   Texas--Trans-Pecos region
   Big Bend National Park, TX
   ranching
   Alpine, TX (local history)
   Sul Ross State University (records)
   mining
   Native Americans
   Fort Davis, TX (local history)
   banking
   religion

INCLUSIVE DATES: ca. 1711-
COLLECTION FORMATS: 992 cubic feet manuscript collections, 176 cubic feet institution's records, 8073 volumes books, 8 cubic feet pamphlets, 25 films/videotapes, 15,000 photographs, 415 maps, 186 oral histories, 960 senior theses, 1450 titles sheet music and sound recordings
COLLECTION ACCESS: card catalog, guide, registers, container lists, computerized finding aids (used by staff)
SOFTWARE/SYSTEM: dBase III+
ACQUISITION REPORTED TO: NUCMC (after processing)
STAFF (FTE): 1 general archival, .25 volunteer, 1 clerical, 1 student
INSTITUTIONAL SUPPORT FOR PROFESSIONAL DEVELOPMENT: tuition
SPECIAL SERVICES/PROGRAMS: exhibits, tours

FACILITIES/EQUIPMENT/PRESERVATION: temperature controls
PATRON USE STATISTICS: 555 in-house patrons, 23 telephone, 14 mail reference requests, 208 collections used (manuscripts only; 1150 total for all materials), 2146 reference photocopies

NHPRC TX14-720

Diocesan Pastoral Center
1800 N. Spring Street, Amarillo, TX 79107
P. O. Box 5644, Amarillo, TX 79117-5644

TEL: (806) 383-2243
FAX: (806) 383-8452

REPORTED BY: Sister Christine Jensen, Archivist
TYPE OF INSTITUTION: archives (religious)

HOURS: M-F 10-4
ACCESS: appointment
SERVICES: photocopies (small fee for copies), other

PRIMARY COLLECTION FOCUS: holdings of the Diocese of Amarillo
  Catholic Church
  Diocese of Amarillo
  religion

INCLUSIVE DATES: 1927-
COLLECTION FORMATS: manuscript collections, institution's records, books, pamphlets, photographs
COLLECTION ACCESS: not described
STAFF (FTE): 1 general archival
INSTITUTIONAL SUPPORT FOR PROFESSIONAL DEVELOPMENT: dues, meetings, mailings, telephone, facilities
PATRON USE STATISTICS: user statistics not kept

NHPRC TX21-690

Brazoria County Historical Museum
100 East Cedar
Angleton, TX 77515

TEL: (409) 849-5711 x1208

REPORTED BY: Linda Wood, Research Library Coordinator
TYPE OF INSTITUTION: museum (state, county/local)

HOURS: M-F 8-5
ACCESS: open
SERVICES: in-person, mail, phone, fee, copies, photographs

PRIMARY COLLECTION FOCUS: history of Brazoria County and Texas
  Brazoria County, TX (local history)
  genealogy

INCLUSIVE DATES: 1800s-
COLLECTION FORMATS: 750 books, 5 films, 300 photographs, 50 maps, 200 oral histories
  video & slide shows circulate
COLLECTION ACCESS: Card catalog
STAFF (FTE): 1 professional
FACILITIES/EQUIPMENT/PRESERVATION: temperature controls, fire detection controls, fire extinguishing system, disaster preparedness plan

PATRON USE STATISTICS: user statistics not kept

Angleton: Brazoria County Library System: NHPRC TX35-90

Fielder Museum and Historic Cabins **TEL**: (817) 460-4001
1616 West Abram Street
Arlington, TX 76013

REPORTED BY: Dorothy Rencurrel, Interim Director
TYPE OF INSTITUTION: Archives, Historical Society (non-profit organization with some funding from city)

HOURS: W-F, 10-4; Sa-Su, 1:30-4:30
ACCESS: open
SERVICES: in person reference, mail, phone, fee (usually postage/copy), copies (fee)

PRIMARY COLLECTION FOCUS: Heritage of the City of Arlington & surrounding areas
    Arlington, TX (local history)

COLLECTION FORMATS: ca. 100 photographs, 5 maps, 2 oral histories
COLLECTION ACCESS: computerized finding aids (used by staff)
SOFTWARE/SYSTEM: Tandy
STAFF (FTE): volunteer/docent, clerical [number not reported]
SPECIAL SERVICES/PROGRAMS: exhibits, classes, newsletter, fund raising, lectures
FACILITIES/EQUIPMENT/PRESERVATION: temperature controls, humidity controls, fire detection controls,
    fire extinguishing system, disaster preparedness plan
PATRON USE STATISTICS: 150 in-house patrons, 500 telephone, 100 mail reference requests, 75
    collections used

University of Texas at Arlington Libraries - Special Collections **TEL**: (817) 273-3393
701 S. College **FAX**: (817) 794-5797
Box 19497
Arlington, TX 76019-0497

REPORTED BY: Shirley R. Rodnitzky, Special Collections Archivist
TYPE OF INSTITUTION: library (academic)

HOURS: M-F, 8-5; Sa 10-2; closed Sa/Su during intersessions; closed major holidays
ACCESS: open
SERVICES: in-person reference, mail, phone, photocopies, photographs
RESTRICTIONS: 30 minutes research limit for mail & phone reference

PRIMARY COLLECTION FOCUS: Texas

    Texas--history
    politics
    labor unions
    Mexican War
    University of Texas at Arlington (records)
    Mexico
    cartography
    Southwestern U.S.
    Robertson Colony (Texas)
    Honduras

INCLUSIVE DATES: 1493-
COLLECTION FORMATS: 3763 manuscript collections & institution's records, 26,061 books & pamphlets, 25 films, 239 volumes government records, 423,602 photographs, 5600 maps, 111 oral histories, 1892 titles, other (sheet music, broadsides, newspapers)
COLLECTION ACCESS: card catalog, guide, register, on-line computerized finding aids access
SOFTWARE/SYSTEM: NOTIS system
ACQUISITION REPORTED TO: NUCMC, OCLC, journal(s), SSA Newsletter
STAFF (FTE): 2 administrative, 5 general archival, 1 photo curator, 1 librarian, 1 historian, 2 clerical, 5 student, intern (number varies)
INSTITUTIONAL SUPPORT FOR PROFESSIONAL DEVELOPMENT: tuition, meetings, mailings, telephone, use of facilities, clerical
SPECIAL SERVICES/PROGRAMS: exhibits, tours, newsletter, fund raising, lectures
FACILITIES/EQUIPMENT/PRESERVATION: temperature controls, fire detection controls, preservation lab, disaster preparedness plan
PATRON USE STATISTICS: 2114 in-house patrons, 1106 telephone, 181 mail reference requests, 371 reference photocopies

NHPRC TX42-810

Austin Presbyterian Theological Seminary - Stitt Library
100 East 27th Street
Austin, TX 78705

TEL: (512) 472-6736
FAX: (512) 479-0738

REPORTED BY: Dr. Valerie R. Hotchkiss, Library Director
TYPE OF INSTITUTION: library (religious)

HOURS: M-Th 8am-11pm; F 8-5; Sa 10-5; Su 3-8
ACCESS: open
SERVICES: in-person, mail, phone

PRIMARY COLLECTION FOCUS: Southwestern Presbyterianism; communion tokens
    religion
    Presbyterian Church
    church history

VOLUME: 150 linear feet
COLLECTION FORMATS: ca. 15-20 linear feet manuscript collections, 6-10 linear feet institution's records, 138,000 books, ca. 10-15 linear feet pamphlets, ca. 250 photographs, ca. 10,000 communion tokens
COLLECTION ACCESS: card catalog
ACQUISITION REPORTED TO: OCLC
STAFF: 6.5 FTE (2 professional) but none dedicated to archives
INSTITUTIONAL SUPPORT FOR PROFESSIONAL DEVELOPMENT: tuition, dues, meetings, mailings, facilities
SPECIAL SERVICES/PROGRAMS: exhibits, tours, newsletter, fund raising
FACILITIES/EQUIPMENT/PRESERVATION: fire detection controls, fire extinguishing system,
PATRON USE STATISTICS: not kept for archives in particular

NHPRC TX56-30

Austin Public Library - Austin History Center
810 Guadalupe Street
P. O. Box 2287
Austin, TX 78768-2287

TEL: (512) 499-7480
FAX: (512) 499-7516

REPORTED BY: Jan Hudson Berry, Associate Archivist
TYPE OF INSTITUTION: archives, library (city)

HOURS: M-Th 9-9, F-Sa 9-6, Su 12-6
ACCESS: open (Records Management not open to general public)
SERVICES: in-person, mail, phone, copies, photograph (fee)

PRIMARY COLLECTION FOCUS: historical and current information on Austin & Travis County
    Austin, TX
    Travis County, TX (local history)

INCLUSIVE DATES: 1830-
COLLECTION FORMATS: 2000 linear feet manuscript collections, 58,000 books, 1500 serials, 190,000 pamphlets, 1800 films, 600,000 photographs, 1000 maps, 800 (sound) oral histories, 11,500 slides, 25,500 drawings & architectural documents
COLLECTION ACCESS: card catalog, registers, newspaper index, computerized finding aids (used by staff, patrons)
SOFTWARE/SYSTEM: DOBIS, locally developed
ACQUISITION REPORTED TO: OCLC
STAFF (FTE): 2 administrative, 1 general archival, .75 map curator, 1 photo archivist, 4.8 other professional, 20-25 volunteer/docent, 2.5 clerical, .5 photo restoration technician
INSTITUTIONAL SUPPORT FOR PROFESSIONAL DEVELOPMENT: tuition
SPECIAL SERVICES/PROGRAMS: exhibits, tours, newsletter, fund raising, lectures, Waterloo Press has published books, maps, posters, postcards
FACILITIES/EQUIPMENT/PRESERVATION: temperature controls, humidity controls (vault only), fire detection controls
PATRON USE STATISTICS: 15,000 in-house patrons, 11,000 telephone patrons, 250 mail reference requests

NHPRC TX56-50

Catholic Archives of Texas
1600 N. Congress Avenue
P.O. Box 13327 Capitol Station
Austin, TX 78711

TEL: (512) 476-4888

REPORTED BY: Kinga Perzynska, Archivist
TYPE OF INSTITUTION: archives (religious)

HOURS: M-F 8-5
ACCESS: appointment
SERVICES: In-person, mail, phone, fee (donations), photocopies, sacramental records, photocopies

PRIMARY COLLECTION FOCUS: central depository for records and documents pertaining to the activities of the Catholic Church in Texas
    Catholic Church
    Texas Catholic Conference
    Knights of Columbus
    religion
    church history

INCLUSIVE DATES: 16th century-
VOLUME: 1250 linear feet
COLLECTION FORMATS: 440 linear feet manuscript collections, 500 linear feet institution's records, 170 linear feet books, 20,000 linear feet films, 501 linear feet photographs, 10 linear feet oral histories, 60 linear feet personal papers
COLLECTION ACCESS: card catalog, registers, container lists, computerized finding aids (used by staff)

SOFTWARE/SYSTEM: CAT Alpha-4 database
STAFF (FTE): general archival, volunteer/docent [numbers not specified]
INSTITUTIONAL SUPPORT FOR PROFESSIONAL DEVELOPMENT: tuition, memberships, meetings registration/travel, mailings, telephone, facilities, clerical
SPECIAL SERVICES/PROGRAMS: exhibits, tours, classes, lectures, meetings
FACILITIES/EQUIPMENT/PRESERVATION: temperature controls, humidity controls, fire detection controls, fire extinguishing system
PATRON USE STATISTICS: 20 in-house patrons, 300 telephone, 250 mail reference requests, 272 collections used, 100 reference photocopies, 100 microfilm/fiche copies

NHPRC TX56-110

Charles E. Stevens American Atheist Library and Archives
7215 Cameron Road, Austin, TX 78752
P. O. Box 14505, Austin, TX 78761

TEL: (512) 458-1271
FAX: (512) 467-9525

REPORTED BY: Robin Murray-O'Hair, Director
TYPE OF INSTITUTION: archives, library (special)

HOURS: by appointment
ACCESS: by appointment
SERVICES: mail, copies

PRIMARY COLLECTION FOCUS: atheism, free thought, and dissent to religion
   atheism
   free thought
   religion

INCLUSIVE DATES: 1660-
VOLUME: 100,000+
COLLECTION FORMATS: 500 manuscript collections, 50,000 institution's records, 80,000 books, 20,000 pamphlets, 1000 films, 2000 photographs, 100 oral histories
COLLECTION ACCESS: not described
STAFF (FTE): 2
FACILITIES/EQUIPMENT/PRESERVATION: temperature controls, humidity controls, fire detection controls
PATRON USE STATISTICS: ca. 20 in-house patrons, ca. 100 telephone, ca. 500 mail reference requests, ca. 100 reference photocopies

---

Harry Ransom Humanities Research Center
21st Street & Guadalupe
P. O. Drawer 7219, The University of Texas at Austin
Austin, TX 78713-7219

TEL: (512) 471-9119
FAX: (512) 471-9646

REPORTED BY: Cathy Henderson, Research Librarian
TYPE OF INSTITUTION: library (academic)

HOURS: M-F 9-5; Sa 9-12
ACCESS: Open
SERVICES: in-person reference, mail, phone, photocopies, microfilm, photographs

PRIMARY COLLECTION FOCUS: 19th and 20th century English, American & French literature; film, theater arts, history of photography
   literary manuscripts
   literature

film
photography, history of
theater
science, history of

INCLUSIVE DATES: papyri-present
VOLUME: 27,000 linear feet
COLLECTION FORMATS: 30 million manuscript collections, 1 million books, 852 linear feet pamphlets, 850,000 running feet films, 5 million photographs, 100 maps
COLLECTION ACCESS: card catalog, guide, registers, container lists, computerized finding aids (used by staff, patrons)
SOFTWARE/SYSTEM: RLIN and Microsoft Word
ACQUISITION REPORTED TO: guide, journal(s)
STAFF (FTE): 7 administrative, 10 general archival, 12 preservation, 2 photo, 1 outreach, 5 curators, 30 volunteer/docent, 30 clerical, 15 student, 7 interns
INSTITUTIONAL SUPPORT FOR PROFESSIONAL DEVELOPMENT: meetings
SPECIAL SERVICES/PROGRAMS: exhibits, tours, classes, newsletter, fund raising, lectures
FACILITIES/EQUIPMENT/PRESERVATION: temperature controls, humidity controls, fire detection controls, fire extinguishing system, preservation lab, disaster preparedness plan
PATRON USE STATISTICS: 12,000 in-house patrons,

NHPRC TX56-890

Jollyville-Pond Springs Historical Assoc **TEL**: (512) 258-5688
c/o Karen R. Thompson, 7203 South Ute Trail
Austin, TX 78729

REPORTED BY: Karen R. Thompson, President
TYPE OF INSTITUTION: historical collection (private - made available to public)

HOURS: as needed
ACCESS: appointment
SERVICES: in-person, mail, phone

PRIMARY COLLECTION FOCUS: history of Jollyville-Pond Springs, Williamson Co., people of Republic of Texas

Jollyville-Pond Springs, TX (local history)
Williamson County, TX (local history)
Texas, Republic of

INCLUSIVE DATES: 1820s-
COLLECTION FORMATS: manuscript collections, books, pamphlets, photographs, maps, oral histories
COLLECTION ACCESS: varies
STAFF (FTE): volunteer/docent [number not specified]
SPECIAL SERVICES/PROGRAMS: tours, classes, newsletter, lectures
PATRON USE STATISTICS: in-house patrons, telephone, mail [number not specified]

Lyndon B. Johnson Library and Museum **TEL**: (512) 482-5137
2313 Red River **FAX**: (512) 478-9104
Austin, TX 78705

REPORTED BY: Christina E. Houston, Supervisory Archivist
TYPE OF INSTITUTION: museum, archives (federal)

HOURS: Archives: M-F 9-5; Museum: M-Su 9-5, except Christmas Day
ACCESS: museum, open; archives, by appointment
SERVICES: in-person reference, mail, phone, photocopies, copies of audiovisual materials (photographs, audio/videotapes, film)

PRIMARY COLLECTION FOCUS: career, administration, family, and friends of Lyndon B. Johnson
    Johnson, Lyndon Baines
    U.S.--government
    U.S.--politics
    congressional papers
    U.S.--presidents
    U.S.--vice-presidents
    Texas--politics

INCLUSIVE DATES: 1908-
VOLUME: 40 million pages
COLLECTION FORMATS: 37 million item manuscript collections, 10 feet institution's records, 20,838 books, 24,081 pamphlets, 1 million feet films, 16,000 videos, 3 million pages government records, 600,000 photographs, 54,000 pages oral histories; oral history transcripts, finding aids, Task Force Reports, and symposia proceedings circulate.
COLLECTION ACCESS: card catalog, guide, registers, container lists, computerized finding aids (used by staff; by patrons in printed form)
SOFTWARE/SYSTEM: WordPerfect and Paradox
ACQUISITION REPORTED TO: Journals, NEWS FROM THE ARCHIVES (NARA publication)
STAFF (FTE): 5 administrative, 12 general archival (including archivists and archives technicians), 1 photo curator, 1 outreach, 1 A/V (photo curator and A/V officer are the same person), 1 museum curator, 1 museum registrar, 6 volunteer/docent (in archives), 2 clerical (including archives aides), 4 students
INSTITUTIONAL SUPPORT FOR PROFESSIONAL DEVELOPMENT: tuition, meetings, facilities
SPECIAL SERVICES/PROGRAMS: exhibits, tours, classes (occasional University of Texas history/government/or economics classes meet at library), newsletter, "Friends of the LBJ Library" (LBJ Foundation), fundraising: LBJ Foundation, lectures
FACILITIES/EQUIPMENT/PRESERVATION: temperature controls, humidity controls, fire detection controls, fire extinguishing system, disaster preparedness plan
PATRON USE STATISTICS: 388 (new in-house researchers), 2905 telephone, 2257 mail reference requests, 27,260 reference photocopies, 200 microfilm/fiche copies

NHPRC TX56-520

St. Edward's University Archives
C/M Box 1062, 3001 South Congress Avenue
Austin, TX 78704

TEL: (512) 448-8476
FAX: (512) 448-8737

REPORTED BY: Ingrid Karklins, University Archivist
TYPE OF INSTITUTION: archives (academic)

HOURS: vary; currently M-W 10:30-2:30; Th 1-7:30
ACCESS: general
SERVICES: in-person, mail, phone, photocopies, photographs (all reproductions require a fee)

PRIMARY COLLECTION FOCUS: history of St. Edward's University
    St. Edward's University (records)
    education
    Congregation of the Holy Cross
    St. Edward's High School (records)
    St. Edward's College & Military Academy (records)
    Catholic Church

INCLUSIVE DATES: ca 1870-
VOLUME: 1500 linear feet
COLLECTION FORMATS: 5% manuscript collections, 95% institution's records, 200 volumes books, 20 (?) reels films, 500 (?) linear feet photographs (still processing), 700 items maps & architectural materials, 100 tapes
COLLECTION ACCESS: card catalog, registers, computerized finding aids (used by staff)
SOFTWARE/SYSTEM: Microsoft Works: word processor and database
STAFF (FTE): .5 general archival, 2.5 student
INSTITUTIONAL SUPPORT FOR PROFESSIONAL DEVELOPMENT: tuition, dues, meetings registration/travel mailings, telephone, facilities, clerical
SPECIAL SERVICES/PROGRAMS: exhibits
FACILITIES/EQUIPMENT/PRESERVATION: temperature controls
PATRON USE STATISTICS: 150 in-house patrons, 60 telephone, 25 mail reference requests

NHPRC TX56-720

Texas General Land Office, Archives & Records Division **TEL**: (512) 463-5277
1700 N. Congress Ave.
Austin, TX 78701

REPORTED BY: Michael T. Moore, Archivist
TYPE OF INSTITUTION: archives (state)

HOURS: M-F 7:30-6:00
ACCESS: Open
SERVICES: in-person reference, mail, phone, photocopies

PRIMARY COLLECTION FOCUS: records of public Texas land grants
    land grants--Texas
    Texas--public lands
    Texas--settlement
    Texas--surveying

INCLUSIVE DATES: 1750-
VOLUME: 5700 linear feet
COLLECTION FORMATS: 120 linear feet institution's records, 600 books, 5568 linear feet government records, 1200 maps
COLLECTION ACCESS: card catalog, guide, registers, container lists, computerized finding aids (used by staff)
SOFTWARE/SYSTEM: Q&A
STAFF (FTE): 1 general archival
SPECIAL SERVICES/PROGRAMS: exhibits, tours, lectures
FACILITIES/EQUIPMENT/PRESERVATION: temperature controls, fire detection controls, fire extinguishing system, disaster preparedness plan
PATRON USE STATISTICS: 1236 in-house patrons, 3444 telephone, 2052 mail reference requests, 8 collections used, 29,000 reference photocopies

---

Texas Memorial Museum **TEL**: (512) 471-1604
2400 Trinity Street **FAX**: (512) 471-4794
Austin, TX 78705

REPORTED BY: Elaine Sullivan, Collections Manager, Anthropology & History Division
TYPE OF INSTITUTION: museum (state--University of Texas)

HOURS: M-F 9-5; Sa 10-5; Su 1-5
ACCESS: collections not on exhibit are available to researchers, students, and professors by appointment only
SERVICES: mail, phone, photographic services for exhibits, publications

PRIMARY COLLECTION FOCUS: Texas history; ethnology worldwide with emphasis on Texas, SW, Mexico, Central, and South America; museum archives
    Texas Memorial Museum (records)
    geology
    paleontology
    archaeology
    Texas--ethnology
    Southwestern U.S.
    Mexico
    Central America
    South America

INCLUSIVE DATES: 1830-
COLLECTION FORMATS: 1 linear foot manuscript collections, 3 file cabinets institution's records, 10,000 photographs, ca. 75 maps
COLLECTION ACCESS: container lists, not described
STAFF (FTE): 5 administrative, 1 curator, 1 collection manager for history & anthropology
    3 volunteer/docent, 2 student
INSTITUTIONAL SUPPORT FOR PROFESSIONAL DEVELOPMENT: meetings registration/travel (as budget permits)
SPECIAL SERVICES/PROGRAMS: exhibits, classes (through university), lectures
FACILITIES/EQUIPMENT/PRESERVATION: temperature controls, fire detection controls, fire extinguishing system, preservation lab
PATRON USE STATISTICS: 10 collections used, 20 photographic requests

---

Texas State Library - Archives Division
1201 Brazos
P. O. Box 12927
Austin, TX 78711

TEL: (512) 463-5480
FAX: (512) 323-6100

REPORTED BY: Michael R. Green, Reference Archivist
TYPE OF INSTITUTION: archives (state)

HOURS: M-F 8-5
ACCESS: Open
SERVICES: in-person reference, mail, phone, copies, photographs
RESTRICTIONS: some materials restricted by nature or donation

PRIMARY COLLECTION FOCUS: State of Texas records
    Texas--government
    Texas--history
    Texas--judicial records
    Texas--executive records
    Texas--legislative records
    Texas--state agency records
    Texas, Republic of
    Nacogdoches Archives (1733-1836)
    Texas--Spanish Colonial era
    Texas--Mexican era

INCLUSIVE DATES: 1682-
VOLUME: 27,000 cubic feet
COLLECTION FORMATS: 1623 cubic feet manuscript collections, 45 cubic feet institution's records, 36,000

volumes books, ca. 25,000 cubic feet government records, 404 cubic feet photographs, 439 cubic feet maps, 84 cubic feet artifacts
COLLECTION ACCESS: card catalog, registers, container lists, computerized finding aids (used by staff, patrons)
ACQUISITION REPORTED TO: journal(s)
STAFF (FTE): 3 administrative, 1 preservation, 1 photo curator, 1 outreach officer, 2 reference, 4 processors, 5 clerical
SPECIAL SERVICES/PROGRAMS: exhibits, tours, lectures
FACILITIES/EQUIPMENT/PRESERVATION: fire detection controls, fire extinguishing system, preservation lab, disaster preparedness plan
PATRON USE STATISTICS: 12,587 in-house patrons, 6359 telephone, 7625 mail reference requests, 29,167 collections used, 132,824 reference photocopies

NHPRC TX56-800

University of Texas at Austin - Center for American History
SRH2.109, University of Texas at Austin
Austin, TX 78713-7330

TEL: (512) 495-4515
FAX: (512) 495-4542

REPORTED BY: Alison Beck, Head, Archives & Manuscripts
TYPE OF INSTITUTION: archives, library, museum (academic)

HOURS: M-Sa 9-5
ACCESS: Open
SERVICES: in-person reference, mail, phone, photocopies, hardcopy microprints from microfilm; microfilm; photographs - prints & slides

PRIMARY COLLECTION FOCUS: history of Texas, the South, the Southwest, and Rocky Mountain West
   Texas--history
   Southern U.S.
   U.S.--Congress
   Southwestern U.S.
   University of Texas at Austin (records)
   agriculture
   politics
   education
   military history
   commerce

COLLECTION FORMATS: 33,000 linear feet manuscript collections, 147,000 books, pamphlets (not separate), 85 films, 450,000 photographs, 32,000 maps, 2,000 tapes oral histories, 18,000 reels microfilm, 1050 videocassettes, 28,000 phonodiscs, 4500 phonotapes
COLLECTION ACCESS: card catalog, repository, registers, container lists, computerized finding aids (used by staff, patrons)
ACQUISITION REPORTED TO: NUCMC, OCLC
STAFF (FTE): 2 administrative, 4 general archival, 1 preservation, 1 photo curator, 1 exhibits coordinator, 3 Texas Newspapers Project staff, 3 oral history staff, 5 reference staff,
   15 volunteer/docent, 7 clerical, 5-10 students (periodically), 1 intern
INSTITUTIONAL SUPPORT FOR PROFESSIONAL DEVELOPMENT: tuition, meetings registration/travel
SPECIAL SERVICES/PROGRAMS: exhibits, tours, newsletter, lectures
FACILITIES/EQUIPMENT/PRESERVATION: temperature controls, fire detection controls, fire extinguishing system, preservation lab, disaster preparedness plan
PATRON USE STATISTICS: 12,000 in-house patrons, 5500 telephone, 500 mail reference requests, 2000 collections used, 175,000 reference photocopies, 118 rolls microfilm/fiche

NHPRC TX56-850 [note name change]

SSA Institutional Directory

Austin: Archives of the Episcopal Church, USA: NHPRC TX56-25

Austin: Daughters of the Republic of Texas, Inc.: NHPRC TX56-160

Austin: Elisabet Ney Museum: NHPRC TX56-200

Austin: Lutheran Church in America: NHPRC TX56-490

Austin: Texas Parks and Wildlife Department, Records Section: NHPRC TX56-780

Austin: Texas State Historical Association: NHPRC TX56-790

Austin: University of Texas, Nettie Lee Benson Latin American Collection: NHPRC TX56-860

Bastrop: Bastrop County Historical Society: NHPRC TX63-80

Matagorda County Museum
2100 F Street
Bay City, TX 77414
TEL: (409) 245-7502

REPORTED BY: Anne W. Goda, Director
TYPE OF INSTITUTION: archives, museum (county/local, non-profit)

HOURS: Museum: T-Sa 10-4; Su 1-4. Archives: by appt.
ACCESS: appointment
SERVICES: in-person reference, mail, photocopies

PRIMARY COLLECTION FOCUS: history of Matagorda County; Matagorda family genealogies
 Matagorda County, TX (local history)
 genealogy

COLLECTION FORMATS: manuscript collections, books, pamphlets, government records, photographs, maps, oral histories, newspapers
COLLECTION ACCESS: not described
STAFF (FTE): ca. 10 volunteers
INSTITUTIONAL SUPPORT FOR PROFESSIONAL DEVELOPMENT: meetings
SPECIAL SERVICES/PROGRAMS: exhibits, tours (school), newsletter, fund raising, lectures
FACILITIES/EQUIPMENT/PRESERVATION: temperature controls, other
PATRON USE STATISTICS: user statistics not kept

Beaumont Heritage Society
2985 French Road
Beaumont, TX 77706
TEL: (409) 898-0348

REPORTED BY: not listed
TYPE OF INSTITUTION: historical society, museum (non-profit corporation)

HOURS: T-Sa 10-4; Su 1-4; closed major holidays
ACCESS: open to general public
SERVICES: in-person reference

PRIMARY COLLECTION FOCUS: historical site and artifacts
 Beaumont, TX (local history)

INCLUSIVE DATES: 1845-1860

COLLECTION FORMATS: institution's records, 200+ books, pamphlets, films, ca. 75 photographs (includes slides), some oral histories
COLLECTION ACCESS: card catalog (books)
STAFF (FTE): 2 administrative
INSTITUTIONAL SUPPORT FOR PROFESSIONAL DEVELOPMENT: meetings registration/travel (for staff)
SPECIAL SERVICES/PROGRAMS: exhibits, tours, classes, newsletter, fund raising, lectures
FACILITIES/EQUIPMENT/PRESERVATION: temperature controls, humidity controls, fire detection controls, fire extinguishing system, disaster preparedness plan

---

McFaddin-Ward House
1906 McFaddin Avenue
725 Third Street
Beaumont, TX 77701

TEL: (409) 832-1906
FAX: (409) 832-3483

REPORTED BY: Jessica Foy, Curator of Collections
TYPE OF INSTITUTION: museum (private)

HOURS: T-Sa 10-4; Su 1-4; closed M
ACCESS: museum: Open; archives: by appointment only
SERVICES: in person reference, photocopies, photographs (in some cases)
RESTRICTIONS: must have appointment (M-F 8:30-4:30)

PRIMARY COLLECTION FOCUS: Southeastern Texas
　　McFaddin family
　　Ward family
　　Beaumont, TX (local history)
　　rice industry
　　ranching
　　Texas, Southeast

INCLUSIVE DATES: ca. 1890 (some earlier) - 1982
COLLECTION FORMATS: ca. 120 feet manuscript collections, books, photographs, oral histories, postcards
COLLECTION ACCESS: registers
FACILITIES/EQUIPMENT/PRESERVATION: temperature controls, humidity controls, fire detection controls, disaster preparedness plan

---

Tyrrell Historical Library
695 Pearl Street, Beaumont, TX 77701
Box 3827, Beaumont, TX 77704

TEL: (409) 833-2759
FAX: (409) 833-5828

REPORTED BY: Marcus C. Robbins, Archivist
TYPE OF INSTITUTION: library (city)

HOURS: T-Sa 9-6
ACCESS: Open
SERVICES: in-person reference, mail, phone, copies, photographs

PRIMARY COLLECTION FOCUS: history of Beaumont and Jefferson County
　　Beaumont, TX (local history)
　　Jefferson County, TX (local history)
　　genealogy

INCLUSIVE DATES: 1835-1991
VOLUME: 1000 cubic feet

COLLECTION FORMATS: 500 cubic feet manuscript collections, 200 cubic feet institution's records, 100 cubic feet government records, 100 cubic feet photographs, 100 cubic feet maps
COLLECTION ACCESS: guide, registers
SOFTWARE/SYSTEM: MicroMARC:AMC (presently coding; system not yet on line); used by staff
STAFF (FTE): administrative, general archival, volunteer/docent [numbers not reported]
INSTITUTIONAL SUPPORT FOR PROFESSIONAL DEVELOPMENT: meetings, in-house workshops, use of facilities
SPECIAL SERVICES/PROGRAMS: exhibits, tours, classes, lectures
FACILITIES/EQUIPMENT/PRESERVATION: temperature controls, humidity controls, fire detection controls, preservation lab, disaster preparedness plan
PATRON USE STATISTICS: 10,350 in-house patrons, 1600 telephone, 51 mail reference requests, 55 collections used, 25,420 reference photocopies, 2087 microfilm/fiche copies

NHPRC TX70-770

Bellaire Historical Society
5111 Jessamine, Bellaire, TX 77401
P. O. Box 854, Bellaire, TX 77402

TEL: not reported

REPORTED BY: Jeff Dunn, Director and Past President
TYPE OF INSTITUTION: historical society (city)

HOURS: Archives are located in Bellaire City Library, open M-F, 9-5, Sa, 9-1
ACCESS: open by appointment only
SERVICES: photocopy machine available in Library

PRIMARY COLLECTION FOCUS: City of Bellaire, Westmoreland Farms
    Bellaire, TX
    Westmoreland Farms, TX

INCLUSIVE DATES: 1908-
VOLUME: four filing cabinets
COLLECTION FORMATS: manuscript collections, institution's records, books, pamphlets, films photographs, maps, oral histories
COLLECTION ACCESS: partially indexed; card catalog in progress
SPECIAL SERVICES/PROGRAMS: exhibits, newsletter, fund raising, lectures
FACILITIES/EQUIPMENT/PRESERVATION: temperature controls, fire detection controls, fire extinguishing system in library
PATRON USE STATISTICS: user statistics not kept

Belton City Library
301 East 1st Avenue
Belton, TX 76513

TEL: (817) 939-1161

REPORTED BY: Lena Armstrong, Librarian
TYPE OF INSTITUTION: library (city)

HOURS: M-F 12-5; Sa 9-1
ACCESS: open
SERVICES: in-person, mail, photocopies

PRIMARY COLLECTION FOCUS: history and genealogy of Belton and Bell County
    Bell County, TX (local history)
    Belton, TX (local history)

genealogy

INCLUSIVE DATES: 1920- (newsclippings)
VOLUME: approximately 1200 folders
COLLECTION FORMATS: 1800 photographs, newsclippings, biographical & genealogical files
COLLECTION ACCESS: not described
STAFF (FTE): 2 Clerical
PATRON USE STATISTICS: user statistics not kept

Heritage Museum
510 Scurry
Big Spring, TX 79720

TEL: (915) 267-8255

REPORTED BY: not listed
TYPE OF INSTITUTION: museum (county/local)

HOURS: T-F 9-5; Sa 10-5
ACCESS: Open
SERVICES: in-person, mail, phone, photocopies

PRIMARY COLLECTION FOCUS: railroads, longhorn cattle
    railroads
    cattle industry

COLLECTION FORMATS: 500 books, 200 pamphlets, 1 film, 4000 photographs, 100 oral histories
COLLECTION ACCESS: card catalog
STAFF (FTE): 1 administrative, 3 volunteer/docent
INSTITUTIONAL SUPPORT FOR PROFESSIONAL DEVELOPMENT: dues, facilities
SPECIAL SERVICES/PROGRAMS: exhibits, tours, classes, newsletter, fund raising, lectures
FACILITIES/EQUIPMENT/PRESERVATION: temperature controls, humidity controls
PATRON USE STATISTICS: 3 in-house patrons

Texas Baptist Historical Center - Museum
Rt 5, Box 222
Brenham, TX 77833

TEL: (409) 836-5117

REPORTED BY: Director
TYPE OF INSTITUTION: archives, library, museum (county/local, religious)

HOURS: W-Sa 10-4
ACCESS: Open
SERVICES: in-person reference, phone

PRIMARY COLLECTION FOCUS: Sam Houston, Baylor University, Old Independence Baptist Church
    Houston, Sam
    Baylor University
    Old Independence Baptist Church
    religion
    church history

INCLUSIVE DATES: 1823-

COLLECTION FORMATS: 250 manuscript collections, 5 institution's records, 250 books, 2 pamphlets, 1 film, 200 photographs, 3 maps, 1 oral histories
COLLECTION ACCESS: registers, computerized finding aids
STAFF (FTE): 1 (does administration, archives, preservation, etc.), 1 volunteer/docent, 1 clerical
SPECIAL SERVICES/PROGRAMS: exhibits, lectures
FACILITIES/EQUIPMENT/PRESERVATION: other

Bryan Public Library
201 East 26th Street
Bryan, TX 77803

TEL: (409) 779-3311

REPORTED BY: Nancy McCraw Ross, Reference Librarian
TYPE OF INSTITUTION: library (city)

HOURS: not reported
ACCESS: open
SERVICES: in-person, mail, phone, photocopies

PRIMARY COLLECTION FOCUS: Brazos Valley history
    Brazos Valley, TX--history
    genealogy

COLLECTION FORMATS: manuscript collections, institution's records, books, pamphlets
    films, photographs, maps, oral histories
COLLECTION ACCESS: card catalog
STAFF (FTE): administrative [number not specified]
INSTITUTIONAL SUPPORT FOR PROFESSIONAL DEVELOPMENT: tuition, meetings
SPECIAL SERVICES/PROGRAMS: exhibits, tours, lectures
PATRON USE STATISTICS: statistics not kept specifically for archives

---

Panhandle-Plains Historical Museum Research Center
2401 4th Avenue
Box 967, W. T. Station
Canyon, TX 79016

TEL: (806) 656-2261
FAX: (806) 656-2250

REPORTED BY: Claire R. Kuehn, Archivist/Librarian
TYPE OF INSTITUTION: Library & Archives in the Museum (state)

HOURS: M-F 9-12, 1-5
ACCESS: Open
SERVICES: in person reference, mail, phone, fee (if extensive), copies, photographs

PRIMARY COLLECTION FOCUS: Texas and Southwest history
    ranching
    Native Americans
    archaeology
    Texas Panhandle--settlement and development
    ethnology
    textiles
    windmills
    fine arts
    congressional papers
    museum science

COLLECTION FORMATS: 10,000 cubic feet manuscript collections, 17,500 books, 500 cubic feet pamphlets, 200 films, 2000 cubic feet government records, 250,000 photographs, 2500 maps, 1000 oral histories
COLLECTION ACCESS: card catalog, registers, computerized finding aids (used by staff)
SOFTWARE/SYSTEM: Q&A
STAFF (FTE): 1 administrative, 1 general archival, 5 volunteer/docent, 2 students
INSTITUTIONAL SUPPORT FOR PROFESSIONAL DEVELOPMENT: meetings registration/travel, telephone, facilities
SPECIAL SERVICES/PROGRAMS: exhibits, tours, classes, fund raising, lectures
FACILITIES/EQUIPMENT/PRESERVATION: temperature controls, fire detections controls, preservation lab
PATRON USE STATISTICS: 1500 in-house patrons, 500 telephone, 500 mail reference requests

NHPRC TX128-640

Chappell Hill Historical Society & Museum
Church Street
P. O. Box 211
Chappell Hill, TX 77426

TEL: (409) 836-6033

REPORTED BY: Peggy Guire, museum secretary
TYPE OF INSTITUTION: historical society, library, museum (county/local, city)

HOURS: museum Sa 10-4, Su 12-4; library by apppointment
ACCESS: open to the public
SERVICES: in-person, mail, fee, photocopies

PRIMARY COLLECTION FOCUS: history and genealogy of Washington County

    Washington County, TX (local history)
    genealogy
    Soule University (records)
    Chappell Hill Female College (records)
    Austin, Stephen F.
    Crockett family papers
    architecture

INCLUSIVE DATES: 1847-1960
COLLECTION FORMATS: manuscript collections, institution's records, books, oral histories
COLLECTION ACCESS: card catalog, registers, container lists, computerized finding aids (in process, used by staff)
SOFTWARE/SYSTEM: Microsoft Works
ACQUISITION REPORTED TO: guide
STAFF (FTE): 1 administrative, 1 general archival, 25 volunteer/docent
INSTITUTIONAL SUPPORT FOR PROFESSIONAL DEVELOPMENT: tuition; payment for meetings/travel; use of facilities
SPECIAL SERVICES/PROGRAMS: exhibits, tours, classes, newsletter, fund raising
FACILITIES/EQUIPMENT/PRESERVATION: temperature controls, humidity controls, fire detection controls, fire extinguishing system
PATRON USE STATISTICS: 15 in-house patrons, other user statistics not kept

---

Layland Museum
201 N Caddo
Cleburne, TX 76031

TEL: (817) 645-0940

REPORTED BY: Mabel McCall, staff

TYPE OF INSTITUTION: museum (city)

HOURS: M-F 9-5; Sa 9-1
ACCESS: Open
SERVICES: in-person reference, mail, phone, photocopies

PRIMARY COLLECTION FOCUS: history of Cleburne and Johnson County
    Cleburne, TX (local history)
    Johnson County, TX (local history)

COLLECTION FORMATS: 3 manuscript collections, books, pamphlets, 500-600 photographs, maps
COLLECTION ACCESS: card catalog
STAFF (FTE): 1 administrative, 1 volunteer/docent, 1 clerical, 1 "Green Thumb Worker"
INSTITUTIONAL SUPPORT FOR PROFESSIONAL DEVELOPMENT: memberships, meetings, facilities
SPECIAL SERVICES/PROGRAMS: exhibits, tours, fund raising, lectures
FACILITIES/EQUIPMENT/PRESERVATION: temperature controls, fire detection controls

---

Colorado City: Mitchell County Public Library: NHPRC TX189-520

Nesbitt Memorial Library
529 Washington Street
Columbus, TX 78934

TEL: (409) 732-5514

REPORTED BY: Bill Stein, Archivist
TYPE OF INSTITUTION: archives, library (county/local, city)

HOURS: M-F 8-5:30; Sa 10-2
ACCESS: Open
SERVICES: in-person reference, photocopies

PRIMARY COLLECTION FOCUS: Colorado County history
    Colorado County, TX (local history)
    genealogy

COLLECTION FORMATS: 150 feet manuscript collections, 1500 books, 750 vertical files pamphlets, 1000
    photographs, 75 maps, 10-15 oral histories, 250 rolls microfilm
COLLECTION ACCESS: card catalog, guide, computerized finding aids (used by staff), not described
STAFF (FTE): 1 general archival
ACQUISITION REPORTED TO: journal of county history
FACILITIES/EQUIPMENT/PRESERVATION: temperature controls, humidity controls, fire detection controls,
    fire extinguishing system
PATRON USE STATISTICS: user statistics not kept

East Texas State University,
Archives, James G. Gee Library
ET Station
Commerce, TX 75429

TEL: (903) 886-5737

REPORTED BY: James Conrad, University Archivist & Coordinator of Oral History
TYPE OF INSTITUTION: archives (academic)

HOURS: M-F 8-5
ACCESS: Open

SERVICES: in-person, mail, photocopies

PRIMARY COLLECTION FOCUS: Northeast Texas; printing arts; Texas politics, agricultural history, education
    agriculture
    education
    politics--Texas
    East Texas State University (records)
    literature--Texas writers
    African Americans
    cotton
    medicine, history of
    Native Americans
    Texas, East

INCLUSIVE DATES: 1846-1950
VOLUME: 1200 cubic feet
COLLECTION FORMATS: 200 cubic feet manuscript collections, 1020 cubic feet institution's records, 10,000 books, 20,000 pamphlets, 100 films, 550 government records, 11,530 photographs, 140 maps, 307 oral histories
COLLECTION ACCESS: card catalog, registers, container lists
ACQUISITION REPORTED TO: NUCMC, OCLC
STAFF (FTE): 1 administrative, 1 clerical, 5 students
INSTITUTIONAL SUPPORT FOR PROFESSIONAL DEVELOPMENT: tuition, telephone, facilities, clerical
SPECIAL SERVICES/PROGRAMS: exhibits
FACILITIES/EQUIPMENT/PRESERVATION: temperature controls, humidity controls, fire detection controls, fire extinguishing system, disaster preparedness plan
PATRON USE STATISTICS: 400 in-house patrons, 140 telephone, 60 mail reference requests, 30 collections used, 1000 reference photocopies, 11 microfilm/fiche copies

NHPRC TX210-200

Corpus Christi Museum of Science & History
1900 North Chaparral
Corpus Christi, TX 78401

TEL: (512) 883-2862
FAX: (512) 884-7392

REPORTED BY: Patricia Murphy, Museum Librarian
TYPE OF INSTITUTION: museum (city)

HOURS: T-S 10-5; Su 1-5
ACCESS: by appointment
RESTRICTIONS: in-house use only

PRIMARY COLLECTION FOCUS: Corpus Christ and South Texas history
    Corpus Christi, TX (local history)
    South Texas--history

INCLUSIVE DATES: 1850s-
VOLUME: 1166.5 cubic feet
COLLECTION FORMATS: 47 cubic feet manuscript collections, 6 cubic feet institution's records, 292 cubic feet books, 117 cubic feet pamphlets, 12 cubic feet films, 677 cubic feet photographs, 6 cubic feet maps, 12 cubic feet oral histories
COLLECTION ACCESS: card catalog, registers, computerized finding aids (used by staff, patrons)
SOFTWARE/SYSTEM: dBase IV
STAFF (FTE): 1 librarian, 22 volunteer/docent
INSTITUTIONAL SUPPORT FOR PROFESSIONAL DEVELOPMENT: tuition, meetings registration/travel, mailings, telephone, facilities, use of clerical staff
SPECIAL SERVICES/PROGRAMS: exhibits, tours, classes, newsletter, fund raising, lectures

FACILITIES/EQUIPMENT/PRESERVATION: temperature controls, humidity controls, fire detection controls, disaster preparedness plan
PATRON USE STATISTICS: user statistics not kept

Corpus Christi Public Library
805 Comanche
Corpus Christi, TX 78401

TEL: (512) 880-7030
FAX: (512) 880-7046

REPORTED BY: Margaret Rose [title not specified]
TYPE OF INSTITUTION: library (city)

HOURS: M-Th 9-9; F-Sa 9-6; closed Su
ACCESS: open
SERVICES: in-person, mail, phone, photocopies

PRIMARY COLLECTION FOCUS: history of Corpus Christi and Nueces County, South Texas history and genealogy
    Corpus Christi, TX (local history)
    South Texas--history
    Nueces County, TX (local history)
    genealogy

INCLUSIVE DATES: 1519 - present
COLLECTION FORMATS: 5000 books, 500 items government records, 750 photographs
    50 maps, 65 tapes, oral histories
COLLECTION ACCESS: card catalog
ACQUISITION REPORTED TO: OCLC, guide
STAFF (FTE): 1 administrative, .5 clerical
PATRON USE STATISTICS: user statistics not kept

NHPRC TX217-480

Special Collections & Archives Dept
Corpus Christi State University Library
6300 Ocean Drive
Corpus Christi, TX 78412

TEL: (512) 994-2300
FAX: (512) 994-2623

REPORTED BY: Thomas H. Kreneck, Ph.D, Special Collections Lib/Arch
TYPE OF INSTITUTION: library (academic)

HOURS: M-F 8-5, and by appointment
ACCESS: open
SERVICES: in-person, mail (limited), phone (limited), copies

PRIMARY COLLECTION FOCUS: history of Corpus Christi and South Texas
    Corpus Christi, TX (local history)
    South Texas--history

INCLUSIVE DATES: nineteenth and twentieth centuries
VOLUME: 12,000 volumes & 1000 linear feet manuscript collections
COLLECTION FORMATS: manuscript collections, institution's records, books, pamphlets, films
    photographs, maps, oral histories
COLLECTION ACCESS: card catalog, container lists, computerized finding aids (used by staff)
SOFTWARE/SYSTEM: ASK SAM

ACQUISITION REPORTED TO: OCLC, journal(s)
STAFF (FTE): 1 administrative, 1 general archival, 1 volunteer/docent, 4 students (work study)
INSTITUTIONAL SUPPORT FOR PROFESSIONAL DEVELOPMENT: meetings registration/travel, mailings, telephone, facilities, clerical
SPECIAL SERVICES/PROGRAMS: exhibits
FACILITIES/EQUIPMENT/PRESERVATION: temperature controls, humidity controls, fire detection controls, disaster preparedness plan
PATRON USE STATISTICS: in the process of being assembled

Discover Houston County Visitors Center/Museum **TEL**: (409) 544-9520
303 South First
629 North Fourth
Crockett, TX 75835

REPORTED BY: Eliza H. Bishop, President of Board; Curator
TYPE OF INSTITUTION: museum, visitors center (county/local)

HOURS: W 1-4; other days by appointment
ACCESS: open
SERVICES: in-person, mail, phone, photocopies

PRIMARY COLLECTION FOCUS: history of Houston County and its communities
    Houston County, TX (local history)

INCLUSIVE DATES: 1847-
VOLUME: approximately 900 items
COLLECTION FORMATS: 40 manuscript collections, 57 books, 500+ pamphlets, 200+ photographs
COLLECTION ACCESS: card catalog, registers
ACQUISITION REPORTED TO: journals
STAFF (FTE): 8 volunteer/docent
INSTITUTIONAL SUPPORT FOR PROFESSIONAL DEVELOPMENT: dues, workshops, use of facilities
SPECIAL SERVICES/PROGRAMS: exhibits, tours, lectures
FACILITIES/EQUIPMENT/PRESERVATION: temperature controls, disaster preparedness plan
PATRON USE STATISTICS: user statistics not kept

Crockett: Historical and Cultural Activities Center: NHPRC TX228-320

Crosby County Pioneer Memorial Museum Community Center **TEL**: (806) 675-2331
101 Main
P. O. Box 386
Crosbyton, TX 79322

REPORTED BY: Verna Anne Wheeler, Executive Director
TYPE OF INSTITUTION: museum (county/local, city)

HOURS: T-Sa 9-12, 1-5
ACCESS: open; staff provides specific information & individualized help
SERVICES: mail, fee, photocopies

PRIMARY COLLECTION FOCUS: history of Crosby County and lower Panhandle and South Plains
    Crosby County, TX (local history)
    Panhandle, TX (local history)
    South Plains--history

INCLUSIVE DATES: 1890-
VOLUME: 660 vols of regional Texana and six vertical files
COLLECTION FORMATS: microfilm (Crosby County News), photographs
COLLECTION ACCESS: computerized finding aids (photographs only, used by staff)
STAFF (FTE): 1 clerical
INSTITUTIONAL SUPPORT FOR PROFESSIONAL DEVELOPMENT: tuition, dues, meetings registration/travel, use of clerical staff
SPECIAL SERVICES/PROGRAMS: exhibits, tours
FACILITIES/EQUIPMENT/PRESERVATION: temperature controls, disaster preparedness plan
PATRON USE STATISTICS: user statistics not kept

NHPRC TX321-120

Cuero: De Witt County Historical Museum: NHPRC TX245-160

Dallas Historical Society
3939 Grand Avenue (Fair Park), Dallas, TX 75210
P. O. Box 150038, Dallas, TX 75315

TEL: (214) 421-4500
FAX: (214) 421-7500

REPORTED BY: Dr. Michael V. Hazel, Deputy Director
TYPE OF INSTITUTION: historical society (private non-profit)

HOURS: Tu-Sa 9-5; Su 1-5; closed Mon
ACCESS: open (appointment advised)
SERVICES: in-person, mail, phone, copies
RESTRICTIONS: phone & mail reference by staff limited to 15 minutes per request

PRIMARY COLLECTION FOCUS: history of Dallas, Dallas County, North Texas & Texas
    Dallas, TX (local history)
    Dallas County, TX (local history)
    North Texas--history

COLLECTION FORMATS: 1.5 million pieces manuscript collections, 8000 books, 2500 pamphlets, 5000 photographs, 500 maps
COLLECTION ACCESS: card catalog
STAFF (FTE): 1 administrative, 1 registrar, 1 research assistant, 2 volunteer/docent
INSTITUTIONAL SUPPORT FOR PROFESSIONAL DEVELOPMENT: tuition, meetings
SPECIAL SERVICES/PROGRAMS: exhibits, tours, newsletter, fund raising, lectures
FACILITIES/EQUIPMENT/PRESERVATION: temperature controls, humidity controls, fire detection controls, fire extinguishing system
PATRON USE STATISTICS: 150 in-house patrons, 500 telephone, 100 mail reference requests

NHPRC TX252-150

Dallas Museum of Art Library
1717 N. Harwood Street
Dallas, TX 75201

TEL: (214) 922-1276
FAX: (214) 954-0174

REPORTED BY: not identified
TYPE OF INSTITUTION: museum (city)

HOURS: not reported
ACCESS: open

SERVICES: in-person, mail, phone

PRIMARY COLLECTION FOCUS: documents related to the history of the museum
    art
        Dallas Museum of Art (records)

INCLUSIVE DATES: 1904-83
COLLECTION FORMATS: 18 linear feet manuscript collections, 25,000 books, ca. 140 linear feet pamphlets
COLLECTION ACCESS: card catalog, computerized finding aids (used by staff)
SOFTWARE/SYSTEM: dBase III, Filemaker
ACQUISITION REPORTED TO: OCLC
STAFF: 1 administrative, 8 volunteer/docent, 1 clerical
INSTITUTIONAL SUPPORT FOR PROFESSIONAL DEVELOPMENT: dues, meetings registration/travel, mailings, facilities
SPECIAL SERVICES/PROGRAMS: fund raising, lectures
FACILITIES/EQUIPMENT/PRESERVATION: temperature controls, humidity controls, fire detection controls, fire extinguishing system, preservation lab, disaster preparedness plan
PATRON USE STATISTICS: 912 in-house patrons, 2850 telephone, 4 mail reference requests, 12 reference copies

---

Dallas Public Library - Texas/Dallas History & Archives Division   **TEL**: (214) 760-1435
1515 Young Street
Dallas, TX 75201

REPORTED BY: Carol Roark, Archivist
TYPE OF INSTITUTION: library (city)

HOURS: M-Th 9-9; F-Sa 9-5; Su 1-5
ACCESS: open
SERVICES: in-person reference, mail, phone, copies, microfilm, microfiche, photographs
RESTRICTIONS: original photographs may not be photocopied, some collections require permission of donor for use or publication

PRIMARY COLLECTION FOCUS: history of Dallas and Dallas County
      Dallas, TX (local history)
      Dallas County, TX (local history)

INCLUSIVE DATES: 1809-
COLLECTION FORMATS: 3000 linear feet manuscript collections, 200 linear feet inst, 50,000 books, 2,500 pamphlets, 30 films, 3000 government records, 350,000+ photographs, 6000 maps, 310 oral histories
COLLECTION ACCESS: registers, DPL's "Master Bibliographic Data Base" computerized finding aids catalog - for books and periodicals
SOFTWARE/SYSTEM: DPL's Master Bibliographic Data Base
ACQUISITION REPORTED TO: OCLC
STAFF (FTE): 1 general archival, 1 map, 1 photo, 2 librarian, 6 volunteer/docent, 1 clerical, 2.5 library associate
INSTITUTIONAL SUPPORT FOR PROFESSIONAL DEVELOPMENT: tuition (% varies), meetings/travel (partial), workshops, mailings, facilities, clerical (for selected projects)
SPECIAL SERVICES/PROGRAMS: exhibits, lectures
FACILITIES/EQUIPMENT/PRESERVATION: temperature controls, humidity controls, fire detection controls, fire extinguishing system, preservation lab in building; no funds to staff, disaster preparedness plan
PATRON USE STATISTICS: 18,183 in-house patrons, 4782 telephone, 417 mail reference requests, 207 archives patrons, 485 map patrons, 134 county records patrons
NHPRC TX252-170

Texas Instruments Incorporated TEL: (214) 995-4458
13510 North Central Expressway, Dallas, TX 75243
P. O. Box 655474, MS-233, Dallas, TX, 75265

REPORTED BY: Ann Westerlin, Manager, Corporate Archives
TYPE OF INSTITUTION: archives (business)

HOURS: M-F 8-5
ACCESS: not open
SERVICES: mail, phone

PRIMARY COLLECTION FOCUS: evolution of activities & philosophy of Texas Instruments Incorporated
    business history
    Texas Instruments Incorporated

INCLUSIVE DATES: 1923-
VOLUME: 1250 cubic feet
COLLECTION ACCESS: registers, finding aids
STAFF (FTE): 1 administrative, 1 secretary
INSTITUTIONAL SUPPORT FOR PROFESSIONAL DEVELOPMENT: tuition, dues, meetings
SPECIAL SERVICES/PROGRAMS: tours
FACILITIES/EQUIPMENT/PRESERVATION: temperature controls, humidity controls, fire extinguishing
    system, disaster preparedness plan
PATRON USE STATISTICS: 981 in-house patrons, 155 telephone

Dallas: Bishop College: NHPRC TX252-80

Dallas: Diocese of Dallas of the Episcopal Church: NHPRC TX252-200

Dallas: Historic Preservation Leaugue: NHPRC TX252-320

Dallas: Society of Independent Professional Earth Scientists: NHPRC TX252-322

Dallas: Southern Methodist University, Perkins School of Theology: NHPRC TX252-760

Dallas: Southern Methodist University, Science/Engineering Library: NHPRC TX252-770

Dallas: Southern Methodist University, Underwood Law Library: NHPRC TX252-780

Wise County Heritage Museum TEL: (817) 627-5586
1602 S. Trinity
P. O. Box 427
Decatur, TX 76234

REPORTED BY: Mrs. Rosalie Gregg, Executive Director
TYPE OF INSTITUTION: archives, historical society

HOURS: M-Sa 9-4; Su 1:30-5
ACCESS: Open
SERVICES: mail, phone, photocopies, microfilm
RESTRICTIONS: no volumes are checked out

PRIMARY COLLECTION FOCUS: history and genealogy of Wise County
    Wise County, TX (local history)

genealogy

COLLECTION FORMATS: films, photographs, oral histories
ACQUISITION REPORTED TO: members
STAFF (FTE): 1 administrative, 14 volunteer/docent (2 work under Green Thumb, Inc.)
SPECIAL SERVICES/PROGRAMS: exhibits, tours, newsletter
FACILITIES/EQUIPMENT/PRESERVATION: fire extinguishing system
PATRON USE STATISTICS: 1000 in-house patrons, other user statistics not kept

NHPRC TX259-880

Deer Park: San Jacinto Museum of History Association: NHPRC TX266-720)

Whitehead Memorial Museum
1308 S. Main Street
Del Rio, TX 78840

TEL: none reported

REPORTED BY: Richard A. Thompson, executive director
TYPE OF INSTITUTION: museum (county/local, city)

HOURS: Tu-Sa 9-4:30 year-round
ACCESS: Open
SERVICES: in-person reference, mail, phone

PRIMARY COLLECTION FOCUS: area culture and history
    railroads
    ranching
    military history
    medicine, history of
    Brinkley, John
    Del Rio, TX (local history)
COLLECTION FORMATS: 20 manuscript collections, 50 books, 100 pamphlets, 20 films, 1000 photographs, 100 maps, 10 oral histories
COLLECTION ACCESS: guide, registers
STAFF (FTE): administrative, volunteer/docent [numbers not reported]
INSTITUTIONAL SUPPORT FOR PROFESSIONAL DEVELOPMENT: telephone, facilities
SPECIAL SERVICES/PROGRAMS: exhibits, tours, lectures
FACILITIES/EQUIPMENT/PRESERVATION: fire extinguishing system
PATRON USE STATISTICS: 5000 in house patrons, 200 telephone, 50 mail reference requests, 10 collections used, 50 reference photocopies

---

Denison: Denison Public Library: NHPRC TX273-160

The American Donkey and Mule Society
2901 North Elm
Denton, TX 76201

TEL: (817) 382-6845

REPORTED BY: Betsy Hutchins, Member Services Officer (co-founder)
TYPE OF INSTITUTION: other: breeders' association

HOURS: by appointment; archives are in her home
ACCESS: appointment

SERVICES: in-person, mail, phone
RESTRICTIONS: staff do not do research

PRIMARY COLLECTION FOCUS: donkeys and mules
    donkeys
    mules

VOLUME: uncataloged; 25 years' worth of material
COLLECTION FORMATS: books, pamphlets, films, photographs
COLLECTION ACCESS: not described
STAFF (FTE): 1 volunteer/docent
ACQUISITION REPORTED TO: magazine, registries (a society with members)

Texas Woman's University
Special Collections
P. O. Box 23715
Denton, TX 76204-1715

TEL: (817) 898-3751
FAX: (817) 898-3726

REPORTED BY: Dawn Letson, Head of Special Collections
TYPE OF INSTITUTION: archives, library (state, academic)

HOURS: M-F 8-5
ACCESS: Open
SERVICES: in-person reference, mail, photocopies, photographs

PRIMARY COLLECTION FOCUS: women's history and women's issues
    women
    Texas--women
    Texas--women's organizations
    military history
    women in military
    Texas Woman's University (records)

INCLUSIVE DATES: 1850-
VOLUME: 2000 cubic feet
COLLECTION FORMATS: 1000 cubic feet manuscript collections, 1000 cubic feet institution's records, 42,000 books (some circulate), 200 films, 20,000 photographs, 100 oral histories
COLLECTION ACCESS: guide, register, container lists, computerized finding aids (used by staff), online catalog & OCLC
ACQUISITION REPORTED TO: NUCMC, OCLC
STAFF (FTE): 1 administrative, .5 volunteer/docent, 2 clerical, 4 student
INSTITUTIONAL SUPPORT FOR PROFESSIONAL DEVELOPMENT: tuition (workshops), meetings registration/travel, telephone, facilities, clerical
SPECIAL SERVICES/PROGRAMS: exhibits, tours, fund raising, lectures
FACILITIES/EQUIPMENT/PRESERVATION: temperature controls, humidity controls, fire detection controls, fire extinguishing system
PATRON USE STATISTICS: 500 in-house patrons, 75 telephone, 50 mail, 966 folders used (folders counted, not collections)

University of North Texas Archives
Box 5188 NT Station
Denton, TX 76203

TEL: (817) 565-2766

REPORTED BY: Richard L. Himmel, University Archivist

TYPE OF INSTITUTION: archives (academic)

HOURS: M-F 8-5
ACCESS: Open
SERVICES: in-person reference, mail, phone, copies, photographs

PRIMARY COLLECTION FOCUS: politics/industry in north central Texas; history of University of North Texas
- agriculture
- women--equal rights
- industry
- military history
- politics
- Texas, North Central
- labor unions
- business history
- Civil War
- University of North Texas (records)

INCLUSIVE DATES: 1850s-
VOLUME: 2836 linear feet
COLLECTION FORMATS: 1200 linear feet manuscript collections, 1050 linear feet institution's records, 70 linear feet books, 10 linear feet pamphlets, 238 linear feet film, 113 linear feet government records, 92 linear feet photographs, 5 linear feet maps, 58 linear feet oral histories
COLLECTION ACCESS: card catalog, guide, computerized finding aids (used by staff)
SOFTWARE/SYSTEM: dBase III plus for university photographs
ACQUISITION REPORTED TO: NUCMC, OCLC
STAFF (FTE): 1 administrative, 1 clerical
INSTITUTIONAL SUPPORT FOR PROFESSIONAL DEVELOPMENT: tuition, meetings registration/travel
SPECIAL SERVICES/PROGRAMS: exhibits, classes, lectures
FACILITIES/EQUIPMENT/PRESERVATION: temperature controls, fire detection controls, fire extinguishing system, disaster preparedness plan
PATRON USE STATISTICS: 537 in-house patrons, 141 telephone, 28 mail reference requests

NHPRC TX280-540

The University of Texas-Pan American
1201 West University Drive
Edinburg, TX 78539-2999

TEL: (512) 381-2799
FAX: (512) 381-5196

REPORTED BY: George R. Gause, Jr., Special Collections Librarian
TYPE OF INSTITUTION: library (academic)

HOURS: M-F 8-5
ACCESS: Open
SERVICES: in-person reference, mail, photocopies, monographs circulate when held in duplicate

PRIMARY COLLECTION FOCUS: South Texas, Mexico (Tamaulipas, N. Leon, Coahuila)
- Texas, South
- Mexico
- Tamaulipas, Mexico
- Nuevo Leon, Mexico
- Coahuila
- Rio Grande Valley (local history)

COLLECTION FORMATS: 5140 monographs, 2327 feet manuscript collections, 254 films 92 photographs, 6425 maps, 857 oral histories
COLLECTION ACCESS: card catalog, registers, computerized finding aid (used by staff, patrons)

SOFTWARE/SYSTEM: WordPerfect, Word Star, Pro-Cite
ACQUISITION REPORTED TO: OCLC
STAFF (FTE): .5 administrative, 1 clerical
INSTITUTIONAL SUPPORT FOR PROFESSIONAL DEVELOPMENT: mailings, telephone, use of facilities
SPECIAL SERVICES/PROGRAMS: exhibits, tours, lectures/presentations
FACILITIES/EQUIPMENT/PRESERVATION: temperature controls, humidity controls, fire extinguishing system (partial)
PATRON USE STATISTICS: 881 in-house patrons, 550 telephone, 15 mail reference requests, 79 collections used, 1329 reference photocopies, 32 microfilm/fiche

NHPRC TX319-640

Schleicher County Museum
Box 114
Eldorado, TX 76936

TEL: none reported

REPORTED BY: not reported
TYPE OF INSTITUTION: museum (county/local)

HOURS: Tu 9-12; W 2-5; F 2-5
ACCESS: Open
SERVICES: not reported

PRIMARY COLLECTION FOCUS: history and genealogy of Schleicher County
    Schleicher County, TX (local history)
    genealogy

COLLECTION FORMATS: institution's records, photographs, maps
STAFF (FTE): volunteer/docent [number not reported]
INSTITUTIONAL SUPPORT FOR PROFESSIONAL DEVELOPMENT: dues
SPECIAL SERVICES/PROGRAMS: exhibits, tours
FACILITIES/EQUIPMENT/PRESERVATION: fire extinguishing system

Chamizal National Memorial
800 South San Marcial
El Paso, TX 79905

TEL: (915)532-7273
FAX: (915)532-7240

REPORTED BY: Robert K. Devine, Park Curator
TYPE OF INSTITUTION: National Park Service (federal)

HOURS: M-F 8-5
ACCESS: by appointment only
SERVICES: in-person reference
RESTRICTIONS: fax 2 pages only

PRIMARY COLLECTION FOCUS: Chamizal National Memorial, theatre, art, Mexico
    theater
    art--paintings--Twentieth Century
    Mexico
    Chamizal National Memorial, TX
    parks and monuments, federal

COLLECTION FORMATS: 1109 institution's records, 1500 films/videotapes, government records, 500 photographs, 50 maps, musical tapes

COLLECTION ACCESS: registers/inventories
STAFF (FTE): 1 curator
SPECIAL SERVICES/PROGRAMS: exhibits
FACILITIES/EQUIPMENT/PRESERVATION: humidity controls, fire extinguishing system

---

El Paso County Historical Society
603 W. Yandell
P.O. Box 28
El Paso, TX 79940

TEL: (915) 533-3603

REPORTED BY: William Latham, Curator
TYPE OF INSTITUTION: historical society (private)

HOURS: Tu 9:30-2 or by appointment
ACCESS: open to the general public
SERVICES: in-person, mail & phone reference, photocopies, photographic reproduction

PRIMARY COLLECTION FOCUS: Southwest U.S. & Northern Mexico history; emphasis on El Paso
    El Paso, TX (local history)
    architecture--El Paso, TX
    New Mexico
    Mexico, Northern

INCLUSIVE DATES: ca. 1860-present
COLLECTION FORMATS: 30 linear feet manuscript collections, 3 feet institution's records, 4,000 books, 9,500 photographs, 100 maps
COLLECTION ACCESS: card catalog
STAFF (FTE): 3 volunteers
INSTITUTIONAL SUPPORT FOR PROFESSIONAL DEVELOPMENT: use of facilities, payment for telephone use
SPECIAL SERVICES/PROGRAMS: exhibits, lectures/presentations
FACILITIES/EQUIPMENT/PRESERVATION: fire detection, fire extinguishing system
PATRON USE STATISTICS: 40 in-house patrons, 40 mail reference requests

---

El Paso Public Library, Southwest Collection
501 N. Oregon
El Paso, TX 79901

TEL: (915)543-5440
FAX: (915)543-5410

REPORTED BY: Wayne Daniel, Librarian
TYPE OF INSTITUTION: library (city)

HOURS: (reference service hours) M-Th 10-8, F-Sa 10-5:30
ACCESS: open to general public; archives by appointment only
SERVICES: in-person, mail, phone reference; photocopies, photographic reproduction

PRIMARY COLLECTION FOCUS: El Paso, Texas, New Mexico, Arizona, Northern Mexico
    El Paso, TX (local history)
    architecture--El Paso, TX
    New Mexico
    Arizona
    Mexico, Northern
    Mexican Revolution

COLLECTION FORMATS: 273 linear feet manuscript collections, 27,800 books, 20,000 photos, 1200 maps,

700 sets architectural drawings
COLLECTION ACCESS: card catalog, inventories, computerized finding aids (used by staff)
SOFTWARE/SYSTEM: R:Base
ACQUISITION REPORTED TO: OCLC
STAFF (FTE): 1 librarian, 2 library assistants, 0.2 volunteer, 0.2 student
INSTITUTIONAL SUPPORT FOR PROFESSIONAL DEVELOPMENT: tuition/registration reimbursement, use of facilities
SPECIAL SERVICES/PROGRAMS: exhibits
FACILITIES/EQUIPMENT/PRESERVATION: temperature controls, fire detection controls, fire extinguishing system
PATRON USE STATISTICS: 6171 in house patrons, 2645 telephone, 105 mail reference requests

NHPRC TX326-210

El Paso Times Inc.
300 N. Campbell
P.O. Box 20
El Paso, TX 79999

TEL: (915)546-6179
FAX: (915)546-6415

REPORTED BY: Judy Soles, Librarian
TYPE OF INSTITUTION: library (special)

HOURS: weekdays 6am-11pm
ACCESS: not open to the general public

PRIMARY COLLECTION FOCUS: El Paso Times and Herald Post newspapers clippings, photos
El Paso, TX
El Paso Times Newspaper
El Paso Herald Post Newspaper
El Paso, TX (local history)

INCLUSIVE DATES: 1940s - present
VOLUME: 200,000 files
COLLECTION FORMATS: 2,000,000 items institution's records, 100,000 photographs
COLLECTION ACCESS: not described
STAFF (FTE): 2 administrative
FACILITIES/EQUIPMENT/PRESERVATION: fire detection controls, fire extinguishing system
PATRON USE STATISTICS: 10,000 in-house patrons, 1000 telephone, 1000 mail reference requests, 10,000 reference photocopies, 2000 microfilm/fiche

---

University of Texas at El Paso
Library, Special Collections Department
El Paso, TX 79968-0582

TEL: (915)747-5697
FAX: (915)747-5327

REPORTED BY: Ann Massmann, Acting Head; Claudia Rivers
TYPE OF INSTITUTION: library (academic)

HOURS: M,T,Th,F 8-5, W 8am-9pm, Sa 10-2
ACCESS: open to the general public
SERVICES: in-person, mail & phone reference, photocopies, photographic reproduction

PRIMARY COLLECTION FOCUS: El Paso, Southern New Mexico & Northern Mexico; printing
El Paso, TX
New Mexico, Southern

Mexico, Northern
Mexico--Spanish Colonial period
Mexican Revolution
military history
printing arts
Texas Regional Historical Resource Depository
railroads
U.S.-Mexico border

INCLUSIVE DATES: 1490 - present
VOLUME: 3,000 linear feet plus 51,000 volumes
COLLECTION FORMATS: 2,000 feet manuscript collections, 50 feet institution's records, 50,000 books, 500 feet government records, 50 feet photographs, 40 maps, 800 oral histories, 2400 microfilm
COLLECTION ACCESS: card catalog, computerized finding aids (used by staff and patrons), inventories, guides
SOFTWARE/SYSTEM: NOTIS, Paradox
ACQUISITION REPORTED TO: OCLC
STAFF (FTE): 1 administrative, 1 general archival, .5 curator, 1 clerical, 10 students, 1-3 interns
INSTITUTIONAL SUPPORT FOR PROFESSIONAL DEVELOPMENT: reimbursement for courses; reimbursement for travel, payment for mailings, telephone; use of facilities, clerical staff
SPECIAL SERVICES/PROGRAMS: exhibits, tours, classes, lectures/presentations
FACILITIES/EQUIPMENT/PRESERVATION: temperature controls, humidity controls, fire detection controls, fire extinguishing system
PATRON USE STATISTICS: 6200 in-house patrons, 300 telephone, 1000 collections used

NHPRC TX326-800

El Paso: Diocese of the Rio Grande, Protestant Episcopal Church: NHPRC TX326-160

El Paso: University of Texas, El Paso Centennial Museum, Mss Collection: NHPRC TX326-770

El Paso: University of Texas, Institute of Oral History: NHPRC TX326-780

Fort Stockton: Annie Riggs Memorial Museum: NHPRC TX367-40

Floyd County Historical Museum **TEL**: (806) 983-2415
105 East Missouri Street
Box 304
Floydada, TX 79235

REPORTED BY: Nancy Marble, board member-volunteer
TYPE OF INSTITUTION: museum (county/local)

HOURS: M-F 1-5
ACCESS: Open
SERVICES: mail, phone, photocopies

PRIMARY COLLECTION FOCUS: Floyd County history and genealogy
Floyd County, TX (local history)
genealogy

INCLUSIVE DATES: 1890-
COLLECTION FORMATS: photographs, county newspaper collection, family papers
COLLECTION ACCESS: card catalog
STAFF (FTE): 2 volunteer/docent, 2 other: "Green Thumb Workers"
SPECIAL SERVICES/PROGRAMS: exhibits, tours, newsletter

PATRON USE STATISTICS: mail reference, photocopies [numbers not reported]

Third Cavalry Museum **TEL**: (915) 568-1922
Attn: ATZC-DPT-MM
Fort Bliss, TX 79916-5300

REPORTED BY: Dick Fritz, Curator
TYPE OF INSTITUTION: museum (federal)

HOURS: M-F, 9-4:30
ACCESS: open
SERVICES: in-person, mail, phone, photocopies

PRIMARY COLLECTION FOCUS: history 3d Regiment U.S. Cavalry, Regiment of Mounted Riflemen, 3d
   Armored Cavalry, Regiment of 3d Cavalry Group (Mecz.)
   military history
   U.S. Army--3d Cavalry Regiment
   U.S. Army--Regiment of Mounted Riflemen
   U.S. Army--3d Armored Cavalry Regiment
   U.S. Army--3d Cavalry Group (Mecz)

INCLUSIVE DATES: 1846-
VOLUME: small
COLLECTION FORMATS: institution's records, books, pamphlets, films
      government records, photographs, maps, oral histories
COLLECTION ACCESS: card, registers
ACQUISITION REPORTED TO: Office of the Chief of Military History
STAFF (FTE): 1 curator
SPECIAL SERVICES/PROGRAMS: exhibits, classes, lectures
FACILITIES/EQUIPMENT/PRESERVATION: temperature controls, fire detection controls, preservation lab,
      disaster preparedness plan
PATRON USE STATISTICS: ca. 150 (mainly persons within the regiment) in-house patrons, 135 telephone,
      96 mail reference requests

U.S. Army Air Defense Artillery Museum **TEL**: (915) 568-5412
Attn: ATZC-DPT-MM
Fort Bliss, TX 79916-5300

REPORTED BY: Tim O'Gorman, Curator
TYPE OF INSTITUTION: museum (federal)

HOURS: daily 9-4:30; closed Christmas, New Years, Easter Sunday, Thanksgiving
ACCESS: Open
SERVICES: in-person reference, mail, phone, copies, photographs
RESTRICTIONS: photocopies limited at discretion of staff; photographs reproduced minimum of 6

PRIMARY COLLECTION FOCUS: materials and documents relating to Air Defense Artillery
      anti-aircraft artillery
      U.S. Army
      military history

INCLUSIVE DATES: 1917-
VOLUME: 7000+ artifacts/documents
COLLECTION FORMATS: 700 books, 500 pamphlets, 150 films, 300 government records, 3000 photographs

100 maps, 10 oral histories
COLLECTION ACCESS: card catalog
ACQUISITION REPORTED TO: Chief, U.S. Army Center of Military History
STAFF (FTE): 2 museum staff, 1 training NCO
INSTITUTIONAL SUPPORT FOR PROFESSIONAL DEVELOPMENT: tuition, memberships, meetings travel, in-house workshops, mailings, telephone, use of facilities and clerical staff
SPECIAL SERVICES/PROGRAMS: exhibits, tours, classes, lectures
FACILITIES/EQUIPMENT/PRESERVATION: temperature controls, humidity controls, fire detection controls, fire extinguishing system, preservation lab, disaster preparedness plan
PATRON USE STATISTICS: 150 in-house patrons, 75 telephone, 75 mail reference requests, 25 collections used, 50 reference photocopies

---

Fort Davis National Historic Site
P. O. Box 1456
Fort Davis, TX 79734

TEL: (915) 426-3164
FAX: (915) 426-3122

REPORTED BY: Elaine Harmon, Museum Technician
TYPE OF INSTITUTION: historic site (federal)

HOURS: daily 8-5
ACCESS: open
SERVICES: in-person, mail, phone, photocopies, fee for photocopying if in volume

PRIMARY COLLECTION FOCUS: Indian Wars; West Texas fort protecting frontier (1854-1891)
  Indian Wars
  Western frontier
  Fort Davis, TX (local history)
  military history
  frontier history
  parks and monuments, federal

INCLUSIVE DATES: 1854-1961
COLLECTION FORMATS: 10,000 items manuscript collections, 5,000 institution's records, 155 rare books, 1000 pamphlets, ca. 50 films, 750 photographs, 250 maps, 10,000 militaria
COLLECTION ACCESS: computerized finding aids (used by staff)
SOFTWARE/SYSTEM: Automated National Catalog System devised by the National Park Service using a dBase foundation
ACQUISITION REPORTED TO: guide
STAFF (FTE): 1 preservation, 1 seasonal aid, 2 student (Youth Conservation Corps)
INSTITUTIONAL SUPPORT FOR PROFESSIONAL DEVELOPMENT: tuition
SPECIAL SERVICES/PROGRAMS: exhibits, tours, lectures
FACILITIES/EQUIPMENT/PRESERVATION: temperature controls, humidity controls, fire detection controls, fire extinguishing system
PATRON USE STATISTICS: 10 in-house patrons, 200 mail reference requests, 75 collections used, 200 microfilm/fiche copies

---

Fort Sam Houston Museum
Building 123
Fort Sam Houston Museum, AFZG-PTM-M
Fort Sam Houston, TX 78234-5000

TEL: (512) 221-0019

REPORTED BY: John Manguso, Museum Director

TYPE OF INSTITUTION: museum with historical site of 500+ acres (federal)

HOURS: W-Su 10-4
ACCESS: Open
SERVICES: in-person, mail, phone, copies
RESTRICTIONS: priority is to inquiries from U.S. Army agencies, federal and state agencies; all others

PRIMARY COLLECTION FOCUS: Artifacts and materials related to the presence of the U.S. Army within this
    region since 1845
    U.S. Army
    Fort Sam Houston, TX
    military history
    parks and monuments, federal

INCLUSIVE DATES: 1845-
VOLUME: 975 cubic feet
COLLECTION FORMATS: 25 institution's records, 150 cubic feet books, 10 cubic feet films
    200 government records, 100 cubic feet photographs, 500 maps
COLLECTION ACCESS: not described
STAFF (FTE): 1 curator, 2 museum technician, 1 exhibit specialist, 2 volunteer/docent
INSTITUTIONAL SUPPORT FOR PROFESSIONAL DEVELOPMENT: tuition
SPECIAL SERVICES/PROGRAMS: exhibits, tours, classes, lectures
FACILITIES/EQUIPMENT/PRESERVATION: temperature controls, humidity controls, fire extinguishing
    system, disaster preparedness plan
PATRON USE STATISTICS: user statistics not kept

Amon Carter Museum
3501 Camp Bowie Blvd., Fort Worth, TX 76107
P. O. Box 2365, Fort Worth, TX 76113-2365

TEL: (817) 738-1933
FAX: (817) 377-8523

REPORTED BY: Paula Stewart, Archivist
TYPE OF INSTITUTION: museum (American art)

HOURS: Archives: M-F, 9:30-4:30; Museum--Offices: M-F, 9-5; Galleries, T-Sa, 10-5; Su, 12/1-5
ACCESS: access policy not yet determined; call/write for information

PRIMARY COLLECTION FOCUS: institutional archives; papers of Amon G. Carter, Sr.; papers of several
    photographers, including Laura Gilpin and Eliot Porter
    Amon Carter Museum (records)
    Carter, Amon G.
    art
    photography, history of
    Gilpin, Laura
    Porter, Eliot

INCLUSIVE DATES: 1959-
COLLECTION FORMATS: 250 linear feet manuscript collections, 500+ linear feet institution's records, books,
    pamphlets, films, 25 linear feet photographs, oral histories, other
COLLECTION ACCESS: not described; however, once processed, collections at least should be inventoried
    to file folder level
ACQUISITION REPORTED TO: RLIN, journal(s)
STAFF (FTE): 1 administrative, 1 general archival, 1 intern
INSTITUTIONAL SUPPORT FOR PROFESSIONAL DEVELOPMENT: tuition, meetings registration/travel,
    mailings, telephone, use of facilities & clerical
SPECIAL SERVICES/PROGRAMS: fund raising
FACILITIES/EQUIPMENT/PRESERVATION: temperature controls, humidity controls, fire detection controls,
    fire extinguishing system, limited in-house preservations facilities; access to independent preservation

lab, disaster preparedness plan
PATRON USE STATISTICS: not available at this time

NHPRC TX374-40

Cattleman's Museum
1301 West 7th Street
Fort Worth, TX 76102

TEL: (817) 332-7064
FAX: (817) 332-5446

REPORTED BY: Carol Williams, Foundation/Museum Coordinator
TYPE OF INSTITUTION: museum (non-profit foundation)

HOURS: M-F 8:30-4:30
ACCESS: by appointment
SERVICES: in-person, mail, phone, fee, copies, photograph reproduction

PRIMARY COLLECTION FOCUS: cattle and ranching industry history
- cattle industry
- ranching
- brands--cattle
- trail drives
- cowboys
- Texas & Southwest Cattle Raisers Association

INCLUSIVE DATES: late 1800s-
COLLECTION FORMATS: 120 volumes institution's records, 1000 books, 100 pamphlets, 100 films 25,000 photographs
COLLECTION ACCESS: card catalog, guide, registers
STAFF (FTE): 1 administrative, 1 administrative fund raiser, 1 coordinator of other activities 10 clerical
SPECIAL SERVICES/PROGRAMS: exhibits, tours, classes, fund raising, lectures
FACILITIES/EQUIPMENT/PRESERVATION: fire detection controls
PATRON USE STATISTICS: ca. 250 requests/year (includes all categories)

Fort Worth Public Library
Genealogy/Local History
300 Taylor
Fort Worth, TX 76102

TEL: (817) 871-7740

REPORTED BY: Kenneth N. Hopkins, Archivist
TYPE OF INSTITUTION: library (city)

HOURS: M-W 9-9; Th-F, 9-6; Sa 10-6
ACCESS: Open
SERVICES: in-person, mail, photocopies, photographic reproduction
RESTRICTIONS: fragile materials cannot be copied; a few collections require permission from donor to examine

PRIMARY COLLECTION FOCUS: Fort Worth and Tarrant County history and genealogy
- Fort Worth, TX (local history)
- Tarrant County, TX (local history)
- genealogy

INCLUSIVE DATES: 1849-
VOLUME: 625 cubic feet

COLLECTION FORMATS: 450 cubic feet manuscript collections, 25 cubic feet institution's records, 3000 volumes books, 75 cubic feet pamphlets/clippings, 10 cubic feet films, 20 cubic feet photographs, 10 cubic feet maps, 5 cubic feet oral histories, 30 cubic feet cartoons, editorials
COLLECTION ACCESS: card catalog, registers, container lists
ACQUISITION REPORTED TO: journals(s)
STAFF (FTE): 1 general archival, 1 preservation, 10 volunteer/docent
INSTITUTIONAL SUPPORT FOR PROFESSIONAL DEVELOPMENT: use of clerical staff
SPECIAL SERVICES/PROGRAMS: exhibits
FACILITIES/EQUIPMENT/PRESERVATION: temperature controls, fire detection controls, fire extinguishing system, preservation lab
PATRON USE STATISTICS: user statistics not kept

NHPRC TX374-250

National Archives and Record Center - Southwest Region   **TEL**: (817) 334-5525
501 West Felix Street, Building 1
P. O. Box 6216
Fort Worth, TX 76115

REPORTED BY: Kent Carter, Director
TYPE OF INSTITUTION: archives (federal)

HOURS: M-F 8-4
ACCESS: Open
SERVICES: in-person reference, photocopies

PRIMARY COLLECTION FOCUS: records of federal agencies
    U.S.--government
    Southwestern U.S.
    Native Americans
    Bureau of Indian Affairs
    U.S.--legal records

INCLUSIVE DATES: 1806-1989
VOLUME: 65,137
COLLECTION FORMATS: government records
COLLECTION ACCESS: guide, registers
ACQUISITION REPORTED TO: journal(s)
STAFF (FTE): 8 general archival, 70 volunteer
FACILITIES/EQUIPMENT/PRESERVATION: temperature controls, humidity controls, fire detection controls, fire extinguishing system, disaster preparedness plan
PATRON USE STATISTICS: 9600 in-house patrons, 20,000 telephone requests, 3600 mail reference requests, 40,000 reference photocopies, 5000 microfilm/fiche copies

NHPRC TX375-550

Southwestern Baptist Theological Seminary   **TEL**: (817) 923-1921 x3330
2001 West Seminary Drive   **FAX**: (817) 923-1921 x2810
Box 22000
Fort Worth, TX 76122-2490

REPORTED BY: Alan J. Lefever, Archivist/Special Collections Librarian
TYPE OF INSTITUTION: archives (religious)

HOURS: M-F 8-12, 1-5

ACCESS: Open
SERVICES: in-person reference, mail, phone, photocopies

PRIMARY COLLECTION FOCUS: Texas Baptist history and archives for the seminary
   religion
   Baptist Church
   Southwestern Baptist Theological Seminary (records)
   church history

INCLUSIVE DATES: 1830s-
VOLUME: 3497 linear feet
COLLECTION FORMATS: 2,375 linear feet manuscript collections, institution's records, books, pamphlets, films, 60,818 photographs, oral histories
COLLECTION ACCESS: card catalog, computerized finding aids (used by staff)
SOFTWARE/SYSTEM: dBase
ACQUISITION REPORTED TO: journal(s)
STAFF (FTE): 1 administrative, 1 clerical, 1 student
INSTITUTIONAL SUPPORT FOR PROFESSIONAL DEVELOPMENT: tuition, memberships, meetings registration/travel, telephone, use of facilities, clerical
SPECIAL SERVICES/PROGRAMS: exhibits
FACILITIES/EQUIPMENT/PRESERVATION: fire extinguishing system
PATRON USE STATISTICS: 69 telephone patrons, 315 mail reference requests
NHPRC TX374-720

Tarrant County Black Historical & Genealogical Society   **TEL**: (817) 332-6049
4751 Ramey Avenue
Fort Worth, TX 76105

REPORTED BY: Lenora Rolla, Director
TYPE OF INSTITUTION: archives, historical society, library, museum (county/local)

HOURS: M-F 11-5; other times by appointment
ACCESS: Open
SERVICES: in-person reference, mail, phone

PRIMARY COLLECTION FOCUS: Black culture and heritage
   African Americans
   genealogy
   Tarrant County, TX

COLLECTION FORMATS: institution's records, 1000 films, 1000 photographs, 40 maps
COLLECTION ACCESS: card catalog, container lists
STAFF (FTE): 1 photo curator (volunteer), 4 other volunteer/docent, 2 clerical (volunteer)
INSTITUTIONAL SUPPORT FOR PROFESSIONAL DEVELOPMENT: meetings, workshops, mailings, facilities, clerical
SPECIAL SERVICES/PROGRAMS: exhibits, tours, classes, newsletter, other
FACILITIES/EQUIPMENT/PRESERVATION: fire extinguishing system
PATRON USE STATISTICS: 110 in-house patrons, 200 telephone, 20 mail reference requests, 15 collections used, 50 reference photocopies, 150 microfilm/fiche copies

---

Texas Christian University - Mary Couts Burnett Library   **TEL**: (817) 921-7108
2800 South University Drive   **FAX**: (817) 921-7447
P. O. Box 32904
Fort Worth, TX 76129

REPORTED BY: Roger L. Rainwater, Special Collections Librarian
TYPE OF INSTITUTION: library (academic)

HOURS: Special Collections: M-F 8-5, advisable to call ahead to make sure the department will be open, especially during intersessions and holidays
ACCESS: by appointment
SERVICES: in-person reference, mail, phone, photocopies

PRIMARY COLLECTION FOCUS: History of Texas Christian University, Fort Worth (to a lesser extent), and Texas (to an even lesser extent)
Texas Christian University (records)
Fort Worth, TX
Texas--history
education

INCLUSIVE DATES: ca. 1860-
COLLECTION FORMATS: manuscript collections, institution's records, books, pamphlets, films, photographs, maps
COLLECTION ACCESS: card catalog, registers, container lists, computerized finding aids (used by staff), not described
SOFTWARE/SYSTEM: DRA ATLAS system, WordPerfect, Pro-Cite
STAFF (FTE): 1 administrative, 1 general, 1 volunteer/docent, 1 clerical, 1 student
INSTITUTIONAL SUPPORT FOR PROFESSIONAL DEVELOPMENT: meetings registration/travel
SPECIAL SERVICES/PROGRAMS: exhibits
FACILITIES/EQUIPMENT/PRESERVATION: temperature controls, humidity controls, fire detection controls, disaster preparedness plan
PATRON USE STATISTICS: user statistics not kept

NHPRC TX374-750

Admiral Nimitz Museum State Historical Park
328 E. Main Street
P. O. Box 777
Fredericksburg, TX 78624

TEL: (512) 997-4379
FAX: (512) 997-8092

REPORTED BY: Paula Ussery, Curator of Collections
TYPE OF INSTITUTION: archives library, museum (state)

HOURS: open 364 days a year, 8-5; closed Christmas Day
ACCESS: open (appointment preferred)
SERVICES: in-person, mail, phone, photocopies

PRIMARY COLLECTION FOCUS: life of Fleet Admiral Chester W. Nimitz; WWII in Pacific
Nimitz, Chester William
naval history
World War 1939-1945--Pacific Theater
U.S. Navy
World War 1939-1945--home front
Pacific Ocean
warships

INCLUSIVE DATES: 1941-45
COLLECTION FORMATS: 70 linear feet manuscript collections, 236 linear feet books, 12 linear feet pamphlets, 25 linear feet films, 15 linear feet photographs, 9 linear feet maps, 2 linear feet oral histories
COLLECTION ACCESS: card catalog, container lists
STAFF (FTE): 1 curator, 2 volunteer/docent, 1 clerical, 1 student

INSTITUTIONAL SUPPORT FOR PROFESSIONAL DEVELOPMENT: dues, meetings, telephone, use of facilities
SPECIAL SERVICES/PROGRAMS: exhibits, newsletter, fund raising, lectures
FACILITIES/EQUIPMENT/PRESERVATION: temperature controls, fire detection controls
PATRON USE STATISTICS: 8 in-house patrons, 21 telephone, 41 mail reference requests, 55 reference photocopies

---

Gillespie County Historical Society
312 West San Antonio
P. O. Box 765
Fredericksburg, TX 78624

TEL: (512) 997-2835

REPORTED BY: Blanca Matern, Collection/Registrar, Museum
TYPE OF INSTITUTION: archives, historical society, (self-sustaining)

HOURS: Museum: Weekdays, 10-5; Sun 1-5; closed all day Tuesdays and Winter Dec 15-Mar 15
SERVICES: office hours, 8-5
ACCESS: open
SERVICES: in-person, mail, phone, photocopies

PRIMARY COLLECTION FOCUS: living history center, documents, photographs, Vereins Kirche Archives
    Germans--Texas
    Gillespie County, TX (local history)
    church history

INCLUSIVE DATES: 1846-1920
VOLUME: 10,000+ (including artifacts)
COLLECTION FORMATS: manuscript collections, institution's records, books, pamphlets, government records, photographs, maps, local census records (1850,-60,-70), church records
COLLECTION ACCESS: registers
STAFF (FTE): administrative, general archival, preservation, 10 volunteer/docent, 1 clerical, 2 other
SPECIAL SERVICES/PROGRAMS: exhibits, tours, newsletter, fund raising
FACILITIES/EQUIPMENT/PRESERVATION: temperature controls, humidity controls, fire detection controls, disaster preparedness plan
PATRON USE STATISTICS: in-house, other [number not specified]

NHPRC TX381-280

Gainesville: Cooke County Heritage Society, Inc.: NHPRC TX390-140

Center for 20th Century Texas Studies (Moody Mansion & Museum)
2618 Broadway
P. O. Box 1300
Galveston, TX 77550

TEL: (409) 762-9693
FAX: (409) 762-7055

REPORTED BY: not given
TYPE OF INSTITUTION: museum (non-profit foundation)

ACCESS: not yet open to the general public
SERVICES: mail, phone, fee, copies, photographs
RESTRICTIONS: for use in interpretive programs & publications (with credit)

PRIMARY COLLECTION FOCUS: Moody family of Galveston
>banking
>Moody family
>ranching
>U.S.--politics
>Texas--politics
>Galveston, TX
>genealogy
>politics

INCLUSIVE DATES: 1790-1986
VOLUME: 1500 linear feet
COLLECTION FORMATS: 50 linear feet institution's records, 1500 books, 60 linear feet pamphlets, 10 films, 11,000 photographs, 25 oral histories
COLLECTION ACCESS: computerized finding aids (used by staff)
SOFTWARE/SYSTEM: QUIXIS
STAFF (FTE): 1 general archival
INSTITUTIONAL SUPPORT FOR PROFESSIONAL DEVELOPMENT: tuition, memberships, meetings registration/travel, use of facilities
SPECIAL SERVICES/PROGRAMS: newsletter, lectures
FACILITIES/EQUIPMENT/PRESERVATION: temperature controls, humidity controls, fire detection controls, fire extinguishing system, disaster preparedness plan

---

1847 Powhatan House
The Galveston Garden Club, Inc.
3427 Avenue O
Galveston, TX 77550

TEL: (409) 763-0077

REPORTED BY: Evangeline Loessin Whorton, House Chairman
TYPE OF INSTITUTION: private landmark (historic residence owned by civic organization)

HOURS: each Sat 1:30 and 3:30, and at all other hours for groups by advance arrangements
ACCESS: open (call for schedule), appointment at other times
SERVICES: in-person, phone

PRIMARY COLLECTION FOCUS: documents and personal papers of the John Seabrook Sydnor and Caroline Willis Ladd families
>Sydnor, John Seabrook
>Ladd, Caroline Willis
>genealogy
>Civil War
>Powhatan House, TX
>family history

INCLUSIVE DATES: 1840-
COLLECTION FORMATS: manuscript collections, institution's records, books, pamphlets, government records, maps, 2 oral histories
COLLECTION ACCESS: registers, not described
ACQUISITION REPORTED TO: guide, journal(s)
STAFF (FTE): preservation, volunteer/docent [numbers not reported]
INSTITUTIONAL SUPPORT FOR PROFESSIONAL DEVELOPMENT: memberships
SPECIAL SERVICES/PROGRAMS: tours, classes, fund raising, lectures
FACILITIES/EQUIPMENT/PRESERVATION: temperature controls, humidity controls, fire detection controls, fire extinguishing system, disaster preparedness plan
PATRON USE STATISTICS: 100 in-house patrons, 50 telephone, 15 mail reference requests

Rosenberg Library - Galveston & Texas History Center
2310 Sealy Avenue
Galveston, TX 77550

TEL: (409) 763-8854
FAX: (409) 763-0275

REPORTED BY: Casey Edward Greene, Assistant Archivist
TYPE OF INSTITUTION: library (privately operated though receives public funds)

HOURS: Library: M-Th, 9-9; F-Sa, 9-6; open Su 1-5 during Sept-May. GTHC: Tu-Sa 9-5.
ACCESS: Open
SERVICES: in-person reference, mail, phone, fee, photocopies, photographs. $5.00 research fee for mail requests. Commercial and scholarly use fees for photo publication orders.

PRIMARY COLLECTION FOCUS: Galveston, Galveston County, TX through 1865 (esp. Republic of Texas);
    Nicholas Clayton
    Galveston, TX (local history)
    Galveston County, TX (local history)
    Upper Gulf Coast
    Clayton, Nicholas J.
    architecture
    Civil War
    Texas, Republic of

INCLUSIVE DATES: 1506-
COLLECTION FORMATS: 2100 linear feet manuscript collections, 12,700 books, 63,000 pamphlets, ca. 500 films, 25,000 photographs, 1500 maps, 125 oral histories, 1000 volumes newspapers, 1000 architectural drawings, 1000 volumes periodicals
COLLECTION ACCESS: card catalog, guide, registers, computerized finding aids (used by staff)
SOFTWARE/SYSTEM: MARCON II
ACQUISITION REPORTED TO: NUCMC, journal(s): SSA Newsletter (infrequently)
STAFF (FTE): 1 administrative, 1 general archival, .5 library assistant, 1 clerical
INSTITUTIONAL SUPPORT FOR PROFESSIONAL DEVELOPMENT: tuition, meetings registration/travel, mailings, telephone, use of facilities and clerical staff
SPECIAL SERVICES/PROGRAMS: exhibits, tours, fund raising, lectures, publications (books), History Fair sponsor
FACILITIES/EQUIPMENT/PRESERVATION: temperature controls, disaster preparedness plan
PATRON USE STATISTICS: 4200 (includes telephone and mail), 250 collections used

NHPRC TX397-690

Truman G. Blocker, Jr., History of Medicine Collection
Moody Medical Library
University of Texas Medical Branch
9th & Market Streets
University of Texas Medical Branch
Galveston, TX 77550

TEL: (409) 772-2397
FAX: (409) 765-9852

REPORTED BY: Inci A. Bowman, Curator
TYPE OF INSTITUTION: library (state, academic)

HOURS: M-F 8-12, 1-5
ACCESS: Open
SERVICES: in person reference, mail, phone, photocopies, photographs, slides

PRIMARY COLLECTION FOCUS: history of medicine and allied sciences
    medicine, history of
    physicians
    health sciences

University of Texas Medical Branch (records)

INCLUSIVE DATES: 15-20th centuries for entire collection
COLLECTION FORMATS: 375 linear feet manuscript collections & institution's records, 18,000 books (rare) & pamphlets, 6000 photographs, 6000 prints, 1600 artifacts
COLLECTION ACCESS: card catalog, registers, container lists, computerized finding aids (used by staff, patrons), rare book collection is included in Library's online catalog
STAFF (FTE): 1 administrative, 1.5 clerical
INSTITUTIONAL SUPPORT FOR PROFESSIONAL DEVELOPMENT: tuition, meetings, registration/travel, mailings, use of facilities and clerical staff
SPECIAL SERVICES/PROGRAMS: exhibits, tours, lectures
FACILITIES/EQUIPMENT/PRESERVATION: temperature controls, humidity controls, fire detection controls, fire extinguishing system, disaster preparedness plan
PATRON USE STATISTICS: in-house, telephone, mail, reference photocopies [numbers not specified]
NHPRC TX397-790

Southwestern University
A. Frank Smith, Jr., Library Center
Box 770
Georgetown, TX 78627-0770

TEL: (512) 863-1561
FAX: (512) 863-1155

REPORTED BY: Norma Siviter Assadourian, Head, Special Collections
TYPE OF INSTITUTION: library (academic)

HOURS: M-F 9:30-4:30, closed holidays
ACCESS: Open
SERVICES: in-person reference, mail, phone, photocopies
RESTRICTIONS: John G. Tower Senate papers available as processed

PRIMARY COLLECTION FOCUS: Edward A. Clark Texana Collection, John G. Tower Archives, American
    literature
    Tower, John Goodwin
    Clark, Edward A.
    literary manuscripts
    Texana
    congressional papers
    Bush, George
    Methodist Church

INCLUSIVE DATES: 1778-present
VOLUME: 14,990 books, 4500 maps, ca. 1200 linear feet Tower Archives
COLLECTION FORMATS: 2000 linear feet manuscript collections, ca. 12 linear feet films, ca. 1000+ photographs, 4500 maps, 96 oral histories, ca. 20 linear feet other
COLLECTION ACCESS: card catalog, guide, registers, container lists, computerized finding aids
SOFTWARE/SYSTEM: Pro-Cite currently used by staff only, DYNIX used by staff and patrons
ACQUISITION REPORTED TO: OCLC
STAFF (FTE): 1 administrative, 1 general archival, 2 clerical, 1.2 student
INSTITUTIONAL SUPPORT FOR PROFESSIONAL DEVELOPMENT: tuition, meetings registration/travel (partial), telephone, facilities
SPECIAL SERVICES/PROGRAMS: exhibits
FACILITIES/EQUIPMENT/PRESERVATION: fire detection controls, fire extinguishing system, preservation lab (in process)
PATRON USE STATISTICS: not reported
NHPRC TX404-120

Texas Wendish Heritage Museum **TEL**: (409) 366-2441
FM 2239, Serbin, TX
Rt 2, Box 155
Giddings, TX 78942

REPORTED BY: Daphne Dalton Garrett, Archivist
TYPE OF INSTITUTION: archives, library, museum (ethnic heritage)

HOURS: Su-F 1-5
ACCESS: Museum & Library open; Archives by appointment
SERVICES: mail, photocopies, photographs (fee for copies & photo duplication)

PRIMARY COLLECTION FOCUS: Wendish heritage in Texas
    Wends

INCLUSIVE DATES: 1555-1990
COLLECTION FORMATS: 16.69 cubic feet manuscript collections, 15.45 cubic feet institution's records, 800 books, pamphlets, 3000 photographs, 2 maps, 1 oral histories, 13.47 cubic feet newspapers
COLLECTION ACCESS: registers, container lists, computerized finding aid (used by staff)
SOFTWARE/SYSTEM: Professional File (in progress)
STAFF (FTE): general archival, photo curator (volunteer)
INSTITUTIONAL SUPPORT FOR PROFESSIONAL DEVELOPMENT: tuition, meetings
SPECIAL SERVICES/PROGRAMS: exhibits, tours, newsletter, lectures
FACILITIES/EQUIPMENT/PRESERVATION: temperature controls, humidity controls

---

Upshur County Library **TEL**: (903) 843-5001
702 West Tyler Street
Gilmer, TX 75644

REPORTED BY: Joyce Morrison, County Librarian
TYPE OF INSTITUTION: library (county/local)

HOURS: M-F 8-6; Sa 9-1
ACCESS: Open
SERVICES: in-person reference, copies, microform copier

PRIMARY COLLECTION FOCUS: history and genealogy of Upshur County
    Upshur County, TX (local history)
    genealogy

COLLECTION FORMATS: 89 manuscript collections, 69 books, 12 cassettes oral histories
STAFF (FTE): 8 hr/wk volunteer/docent

Grapevine Public Library **TEL**: (817) 481-0336
1201 South Main **FAX**: (817) 481-0474
Grapevine, TX 76051

REPORTED BY: Jerre Williams, Reference Librarian
TYPE OF INSTITUTION: library (city)

HOURS: M Tu Th 10-8; W F 10-6; Sa 10-5
ACCESS: Open
SERVICES: in-person, mail, phone, photocopies

PRIMARY COLLECTION FOCUS: genealogy and local history of Grapevine area
    Grapevine, TX (local history)
    genealogy

VOLUME: 1 file d
COLLECTION FORMATS: books, 26 oral histories, manuscripts, photographs
COLLECTION ACCESS: computerized finding aids (used by staff and patrons)
SOFTWARE/SYSTEM: local in-house program
INSTITUTIONAL SUPPORT FOR PROFESSIONAL DEVELOPMENT: tuition (100%), dues, meetings, clerical
SPECIAL SERVICES/PROGRAMS: classes, lectures
FACILITIES/EQUIPMENT/PRESERVATION: other
PATRON USE STATISTICS: user statistics not kept

NHPRC TX439-280

Harlingen: Harlingen Public Library: NHPRC TX446-320

Depot Museum   **TEL**: (903)657-4303
514 N. High St.
Henderson, TX 75652

REPORTED BY: not listed
TYPE OF INSTITUTION: museum (county/local)

HOURS: M-F 9-5, Sa 9-1
ACCESS: open to the general public
SERVICES: in-person and mail reference, photocopies

PRIMARY COLLECTION FOCUS: Rusk County, Texas, History
    Rusk County, TX (local history)
    business history
    genealogy

INCLUSIVE DATES: 1840-1950
COLLECTION FORMATS: photographs, maps
COLLECTION ACCESS: card catalog
STAFF (FTE): 1 administrative, 5 volunteer/docent
FACILITIES/EQUIPMENT/PRESERVATION: fire detection controls
PATRON USE STATISTICS: user statistics not kept

National Cowgirl Hall of Fame & Western Heritage Center   **TEL**: (806)364-5252
515 Avenue B
P.O. Box 1742
Hereford, TX 79045

REPORTED BY: Virginia Artho, Assistant Director
TYPE OF INSTITUTION: archives, library, museum (special)

HOURS: M-F 9-5
ACCESS: open to the general public
SERVICES: in-person, mail & phone reference; fee; photocopies, photographic reproduction
RESTRICTIONS: copyrighted material

PRIMARY COLLECTION FOCUS: papers and memorabilia of over 600 Western women
women--Western U.S.
cowgirls
cattle industry

COLLECTION FORMATS: manuscript collections, institution's records, books/serials, pamphlets/ephemera, films/videos, photographs, oral histories
COLLECTION ACCESS: card catalog, registers/inventories, container lists
STAFF (FTE): 2 directors, volunteer/docent, 3 clerical
INSTITUTIONAL SUPPORT FOR PROFESSIONAL DEVELOPMENT: use of facilities, equipment, and clerical staff
SPECIAL SERVICES/PROGRAMS: exhibits, tours, newsletter, fundraising/endowment, lectures/presentations, magazine
FACILITIES/EQUIPMENT/PRESERVATION: temperature controls, fire extinguishing system
PATRON USE STATISTICS: user statistics not kept

Hillsboro: Hill Junior College" NHPRC TX476-320

Harris County Medical Archive **TEL**: (713)795-4200
Houston Academy of Medicine-Texas Medical Center Library **FAX**: (713)790-7052
1133 M.D. Anderson Blvd.
Houston, TX 77030

REPORTED BY: Elizabeth Borst White, Director, Historical Research Center
TYPE OF INSTITUTION: library (private medical library)

HOURS: M-F 9-12, 1-5, weekends by appointment
ACCESS: open to the general public
SERVICES: in-person, mail, & phone reference, photocopies, other
RESTRICTIONS: in depth research for library card holders only

PRIMARY COLLECTION FOCUS: health care & clinical medicine in Harris County, Texas
medicine--Harris County, TX
physicians--Harris County, TX
rheumatology
Hench, Philip
Atomic Bomb Casualty Commission

INCLUSIVE DATES: 1920 - present
COLLECTION FORMATS: 2800 linear feet manuscript collections, 10,000 books, 100 films, 50,000 photographs, 10 oral histories
COLLECTION ACCESS: computerized finding aids (used by staff), registers, on line catalog
SOFTWARE/SYSTEM: Paradox, WordPerfect, Lotus
ACQUISITION REPORTED TO: OCLC
STAFF (FTE): 1 administrative, 1 general archival, 1 photo curator, .5 clerical
INSTITUTIONAL SUPPORT FOR PROFESSIONAL DEVELOPMENT: reimbursement for tuition/registration, courses, meeting registration & travel, payments for mailings, telephone, facilities
FACILITIES/EQUIPMENT/PRESERVATION: temperature controls, humidity controls, fire detection, fire extinguishing system, disaster preparedness plan
PATRON USE STATISTICS: 2500 reference photocopies

Houston Fire Museum **TEL**: (713)524-2526
2403 Milam St.
Houston, TX 77006

REPORTED BY: Tom McDonald
TYPE OF INSTITUTION: museum (city)

HOURS: T-Sa 10-4
ACCESS: open to the general public
SERVICES: in-person, mail and phone reference, photocopies

PRIMARY COLLECTION FOCUS: fire fighting
    firefighting
    Houston, TX--Fire Department
    fire departments--history

INCLUSIVE DATES: 1750-present
COLLECTION FORMATS: 6 feet manuscript collections, institution's records, 150 books, 30 pamphlets, 5 oral histories, 40 films/videotapes, 6 government records, 2000 photographs, 25 maps
COLLECTION ACCESS: not described
STAFF (FTE): 1 administrative, 1 curator
INSTITUTIONAL SUPPORT FOR PROFESSIONAL DEVELOPMENT: tuition/registration reimbursement for courses, payment of dues, reimbursement for professional meetings
SPECIAL SERVICES/PROGRAMS: exhibits, newsletter, lectures/presentations
FACILITIES/EQUIPMENT/PRESERVATION: fire detection controls
PATRON USE STATISTICS: 14,200 in-house patrons

Houston Public Library, Houston Metropolitan Research Center   **TEL**: (713)247-1661
500 McKinney
Houston, TX 77002

REPORTED BY: Dr. Louis J. Marchiafava, Archivist
TYPE OF INSTITUTION: library, archives and manuscripts collections

HOURS: M-F 9-6, processed collections available M-Sa 9-6
ACCESS: open to the general public
SERVICES: in-person, mail, and phone reference, photocopies

PRIMARY COLLECTION FOCUS: history of Houston metropolitan region
    Houston, TX (local history)
    Mexican Americans
    African Americans
    architecture
    civic organizations
    business history
    religious organizations
    Texas Regional Historical Resource Depository

INCLUSIVE DATES: 1830s - present
VOLUME: 21,000 linear feet
COLLECTION FORMATS: 548 manuscript collections, 1.5 million photographs, 600 oral histories
COLLECTION ACCESS: container lists, card index
STAFF (FTE): 2 administrative, 2 general archival/preservation, 1 photo curator, 8 volunteer/docent, 1 clerical, 2 students, 2 interns
INSTITUTIONAL SUPPORT FOR PROFESSIONAL DEVELOPMENT: tuition/registration reimbursement for courses, workshops, reimbursement for professional meeting (registration & travel)
FACILITIES/EQUIPMENT/PRESERVATION: temperature controls, humidity controls, fire extinguishing system, disaster preparedness plan
PATRON USE STATISTICS: 2846 in-house patrons, 5759 telephone, 172 mail reference requests, 5692 collections used

NHPRC TX483-320

Museum of Fine Arts, Houston **TEL**: (713)639-7520
1001 Bissonnet **FAX**: (713)639-7595
P.O. Box 6826
Houston, TX 77265

REPORTED BY: Kathleen Robinson, Archivist
TYPE OF INSTITUTION: archives, museum (city)

HOURS: M-F 10-4:30
ACCESS: public access by appointment only
SERVICES: in-person, mail, & phone reference, photocopies, other
RESTRICTIONS: fees for photocopies & photographs, not all records/collections

PRIMARY COLLECTION FOCUS: Museum of Fine Arts, Houston
- Museum of Fine Arts, Houston, TX (records)
- Contemporary Arts Museum--Houston, TX
- Garden Club of Houston, TX
- art--schools
- art--exhibitions
- architecture--art museums
- museums--education
- Bayou Bend Collection--Houston, TX
- Hogg, Ima
- art museums

INCLUSIVE DATES: 1882 - present
VOLUME: 1800 cubic feet
COLLECTION FORMATS: 125 cubic feet manuscript collections, 1650 cubic feet institution's records, 25 cubic feet ephemera, 400 films, 10,000 photographs, 800 audio tapes
COLLECTION ACCESS: card catalog, container lists, registers
ACQUISITION REPORTED TO: RLIN
STAFF (FTE): 1 administrative, 1 general archival, .5 volunteer, .5 clerical, .5 intern
INSTITUTIONAL SUPPORT FOR PROFESSIONAL DEVELOPMENT: tuition/registration reimbursement for courses, payment of dues, reimbursement for meeting registration & travel, workshops, mailings, use of facilities
FACILITIES/EQUIPMENT/PRESERVATION: temperature controls, humidity controls, fire detection controls, fire extinguishing system
PATRON USE STATISTICS: 785 in-house patrons

National Aeronautics and Space Administration, History Office **TEL**: (713)483-6715
Lyndon B. Johnson Space Center **FAX**: (713)483-2726
Code JM12
Houston, TX 77058

REPORTED BY: Ms. Joey P. Kuhlman, Archivist
TYPE OF INSTITUTION: archives (federal)

HOURS: M-F 8-4:30
ACCESS: public access by appointment only
SERVICES: in-person, mail, & phone reference, photocopies
RESTRICTIONS: requests for documents of over 50 pp. handled through Freedom of Information Act

PRIMARY COLLECTION FOCUS: U.S. manned space flight
  Johnson Space Center, Houston, TX (records)
  NASA - Space Shuttle
  NASA - Space Station
  NASA - Apollo Project
  NASA - Gemini Project
  NASA - Mercury Project
  NASA - Skylab Project
  NASA - Apollo-Soyuz Test Project
  National Aeronautics and Space Administration
  aeronautics
  astronauts
  space exploration

INCLUSIVE DATES: 1958 - present
VOLUME: 2600 linear feet
COLLECTION FORMATS: 2500 feet government records, 100 feet oral histories
COLLECTION ACCESS: repository guide, registers/inventories, computerized finding aids (used by staff)
SOFTWARE/SYSTEM: TextDBMS (full text database management)
ACQUISITION REPORTED TO: NASA Headquarters History Division
STAFF (FTE): 1.5 general archival, .5 part time, 1 clerical
INSTITUTIONAL SUPPORT FOR PROFESSIONAL DEVELOPMENT: tuition/registration reimbursement for courses, payment for mailings, use of facilities, payment for telephone use
FACILITIES/EQUIPMENT/PRESERVATION: temperature controls, fire extinguishing system
PATRON USE STATISTICS: 45 in-house patrons, 456 telephone, 86 mail reference requests,
  43 (all) collections used,
NHPRC TX483-560

Rice University Library, Woodson Research Center
6100 So. Main St.
Houston, TX 77251-1891

TEL: (713)527-8101, ext. 2586
FAX: (713)523-4177

REPORTED BY: Nancy L. Boothe, Director, Woodson Research Center
TYPE OF INSTITUTION: archives, library (academic)

HOURS: M-F 9-5
ACCESS: open to the general public
SERVICES: in-person, mail, & phone reference, photocopies

PRIMARY COLLECTION FOCUS: university archives, manuscript collections & rare books
  Rice University, Houston, TX (records)
  Texas--history
  Civil War
  space--history
  science, history of
  politics--20th century, U.S.
  literature--U.S. authors
  drama--18th century, British
  aeronautics
  naval history--17th and 18th centuries, British

COLLECTION FORMATS: 1725 cubic feet manuscript collections, 841 cubic feet institution's records, 26,854 books, 965 cubic feet government records, 8481 photographs, 132 maps, 1281 architectural records
COLLECTION ACCESS: card catalog, container lists, registers/inventories
STAFF (FTE): 1 administrative, 1.5 volunteer/docent, .5 student, 3 library assistants
INSTITUTIONAL SUPPORT FOR PROFESSIONAL DEVELOPMENT: tuition/registration reimbursement for courses, reimbursement for meetings (registration & travel)

SPECIAL SERVICES/PROGRAMS: exhibits, tours, classes, lectures/presentations
FACILITIES/EQUIPMENT/PRESERVATION: temperature controls, humidity controls, fire detection controls,
PATRON USE STATISTICS: 525 in-house patrons, 1338 collections used, 24780 reference photocopies

NHPRC TX 483-690

Texas Southern University, Special Collections
3100 Cleburne
Houston, TX 77004

TEL: (713)527-7149

REPORTED BY: Sandra Martin-Parham, Archivist/Coordinator of Special Collections
TYPE OF INSTITUTION: archives, library (academic)

HOURS: M-F 8-5
ACCESS: open to the general public
SERVICES: in-person, mail, and phone reference, photocopies, photographs

PRIMARY COLLECTION FOCUS: African Americans; Heartman Collection; Barbara Jordan Archives
   Jordan, Barbara
   African Americans
   history--African Americans
   jazz

COLLECTION ACCESS: card catalog, computerized finding aids (used by patrons), registers/inventories
ACQUISITION REPORTED TO: OCLC
STAFF (FTE): 1 administrative, 1 clerical, 1 student
INSTITUTIONAL SUPPORT FOR PROFESSIONAL DEVELOPMENT: tuition/registration reimbursement for
   courses, reimbursement for meetings, payment for mailings, phone, facilities, use of clerical
SPECIAL SERVICES/PROGRAMS: exhibits, tours, lectures/presentations
FACILITIES/EQUIPMENT/PRESERVATION: temperature controls, fire detection controls, fire extinguishing
   system, disaster plan

NHPRC TX 483-820

University of Houston - Clear Lake
2700 Bay Area Blvd
Houston, TX 77058

TEL: (713)283-3930

REPORTED BY: Casey Edward Greene, Adjunct University Archivist
TYPE OF INSTITUTION: archives (academic)

HOURS: M 8-5
ACCESS: public access by appointment only

PRIMARY COLLECTION FOCUS: records of the University
   Neuman, Alfred R.
   Stauffer, Thomas M.
   University of Houston - Clear Lake (records)

INCLUSIVE DATES: 1970 - present
COLLECTION FORMATS: 2 feet manuscript collections, 70 feet institution's records, 100 books/serials, 3 feet
   pamphlets/ephemera, 500 photographs.
COLLECTION ACCESS: card catalog, container lists, registers/inventories
STAFF (FTE): .2 general archival

University of Houston Libraries, Special Collections
4800 Calhoun
Houston, TX 77204-2091

TEL: (713)743-9750
FAX: (713)743-9748

REPORTED BY: Pat Bozeman, Head, Special Collections
TYPE OF INSTITUTION: library (academic)

HOURS: M-F 8-5
ACCESS: open to the general public
SERVICES: in-person, mail, & phone reference, photocopies, photographs
RESTRICTIONS: photocopies on a case-by-case basis

PRIMARY COLLECTION FOCUS: Texas history, 20th century literature, University of Houston
  Texas
  history--Texas
  literature--19th century
  literature--20th century
  University of Houston (records)
  printing--fine presses

INCLUSIVE DATES: 18th century to present
COLLECTION FORMATS: 500 linear feet manuscript collections, 600 linear feet institution's records, 13,000 volumes books, 3,000 photographs, 3 videos, 500 maps, 750 linear feet theses/dissertations
COLLECTION ACCESS: card catalog, computerized finding aids (used by staff), registers
SOFTWARE/SYSTEM: WordPerfect 5.1
ACQUISITION REPORTED TO: OCLC, professional journal(s)
STAFF (FTE): 1 administrative, 1.5 general archival, 0.5 Friends of the Libraries,
  0.5 clerical, 0.6 student
INSTITUTIONAL SUPPORT FOR PROFESSIONAL DEVELOPMENT: tuition/registration reimbursement for courses, workshops, reimbursement for meetings; payment for mailings, phone; use of facilities, clerical
SPECIAL SERVICES/PROGRAMS: exhibits, classes, fundraising/endowment, lectures/presentations
FACILITIES/EQUIPMENT/PRESERVATION: temperature controls, humidity controls
PATRON USE STATISTICS: 1,789 in-house patrons, 30-50 collections used, 11,600 reference photocopies

---

Houston: Diocese of Galveston-Houston, Chancery Archives & Research: NHPRC TX483-160

Houston: Harris County Heritage Society: NHPRC TX483-280

Houston: Incarnate Word Convent: NHPRC TX483-322

Houston: Lunar Science Institute, Photo/Map Library: NHPRC TX483-480

Houston: Texas Gulf Coast Historical Association: NHPRC TX483-810

Sam Houston Memorial Museum
1836 Sam Houston Avenue
P.O. Box 2057, SHSU
Huntsville, TX 77341

TEL: (409)294-1832
FAX: (409)294-3577

REPORTED BY: Lois S. Pierce, Acting Director/ Education Coordinator
TYPE OF INSTITUTION: museum (state)

HOURS: T-Su 9-5
ACCESS: open to the general public

SERVICES: in-person and mail reference, photocopies

PRIMARY COLLECTION FOCUS: Sam Houston and early Texas life
    Houston, Sam
    Texas
    Texas, Republic of

COLLECTION FORMATS: manuscript collections, institution's records, pamphlets/ephemera, government records, photographs, maps, oral histories
COLLECTION ACCESS: container lists, registers/inventories
STAFF (FTE): 1 administrative
INSTITUTIONAL SUPPORT FOR PROFESSIONAL DEVELOPMENT: payment of dues for memberships, reimbursement for meetings, registration & travel, mailings, use of facilities, phones & staff
SPECIAL SERVICES/PROGRAMS: exhibits, tours, newsletter, fundraising/endowment, lectures/presentations
FACILITIES/EQUIPMENT/PRESERVATION: fire detection controls

Irving Public Library
801 W. Irving Blvd.
P.O. Box 152288
Irving, TX 75015-2288
TEL: (214)721-2606

REPORTED BY: Elaine Collins, Sr. Librarian's Assistant
TYPE OF INSTITUTION: library (city)

HOURS: M,T,Th 12-9, W 10-9, F & Sa 12-6, Su 2-6
ACCESS: open to the general public
SERVICES: in-person, mail, & phone reference
RESTRICTIONS: self-addressed & stamped envelope for mail reference

PRIMARY COLLECTION FOCUS: Irving local history, genealogy, Southern migration route
    Irving, TX (local history)
    genealogy
    migration - Southern U.S.

INCLUSIVE DATES: 1790-present
COLLECTION FORMATS: 50 institution's records, 1300/25 books/serials, 4 films, 250 government records, 10 photographs, 20 maps, 25 oral histories
COLLECTION ACCESS: card catalog, container lists, computerized finding aids (used by staff and patrons)
SOFTWARE/SYSTEM: DYNIX (books)
ACQUISITION REPORTED TO: OCLC
STAFF (FTE): 1 librarian, 1 librarian assistant, 3 volunteer/docent
INSTITUTIONAL SUPPORT FOR PROFESSIONAL DEVELOPMENT: tuition/registration reimbursement for courses, payment of dues for memberships, reimbursement for meetings, use of facilities
SPECIAL SERVICES/PROGRAMS: exhibits
FACILITIES/EQUIPMENT/PRESERVATION: fire detection controls, fire extinguishing system, disaster preparedness plan

---

University of Dallas, Archives
1845 E. Northgate Drive
Irving, TX 75062
TEL: (214)721-5040

REPORTED BY: Harry A. Butler, Collection Development Librarian
TYPE OF INSTITUTION: library (academic)

HOURS: M-F
ACCESS: public access by appointment only
SERVICES: mail & phone reference

PRIMARY COLLECTION FOCUS: University of Dallas & alumni
  University of Dallas (records)
  architecture
  courthouses--Texas

INCLUSIVE DATES: 1955-present
COLLECTION FORMATS: manuscript collections, institution's records, films, photographs, maps
COLLECTION ACCESS: registers/inventories
STAFF (FTE): 0.1 administrative
INSTITUTIONAL SUPPORT FOR PROFESSIONAL DEVELOPMENT: tuition/registration reimbursement for courses, workshops
PATRON USE STATISTICS: user statistics not kept

University of Dallas, William A. Blakley Library,
Special Collections, 1845 E. Northgate Drive
Irving, TX 75062-4799

TEL: (214)721-5350

REPORTED BY: Claudette Hagle, Director of Public Services
TYPE OF INSTITUTION: library (academic, religious)

HOURS: M-F 9-12, 1-4
ACCESS: open to the general public
SERVICES: in person, mail & phone reference

PRIMARY COLLECTION FOCUS: William Rogers Collection, Willmoore Kendall Collection, Polish and Irish Americans
  Rogers, William
  journalists--foreign correspondents
  Polish Americans
  Irish Americans
  Kendall, Willmoore
  political philosophy
  Texas--politics

COLLECTION FORMATS: 1 linear foot manuscript collections, 50 photographs, 3700 books, 30 audio tapes
COLLECTION ACCESS: card catalog, repository guide, inventories, computerized finding aids (used by staff and patrons)
SOFTWARE/SYSTEM: DYNIX
ACQUISITION REPORTED TO: OCLC
STAFF (FTE): 2 administrative (staffed from reference dept.), 1 clerical
INSTITUTIONAL SUPPORT FOR PROFESSIONAL DEVELOPMENT: tuition/registration for courses, in-house workshops, use of facilities, telephone
SPECIAL SERVICES/PROGRAMS: exhibits, tours, newsletter
FACILITIES/EQUIPMENT/PRESERVATION: temperature controls, humidity controls, fire extinguishing system, preservation lab, disaster preparedness plan
PATRON USE STATISTICS: 40 in-house patrons, 10 telephone, 40 mail reference requests, 40 collections used

---

Baptist Missionary Association Theological Seminary
1410 E. Pine St.
Jacksonville, TX 75766

TEL: (903)586-2501

REPORTED BY: James C. Blaylock, Library Director
TYPE OF INSTITUTION: library (religious)

HOURS: [not reported]
ACCESS: [not reported]
SERVICES: in-person reference, photocopies

PRIMARY COLLECTION FOCUS: materials by & about Baptist Missionary Association of America
    Baptist Missionary Association of America
    Baptist Church

INCLUSIVE DATES: 1950-present
VOLUME: 500
COLLECTION FORMATS: institution's records, books/serials, pamphlets/ephemera, films/video, photographs
COLLECTION ACCESS: card catalog, computerized finding aids (used by staff)
SOFTWARE/SYSTEM: Bib-Base
STAFF (FTE): 1 administrative, 3 clerical
FACILITIES/EQUIPMENT/PRESERVATION: fire extinguishing system
PATRON USE STATISTICS: 30 in-house patrons, other user statistics not kept

---

United Methodist Church, Texas Conference   **TEL**: (903)586-2471
Doornbos Library, Lon Morris College
Jacksonville, TX 75766

REPORTED BY: Betty S. Mallory, Chair, Commission on Archives & History
TYPE OF INSTITUTION: archives (religious)

HOURS: T 1-5, W 9-4, Th 9-12 noon
ACCESS: open to the general public
SERVICES: in-person and mail reference, photocopies

PRIMARY COLLECTION FOCUS: Texas Conference - United Methodist Churches
    United Methodist Church, Texas Conference
    Methodist Church

COLLECTION FORMATS: manuscript collections, internal records, books/serials, pamphlets/
    ephemera, films/videotapes, photographs, oral histories
COLLECTION ACCESS: card catalog
STAFF (FTE): [not reported]
INSTITUTIONAL SUPPORT FOR PROFESSIONAL DEVELOPMENT: payment of dues for professional
    organization, reimbursement for meetings, payment for mailings, payment for telephone use

---

Kilgore College   **TEL**: (903)983-8235
1100 Broadway   **FAX**: (903)983-8239
Kilgore, TX 75662

REPORTED BY: Wade L. Pipkin, Library Director
TYPE OF INSTITUTION: library (academic)

HOURS: M-Th 7:30am-9:30pm, F 7:30-4, Su 2-5
ACCESS: open to the general public
SERVICES: in-person, mail, & phone reference, photocopies

PRIMARY COLLECTION FOCUS: Texana, papers of John Hill

Hill, John (former Texas attorney general)
Texana

INCLUSIVE DATES: 1930 - present
COLLECTION FORMATS: 3 file cabinets, 200 maps, 400 pamphlets, ephemera
COLLECTION ACCESS: card catalog, computerized finding aids (used by staff & patrons)
STAFF (FTE): 4 administrative, 7 clerical, 6 student
INSTITUTIONAL SUPPORT FOR PROFESSIONAL DEVELOPMENT: payment of dues for memberships, reimbursement for meetings, in-house workshops, payment for mailings, use of facilities
SPECIAL SERVICES/PROGRAMS: exhibits, tours, classes, newsletter
FACILITIES/EQUIPMENT/PRESERVATION: temperature controls, fire extinguishing system

---

King Ranch Archives
405 North Sixth Street
P.O. Box 1090
Kingsville, TX 78364-1090

TEL: (512)592-0408
FAX: (512)592-6885

REPORTED BY: Bruce S. Cheeseman, Archivist and Historian
TYPE OF INSTITUTION: archives (business)

HOURS: M-F 8-5
ACCESS: by appointment only
SERVICES: in-person, mail and phone reference; photocopies
RESTRICTIONS: research requests subject to approval

PRIMARY COLLECTION FOCUS: King Ranch history
King Ranch, TX (records)
Texas, South
ranching
agriculture
King, Captain Richard
King, Richard family
cattle industry

INCLUSIVE DATES: 1792-present
VOLUME: 4000 cubic feet
COLLECTION FORMATS: 500 cubic feet manuscript collections, 2500 feet institution's records, 1000 books, 100 feet pamphlets, 16,000 photographs, 450 maps, 65 oral histories
COLLECTION ACCESS: Registers, inventories, computerized finding aids (used by staff)
SOFTWARE/SYSTEM: STAR
ACQUISITION REPORTED TO: professional journals
STAFF (FTE): 1 administrative, 1 general archival, 1 volunteer, 1 student
INSTITUTIONAL SUPPORT FOR PROFESSIONAL DEVELOPMENT: tuition/registration reimbursement, dues for professional memberships, reimbursement for meetings, payment for mailings & phone, use of facilities & clerical staff
SPECIAL SERVICES/PROGRAMS: exhibits, tours, newsletter, lectures/presentations
FACILITIES/EQUIPMENT/PRESERVATION: temperature controls, humidity controls, fire detection controls
PATRON USE STATISTICS: 104 telephone patrons, 35 mail reference requests

---

Kingsville: Texas A & I University, John E. Conner Museum: NHPRC TX529-770

Fayette Public Library/Fayette Heritage Museum & Archives
855 S. Jefferson
La Grange, TX 78945

TEL: (409)968-6418

REPORTED BY: Kathy Carter, Director
TYPE OF INSTITUTION: archives, library, museum (city)

HOURS: T-F 10-5, Sa 10-1, Su 1-5
ACCESS: open to the general public
SERVICES: in-person, mail & phone reference, fee for reference, photocopies

PRIMARY COLLECTION FOCUS: Fayette County, Texas
    Fayette County, TX (local history)

COLLECTION FORMATS: manuscript collections, institution's records, books, pamphlets/ephemera, films/videotapes, government records, photographs, maps, oral histories
COLLECTION ACCESS: card catalog, repository guide, registers/inventories
STAFF (FTE): 1.5 administrative.
INSTITUTIONAL SUPPORT FOR PROFESSIONAL DEVELOPMENT: tuition/registration reimbursement for courses, reimbursement for meeting registration, payment for mailings
SPECIAL SERVICES/PROGRAMS: exhibits
FACILITIES/EQUIPMENT/PRESERVATION: temperature controls, humidity controls, fire detection controls, fire extinguishing system

---

Laredo: Nuevo Santander Museum: NHPRC TX543-560

Conservation Districts Foundation, Davis Conservation Library   **TEL**: (713)332-3404
408 East Main St.   **FAX**: (713)332-5259
P.O. Box 776
League City, TX 77573

REPORTED BY: Ruth Chenhall, Education-Information Specialist
TYPE OF INSTITUTION: library (special, nonprofit)

HOURS: weekdays 8-12, 1-5
ACCESS: open to the general public
SERVICES: in-person reference, photocopies

PRIMARY COLLECTION FOCUS: history of conservation district movement
    National Association of Conservation Districts
    environment--conservation
    conservation--soil and water
    conservation districts

INCLUSIVE DATES: 1930s-present
COLLECTION FORMATS: ca. 500 photographs & slides, 1000 books, 100 films/video
COLLECTION ACCESS: not described
ACQUISITION REPORTED TO: American Agricultural Archives, Iowa State University
STAFF (FTE): 0.5 administrative
INSTITUTIONAL SUPPORT FOR PROFESSIONAL DEVELOPMENT: use of facilities and equipment permitted, payment for telephone use
SPECIAL SERVICES/PROGRAMS: fundraising/endowment
PATRON USE STATISTICS: 10 in-house patrons, 150 telephone, 150 mail reference requests, 10 collections used, other user statistics not kept

---

Levelland: South Plains Museum: NHPRC TX555-720

Sam Houston Regional Library & Research Center TEL: (409)336-8821
FM 1011
Box 310
Liberty, TX 77575-0310

REPORTED BY: Robert L. Schaadt, Director-Archivist
TYPE OF INSTITUTION: archives, library (state, part of the TX State Library-Local Records Division)

HOURS: M-F 8-5, Sa 9-4
ACCESS: open to the general public
SERVICES: in-person, mail, and phone reference, photocopies, photographic reproduction
RESTRICTIONS: fragile materials' access restricted: copies available

PRIMARY COLLECTION FOCUS: history of Southeast Texas
    Texas, Southeast
    Texas Regional Historical Resource Depository
    Daniel, Price
    Dies, Martin
    Houston, Sam
    Lafitte, Jean
    business history--Southeast Texas
    social organizations--Southeast Texas
    families--Southeast Texas

INCLUSIVE DATES: 1820s to present
VOLUME: 16,000 cubic feet
COLLECTION FORMATS: 6,285 feet manuscript collections; 8,211 feet government records; 20 institution's records; 19,292 photographs; 6,304 books; 6,831 maps;
COLLECTION ACCESS: card catalog, container lists, registers/inventories, newsletters
ACQUISITION REPORTED TO: OCLC, professional journals
STAFF (FTE): 1 administrative, 3 general archival, 1 curator, 3 volunteer/docent, 1 clerical, 2 maintenance/security
INSTITUTIONAL SUPPORT FOR PROFESSIONAL DEVELOPMENT: tuition/registration, reimbursement for professional meetings, in-house workshops on a regular basis
SPECIAL SERVICES/PROGRAMS: exhibits, tours, classes, newsletter, fundraising/endowment, lectures/presentations, radio program
FACILITIES/EQUIPMENT/PRESERVATION: temperature controls, humidity controls, fire detection controls, fire extinguishing system, disaster preparedness plan
PATRON USE STATISTICS: 7,517 in-house patrons, 2,963 telephone, 1,905 mail reference requests, 1,520 cubic feet of holdings provided to patrons, 9,519 reference photocopies

NHPRC TX560-720

Margaret Estes Library, LeTourneau University TEL: (903)753-0231
2100 S. Mobberly FAX: (903)237-2732
P.O. Box 7001
Longview, TX 75607

REPORTED BY: Mary Sue Beaty, Assistant Director
TYPE OF INSTITUTION: library (academic)

HOURS: M-Th 8am-11pm, F 8-5, Sa 1-9, Su 1-6
ACCESS: not open to the general public
SERVICES: in-person, mail, & phone reference, ILL

PRIMARY COLLECTION FOCUS: LeTourneau University, missionary activities, inventors
    LeTourneau University, Longview TX (records)

LeTourneau, Robert G.
engineering, mechanical
missionaries
inventors
prisoners of war--German
Harmon General Army Hospital, Texas
hospitals

VOLUME: 251,435 items
COLLECTION FORMATS: 5000 item manuscript collections, 391 institution's records, 100,000 books, 2,136 pamphlets, 173 films, 10,850 government records, 66 photographs
COLLECTION ACCESS: card catalog
ACQUISITION REPORTED TO: specialized/regional guide, IPEDS
STAFF (FTE): 2 administrative, 1 outreach officer, 1 A/V officer, 3 clerical, 3 student
INSTITUTIONAL SUPPORT FOR PROFESSIONAL DEVELOPMENT: reimbursement for professional meeting registration
SPECIAL SERVICES/PROGRAMS: exhibits, other [not specified]
FACILITIES/EQUIPMENT/PRESERVATION: temperature controls, humidity controls, fire detection controls
PATRON USE STATISTICS: 11,504 in-house patrons, 1,645 telephone, 97 mail reference requests

---

Texas Tech University, Southwest Collection
106 Mathematics
Box 4041
Lubbock, TX 79409-1041

TEL: (806)742-3749
FAX: (806)742-0496

REPORTED BY: Cindy Martin, Assistant Director
TYPE OF INSTITUTION: archives, library (academic)

HOURS: M,W,F 9-5, Tu 9-7, Sa 9-1
ACCESS: open to the general public
SERVICES: in-person, mail & phone reference, photocopies, photographs

PRIMARY COLLECTION FOCUS: history of the American Southwest
Texas Tech University (records)
ranching
agriculture
politics
Texas, West
Southwestern U.S.
music
entertainment
petroleum industry
cotton

INCLUSIVE DATES: ca. 1870s-present
COLLECTION FORMATS: 9216 linear feet manuscript collections, 129,800 books/serials, 6000 pamphlets, 3893 oral histories, 1263 films/videotapes, 4222 government records, 128,000 photographs, 2600 maps
COLLECTION ACCESS: card catalog, inventories, online catalog
ACQUISITION REPORTED TO: OCLC
STAFF (FTE): 2 administrative, 6 general archival, 1.5 clerical, 9 student
INSTITUTIONAL SUPPORT FOR PROFESSIONAL DEVELOPMENT: tuition/registration reimbursement, reimbursement for meetings and travel, payment for mailings & telephone use, use of facilities
SPECIAL SERVICES/PROGRAMS: exhibits, fundraising/endowment, lectures/presentations
FACILITIES/EQUIPMENT/PRESERVATION: fire detection controls
PATRON USE STATISTICS: 3000 in-house patrons, 200 telephone, 75 mail reference requests, 9500 collections used

NHPRC TX590-760

The Museum of East Texas TEL: (409)639-4434
504 N. Second St.
Lufkin, TX 75901

REPORTED BY: Nancy Wilson, Curator of Photographic Collections
TYPE OF INSTITUTION: museum

HOURS: T-F 10-5, Sa & Su 1-5
ACCESS: open to the general public
SERVICES: [not specified]

PRIMARY COLLECTION FOCUS: East Texas and Lufkin photographs
    photographs--portraits
    Texas, East
    Lufkin, TX--photographs

COLLECTION FORMATS: 50,000 photographs
STAFF (FTE): 1 administrative, 1 educational director, 1 photo curator, 1 clerical, 1 shop keeper, 0.5 handyman
INSTITUTIONAL SUPPORT FOR PROFESSIONAL DEVELOPMENT: tuition/registration reimbursement, payment of dues for memberships, reimbursement for meetings, payment for mailings, phone, use of facilities
SPECIAL SERVICES/PROGRAMS: exhibits, tours, classes, fundraising/endowment, lectures/presentations
FACILITIES/EQUIPMENT/PRESERVATION: temperature controls, humidity controls, fire detection controls, fire extinguishing system

---

Harrison County Historical Museum TEL: (903)938-2680
Peter Whetsrone Square
Marshall, TX 75670

REPORTED BY: Inez Hatley Hughes Director
TYPE OF INSTITUTION: archives, historical society, library, museum (county/local)

HOURS: T-Sa 9-5, Su 1:30-5
ACCESS: open to the general public
SERVICES: in-person reference, photocopies

PRIMARY COLLECTION FOCUS: history of Harrison County
    Harrison County, TX (local history)
    Caddo Indians
    medicine
    Judaism
    education
    photography
    transportation
    business history
    art
    communication

COLLECTION ACCESS: card catalog
ACQUISITION REPORTED TO: members newsletter
STAFF (FTE): 3 administrative, 1 volunteer

INSTITUTIONAL SUPPORT FOR PROFESSIONAL DEVELOPMENT: payment for mailings, use of facilities permitted, payment for telephone use, use of clerical staff
SPECIAL SERVICES/PROGRAMS: exhibits, tours, newsletter
PATRON USE STATISTICS: in house patrons, telephone, and mail reference requests [number not specified]

Marshall: East Texas Baptist College, Mamye Jarrett Learning Center, Special Collection: NHPRC TX604-220

Old Post Office Museum, Collin County Historical Society
Chestnut at Virginia
McKinney, TX 75069

TEL: (214)542-9457 on Tuesdays

REPORTED BY: Elisabeth R. Pink, Director
TYPE OF INSTITUTION: archives, historical society, library, & museum (county/local)

HOURS: T 1-5, by appointment
ACCESS: open to the general public
SERVICES: mail, phone, & fee reference, copy machine

PRIMARY COLLECTION FOCUS: Collin County History
  Collin County, TX (local history)
  farming
  arts--decorative

INCLUSIVE DATES: ca. 1800 - present
VOLUME: 5000 items
COLLECTION FORMATS: 2 manuscript collections, 30 institution's records, 300 books, 500 photographs, 10 maps, 10 oral histories
COLLECTION ACCESS: card catalog
STAFF (FTE): 10 volunteer/docent
SPECIAL SERVICES/PROGRAMS: exhibits, classes, lectures/presentations
FACILITIES/EQUIPMENT/PRESERVATION: temperature controls, fire extinguishing system, disaster preparedness plan
PATRON USE STATISTICS: 20 telephone patrons, 25 mail reference requests, 25 collections used, 30 reference photocopies

---

Nita Stewart Haley Memorial Library
1805 W. Indiana
Midland, TX 79701

TEL: (915)682-5785
FAX: (915)683-7766

REPORTED BY: Frances N. Stapp, Director/Librarian
TYPE OF INSTITUTION: archives, library, museum, other

HOURS: M-F 9-12, 1-5
ACCESS: open to general public
SERVICES: in-person, mail and phone reference, photocopies

PRIMARY COLLECTION FOCUS: range and cattle industry
  cattle industry
  ranching
  art

COLLECTION FORMATS: manuscript collections, books, pamphlets, films/videotapes, photographs, maps,

oral histories, other
COLLECTION ACCESS: card catalog, registers/inventories
STAFF (FTE): 1 administrative, 1 general archival, 7 volunteer, 1 clerical
SPECIAL SERVICES/PROGRAMS: exhibits, tours, newsletter, fundraising/endowment
FACILITIES/EQUIPMENT/PRESERVATION: temperature controls, humidity controls

---

Midland: Permian Basin Petroleum Musuem, Library, and Hall of Fame; Archives Center: NHPRC TX625-640

Stephen F. Austin State University, Steen Library, Special Collections　　　**TEL**: (409)568-4100
1936 North St.　　　**FAX**: (409)568-4117
Box 13055 SFA Station
Nacogdoches, TX 75962

REPORTED BY: Linda Cheves Nicklas, Special Collections Librarian
TYPE OF INSTITUTION: library (academic)

HOURS: M-F 8-5, Sa 10-6
ACCESS: open to the general public
SERVICES: in-person, mail, and phone reference, photographs
RESTRICTIONS: photocopies limited to 100/wk/patron, 2 hour limit research

PRIMARY COLLECTION FOCUS: East Texas
　　　Texas, East
　　　Texas Regional Historical Resource Depository
　　　Stephen F. Austin State University (records)
　　　forestry
　　　Texas, East--history
　　　Texas, East--literature
　　　lumber industry
　　　business history

INCLUSIVE DATES: ca. 1780 - present
COLLECTION FORMATS: 2,850 linear feet manuscript collections, 305 linear feet institution's records, 4000 photographs, 16800/950 books/serials, 1,000 linear feet government records, 530 maps, 105 oral histories
COLLECTION ACCESS: card catalog, container lists, repository guide
STAFF (FTE): 1 administrative, 1 clerical, 1 student
INSTITUTIONAL SUPPORT FOR PROFESSIONAL DEVELOPMENT: reimbursement for professional meeting(s) registration &/or travel
SPECIAL SERVICES/PROGRAMS: exhibits, tours, lectures/presentations
FACILITIES/EQUIPMENT/PRESERVATION: temperature controls, humidity controls, fire detection controls
PATRON USE STATISTICS: 3000 in-house patrons, 815 telephone, 377 mail reference requests, 12,500 reference photocopies

NHPRC TX632-720

Sterne-Hoya House Library & Museum　　　**TEL**: (409)560-5426
211 S. Lanana
Nacogdoches, TX 75961

REPORTED BY: Dianna Scott, Director
TYPE OF INSTITUTION: library & museum (city)

HOURS: M-Sa 9-12, 2-5
ACCESS: open to the general public
SERVICES: in-person & photocopies

PRIMARY COLLECTION FOCUS: Nacogdoches, Texas, and Sterne-Hoya House
    Nacogdoches, TX (local history)
    Sterne-Hoya House, TX
    Sterne, Eva
    Hoya, Joseph von der
    genealogy

INCLUSIVE DATES: 1815-1900
COLLECTION FORMATS: 10 item manuscript collections, 3 linear feet photographs, 4000 books
COLLECTION ACCESS: card catalog & registers/inventories
STAFF (FTE): 1 administrative, 1 clerical
INSTITUTIONAL SUPPORT FOR PROFESSIONAL DEVELOPMENT: use of facilities and equipment
    permitted
SPECIAL SERVICES/PROGRAMS: exhibits, tours, lectures/presentations
FACILITIES/EQUIPMENT/PRESERVATION: fire detection controls, disaster preparedness plan
PATRON USE STATISTICS: 8,000 in-house patrons, 100 collections used, 20 reference photocopies

---

Nacogdoches: East Texas Historical Association: NHPRC TX632-200

Sophienburg Museum & Archives   **TEL**: (512)625-5656
200 N. Seguin Ave.
New Braunfels, TX 78130

REPORTED BY: Iris T. Schumann, CA, Archivist
TYPE OF INSTITUTION: archives (private, non-profit organization)

HOURS: M-F 10-3
ACCESS: open to the general public
SERVICES: in-person, mail, phone, and fee reference, photocopies, photographs

PRIMARY COLLECTION FOCUS: Comal County, Texas; German settlements & ethnic groups
    Comal County, TX (local history)
    New Braunfels, TX (local history)
    ethnic groups--Texas
    German Immigration Society
    Hispanics--Texas
    African Americans--Texas
    Germans--Texas
    immigration
    genealogy

INCLUSIVE DATES: 1840s - present
VOLUME: 1180 linear feet
COLLECTION FORMATS: 600 feet manuscript collections, 12 feet institution's records, 120 feet books, 150
    maps, 50 reels films, 120 feet government records, 500,000 photographs, 700 oral histories
COLLECTION ACCESS: card catalog, container lists, computerized finding aids (used by staff)
SOFTWARE/SYSTEM: MARCON PLUS
STAFF (FTE): 1 administrative, 1 general archival, 0.5 photo curator, 12 volunteer/docent
INSTITUTIONAL SUPPORT FOR PROFESSIONAL DEVELOPMENT: tuition/registration reimbursement for
    courses, payment of dues, payment for mailings, use of clerical staff
SPECIAL SERVICES/PROGRAMS: classes, newsletter, fundraising/endowment, lectures/presentations

FACILITIES/EQUIPMENT/PRESERVATION: preservation lab
PATRON USE STATISTICS: 600 in-house patrons, 900 telephone, 72 mail reference requests, 1200 collections used, 1200 reference photocopies, 250 microfilm/fiche

NHPRC TX640-720

University of Texas of the Permian Basin Library
4901 East University Blvd.
Odessa, TX 79762-0001

TEL: (915)367-2114
FAX: (915)367-2115

REPORTED BY: Bobbie Jean Klepper, Special Services Librarian
TYPE OF INSTITUTION: library (state)

HOURS: M,W-F 8-12,1-5; T 8-noon
ACCESS: open to the general public
SERVICES: in-person, mail, & phone reference, photocopies, photographs
RESTRICTIONS: reasonable time limit, copyright restrictions

PRIMARY COLLECTION FOCUS: Texana, emphasis on Permian Basin
University of Texas of the Permian Basin (records)
Texas--history
Permian Basin, TX
Shepperd, John Ben
petroleum industry

INCLUSIVE DATES: 1885-present
VOLUME: 600 cubic feet
COLLECTION FORMATS: manuscript collections, institution's records, books, pamphlets, films, government records, photographs, maps, oral histories
COLLECTION ACCESS: card catalog, container lists, computerized finding aids (used by staff)
SOFTWARE/SYSTEM: d-Base III, MARC:AMC, on-line catalog
STAFF (FTE): .5 administrative, .5 clerical, .5 student
INSTITUTIONAL SUPPORT FOR PROFESSIONAL DEVELOPMENT: reimbursement of dues for meetings, registration & travel
PATRON USE STATISTICS: 400 in-house patrons

Odessa: Presidential Museum, Library of the Presidents: NHPRC TX654-640

Orange Public Library
220 N. Fifth St.
Orange, TX 77630

TEL: (409)883-1086
FAX: (409)883-1096

REPORTED BY: Walter Burkhalter, Library Director
TYPE OF INSTITUTION: library (city)

HOURS: M-W 9-9, Th-Sa 9-5
ACCESS: open to the general public
SERVICES: in-person, mail, and phone reference

PRIMARY COLLECTION FOCUS: Orange, Texas local history & genealogy
Orange, TX (local history)
genealogy

INCLUSIVE DATES: 20th century
VOLUME: 72,094 items
COLLECTION FORMATS: 71,000 books/serials, 200 pamphlets/ephemera, 500 films/videotapes, 200 government records
COLLECTION ACCESS: card catalog
STAFF (FTE): 2 administrative, 10 public/technical services
INSTITUTIONAL SUPPORT FOR PROFESSIONAL DEVELOPMENT: payment of dues for memberships, reimbursement for professional meetings, registration and travel
SPECIAL SERVICES/PROGRAMS: classes, newsletter, other [not specified]
FACILITIES/EQUIPMENT/PRESERVATION: temperature controls, fire detection controls, fire extinguishing system, disaster preparedness plan
PATRON USE STATISTICS: 200,000 in-house patrons, 2000 telephone, 100 mail reference requests

---

White Deer Land Museum   **TEL**: (806)669-8041
STREET ADDRESS: 116 S. Cuyler
Box 1556
Pampa, TX 79065

REPORTED BY: Anne Davidson, Curator
TYPE OF INSTITUTION: museum (county/local)

HOURS: [not reported]
ACCESS: open to the general public, also by appointment
SERVICES: [not reported]

PRIMARY COLLECTION FOCUS: general history of Gray County
    Plains Indians--arrowheads
    Gray County, TX (local history)

INCLUSIVE DATES: year around
VOLUME: 2200 items
COLLECTION FORMATS: institution's records, photographs, maps, oral histories
COLLECTION ACCESS: card catalog, registers/inventories
ACQUISITION REPORTED TO: Gray County
STAFF (FTE): 1 administrative, 1 general archival, 1 clerical
SPECIAL SERVICES/PROGRAMS: exhibits, tours, lectures/presentations
FACILITIES/EQUIPMENT/PRESERVATION: fire extinguishing system
PATRON USE STATISTICS: user statistics not kept

Carson County Square House Museum   **TEL**: (806)537-3524
5th and Elsie
P.O. Box 276
Panhandle, TX 79068-0276

REPORTED BY: David L. Hoover-Registrar
TYPE OF INSTITUTION: museum (county/local)

HOURS: M-Sa 8:30-5:30, Su 1-5
ACCESS: open to the general public
SERVICES: in-person, and mail reference
RESTRICTIONS: books may not leave the Museum

PRIMARY COLLECTION FOCUS: Carson County & surrounding counties: culture, history
    Texas

Texas Panhandle
Carson County, TX (local history)
agriculture
natural history
archaeology
military history
education

INCLUSIVE DATES: ca. 1870 to present
COLLECTION FORMATS: 50 item manuscript collections; 500 item institution's records; 1,539 books; 27 videotapes; 18,585 artifacts; 150 government records; 3761 photographs; 88 maps; 51 oral histories; 11,859 other
COLLECTION ACCESS: card catalog, computerized finding aids (used by staff)
SOFTWARE/SYSTEM: Data Ease and WordPerfect 5.1
STAFF (FTE): 1 administrative, 1 general archival, 1 outreach officer, 30 volunteer/docent, 1 clerical
INSTITUTIONAL SUPPORT FOR PROFESSIONAL DEVELOPMENT: tuition/registration reimbursement, reimbursement for meetings, payment for mailings, use of facilities, phone, clerical
SPECIAL SERVICES/PROGRAMS: exhibits, tours, classes, newsletter, fundraising/endowment, lectures/presentations, other [not specified]
FACILITIES/EQUIPMENT/PRESERVATION: temperature controls, humidity controls, fire detection controls, fire extinguishing system, disaster preparedness plan
NHPRC TX691-130

Paris: Paris Junior College, A.M. & Welma Aikin Regional Archives: NHPRC TX695-640

Wayland Baptist University, Van Howeling Memorial Library
1900 W. 7th
Plainview, TX 79072

TEL: (806)296-4737
FAX: (806)296-4736

REPORTED BY: Polly Lackey, Director
TYPE OF INSTITUTION: library (academic)

HOURS: M-Th 8-11am, Fri. 8-5:30, Sa 9-5, Su 2-5
ACCESS: open to the public
SERVICES: in-person, mail, and phone reference, photocopies

PRIMARY COLLECTION FOCUS: university records, Baptist history
Texas--history
Baptist Church
Wayland Baptist University (records)
railroads
Llano Estacado region, TX--history and development

VOLUME: 225 feet
COLLECTION FORMATS: manuscript collections, institution's records, books/serials, ephemera, films/videotapes, photographs, oral histories
COLLECTION ACCESS: card catalog, repository guide
ACQUISITION REPORTED TO: OCLC
STAFF (FTE): .25 administrative
INSTITUTIONAL SUPPORT FOR PROFESSIONAL DEVELOPMENT: use of facilities and equipment, use of clerical staff
PATRON USE STATISTICS: user statistics not kept

NHPRC TX712-880

Port Arthur Public Library
3601 Cultural Center Drive
Port Arthur, TX 77642-3136

TEL: (409)985-8838

REPORTED BY: Yvonne Sutherlin, Volunteer-retired professional
TYPE OF INSTITUTION: library, local history archives (city)

HOURS: M-F 9am-9pm, Sa 9-5, Su 1-5 (closed Sundays during summer)
ACCESS: general public access with approval by reference librarian
SERVICES: in-person, mail, and phone reference, photocopies
RESTRICTIONS: reasonable search & copy time

PRIMARY COLLECTION FOCUS: Port Arthur local history
    Port Arthur, TX (local history)
    Port Arthur, TX--city government
    Texas, Southeast
    Joplin, Janis
    Stilwell, Arthur
    Gates, John W. "Bet-a-Million"

INCLUSIVE DATES: 1893-present
VOLUME: 286 linear feet
COLLECTION FORMATS: manuscript collections, institution's records, books/serials, pamphlets/ephemera, photographs, maps, oral histories, government records, films
COLLECTION ACCESS: card catalog, computerized finding aids (used by staff), registers/inventories
SOFTWARE/SYSTEM: d-Base
STAFF (FTE): 3 administrative, volunteer
INSTITUTIONAL SUPPORT FOR PROFESSIONAL DEVELOPMENT: tuition/registration reimbursement for courses, payment of dues, reimbursement for professional meeting(s), use of facilities
SPECIAL SERVICES/PROGRAMS: exhibits, classes, lectures/presentations
PATRON USE STATISTICS: user statistics not kept

NHPRC TX719-640

Portland: Bell Public Library: NHPRC TX726-80

Prairie View: Prairie View A & M University, W.R. Banks Library: NHPRC TX33-640

National Museum of Communications, Inc.
2001 Plymouth Rock
Richardson, TX 75081

TEL: (214)690-3636
FAX: (214)644-2473

REPORTED BY: Bill Bragg
TYPE OF INSTITUTION: archives, library, museum (special)

HOURS: M-Sa 10-4
ACCESS: open to the general public
SERVICES: in-person, mail, phone, & fee reference, photocopies

PRIMARY COLLECTION FOCUS: history of communications
    communication
    radio
    television
    print media
    telephone
    telegraph

media

INCLUSIVE DATES: B.C.-present
VOLUME: 100,000 items
COLLECTION FORMATS: 200 books, 500 films/videotapes, 90,000 phonograph records
COLLECTION ACCESS: not described
ACQUISITION REPORTED TO: professional journal(s)
STAFF (FTE): 1 administrative
INSTITUTIONAL SUPPORT FOR PROFESSIONAL DEVELOPMENT: payment of dues for professional organization, memberships, use of facilities & equipment permitted
SPECIAL SERVICES/PROGRAMS: exhibits, tours, classes, newsletter, fundraising/endowment, lectures/presentations
FACILITIES/EQUIPMENT/PRESERVATION: temperature controls, fire extinguishing system

---

Richardson Public Library
900 Civic Center Dr.
Richardson, TX 75080

TEL: (214)238-4000

REPORTED BY: Isabel Davis, Reference Librarian/Local Hist. Librarian
TYPE OF INSTITUTION: library (city)

HOURS: M-T 10-9pm, F-Sa 10-6, Su 2-6
ACCESS: public access by appointment only
SERVICES: in-person, mail, & phone reference, photocopies

PRIMARY COLLECTION FOCUS: local history
    Richardson, TX (local history)
    genealogy

INCLUSIVE DATES: 1850-present
COLLECTION FORMATS: manuscript collections, institution's records, books, pamphlets, government records, photographs, maps, oral histories
COLLECTION ACCESS: registers/inventories, not described
STAFF (FTE): [not reported]
INSTITUTIONAL SUPPORT FOR PROFESSIONAL DEVELOPMENT: reimbursement for professional meetings registration & travel
SPECIAL SERVICES/PROGRAMS: tours, Richardson Historical Society meetings
PATRON USE STATISTICS: user statistics not kept

NHPRC TX742-680

Richardson: Rockwell International, Collins Commercial Telecommunications: NHPRC TX742-690

Richardson: University of Texas at Dallas, Special Collections, History of Aviation Collection: NHPRC TX742-800

Fort Bend County Library System
1001 Golfview Drive
Richmond, TX 77469

TEL: (713)342-4455
FAX: (713)341-2688

REPORTED BY: W. M. Von-Maszewski, Department Manager
TYPE OF INSTITUTION: library (county/local)

HOURS: M-F 9-9, F & Sa 9-5, Su 1-5, summer hours differ
ACCESS: open to general public
SERVICES: in-person, mail, and phone reference, fee for reference, photocopies

PRIMARY COLLECTION FOCUS: non-current government records for 5 area counties
    Fort Bend County, TX
    Waller County, TX
    Matagorda County, TX
    Brazoria County, TX
    Wharton County, TX

INCLUSIVE DATES: 1836-1970's
COLLECTION FORMATS: 1200 government records
COLLECTION ACCESS: computerized finding aids (used by staff and patrons)
SOFTWARE/SYSTEM: DYNIX
ACQUISITION REPORTED TO: OCLC
STAFF (FTE): 1 general archival, 2 volunteer, 2 clerical (Genealogy & Local Hist. Dept. only)
INSTITUTIONAL SUPPORT FOR PROFESSIONAL DEVELOPMENT: tuition, reimbursement (registration and travel), workshops, mailings, use of facilities, payment for phone, use of clerical staff
SPECIAL SERVICES/PROGRAMS: exhibits, tours, classes, newsletter
FACILITIES/EQUIPMENT/PRESERVATION: temperature controls, humidity controls, disaster preparedness plan

---

Richmond: Fort Bend County Museum: NHPRC TX749-246

Round Rock Public Library
216 E. Main
Round Rock, TX 78664

TEL: (512)255-3612
FAX: (512)255-6676

REPORTED BY: Ms. Dale L. Ricklefs, Library Director
TYPE OF INSTITUTION: library (city)

HOURS: M-Th 10-9, F-Sa 10-5
ACCESS: open to the general public
SERVICES: in-person, mail, & phone reference, fee reference, photocopies, other

PRIMARY COLLECTION FOCUS: Round Rock, TX
    Round Rock, TX (local history)
    architecture--Round Rock, Texas
    Bass, Sam
    genealogy

INCLUSIVE DATES: 1850 - present
COLLECTION FORMATS: 2 feet manuscript collections, 60 tapes oral histories
COLLECTION ACCESS: computerized finding aids (used by staff and patrons), not described (some)
SOFTWARE/SYSTEM: PICK OS-mainframe unit
ACQUISITION REPORTED TO: specialized/regional guide: CDROM-based regional database
STAFF (FTE): 1 administrative, .25 general archival, .5 preservation, .25 outreach, .25 audio-visual, 4 professional, 3 volunteer/docent, 5 clerical
INSTITUTIONAL SUPPORT FOR PROFESSIONAL DEVELOPMENT: tuition/registration reimbursement for courses, payment of dues, payment for mailings, use of facilities, clerical staff
SPECIAL SERVICES/PROGRAMS: exhibits, tours, newsletter, fundraising/endowment
FACILITIES/EQUIPMENT/PRESERVATION: temperature controls
PATRON USE STATISTICS: 125,000 total in-house, 10 mail reference requests

Winedale Historical Center, University of Texas
Farm Road 2714- Winedale
P.O. Box 11
Round Top, TX 78954

TEL: (409)278-3530
FAX: (409)278-3531

REPORTED BY: Gloria Jaster, Administrative Supervisor
TYPE OF INSTITUTION: historical center (academic--non-profit)

HOURS: (office) M-F 8-5, Sa 9-5, Su 12-5
ACCESS: public access by appointment only
SERVICES: in-person reference

PRIMARY COLLECTION FOCUS: German Texas, architecture, and Round Top, Texas
- Texas--Germans
- Texas--nineteenth century
- German Americans
- Roundtop, TX (local history)
- Fayette County, TX (local history)
- architecture
- arts--decorative
- folk life

INCLUSIVE DATES: 1830-1890
VOLUME: 7,500 items
COLLECTION FORMATS: 15 linear feet manuscript collections, 4 feet institution's records, 1400 books/serials, 6,400 photographs, 8 maps
COLLECTION ACCESS: registers/inventories
STAFF (FTE): 1 administrative, 1 general archival, 1 photo curator, 12 paid docents, 1 clerical, 5 maintenance
SPECIAL SERVICES/PROGRAMS: exhibits, tours, classes, newsletter, lectures/presentations
PATRON USE STATISTICS: 10,000 in-house museum patrons, 20,000 telephone, 500 mail reference requests, 300 collections used, 100 reference photocopies

NHPRC TX754-880

Fort Concho National Historic Landmark
213 East Avenue D
San Angelo, TX 76903-7099

TEL: (915) 657-4441
FAX: (915) 659-2407

REPORTED BY: John Neilson, Historian/Archivist
TYPE OF INSTITUTION: Other: historic site (city)
HOURS: T-Sa, 10-5; Su, 1-5; closed Mondays; Research Library & Archives by appt.
ACCESS: appointment
SERVICES: in person reference, mail, phone, copies, photographic copying service

PRIMARY COLLECTION FOCUS: history of Fort Concho and its environs
- Great Plains
- Fort Concho, TX
- Texas
- Southwestern U.S.
- military history
- farming
- ranching
- politics
- business history
- Ragsdale, M. C.
- physicians

Native Americans
Hispanic Americans
African Americans

INCLUSIVE DATES: 1860-1990 (including museum records)
VOLUME: ca. 5000 cubic feet
COLLECTION FORMATS: 500 cubic feet manuscript collections, 100+ cubic feet institution's records, 7000 books, 200 pamphlets, less than 100 films, 155 rolls of military government records, (microfilm), ca. 10,000 photographs, 300 maps, 220 collections oral histories
COLLECTION ACCESS: guide, registers, container lists (currently in progress)
ACQUISITION REPORTED TO: journal(s), own publications
STAFF (FTE): 1 general archival, 2 volunteer
INSTITUTIONAL SUPPORT FOR PROFESSIONAL DEVELOPMENT: tuition, meetings, telephone, facilities, clerical
SPECIAL SERVICES/PROGRAMS: exhibits, tours, newsletter, lectures/presentations
FACILITIES/EQUIPMENT/PRESERVATION: temperature controls, fire detection controls, disaster preparedness plan (in development)
PATRON USE STATISTICS: 500 in-house patrons, 730 telephone, 350 mail reference requests

NHPRC TX770-240

Archdiocese of San Antonio, Catholic Archives   **TEL**: (210)734-2620
2718 W. Woodlawn   **FAX**: (210)734-2774
P.O. Box 28410
San Antonio, TX 78284-4901

REPORTED BY: Brother Edward Loch, S.M., Archivist
TYPE OF INSTITUTION: archives, museum (religious)

HOURS: M-F 9-12, 1-4
ACCESS: open to the general public
SERVICES: in-person, mail, & phone reference, fee reference, photocopies, microfilm
RESTRICTIONS: some collections are restricted

PRIMARY COLLECTION FOCUS: sacramental records of the Catholic Church in San Antonio
Catholic Church
Archdiocese of San Antonio, TX (records)
Church architecture--San Antonio, TX
Pope John Paul II--1987 visit
Bexar Archives (microfilm)
genealogy

INCLUSIVE DATES: 1703-present
VOLUME: 410 cubic feet
COLLECTION FORMATS: 400 feet institution's records, 1000 books, 20 cubic feet pamphlets, 1000 blueprints, 962 microfilms, 120 videos, 16 cubic feet photographs, 4 oral histories
COLLECTION ACCESS: card catalog, repository guide, registers/inventories
ACQUISITION REPORTED TO: Archdiocese of San Antonio
STAFF (FTE): 1 general archival
INSTITUTIONAL SUPPORT FOR PROFESSIONAL DEVELOPMENT: payment of dues for memberships, reimbursement for meeting registration, in-house workshops, use of facilities
SPECIAL SERVICES/PROGRAMS: exhibits, classes, newsletter
FACILITIES/EQUIPMENT/PRESERVATION: fire detection controls, disaster preparedness plan
PATRON USE STATISTICS: 500 in-house patrons, 2000 telephone, 400 mail reference requests, other user statistics not kept

NHPRC TX777-30

Daughters of the Republic of Texas Library
Alamo Plaza at Crockett St.
P.O. Box 1401
San Antonio, TX 78295-1401

TEL: (210)225-1071 or 225-8155
FAX: (210)229-1343 (Alamo business office)

REPORTED BY: Martha Utterback, Assistant to the Library Director
TYPE OF INSTITUTION: library (historical organization)

HOURS: M-Sa 9-5
ACCESS: open to the general public
SERVICES: in-person, mail & phone reference, photocopies, photographs, other
RESTRICTIONS: usual copyright restrictions regarding complete volume copying

PRIMARY COLLECTION FOCUS: Republic of Texas
- Texas, Republic of
- Texas--history
- Alamo
- San Antonio, Texas--history
- Houston, Sam
- Austin, Stephen F. (family papers)
- Texas--Colonial

INCLUSIVE DATES: 16th century - present
COLLECTION FORMATS: 500 linear feet manuscript collections, 16,000 books/serials, 30,000 photographs, 1000 maps, 1000 pieces artwork
COLLECTION ACCESS: card catalog, container lists, repository guide
STAFF (FTE): 1 administrative, 1 general archival, 1 photo curator, 2 librarian, 3 clerical
INSTITUTIONAL SUPPORT FOR PROFESSIONAL DEVELOPMENT: tuition/registration reimbursement for courses, reimbursement for meetings, use of facilities and equipment
SPECIAL SERVICES/PROGRAMS: occasional newsletter
FACILITIES/EQUIPMENT/PRESERVATION: temperature controls, humidity controls, fire detection controls, fire extinguishing system
PATRON USE STATISTICS: 1500 in-house patrons, 3500 telephone, 900 mail reference

NHPRC TX777-160

Edward H. White II Memorial Museum
Brooks AFB
San Antonio, TX 78235-5000

TEL: (512) 536-2203

REPORTED BY: Fernando Cortez, Curator
TYPE OF INSTITUTION: museum (federal)

HOURS: M-F 8-4; closed holidays
ACCESS: open
SERVICES: in-person, mail, and phone reference, fee, copies (cost cannot exceed $50.00)

PRIMARY COLLECTION FOCUS: history of flight medicine in the U.S. Air Force
- U.S. Air Force
- Brooks AFB (records)
- aviation medicine
- aerospace medicine
- medicine, history of

INCLUSIVE DATES: 1911-
VOLUME: 8000 items
COLLECTION FORMATS: 600 items manuscript collections, 125 items institution's records, 200 books, 450 pamphlets, 200 films, 600 items government records, 3000 photographs, 80 maps, 100 oral histories
COLLECTION ACCESS: not described
STAFF (FTE): photo curator [number not specified], volunteer/docent [number not specified]
INSTITUTIONAL SUPPORT FOR PROFESSIONAL DEVELOPMENT: use of facilities
SPECIAL SERVICES/PROGRAMS: exhibits, tours, fundraising/endowment
FACILITIES/EQUIPMENT/PRESERVATIONS: temperature controls, fire detection controls, fire extinguishing system

---

Incarnate Word College Library
4301 Broadway
San Antonio, TX 78209

TEL: (210)829-3838
FAX: (210)829-6041

REPORTED BY: Mendell D. Morgan, Jr., Library Director
TYPE OF INSTITUTION: library (academic, religious)

HOURS: M-Th 7:45am-10:30pm, F 7:45-5, Sa 11-5, Su 2:30-10:30
ACCESS: public access by appointment only
SERVICES: in-person, mail, and phone reference, photocopies, microforms

PRIMARY COLLECTION FOCUS: Texana, history of Incarnate Word College
 Incarnate Word College, San Antonio, TX (records)
 San Antonio, TX
 Texas--history
 Zavala, Adina de
 Menger family, San Antonio, TX
 Texana

INCLUSIVE DATES: 1880s-present
VOLUME: 100 linear feet
COLLECTION FORMATS: 33 linear feet manuscript collections, 40 linear feet institution's records, 700 books, 15 feet pamphlets/ephemera, 12 feet photographs, 1 film
COLLECTION ACCESS: card catalog
STAFF (FTE): 1 administrative
FACILITIES/EQUIPMENT/PRESERVATION: temperature controls, humidity controls, disaster preparedness plan
PATRON USE STATISTICS: user statistics not kept

San Antonio Public Library
Hertzberg Circus Museum & Collection
210 W. Market
San Antonio, TX 78205

TEL: (210)299-7819
FAX: (210)271-9497

REPORTED BY: Lenore de la Vega, Curator
TYPE OF INSTITUTION: museum (city)

HOURS: Oct-Apr: M-Sa 9-5; May-Sept: M-Sa 9-5, Sun 1-5
ACCESS: public access by appointment only
SERVICES: in-person, mail, & phone reference, photocopies, photographs (usage fee for photographic reproduction)

PRIMARY COLLECTION FOCUS: circuses and circus performers

circuses
circus performers
circus art
side shows
Barnum, P. T.
Roe, E.
Cody, William (Buffalo Bill)
Lind, Jenny

INCLUSIVE DATES: ca. 1700-present
VOLUME: 20,000 items
COLLECTION FORMATS: manuscript collections, institution's records, books, pamphlets, films, photographs, artifacts & posters
COLLECTION ACCESS: card catalog, not described
STAFF (FTE): .5 general archival, .5 preservation, 1 curator, 1.75 clerical
INSTITUTIONAL SUPPORT FOR PROFESSIONAL DEVELOPMENT: tuition/registration reimbursement for courses, reimbursement for meetings, payment for mailings and telephone, use of facilities and clerical
SPECIAL SERVICES/PROGRAMS: exhibits, lectures/presentations, other [not specified]
PATRON USE STATISTICS: user statistics not kept
See NHPRC TX777-720

San Antonio Public Library
203 S. St. Mary's Street
San Antonio, TX 78205

TEL: (210) 299-7813
FAX: (210) 299-7822

REPORTED BY: Jo Myler, Library Services Supervisor, History & Reference Dept.
TYPE OF INSTITUTION: library (city)

HOURS: M-Th 9-9; F-Sa 9-5
ACCESS: open to general public
SERVICES: in person, mail, and phone reference, photocopies
RESTRICTIONS: no in depth research by staff, patrons do own photocopies

PRIMARY C
San Antonio, TX
Texas, South
Bexar County, TX
Texas--history
genealogy

COLLECTION FORMATS: manuscript collections, institution's records, books, pamphlets/ephemera, government records, photographs, maps, oral histories
COLLECTION ACCESS: card catalog, registers/inventories, container lists; most not described
STAFF (FTE): no separate archives staff: 4 professional, 2 para-professionals
INSTITUTIONAL SUPPORT FOR PROFESSIONAL DEVELOPMENT: tuition/registration reimbursement for courses, payment for telephone use
FACILITIES/EQUIPMENT/PRESERVATION: temperature controls, fire detection controls
PATRON USE STATISTICS: user statistics not kept separately
NHPRC TX777-720

Society of Mary, St. Louis Province Archives
St. Mary's University, One Camino Santa Maria
520 Fordham Lane
San Antonio, TX 78228

TEL: (210)436-3777

REPORTED BY: Paul Novosal, Archivist
TYPE OF INSTITUTION: archives (religious)

HOURS: M-F, hours variable
ACCESS: public access by appointment only
SERVICES: in-person, mail, & phone reference, photocopies

PRIMARY COLLECTION FOCUS: Society of Mary, St. Louis Province of
    Catholic Church
    Society of Mary, St. Louis Province of
    St. Mary's University, San Antonio, Texas (records)
    education--Catholic
    missions--San Antonio, TX
    San Antonio, TX (local history)

COLLECTION FORMATS: 400 (items) institution's records, 5,000 books, 45 films, 17,000 photographs, 100 oral histories, maps, ephemera
COLLECTION ACCESS: not described
STAFF (FTE): 1 general archival, 1 researcher
INSTITUTIONAL SUPPORT FOR PROFESSIONAL DEVELOPMENT: tuition/registration reimbursement for courses, reimbursement for meetings registration and travel, payment for mailings, use of facilities
SPECIAL SERVICES/PROGRAMS: exhibits, tours, lectures/presentations
FACILITIES/EQUIPMENT/PRESERVATION: temperature controls, humidity controls, fire detection controls
PATRON USE STATISTICS: user statistics not kept
See NHPRC TC777-670

St. Mary's University, Special Collections   **TEL**: (210)431-2126
1 Camino Santa Maria
San Antonio, TX 78228

REPORTED BY: Brother Robert Wood, S.M.
TYPE OF INSTITUTION: library (academic)

HOURS: hours vary
ACCESS: public access by appointment only

PRIMARY COLLECTION FOCUS: Laredo Archives, San Luis Potosi Archives, borderlands
    U.S.-Mexico border
    borderlands--U.S.-Mexico
    Laredo Archives
    San Luis Potosi Archives
    Texas--history

COLLECTION ACCESS: card catalog, computerized finding aids (used by staff)
STAFF (FTE): 1 general archival
INSTITUTIONAL SUPPORT FOR PROFESSIONAL DEVELOPMENT: reimbursement for professional meetings, registration & travel
FACILITIES/EQUIPMENT/PRESERVATION: temperature controls, humidity controls, fire extinguishing system
PATRON USE STATISTICS: user statistics not kept
NHPRC TX777-670 [see also Society of Mary, St. Louis Province, above]

University of Texas at San Antonio   **TEL**: (210)691-5505
Library, Special Collections   **FAX**: (210)691-4571
6900 North Loop 1604 West
San Antonio, TX 78249-0671

REPORTED BY: Dora Guerra
TYPE OF INSTITUTION: library (academic)

HOURS: M-T 8-12, 12:30-4:30, W 8-12 noon, Th 2:30-6:30
ACCESS: open to the general public
SERVICES: in-person, mail & phone reference, photocopies
RESTRICTIONS: photocopying of fragile material not allowed

PRIMARY COLLECTION FOCUS: San Antonio, Texana, Spanish Colonial history, Southwest
    San Antonio, TX (local history)
    Texas--Colonial
    Texana
    borderlands--U.S.-Mexico
    U.S.-Mexico border
    Southwestern U.S.--history
    Southwestern U.S.--literature
    Mexico--Spanish Colonial period
    Native Americans
    Civil War
    U.S.-Mexican War
    Northwestern U.S.

INCLUSIVE DATES: 1600's-present
VOLUME: 9,085 items
COLLECTION FORMATS: manuscript collections, books/serials, pamphlets, photographs, maps
COLLECTION ACCESS: computerized finding aids (used by staff and patrons)
SOFTWARE/SYSTEM: NOTIS
ACQUISITION REPORTED TO: OCLC
STAFF (FTE): 1 administrative
INSTITUTIONAL SUPPORT FOR PROFESSIONAL DEVELOPMENT: tuition/registration for courses,
    reimbursement for meetings, payment for mailings, use of facilities & clerical staff
SPECIAL SERVICES/PROGRAMS: tours, lectures/presentations
FACILITIES/EQUIPMENT/PRESERVATION: disaster preparedness plan

NHPRC TX777-810

University of Texas Health Science Center
Briscoe Library, Special Collections
7703 Floyd Curl Drive
San Antonio, TX 78284-7940

TEL: (210)567-2400
FAX: (210)567-2490

REPORTED BY: Daniel Jones, Assistant Library Director for Collection Development
TYPE OF INSTITUTION: library (academic)

HOURS: M-F 8-5
ACCESS: appointment preferred
SERVICES: in-person, mail, and phone reference, photocopies

PRIMARY COLLECTION FOCUS: University of Texas Health Science Center and local medical history
    University of Texas Health Science Center, San Antonio, TX (records)
    medicine, history of
    Texas, South--medicine
    nursing
    dentistry
    medical research
    physicians

INCLUSIVE DATES: 1920-present
VOLUME: 312 linear feet
COLLECTION FORMATS: 8 linear feet manuscript collections, 304 linear feet institution's records, 3000 photographs
COLLECTION ACCESS: computerized finding aids (used by staff and patrons)
SOFTWARE/SYSTEM: on-line library catalog
ACQUISITION REPORTED TO: OCLC
STAFF (FTE): .2 administrative
INSTITUTIONAL SUPPORT FOR PROFESSIONAL DEVELOPMENT: payment for mailing & telephone use, use of clerical staff
SPECIAL SERVICES/PROGRAMS: exhibits, lectures/presentations, other [not specified]
FACILITIES/EQUIPMENT/PRESERVATION: temperature controls, humidity controls, fire detection controls, fire extinguishing system, disaster preparedness plan
PATRON USE STATISTICS: 300 in-house patrons, 20 telephone, 100 collections used

NHPRC TX777-790

University of Texas Institute of Texan Cultures, Library
801 S. Bowie
P.O. Box 1226
San Antonio, TX 78294

TEL: (210)226-7651
FAX: (210)222-8564

REPORTED BY: James C. McNutt, Director of Research and Collections
TYPE OF INSTITUTION: library, museum, research institution (state, academic)

HOURS: M-F 9-5 (library)
ACCESS: public access by appointment only
SERVICES: in-person, mail, phone, & fee reference, photocopies, photographs

PRIMARY COLLECTION FOCUS: Texas history, ethnic groups and communities
  Institute of Texan Cultures, University of Texas (records)
  Texas--history
  ethnic groups--Texas
  culture--Texas
  Native Americans
  African Americans
  Mexican Americans
  Asian Americans
  German Americans

INCLUSIVE DATES: prehistory - present
COLLECTION FORMATS: 15 linear feet institution's records, 1,500,000 photographs, 6000 books, 125 linear feet pamphlets, 10 linear feet films, 200 maps, 100 oral histories
COLLECTION ACCESS: card catalog, computerized finding aids (used by staff and patrons)
SOFTWARE/SYSTEM: DataPerfect, Fox Base
ACQUISITION REPORTED TO: OCLC, specialized/regional guide
STAFF (FTE): 1 administrative, 1 general archival, 1 photo curator, 10 volunteer/docent, 1 clerical
INSTITUTIONAL SUPPORT FOR PROFESSIONAL DEVELOPMENT: payment of dues for memberships, reimbursement for meetings registration, payment for telephone use
SPECIAL SERVICES/PROGRAMS: exhibits, tours, classes, newsletter, lectures/presentations
FACILITIES/EQUIPMENT/PRESERVATION: temperature controls, humidity controls, fire detection controls, fire extinguishing system
PATRON USE STATISTICS: 3500 in-house patrons, 6000 telephone, 3000 mail reference requests, 24,000 reference photocopies, 150 microfilm/fiche copies

Witte Museum
3801 Broadway
P.O. Box 2601
San Antonio, TX 78299-2601

TEL: (210)820-2153

REPORTED BY: Rebecca Huffstutler, Curatorial Assistant
TYPE OF INSTITUTION: museum (city/private)

HOURS: M, W-Su 10-5, Tu 10-9pm
ACCESS: public access by appointment only
SERVICES: in-person, mail, phone, & fee reference, photocopies, photographs
RESTRICTIONS: copyright regulations on photographs & slides

PRIMARY COLLECTION FOCUS: Witte Museum, San Antonio and Texas history & artists
    San Antonio, TX (local history)
    Witte Museum, San Antonio, TX (records)
    Texas--history
    artists--Texas
    architecture

INCLUSIVE DATES: 19th & 20th centuries
COLLECTION FORMATS: 45 linear feet manuscript collections, 3 feet institution's records, 8 feet pamphlets/ephemera, 91 feet photographs, 20-25 maps
COLLECTION ACCESS: card catalog, container lists
STAFF (FTE): 1 curatorial assistant
FACILITIES/EQUIPMENT/PRESERVATION: fire detection controls
PATRON USE STATISTICS: user statistics not kept

San Antonio: Bexar County Archives: NHPRC TX777-80

San Antonio: Our Lady of the Lake University, Texana Collection: NHPRC TX777-620

San Antonio: Protestant Episcopal Church in the Diocese of West Texas, Cathedral House Archives: NHPRC TX777-640

San Antonio: San Antonio Conservation Society, Library: NHPRC TX777-700

San Antonio: San Antonio Museum Association, Research Library: NHPRC TX777-710

San Antonio: Trinity University, Special Collections: NHPRC TX777-760

Southwest Texas State University, Alkek Library
Southwestern Writers Collection
San Marcos, TX 78666-4604

TEL: (512)245-2313
FAX: (512)245-3002

REPORTED BY: Rene LeBlanc, Assistant to Head of Special Collection
TYPE OF INSTITUTION: library (academic)

HOURS: M-F 8-5
ACCESS: open to the general public
SERVICES: in-person & mail reference, photocopies
RESTRICTIONS: some materials may not be copied without permission

PRIMARY COLLECTION FOCUS: works of Southwestern authors and artists
    Southwestern U.S.--literature
    music

art
authors--Southwestern U.S.

INCLUSIVE DATES: 1555, 1870 - present
COLLECTION FORMATS: 560 cubic feet manuscript collections, 20 cubic feet institutional records, 350 linear feet books, 20 cubic feet pamphlets, 10 linear feet audio/visual, 10 linear feet photographs, 5 feet maps
COLLECTION ACCESS: card catalog, registers/inventories, container lists, computerized finding aids (used by staff), OPAC
SOFTWARE/SYSTEM: MS Word, Works
ACQUISITION REPORTED TO: OCLC
STAFF (FTE): 1 administrative, 2 clerical, 2 student
INSTITUTIONAL SUPPORT FOR PROFESSIONAL DEVELOPMENT: tuition/registration reimbursement, reimbursement for meetings & travel, payment for mailings & phone, use of facilities & clerical
SPECIAL SERVICES/PROGRAMS: exhibits, tours, lectures/presentations
FACILITIES/EQUIPMENT/PRESERVATION: temperature controls, humidity controls, fire detection controls, fire extinguishing system, disaster preparedness plan
PATRON USE STATISTICS: user statistics not kept
NHPRC TX791-730

Santa Fe Area Historical Foundation
11225 Highway 6, Hitchcock, TX 77563
P. O. Box 275, Santa Fe, TX 77517
TEL: (409) 925-3009

REPORTED BY: Charles C. Meek, Director
TYPE OF INSTITUTION: historical society, museum (local)

HOURS: third Sunday of month, 2-4; special events, by appointment
ACCESS: Open
SERVICES: in-person reference, mail

PRIMARY COLLECTION FOCUS: Early Galveston County mainland communities along the Gulf, Colorado & Santa Fe Railroad (Hitchcock, Alta Loma, Arcadia, Algoa)
Galveston County, TX
Hitchcock, TX
Alta Loma, TX
Algoa, TX
Arcadia, TX

INCLUSIVE DATES: 1890-1950
VOLUME: 500 items (regularly added to)
COLLECTION FORMATS: photographs
COLLECTION ACCESS: registers
STAFF (FTE): 5 volunteer/docent
SPECIAL SERVICES/PROGRAMS: exhibits, tours, lectures
PATRON USE STATISTICS: user statistics not kept

Big Thicket Museum
FM 770
P.O. Box 198
Saratoga, TX 77585
TEL: (409)274-5000

REPORTED BY: Jim Bell, Museum Director
TYPE OF INSTITUTION: museum (regional-7 counties, a non-profit organization)

HOURS: T-Sa 9-5, Su 1-5
ACCESS: open to the general public
SERVICES: in-person, mail, and phone reference, photocopies, fee

PRIMARY COLLECTION FOCUS: Big Thicket residents, natural history
    Big Thicket National Preserve, TX
    natural history

INCLUSIVE DATES: Twentieth Century
VOLUME: not completely cataloged
COLLECTION FORMATS: 30 manuscripts, numerous books/serials, numerous pamphlets, videotapes/films, 500 photographs, maps, 200 oral histories
COLLECTION ACCESS: card catalog, container lists
STAFF (FTE): administrative, general archival, volunteer, clerical [numbers not specified]
INSTITUTIONAL SUPPORT FOR PROFESSIONAL DEVELOPMENT: tuition
SPECIAL SERVICES/PROGRAMS: exhibits, tours, classes, newsletter, lectures/presentations
FACILITIES/EQUIPMENT/PRESERVATION: temperature controls
PATRON USE STATISTICS: user statistics not kept until 1992

Mutual UFO Network, Inc. (MUFON)   **TEL**: (512)379-9216
103 Oldtowne Rd.
Seguin, TX 78155-4099

REPORTED BY: Walter H. Andrus, Jr., International Director
TYPE OF INSTITUTION: library (Texas non-profit corporation, tax exempt)

HOURS: M-F 9-5
ACCESS: public access by appointment only
SERVICES: in-person reference & photocopies (fee for photocopies)

PRIMARY COLLECTION FOCUS: unidentified flying objects, related phenomena
    unidentified flying objects
    UFOs
    abductions--unidentified flying objects
    animals--mutilation
    crop circles
    Bigfoot

COLLECTION FORMATS: 800 books, 200 films, 7000 government records, 400 photographs
COLLECTION ACCESS: not described
STAFF (FTE): 1 administrative, 3 clerical
SPECIAL SERVICES/PROGRAMS: newsletter, other [not specified]
PATRON USE STATISTICS: 100 in-house patrons, 500 telephone, 300 mail reference requests, 200 reference photocopies

---

Seguin: Texas Lutheran College, Blumberg Memorial Library: NHPRC TX797-760

Austin College Archives   **TEL**: (903)813-2476
900 N. Grand, Suite 6 G   **FAX**: (903)813-3199
Sherman, TX 75090

REPORTED BY: Laura McLemore, Archivist
TYPE OF INSTITUTION: archives, college (academic)

HOURS: M-W 8:30-4:30, Tu-Th 9-12 noon, F by appointment
ACCESS: open to the general public
SERVICES: in-person, mail, and phone reference, photocopies, photographs
RESTRICTIONS: as imposed by statute, donor or policy

PRIMARY COLLECTION FOCUS: Austin College and Texas history
    Austin College, Sherman, TX (records)
    Texas--history
    Texas, Republic of

INCLUSIVE DATES: 1836-present
VOLUME: 1000 cubic feet
COLLECTION FORMATS: 400 feet manuscript collections, 500 feet institution's records, 50 feet photographs, 20 feet books/serials, 10 feet pamphlets/ephemera, 20 feet videos
COLLECTION ACCESS: container lists, computerized finding aids (used by staff and patrons), registers
SOFTWARE/SYSTEM: NOTIS
ACQUISITION REPORTED TO: OCLC
STAFF (FTE): 1 general archival, 1 volunteer/docent, 1 student
INSTITUTIONAL SUPPORT FOR PROFESSIONAL DEVELOPMENT: tuition/registration reimbursement, payment of dues for memberships, reimbursement for professional meetings, use of facilities
SPECIAL SERVICES/PROGRAMS: exhibits, lectures/presentations, other [not specified]
FACILITIES/EQUIPMENT/PRESERVATION: humidity controls, disaster preparedness plan
PATRON USE STATISTICS: 31 in-house patrons, 28 telephone, 7 mail reference requests, 26 collections used, 32 reference photocopies

---

Sherman Public Library, Local History Department
421 N. Travis
Sherman, TX 75090-5975

TEL: (903)892-7240
FAX: (903)892-7101

REPORTED BY: Jacqueline Banfield, Assistant Library Director
TYPE OF INSTITUTION: library (city)

HOURS: MWF 9-6; Tu,Th 9-9; Sa 9-5
ACCESS: public access by appointment only
SERVICES: in-person & mail reference, photocopies

PRIMARY COLLECTION FOCUS: Grayson County
    Grayson County, TX (local history)
    Sherman, TX (local history)

INCLUSIVE DATES: 1884-1978
VOLUME: 257 items
COLLECTION FORMATS: 85 films, 172 government records
COLLECTION ACCESS: repository guide
STAFF (FTE): not reported
PATRON USE STATISTICS: 340 reference photocopies

Railroad & Pioneer Museum
710 Jack Baskin St.
P.O. Box 5126
Temple, TX 76505-5126

TEL: (817)778-6873
FAX: (817)770-5582

REPORTED BY: Mary Lynn Irving, Director

TYPE OF INSTITUTION: archives, museum (city)

HOURS: T-F 1-4, Sa 10-4
ACCESS: open to the general public
SERVICES: in-person, mail, & phone reference, photocopies
RESTRICTIONS: research under supervision, in-house only

PRIMARY COLLECTION FOCUS: Texas railroads, Central Texas and Temple history
    Temple, TX (local history)
    Texas, Central--history
    railroads
    U.S.--railroads
    Texas--railroads
    Canada--railroads
    Mexico--railroads
    Gulf, Colorado & Santa Fe Railroad
    Bell County, TX (local history)

INCLUSIVE DATES: 1836-present
VOLUME: 25,000 pieces
COLLECTION FORMATS: 250 institution's records, 3,000 books, 20,000 pamphlets, 20 films, 250 government records, 1,000 photographs, 500 maps, 10 oral histories
COLLECTION ACCESS: card catalog, registers/inventories, computerized finding aids (used by staff)
SOFTWARE/SYSTEM: In-house program & WordPerfect
STAFF (FTE): 1 administrative, 5 volunteers, 1 clerical, 2 student
INSTITUTIONAL SUPPORT FOR PROFESSIONAL DEVELOPMENT: tuition/registration reimbursement, payment of dues for meetings, payment for mailings, telephone, use of facilities & clerical staff
SPECIAL SERVICES/PROGRAMS: exhibits, tours, classes, newsletter, fundraising/endowment, lectures/presentations, other [not specified]
FACILITIES/EQUIPMENT/PRESERVATION: temperature controls, fire detection controls, fire extinguishing system, disaster preparedness plan
PATRON USE STATISTICS: 18,447 in-house patrons, 5,000 telephone, 100 mail reference requests, 500 collections used, 500 reference photocopies

NHPRC TX851-690

Scott and White Archives
Santa Fe Center, 600 South 25th St.
Temple, TX 76504

TEL: (817)771-8205

REPORTED BY: Michelle M. Mears, Archivist
TYPE OF INSTITUTION: archives (hospital)

HOURS: M-F 8-5 (call first)
ACCESS: open to the general public
SERVICES: in-person, mail, and phone reference, photocopies

PRIMARY COLLECTION FOCUS: Scott and White Memorial Hospital
    hospitals
    Scott and White Memorial Hospital, TX (records)
    Scott and White Clinic, TX
    Santa Fe Railroad Hospital, TX
    Temple Sanitarium, TX
    Scott and White School of Nursing, TX
    medicine, history of

INCLUSIVE DATES: 1891-present

VOLUME: 300 linear feet
COLLECTION FORMATS: 24 feet manuscript collections, 165 feet institution's records, 24 feet books/serials, 24 feet photographs, 12 feet maps, 3 feet oral histories, 48 feet artifacts
COLLECTION ACCESS: registers/inventories, computerized finding aids (used by staff)
SOFTWARE/SYSTEM: Minaret
STAFF (FTE): 1 administrative
INSTITUTIONAL SUPPORT FOR PROFESSIONAL DEVELOPMENT: tuition/registration reimbursement, payment of dues for memberships, reimbursement for meetings, payment for mailings, use of facilities & phone
SPECIAL SERVICES/PROGRAMS: exhibits, tours, lectures/presentations
FACILITIES/EQUIPMENT/PRESERVATION: fire detection controls, fire extinguishing system, disaster preparedness plan
PATRON USE STATISTICS: 20 in-house patrons, 25 telephone, 10 mail reference requests, 7 collections used, 5 reference photocopies

---

Slavonic Benevolent Order of the State of Texas (SPJST), Pioneer Museum **TEL**: (817)773-1575
520 North Main
P.O. Box 100
Temple, TX 76503

REPORTED BY: Dorothy Pechal, Museum Curator
TYPE OF INSTITUTION: archives, library, museum (business, fraternal benefit society)

HOURS: M-F 8-12, 1-5
ACCESS: open to the general public
SERVICES: in-person, mail, & phone reference, photocopies

PRIMARY COLLECTION FOCUS: Czechoslovakian heritage
    Czechoslovakia
    Czechoslovakian culture
    Catholic Church
    Moravian Church
    genealogy--Czechoslovakia
    Slavonic benevolent societies
    philanthropies

INCLUSIVE DATES: 1897-1940s
COLLECTION FORMATS: manuscript collections, institution's records, 23000 books, 30 films, government records, 5000 photographs, 10 maps, microfilm
COLLECTION ACCESS: card catalog, container lists, computerized finding aids (used by staff)
SOFTWARE/SYSTEM: Roots and P.A.F.
ACQUISITION REPORTED TO: Supreme Lodge
STAFF (FTE): 1 administrative
INSTITUTIONAL SUPPORT FOR PROFESSIONAL DEVELOPMENT: payment for mailings, use of facilities & equipment
SPECIAL SERVICES/PROGRAMS: exhibits, tours, lectures/presentations
FACILITIES/EQUIPMENT/PRESERVATION: temperature controls, humidity controls, fire detection controls, fire extinguishing, preservation lab, disaster preparedness plan
PATRON USE STATISTICS: 2500 in-house patrons, 300 telephone, 40 mail reference requests, 225 collections used, 100 reference photocopies, 50 microfilm/fiche

---

Texarkana Museum System **TEL**: (903)793-4831
219 State Line Ave.
P.O. Box 2343
Texarkana, TX 75501

REPORTED BY: Jeanette Winters, Collections Manager
TYPE OF INSTITUTION: museum

HOURS: Tu-F 10-4
ACCESS: public access by appointment only
SERVICES: mail and phone reference, photocopies

PRIMARY COLLECTION FOCUS: Texarkana area history
    Bowie County, TX (local history)
    Miller County, AZ
    Texarkana, TX (local history)
    pioneers--Texarkana, TX
    railroads
    Texas and Pacific Railroad

INCLUSIVE DATES: 1850-present
COLLECTION FORMATS: 10 linear feet manuscript collections, 10,000 photographs, 750 maps, 250 oral histories, books/periodicals
COLLECTION ACCESS: card catalog
STAFF (FTE): 6 administrative, 95 volunteer, 4 clerical, 3 student
INSTITUTIONAL SUPPORT FOR PROFESSIONAL DEVELOPMENT: in-house workshops on a regular basis, use of facilities and equipment permitted
SPECIAL SERVICES/PROGRAMS: exhibits, tours, newsletter, fundraising/endowment, lectures/presentations
FACILITIES/EQUIPMENT/PRESERVATION: temperature controls, humidity controls, fire detection controls, fire extinguishing system
NHPRC TX865-750 [note name change]

Smith County Historical Society   **TEL**: (903)592-5993
125 S. College
Tyler, TX 75702

REPORTED BY: Virginia Buchanan-Archivist
TYPE OF INSTITUTION: archives, historical society (county/local)

HOURS: W & 1st Sa 1-4:30
ACCESS: open to the general public
SERVICES: in-person, mail, and phone reference, photocopies (photocopy and mailing fee)

PRIMARY COLLECTION FOCUS: historical data on Smith County, Texas
    Smith County, TX (local history)
    Civil War
    military camps
    church history
    business history

INCLUSIVE DATES: Pre-1846 - present
COLLECTION FORMATS: books/serials, photographs, and maps
COLLECTION ACCESS: card catalog, registers/inventories, computerized finding aids (used by staff), index
STAFF (FTE): 8 volunteer/docents
SPECIAL SERVICES/PROGRAMS: exhibits, newsletter, fundraising/endowment
FACILITIES/EQUIPMENT/PRESERVATION: temperature controls, fire detection controls, fire extinguishing system
PATRON USE STATISTICS: 600 in-house patrons, 100 telephone, 100 mail reference requests
NHPRC TX890-720

Congregation of the Incarnate Word & Blessed Sacrament TEL: (512)575-2266
1101 N.E. Water St.
Victoria, TX 77901-9298

REPORTED BY: Sister M. Andrea Hubnik, IWBS
TYPE OF INSTITUTION: Headquarters for Congregation (religious)

HOURS: M-F 8:30-4:30
ACCESS: not open to the general public; by special appointment
SERVICES: mail and fee reference, photocopies

PRIMARY COLLECTION FOCUS: history of Congregation, members of Congregation
    Congregation of the Incarnate Word & Blessed Sacrament, TX (records)
    Catholic Church
    missions

INCLUSIVE DATES: 17th century - present
COLLECTION FORMATS: manuscript collections, institution's records, books/serials, pamphlets/
    ephemera, films/videotapes, photographs, oral histories
COLLECTION ACCESS: container lists
SPECIAL SERVICES/PROGRAMS: exhibits, tours, newsletter

Victoria Regional Museum Association, McNamara House TEL: (512)575-8227
502 N. Liberty
Victoria, TX 77901

REPORTED BY: Carla Hurt, Curator
TYPE OF INSTITUTION: museum (private non-profit)

HOURS: Th-F 12-5, Sa & Su 1-5
ACCESS: open to the general public, public access by appointment
SERVICES: in-person reference

PRIMARY COLLECTION FOCUS: late 19th century and early 20th century Victoria TX
    Victorian era
    Victoria, TX (local history)
    consumerism--Victorian era

INCLUSIVE DATES: ca. 1870 - ca. 1920
COLLECTION FORMATS: 10,000 manuscript collections, 50 institution's records, 125 photographs,
    15 maps
COLLECTION ACCESS: not described
STAFF (FTE): 1 administrative, 1 clerical
SPECIAL SERVICES/PROGRAMS: exhibits, tours, newsletter, fundraising/endowment,
    lectures/presentations
FACILITIES/EQUIPMENT/PRESERVATION: temperature controls, humidity controls, fire detection controls,
    fire extinguishing system
PATRON USE STATISTICS: user statistics not kept

Victoria: Victoria College, Library, Local History Collection: NHPRC TX923-840

Baylor University, Strecker Museum TEL: (817)755-1110
P.O. Box 97154
Waco, TX 76798-7154

REPORTED BY: T. Lindsay Baker
TYPE OF INSTITUTION: museum (academic)

HOURS: M-F 9-4, Sa 10-3
ACCESS: open to the general public
SERVICES: in-person reference

PRIMARY COLLECTION FOCUS: Strecker Museum, Texas history, natural history
    Strecker Museum, Waco, TX (records)
    natural history
    Texas--history

INCLUSIVE DATES: 1880-present
COLLECTION FORMATS: manuscript collections, institution's records, 42,000 photographs, 5,000 books, 40 linear feet ephemera, 100 films, 10 maps
COLLECTION ACCESS: registers/inventories
STAFF (FTE): 1 administrative, 1 curator, .5 photo curator, 4 students
INSTITUTIONAL SUPPORT FOR PROFESSIONAL DEVELOPMENT: tuition/registration reimbursement for courses, workshops, reimbursement for professional meetings registration & travel
SPECIAL SERVICES/PROGRAMS: exhibits, classes, newsletter, lectures/presentations
FACILITIES/EQUIPMENT/PRESERVATION: fire detection controls, fire extinguishing system
PATRON USE STATISTICS: user statistics not kept

See NHPRC TX933-80

Baylor University, The Texas Collection
P.O. Box 97142
Waco, TX 76798-7142

TEL: (817)755-1268
FAX: (817)755-1368

Closed for renovation, call for further information.

NHPRC TX 933-80

Waco: Baylor University, Armstrong-Browning Library: NHPRC TX933-65

Washington: Star of the Republic Museum: NHPRC TX940-720

Waxahachie: Southwestern Assemblies of God College, Nelson Memorial Library: NHPRC TX947-720

Wichita Falls: Midwestern State University, Moffett Library: NHPRC TX968-520

Yorktown Historical Society
Main & Eckhardt Streets
P.O. Box 884
Yorktown, TX 78164

TEL: (512)564-2174

REPORTED BY: not given
TYPE OF INSTITUTION: historical society (county/local)

HOURS: Th & Su 2:30-4:30
ACCESS: open to the general public
SERVICES: in-person and mail reference

PRIMARY COLLECTION FOCUS: Yorktown, Texas history, Old Indianola Trail

Yorktown, TX (local history)
Old Indianola Trail, TX
cemeteries
architecture
York, Captain John
Dewitt County, TX (local history)

INCLUSIVE DATES: 1848-present
COLLECTION FORMATS: 5 feet manuscript collections, 3 feet institution's records, 30 books/serials, 100 pamphlets/ephemera, 500 photographs
COLLECTION ACCESS: container lists
STAFF (FTE): volunteer/docent [number not specified]
SPECIAL SERVICES/PROGRAMS: exhibits, tours
FACILITIES/EQUIPMENT/PRESERVATION: fire extinguishing system
PATRON USE STATISTICS: user statistics not kept

SPECIAL INDEXES

FACILITIES, EQUIPMENT & PRESERVATION

disaster preparedness plan 6, 8, 9, 11, 13, 15, 19, 22, 23, 26, 29, 30, 37, 40, 42, 43, 45, 47, 48, 50, 53, 55, 57, 58, 61-63, 65, 68, 71, 72, 75, 78, 79, 82-84, 86, 88, 90, 92, 94, 99, 100, 104, 109, 112, 127, 130, 132, 133, 136, 139-141, 145-147, 149, 152, 153, 155, 159, 160, 164-167, 170-172, 174, 176, 177, 182-187, 190, 195-199, 201-205, 208, 209, 214, 215, 219, 222, 224, 226, 227, 230, 232, 234, 237, 238, 240, 242-244

fire detection controls 1, 2, 5, 7-17, 20-23, 25-31, 34, 35, 37, 40-45, 47, 48, 53, 55-58, 61-63, 65, 67-69, 71-73, 75-77, 79, 81, 84, 86-105, 107, 108, 110, 112, 113, 115-118, 120, 122, 124, 126, 128, 131, 133-137, 139-141, 146, 147, 149, 152-156, 160-162, 164-174, 176, 177, 180-186, 189, 190, 193-199, 201-203, 205, 207, 209, 210, 212, 214, 217-221, 223, 224, 226, 227, 232-236, 238-240, 243-247

fire extinguishing system 1-3, 5, 6, 8-13, 15-18, 20, 23-28, 30-38, 40, 41, 43-45, 47-49, 52, 55, 57, 58, 61-63, 68, 71-80, 82, 84-92, 95, 97, 98, 101-104, 107, 108, 110, 112, 113, 116-118, 120, 122-125, 128-130, 133, 135, 137, 141, 144, 145, 147-149, 153, 155, 156, 162, 164-167, 169-174, 176, 177, 180-182, 185-194, 196, 197, 199, 200, 203, 205, 208-212, 214-219, 221, 222, 226, 227, 229, 233, 234, 236, 238, 240, 243-248

humidity controls 6-9, 12, 17, 25-27, 30, 31, 34-37, 44, 45, 47, 49-51, 53, 56-58, 60-63, 67, 68, 72, 73, 75, 77, 78, 80, 81, 84, 86-88, 90-92, 97-99, 101, 102, 104, 107, 108, 110, 112, 116-118, 128, 131-133, 135, 136, 140, 141, 146, 147, 149, 153, 155-157, 159, 160, 164, 166, 168-171, 176-178, 180-187, 189, 191, 192, 194, 196, 197, 199, 201-203, 205, 206, 208-210, 212, 213, 215, 217-221, 223, 227, 230, 233, 234, 236, 238, 240, 242, 244-246

preservation lab 11, 36, 37, 43, 47, 49, 60-62, 67, 68, 73, 75, 76, 83, 87, 92, 94, 95, 97, 101, 104, 107, 114, 147, 149, 152, 155, 160, 167, 170, 173, 174, 177, 180, 186, 195, 196, 198, 199, 205, 215, 225, 244

temperature controls 3-10, 12, 13, 15-17, 19, 20, 22, 23, 25-27, 30-37, 40, 42-51, 53, 55-58, 60-63, 67, 68, 71-73, 75-81, 83-95, 97-99, 101-108, 110-113, 116-118, 121, 125, 127-130, 132, 133, 135, 136, 140-143, 145-147, 149, 151-153, 155-162, 164-178, 180-187, 189-191, 193-197, 199, 201-206, 208-213, 215, 217-223, 226, 227, 229, 230, 232-236, 238, 240, 241, 243-246

SOFTWARE, OPACS & BIBLIOGRAPHIC UTILITIES

AMC 97, 151, 152, 177, 225 (see also "Marc:AMC" and "MicroMarc: AMC")
Apple Works 2
Archives Maintenance Software 81
Argus/Questor 116
AskSam 102, 183
Automated National Catalog System 13, 42, 58, 196
BIB-Base 34, 216
Bibliofile 128
CARL 37, 150-152
CAT-Alpha-4 88, 169
ClarisWorks 9, 48
Clipper 47
CLSI 29, 53, 129
d-Base 11, 13, 14, 22, 41, 42, 45, 75, 94, 145, 164, 182, 186, 190, 196, 200, 225, 228
DataEase 227
Data Trek 132
Databridge 49, 60, 114, 164, 182, 186, 190, 196, 200
DataPerfect 88, 162, 238
Deskmate 85
DOBIS 82, 168
Documaster 30
DPL's Master Bibliographic Data Base 186
DRA ATLAS 201
DYNIX 95, 141, 205, 214, 215, 230
FileMaker 9, 52, 186
Filepro 48
First Choice 15, 87
Follett Circulation Plus 65
Foxbase 48
Galaxy 76, 129
Hypercard 112
INFO 42
Infoware 43
Inmagic 44, 130, 134
Innopac 114, 117
Innovative Interfaces 140
Lias-TV 160
Lotus-Magellan 40
MacCards 112
Macintosh Custom 46
Marcive 29
MARCON 37, 204, 224
Marc:AMC 225
MicroMARC:AMC 23, 63, 97, 108, 110, 151, 177
Microsoft Works 24, 112, 127, 172, 180
Minaret 118, 153, 244
Microsoft Word 240
NOTIS 73, 99, 102, 145, 155, 158, 167, 194, 237, 242
NUCMC 36, 45, 53, 73, 87, 90, 93, 97-99, 103, 156, 164, 167, 174, 182, 189, 190, 204
Nutplus 136
OCLC 11, 29, 36, 37, 44, 45, 51, 53, 57, 61, 65, 73, 76, 78, 82, 93, 95, 98, 99, 102, 103, 106, 114, 124, 125, 128, 130, 132, 134, 140, 145, 146, 149, 155, 158, 160, 162, 167, 168, 174, 182-184, 186, 189-191, 193, 194, 205, 208, 212-215, 219, 220, 227, 230, 237, 238, 240, 242
OPAC 125, 160, 225, 240 (see also specific name of system)
Oracle 34
P.A.F 244
Paradox 11, 25, 100, 120, 135, 171, 194, 208
PC-File 160
Photoarchivist 113
Prism 114
Pro-Cite 78, 102, 127, 201, 205
Professional File 206
Q&A 37, 172, 180
Questor's Argus/Muse 26
Quixis 90, 203
R:Base 122, 193
Red Ball 81
Reflex 2 135
RLIN 44, 73, 130, 152, 170, 197, 210
Roots 244
SAS 152
SIRSI 106
Smart 25
STAR 191, 217, 247
TextDBMS 211
Willoughby's MIMSY 61
Wordstar 191
WordPerfect 11, 36, 40, 45, 82, 87, 88, 101, 131, 147, 151, 160, 162, 171, 191, 201, 208, 213, 227, 243

SPECIAL SERVICES & PROGRAMS

classes 11, 13, 15, 17, 22, 27, 37, 38, 40, 41, 45, 50, 52, 54, 57, 60, 62, 63, 69, 73, 75, 76, 80, 82, 86, 88, 91, 93, 99, 106, 112, 115, 128-130, 133, 135, 136, 140, 150-153, 155, 156, 162, 166, 169-171, 173, 176-178, 180, 182, 190, 194-198, 200, 203, 207, 212, 213, 217, 219, 221, 222, 224, 226-232, 238, 241, 243, 247

exhibits 1, 2, 4-14, 16, 17, 19, 21, 22, 24, 26, 27, 30, 31, 33-38, 41, 42, 44-46, 49, 50, 52-64, 66-68, 71, 73, 75, 76, 78-80, 82-87, 89-91, 93-95, 97-106, 108, 111-122, 125, 126, 128-130, 132, 135, 136, 138-142, 144-154, 156-164, 166-182, 184-186, 188-202, 204-206, 208, 209, 212-215, 217-224, 226-232, 234-236, 238,

240-248
fundraising 5, 52, 55, 62, 63, 68, 69, 114, 171, 208, 213, 214, 218-221, 223, 224, 227, 229, 230, 234, 243, 245, 246
fund raising 1, 2, 6, 9, 12, 16, 17, 19-21, 27, 34, 37, 38, 44, 45, 48, 54, 56, 73, 75, 83, 91, 94, 95, 97, 112, 115, 119, 121, 122, 124, 129, 130, 136, 142, 145, 149, 151, 152, 161, 162, 166-168, 170, 175-178, 180-182, 185, 186, 189, 197, 198, 202-204
lectures 1, 2, 5-7, 10, 11, 13-17, 19-24, 26, 27, 31, 34-38, 40-50, 52-63, 66-68, 73-75, 79, 80, 82-85, 87, 88, 90-92, 94, 95, 97-100, 102, 104, 106, 109, 111-115, 117, 119-122, 125, 126, 129, 130, 132-136, 139, 140, 145-149, 151, 152, 155, 156, 159-164, 166-182, 184-186, 188-192, 194-198, 202-209, 212-214, 217, 219-224, 226-229, 231, 232, 235-238, 240-247
newsletter 1, 2, 4-7, 14, 16, 17, 19, 21, 22, 24, 26, 27, 31, 33, 34, 38, 45, 49, 51, 52, 55, 56, 60-68, 74, 75, 80, 83, 91, 94, 95, 97-99, 102, 104, 112, 117, 119, 121, 122, 126, 129, 132, 135, 136, 140, 142, 145, 147, 149-152, 155, 157, 161, 162, 166-168, 170, 171, 174-178, 180, 182, 185, 188, 194, 200, 202-204, 206, 208, 209, 214, 215, 217, 219, 221-224, 226, 227, 229-233, 238, 241, 243, 245-247
tours 1, 5-7, 10, 11, 13, 14, 16, 17, 19, 20, 22, 23, 26, 27, 29-38, 40-42, 44-46, 48-50, 52-55, 57, 59, 61, 62, 64, 66-68, 73, 75, 76, 79, 81-88, 90, 91, 94, 95, 98-100, 102-105, 111, 112, 114, 117-122, 124-130, 132-136, 139-142, 144-152, 154-159, 161, 164, 167-172, 174-182, 184, 185, 187-189, 191, 194, 196-198, 200, 202-206, 208, 212, 214, 215, 217, 219, 221-224, 226, 227, 229-232, 234, 236-238, 240, 241, 243-246, 248

SPECIALIZED COLLECTION FORMATS
artifacts 2, 4, 10, 21, 33, 34, 46, 100, 121, 141, 152, 174, 175, 195, 197, 202, 205, 227, 235, 244
ephemera 10, 27, 49-51, 53-58, 60-63, 65, 67, 69, 71-74, 76, 78, 80, 82-84, 86-95, 98, 102-105, 107, 108, 112, 114, 115, 118, 119, 121, 122, 124, 130, 132, 135-138, 140-142, 144, 146, 147, 150, 151, 153, 158-160, 208, 210, 212, 214, 216-218, 226-228, 234-236, 239, 242, 246-248
film 9, 82, 120, 128, 135, 169-171, 178, 179, 190, 234
government records 1, 2, 6, 9, 11, 12, 14-18, 20-23, 27, 29, 32, 34, 36-38, 40, 41, 45, 47-49, 52-54, 56, 58, 60, 65, 67, 69, 73, 74, 76, 77, 81-83, 85-87, 90, 92, 95, 99, 103, 114, 115, 118, 119, 121, 122, 124-126, 129, 131, 132, 135, 139-142, 147, 149, 150, 155, 158-160, 164, 167, 171, 172, 174, 175, 177, 180, 182, 183, 186, 190, 194, 195, 197, 199, 202, 203, 209, 211, 214, 218-220, 223-230, 232, 234, 241-244
institution's records 8, 16
legal records 12, 95, 103, 142, 199 (see also subject index, "law, history of")
literary manuscripts 44, 56, 87, 99, 169, 205 (see also subject index, "literature")
maps 1-18, 20-22, 25, 27-42, 45-51, 53, 54, 56-61, 65-67, 69, 71, 73, 74, 76-78, 82, 84, 86, 87, 90, 91, 95, 97, 100, 101, 103, 104, 106, 108, 109, 112, 114, 115, 118-125, 127, 129, 130, 132-134, 136, 139-142, 144, 147, 149-156, 158-161, 163-168, 170, 172-175, 177, 179-183, 185, 186, 188, 190-192, 194-197, 199-207, 209, 211, 213-215, 217-220, 222-229, 231-241, 243-247
newspapers 5, 15-17, 28, 36, 54, 73, 87, 134, 167, 174, 175, 193, 204, 206
oral histories 1-4, 6-11, 13-18, 20-23, 25-27, 30, 31, 33-41, 44-56, 58, 62, 65-67, 73, 74, 76-80, 82, 83, 86-89, 91, 97, 98, 102-105, 107-109, 112, 114, 115, 117-119, 121-129, 136, 138, 139, 141, 142, 144-147, 151-154, 156-158, 161-171, 174-183, 186, 188-190, 194-197, 199-201, 203-209, 211, 214, 216-218, 220, 222-230, 232, 234-236, 238, 241, 243-246
pamphlets 1-4, 6, 7, 9-18, 20, 21, 25-28, 31-41, 44, 45, 47-51, 53-58, 60-63, 65, 67, 69, 71-74, 76, 78, 80, 82-84, 86-95, 98, 99, 102-105, 107, 108, 112, 114, 115, 117-119, 121-124, 126, 129, 130, 132, 134-138, 140-142, 144, 146, 147, 150, 151, 153, 154, 158-160, 162, 164, 165, 167-171, 174-186, 188-190, 195-206, 208, 209, 212, 214, 216-218, 220, 222, 225, 226, 228, 229, 232, 234, 235, 237-243, 246, 248
photographs 1-18, 20, 21, 23-42, 44-51, 53-67, 69, 71-78, 80-95, 97-109, 112-119, 121-142, 144-150, 152-186, 188-229, 231-248
prints 127, 152, 174, 205
video 44, 76, 86, 120, 128, 165, 216, 218

SPECIALIZED STAFF
audio-visual staff 46, 93, 112, 171, 220
cataloger 102, 129, 134
curator 2, 4, 5, 8, 9, 11-14, 17, 21, 22, 29, 36, 37, 39, 42-47, 56, 58, 60, 68, 85, 86, 89, 91, 95, 98-100, 102, 107, 112-115, 120-122, 125, 129, 133, 135, 136, 138, 143, 144, 147-149, 151-153, 156, 158-160, 167, 168, 171, 173, 174, 176, 184, 191, 192, 194, 195, 197, 200, 201, 204, 206, 208, 209, 219, 221, 224, 226, 231, 233-235, 238, 244, 246, 247
education officer 61, 221
exhibit staff 13, 37, 197
field archivist 56
interns 7, 11, 23, 35-37, 39, 40, 44, 45, 61, 91, 99, 114, 115, 126, 130, 136, 152, 156, 167, 170, 174, 194, 197, 209, 210
map curator 11, 29, 56, 121, 133, 149, 168, 186
microfilm technician 94, 95
oral history staff 114, 174
outreach/ public relations officer 12, 32, 39, 44, 46, 57, 112, 114, 170, 171, 174, 220, 227, 230
photo curator/archivist 2, 9, 11, 17, 21, 28, 37, 39, 40, 42, 44-46, 56, 60, 68, 95, 107, 114, 121, 131, 133, 147, 149, 156, 167, 168, 170, 171, 174, 186, 200, 206, 208, 209, 221, 224, 231, 233, 234, 238, 247
photographer 131
preservation staff 13, 23, 39, 55, 60, 61, 76, 93, 94, 112, 114, 133, 149, 156, 170, 174, 196, 199, 202, 203, 230, 235
student intern 35
volunteer coordinator 37

SUBJECT INDEX

abductions--unidentified flying objects 241
Abilene Christian University 162
Academy of the Sacred Heart 88
Acadia 19, 79, 81, 82
Ada, OK 140
Adams, Ansel 43
Adjutant General Archives 90
aeronautics 210, 211
aerospace industries 112
aerospace medicine 233
AFL-CIO 11
Africa 8, 97
Africa--dance 8
African Americans 52, 68, 75, 94, 97, 98, 104, 114, 182, 200, 209, 212, 224, 232, 238
Africans 97
agriculture 3, 5, 33, 34, 36, 47, 57, 60, 66, 67, 78, 81, 99, 109, 131, 149, 158, 160, 174, 182, 190, 217, 220, 227 (see also "cotton," "rice")
aircraft 55, 195
Ak-Chin 16, 17
Alamo 233
Albuquerque, NM 113-118
Albuquerque--library history 113
Alexandria, LA 71
Alfalfa County, OK 142, 143
Algoa, TX 240
Alpine, TX 164
Alta Loma, TX 240
American frontier 152
American Missionary Association 98
Amon Carter Museum 197
Andy Devine 16
Anglo-American Art Museum 75
animals--mutilation 241
Ansel 43
anthropologists 39, 130
anthropology 8, 26, 39, 42, 87, 100, 114-116, 119, 123, 130, 134, 135, 138, 139, 151, 152, 172, 173 (see also "ethnology")
anthropology of dance 8
anti-aircraft artillery 195
Anti-Horse Thief Association 143
Anti-Thief Association 143
Apache County, AZ 33
Apache Indians 135, 147
Apache Trail 1
Appalachian whites 98
Arcadia, LA 71, 240
archaeology 7, 10, 14, 17, 34, 39, 41, 44, 87, 100, 112, 115, 116, 119, 123, 130, 131, 136, 138, 149, 151, 173, 179, 227
archaeology--pre-Columbian 100
architecture 35, 37, 60, 62, 74, 81, 91, 94, 100, 109, 113, 180, 192, 204, 209-211, 215, 230-232, 239, 248
architecture--art museums 210
architecture--El Paso, TX 192
architecture--Round Rock, TX 230
architecture--twentieth century 62

Arizona 1-16, 18-48, 192
Arizona Bankers Association 36
Arizona Baptist Children's Service 23
Arizona Business Gazette 28
Arizona Cattle Growers Association 36
Arizona Cotton Growers Association 36
Arizona Newspapers, Inc. 28
Arizona Republic 28
Arizona Southern Baptist Convention 22, 23
Arizona State Museum 39, 42, 43
Arizona State University 35-37
Arizona Strip 18
Arizona Supreme Court--judicial records 12
Arizona--communities 21
Arizona--government 23, 29
Arizona--governors 23
Arizona--history 23, 25, 27, 28, 29, 33, 44
Arizona--Jews 40
Arkansas 49-70, 142, 143
Arkansas Baptist State Convention Archives 50
Arkansas College 51
Arkansas River 142
Arkansas River Navigation System 142
Arkansas territory 61
Arkansas--African Americans 68
Arkansas--architecture 62
Arkansas--government and politics 53
Arkansas--health care 63
Arkansas--historic preservation 60
Arkansas--politics 56, 59
Arlington, TX 166
army (see U.S. Army)
art 8, 19, 26, 43, 75, 92, 97, 99, 100, 109, 113, 115, 118, 129, 130, 134, 135, 138, 159, 160, 163, 185, 186, 191, 197, 210, 221, 222, 235, 240
art history 115, 129, 138
art--African 97
art--decorative 222, 231
Artesia, NM 118
artists 24, 26, 53, 87, 130, 138, 239
artists--Native Americans 24
art--performing 8, 89, 94
art--schools 210
Asia--dance 8
Asian Americans 98, 238
astronauts 211
astronomers 9
astronomy 9
atheism 169
Atoka, OK 140
Atomic Bomb Casualty Commission 208
Austin College 242
Austin, Stephen F. 180, 233
Austin, TX 168
aviation 55, 147, 229, 233
aviation medicine 233
Babbitt, Bruce 11

Baja 44
banking 11, 36, 164, 203
Baptist Church 23, 93, 105, 178, 200, 216, 227
Baptist Missionary Association of America 216
Baptists 50
barns 66
Barnum, P.T. 235
Bartlesville, OK 141
Bass, Sam 230
Bataan-Corregidor 121
bathing industry 58 (see also "resorts--health")
Baton Rouge, LA 72
Battle of Mansfield, LA 84
Battle of New Orleans 77, 89
Baylor University 178, 246, 247
Bayou Bend Collection--Houston, TX 210
Beaumont, TX 175, 176
Beaver County, OK 141
Bell County, TX 177, 243
Bellaire, TX 177
Belton, TX 177
Benedictine Order 107
Benson, AZ 1
Bexar Archives (microfilm) 232
Bexar County, TX 235, 239
Big Bend National Park, TX 164
Big Thicket National Preserve, TX 241
Bigfoot 241
Billy the Kid 126
biography 28, 40, 123
biology 14, 31, 117
Bisbee, AZ 2
Blackwell, OK 142
Blaine County, OK 148
Blanchard, OK 157
borderlands--U.S.-Mexico 14, 15, 23, 43, 44, 114, 236, 237 (see also northern Mexico states by name)
Bossier Parish, LA 76, 77
botany--native plants--Southwestern U.S. 119
Bowie County, TX 245
brands--cattle 198
Brazoria County 166, 230
Brazos Valley, TX 179
Brinkley, John 188
British literature 160
Brooks AFB 233
Buffalo Bill (William Cody) 19
Bullock 44
Bureau of Indian Affairs 199
Burleson, Omar 162
Bush, George 205
business history 3, 4, 11, 18, 21, 45, 60, 79, 83, 91, 94, 99, 103, 106, 110, 113, 114, 128, 145, 156, 163, 187, 190, 207, 209, 219, 221, 223, 231, 245
business history--Jewish 21
business records 25, 155
Caddo Indians 221

California--politics 151
Callahan, Harry 44
Camp Cody 121
Canada--railroads 243
Canadian River Valley 148
canals 30, 41 (see also "irrigation," "waterworks")
Caribbean 104
Carlsbad Caverns, NM 119
Carlsbad, NM 119, 120
Carson County, TX 227
Carter, Amon G. 197
cartography (see record formats index, "maps")
Casa Grand Valley Historical Society 3
Casa Grande Ruins 5
Casa Grande Valley, AZ 3
Catholic Church 24, 43, 62, 72, 80-82, 88, 89, 92, 96, 98, 104, 107, 110, 165, 168, 171, 232, 236, 244, 246
cattle, feral 42
cattle industry 145, 178, 198, 208, 217, 222
cavalry 47, 195
Cave Creek Canyon, AZ 31
cemetery and burial records 35, 52, 66, 77, 248
Centenary College 107, 108
Central America 98, 100, 173
Central Arizona Project 12, 40, 41
Central State [OK] University 145
Chacoan archaeology 115
Chambers family 10
Chamizal National Memorial, tx 191
Chandler, AZ 4
Chappell Hill Female College 180
Chaves County, NM 128
Chemehuevi Indians 20
Cherokee Indians 143, 150
Chicanos 37 (see also "Hispanics and Mexican Americans")
Chickasaw Indians 150
Chiricahua history 47
Choctaw Indians 150, 157
Christian Brothers 81
Church architecture--San Antonio, TX 232
church history 23, 24, 27, 83, 103, 107, 153, 163, 167, 168, 178, 200, 202, 245 (see also specific denomination)
Church of Christ 98, 162
circuses 234
civic organizations 56, 114, 209
Civil War 54, 65, 73, 84, 89-91, 99, 108, 151, 190, 203, 204, 211, 237, 245
Clark County, AR 49
Clark, Edward 205
classics 151
Clayton, Nicholas J. 204
Cleburne, TX 180, 181, 212
cliff dwellings 32
Coahuila, Mexico 190

Cochise County Historical and Archaeological Society 7
Cochise County, AZ 2, 6, 7, 38
Cody, William (Buffalo Bill) 19, 235
Colfax County, NM 137
Collin County, TX 222
Colorado 44
Colorado County, TX 181
Colorado River 19, 20, 23, 45
Colorado River Indian Reservation 20
Columbus, NM 121
Comal County, TX 224
commerce 47, 174, 181 (see also "business history")
communication 221, 228 (see also "media")
Congregation of the Holy Cross 171
Congregation of the Incarnate Word and Blessed Sacrament, TX 246
congressional papers 11, 12, 79, 110, 151, 171, 179, 205
conservation--soil and water 218
consumerism--Victorian era 246
Contemporary Arts Museum--Houston 210
Coolidge, AZ 5, 6
Coronado expedition 15
Corpus Christi, TX 182, 183
Correll, J. Lee 48
Corrington, William 108
cotton 3, 23, 36, 67, 182, 220
cowboys 47, 198
cowgirls 208
Crane, R.C. 162
Creek Indians 150
Crittenden County, AR 54
Crockett family papers 180
crop circles 241
Crosby County, TX 184, 185
Cross County, AR 69
Cushing, OK--funeral records 144
Czechoslovakian culture 244
Dallas County, TX 185, 186
Dallas Museum of Art 185, 186
Dallas, TX 185, 186
dance 8
Daniel, Price 219
Davis, OK 144
Del Rio, TX 188
Del Webb Corporation 25
Delta culture 57 (see also "plantation life and culture")
dentistry 237
Desoto Parish, LA 84
Dewitt County, TX 248
diaries and journals--prisons and prisoners 46
Dies, Martin 219
diocese records 62, 72, 80, 82, 165, 232
donkeys 189
drama--18th century, British 211
Duncan, OK 144
Dust Bowl (OK) 148
earth sciences 151
East Baton Rouge, LA 73

East Central [OK] University 140
East Texas State University 181, 182
Eastern New Mexico University, Historical Services 127, 128
ecology 53
economic history 73, 89, 108, 115
Edmond, OK 144, 145
education 3, 55, 61, 81, 88, 96, 99, 109, 117, 125, 136, 145, 156, 162, 171, 174, 182, 201, 210, 213, 218, 221, 227, 236
education--peace 55
El Paso, TX 192, 193
elderly, care of 96
Ellender, Allen J., Senate papers 110
engineering 100, 187, 220
Enid, OK 146, 147
entertainment 220
environment 53, 218
Episcopal Church 25, 153, 175, 187, 194, 239
ethnic communities 114, 136
ethnic groups 57, 103, 224, 238
ethnography (see "ethnology")
ethnohistory 43, 115, 133
ethnology 7, 10, 14, 26, 39, 116, 130, 134, 151, 173, 179
ethnomusicology 35, 48
exploration 15, 145, 159, 211
family history--Jewish 21, 40
family papers 1, 21, 27, 33, 40, 89, 141, 180, 194, 203, 233
Fannin, Paul 36
Far Away Ranch 47
farming 56, 57, 66, 145 222, 231
Farmington 119, 122, 123
Faulkner County, AR 52
Fayette County, TX 218, 231
Federal Writers Project 87, 155
firearms 46
firefighting 26, 209
Five Civilized Tribes 141, 150, 156, 159
Flagstaff, AZ 9
Florida Parishes, LA 79, 106, 107
Floyd County, TX 194
folklife 57, 231
folklore 1, 51, 56, 59, 63
Folsom, NM 123
forestry 223
Fort Bend County, TX 229, 230
Fort Concho, TX 231
Fort Concho Museum 231
Fort Davis, TX 164, 196
Fort Griffin, TX 164
Fort Sam Houston, TX 197
Fort Sill, OK 147
Fort Union, NM 124, 139
Fort Worth, TX 198, 201
fossils 22
free thought 169
frontier history 196
Galveston County, TX 204, 240
Galveston, TX 203, 204
Gammage, Grady 37
Garden Club of Houston, TX 210

Garland County, AR 57
Gates, John W. "Bet-a-Million" 228
gay rights 98
Geary, OK 148
genealogy 1, 29, 30, 49, 50, 52, 58, 59, 61-67, 69, 72, 78, 79, 83, 84, 86-88, 105, 106, 110, 118, 123, 127, 141, 143, 144, 149, 150,165, 175-181, 183, 187, 188, 191, 194, 198, 200, 203, 206, 207, 214, 224, 225, 229, 230, 232, 235, 244
genealogy--Acadian 79
genealogy--Czechoslovakia 244
geology 14, 59, 68, 77, 122, 123, 173
German Americans 107, 202, 224, 231, 238
German Immigration Society 224
Gila County, AZ--prehistory 21
Gilbert, AZ 13
Gillespie County, TX 202
Gilpin, Laura 197
glasswork crafts 46
Goddard, Robert H. 130
Goldwater, Barry, Senator 36
Graham County, AZ 32, 33
Grand Canyon, AZ 11, 14, 23
Grand Canyon University Baptist Foundation of AZ 23
Grant County, NM 136, 150
Grant Parish, LA 78
Grapevine, TX 206, 207
Gray County, TX 226
Grayson County, TX 242
Great Basin, settlement 18
Great Plains 149, 231
Grubbs, Walter 163
Gulf of Mexico 104
Guthrie, OK 148, 149
Hale, John 17
Harmon General Army Hospital, TX 220
Harrison County, TX 221
Hayden, Carl T. 36, 37
health sciences 63, 92, 204 (see also "hospitals," "medicine")
Hench, Philip 208
Henderson State University 49
Hendrix College, AR 52, 53
highways 132
Hill, John 217
Hillary, John 10
Hispanics and Mexican Americans 37, 44, 138, 209, 224, 232, 238
historians 155
historic preservation 3, 60, 74, 95, 154, 187
Hitchcock, TX 240
Hogg, Ima 210
Hohokam culture 5
Honduras 166
Hopi Indians 20
horticulture--Southern United States 87
hospitals 63, 97, 116, 117, 220, 243 (see also "health sciences," "resorts--health")

Hot Springs, AR 57, 58
Houston County, TX 184
Houston, Sam 178, 214, 219, 233
Houston, TX 209
Hoya, Joseph von der 224
Hubbell family, AZ 13
Hubbell Trading Post, AZ 13
Hunt, George W.P., Governor (AZ) 23, 37
immigration 224
Imperial County, CA 45
Incarnate Word College, San Antonio, TX 234
Indian wars 3, 196
industry 11, 58, 68, 78, 79, 82, 108, 122, 145, 147, 159, 160, 176, 178, 190, 198, 208, 217, 220, 222, 223, 225
Institute of Texan Cultures 238
inventors 219, 220
Irish Americans 215
Irish literature 160
irrigation 3, 30, 41
Irving, TX 214
Jackson County, AR 65
jazz 102, 212
Jefferson County, TX 176
Jerome, AZ 15
Jesuitica 43
Johnson County, TX 181
Johnson, Lyndon Baines 171
Johnson Space Center, Houston, TX 210, 211
Jollyville-Pond Springs, TX 170
Joplin, Janis 228
Jordan, Barbara 212
journalism 158
journalists--foreign correspondents 215
Judaism 21, 40, 99, 221
Kansas--politics 151
Kay County, OK 142
Kendall, Willmoore 215
Kennedy Assassination (FBI files) 80, 171
Kerr, Robert S. 157
Kerr-McClellan Waterway 142
King family 217
King Ranch 217
Knights of Columbus 168
La Paz County, AZ 32
labor unions 102, 103, 166, 190
Ladd, Caroline Willis 203
Lafayette, LA 81
Lafitte, Jean 219
Lake Charles, LA 82, 83
Lake Havasu City, AZ 16
Lake Powell, AZ 19
Lampland, C.O.--radiometric work 9
land tenure records 89
Laredo Archives 236
Las Cruces, NM 123, 124
Las Vegas, NM 124, 125
LaSalle Parish, LA 80
Latimer, True H. 162
Latin America 98, 114, 131

Latter Day Saints 1
law 134, 135, 160, 187
lawyers 162, 163
Lea County, NM 127
Lee County, AZ 64
LeTourneau, Robert C. 220
LeTourneau University, Longview, TX 219
life science 151
Lincoln County, NM 125, 126
Lincoln County (NM) War 126
Lincoln Parish, LA 106
Lind, Jenny 235
literature 81, 129, 140, 159, 160, 169, 182, 205, 211, 213, 223, 237, 239
Little Rock 61
livestock (see "cattle," "donkeys," "mules")
Llano Estacado 128, 227
local history 1-4, 6-8, 13, 15-17, 19, 23, 28, 30-35, 37, 38, 45-47, 49-54, 56-58, 60, 61, 63-67, 69, 71, 77-80, 83, 84, 86, 87, 106, 107, 113, 114, 118-128, 136-149, 154, 156, 157, 160, 164-166, 168, 170, 175-177, 180-188, 190-194, 196, 198, 202, 204, 206 207, 209, 214, 218, 221, 222, 224-231, 236, 237, 239, 242, 243, 245, 246, 248
Logan County, OK 149
London Bridge 16
London, Jack 108
Louisiana 61, 71-110
Louisiana College 104, 105
Louisiana Methodist Conference 108
Louisiana State University 71, 73, 75, 79, 92, 108
Louisiana Tech University 105, 106
Louisiana--American Territory 87
Louisiana--Cane River Region 87
Louisiana--colonial 82, 89, 91, 92
Louisiana--cultural history 91
Louisiana--economics 85
Louisiana--French Colonial 87
Louisiana--government 74
Louisiana--history 72, 79, 105
Louisiana--legislative records 74
Louisiana--military history 90
Louisiana--politics 73, 85, 91
Louisiana--religious life 106
Louisiana--social and cultural life 85
Louisiana--social/economic history 73, 89, 108
Lowell Observatory 9
Lowell, Percival--studies of Mars 9
Lower Colorado River 45
Loyola University 92
Lufkin, TX--photographs 221
Luhrs family 37
lumber industry 11, 79, 223
Mammoth, AZ 19
marine sciences 77
Marksville Indians 85
Matagorda County, TX 175, 230
Maxwell, George Hebard 23
McClain County, OK 157

McClintock, James H. 28
McFaddin family 176
McFarland, Ernest W. 12
McLaughlin, Herb and Dorothy 37
McNeese, John 83
McNeese State University 83
media 129, 229 (see also "communication")
medicine 63, 92, 97, 99, 101, 102, 116, 145, 182, 188, 204, 208, 221, 233, 237, 243
Menger family, San Antonio, TX 234
Mesa, AZ 17
Methodist Church 53, 120, 154, 163, 205, 216
Mexican government 125, 133
Mexican Revolution 192, 194
Mexican War (with U.S.) 166
Mexico 2, 7, 18, 39, 43-45, 98, 100, 166, 173, 190-192, 194, 236, 237, 243
Mexico--railroads 243
Mexico--Spanish Colonial period 194, 237
Middle East 131
Midvale, Frank 17
migration--Southern U.S. 214
military history 1, 3, 12, 22, 31, 45, 77, 90, 125, 129, 139, 145, 147, 153, 174, 188-190, 194-197, 227, 231
military--G.I. Bill of Rights 12
Miller County 245
Mimbreno Indians 139
Mimbres Indians 121
minerals 22
mining 1, 2, 5, 15, 16, 18, 19, 22, 23, 31, 37, 39, 42, 45, 46, 131, 136, 137, 164
minorities 53, 68
missionaries 43, 92, 98, 117, 220
missions 25, 117, 236, 246
Mississippi County, AR 66
Mississippi River Valley, lower 73
Mississippi River 57, 73
Mohave Indians 20
Montezuma, Carlos 37
Montgomery County, AR 64
Moody family 203
Moravian Church 244
Morgan City, LA 86
Mormons 1, 11
Morrison, James H., congressional papers 79
mules 189
municipal agencies 39
museum science 179
Museum of the Cherokee Strip 147
Museum of Fine Arts, Houston, TX 210
museums--education 210
music 8, 26, 35, 51, 57, 102, 164, 167, 220, 239
music and graphic arts 8
musicians 56, 102
Nacogdoches Archives (1733-1836) 173
Nacogdoches, TX 223, 224
Natchitoches, LA 87
National Aeronautics and Space Administration 210, 211
National Association of Conservation Districts 218
National Guard 22
National Park Service 5, 13, 14, 42, 58, 115, 131, 191, 196
National Register of Historic Places 60, 74
Native Americans 1, 6, 8, 11, 16, 17, 20, 21, 23, 24, 26, 28-30, 32-35, 37, 39, 41, 42, 44, 46-48, 59, 85, 98, 113-116, 121, 122, 130, 131, 135, 138, 139, 141, 147, 149, 150, 152, 155, 157, 159, 160, 164, 179, 182, 199, 231, 237, 238 (see also specific tribal names)
Native Americans--art 26, 130, 135, 138
Native Americans--law 135, 160
Native Americans--literature 26, 160
Native Americans--musicology 35, 48
natural gas industry 122
natural history 10, 14, 30, 122, 151, 227, 241, 247
natural resources 15, 42, 135
Navajo Indians 20, 48, 119, 135
naval history 201, 211
naval history--17th and 18th centuries, British 211
Neuman, Alfred R. 212
Nevada County, AR 66
New Braunfels, TX 224
New Jersey--politics 151
New Mexico Institute of Mining and Technology 137
New Mexico state government--records 133
New Mexico 40, 44, 112-139, 192, 193
New Mexico--archaeology 115
New Mexico--history 123, 124, 131, 133
New Mexico--Jews 40
New Mexico--Southwestern 121
New Mexico--statutes 123, 135
New Orleans Baptist Theological Seminary 93
New Orleans 77, 81, 88-104, 106
Newhall, Beaumont and Nancy 44
Nicholls State University 110
Nimitz, Chester William 201
No Man's Land (OK) 148
Nogales, AZ 18
nonviolence 55
Northern New Spain 43 (see also "borderlands--U.S.-Mexico")
Northwestern U.S. 237
nuclear waste--depositories 119
Nueces County, TX 183
Nuevo Leon, Mexico 190
nursing 92, 128, 237, 243
observatories--history 9
oil (see "petroleum industry")
Oklahoma 140, 142, 143, 145, 147-149, 151-160
Oklahoma City University 154
Oklahoma City 152-156
Oklahoma County 154
Oklahoma Panhandle 148
Oklahoma State University 140, 158, 159
Oklahoma Territory 155
Oklahoma--agriculture 158
Oklahoma--government 155
Oklahoma--history 140, 145, 155
Oklahoma--literature 140
Oklahoma--politics 151, 155, 158
Oklahoma--townsite case files 145
Old Independence Baptist Church 178
Old Indianola Trail, TX 247, 248
opera 94
Oracle 19
Orange, TX 225
organic farming 57
Otero County, NM 120
Ouachita Baptist University 49, 50
Ozarks--folk music 51
Pacific Ocean 201
Pacific--dance 8
Page, AZ 19
paleobotany 152
paleontology 14, 151, 173
Palfi, Morgan 44
Panhandle, TX 184
parks and monuments 6, 12-15, 18, 32, 34, 47, 58, 77, 115, 131, 139, 191, 196, 197
Pawnee County, OK 156
Payne County, OK--cemetery listss/histories 143
peace--studies 54, 55
Pecos Valley, NM 128
Permian Basin, TX 225
petroleum industry 68, 82, 108, 122, 147, 160, 220, 225
philanthropy 99, 244
philately 41
Phillips University, OK 146
Philmont Ranch and Philmont Scout Ranch 120
Phoenix, AZ 28, 35
Phoenix Gazette 28
photography, history of 43, 113, 131, 149, 169, 170, 197, 221
physicians 97, 101, 116, 204, 208, 231, 237 (see also "health sciences," "medicine")
Pike County, AR 64, 65
Pima, AZ 30
pioneers 1, 11, 17, 18, 30, 31, 47, 117, 145, 149, 160, 245
Pittsburg County, OK 150
Plains Indians 147, 160, 226
plantation life and culture 67, 73, 87, 99, 100, 108, 110
Polish Americans 215
political philosophy 215

Pomerene, AZ 1
Pontotoc County, OK 140
Pope John Paul II--1987 visit to the U.S. 232
Port Arthur, TX 228
Porter, Eliot 197
portraiture 113
postal history 41
Pottawatomie County, OK 157, 158
Powell, John Wesley 20
power systems 30
Powhatan House, TX 203
Presbyterian Church 27, 117, 167
Prescott, AZ 31, 66, 105
printing arts 182, 194
prisoners of war--German 220
prisons and prisoners 46
Pueblo Indians 115, 118, 135
Pulaski County, AR 61
Purcell, OK 157
Quartzsite, AZ 31, 32
race relations 98
Rader, Lloyd E. 145
radio 125, 162, 219, 228
Ragsdale, M.C. 231
railroads 4, 31, 34, 57, 131, 158, 162, 178, 188, 194, 227, 243, 245
ranches--dude (see "tourism--guest ranches")
ranching 1, 5, 11, 16, 18, 23, 31, 34, 39, 46, 145, 160, 163, 164, 176, 179, 188, 198, 203, 217, 220, 222, 231
Randolph County, AR 66
Reconstruction 91
Red River, LA 108
Reed, Stephen 31
religion 50, 60, 62, 93, 99, 112, 117, 119, 162-165, 167-169, 178, 200
religious communities 81, 88, 89, 96, 104 (see also "religion" and names of specific orders)
Remuda Ranch, AZ 46
resorts--health 19, 58
Revolutionary War 65
Rhodes, John J. 37
rice industry 78, 176
Rice University 211
Richardson, TX 229
Rio Grande Valley 190
Riordan family 10
Robertson Colony (Texas) 166
Roe, E. 235
Rogers, William 215
Roman Catholic Church (see Catholic Church)
Roosevelt County, NM 127
Roswell, NM 129
Round Rock, TX 230
Roundtop, TX 231
Runestone, Heavener 157
Rusk County, TX 207
Sabine Parish, LA 84
Sacramento Mountains, NM 120
Saguaro National Monument, AZ 42
Salado culture 32

Saline County, AR 51
Salt River Reclamation Project Dam, AZ 30
San Angelo, TX 231
San Antonio, TX 233-237, 239
San Juan County, NM 119, 123
San Luis Potosi Archives 236
San Pedro Valley, AZ 2
Sandoval County, NM 118
Santa Fe Railroad Hospital, TX 243
Santa Fe Trail 137, 148
Schleicher County, TX 191
science and technology, 9, 112, 170, 211
science fiction 127
Scott and White Memorial Hospital, TX 243
Scottsdale, AZ 33
Seminole Indians 150
Seton, Ernest Thompson 120
Shackelford County, TX 164
Sharp County, AR 50
Shepperd, John Ben 225
Sherman, TX 242
shipping industry--Lake Pontchartrain, LA 79
Sierra County, NM 139
Silver City, NM 137
Simmons, James B. 162
Sisters of Mercy 96
Sisters of the Holy Family 96
Skull Valley, AZ 34
slavery 73, 76 (see also "African Americans," "plantation life and culture")
Slavonic benevolent societies 244
Smith County, TX 245
social agencies--Jewish 21
social history 88, 91, 102, 114, 145
social reform 92
Society of Jesus, New Orleans Province of 92
Society of Mary, St. Louis Province of 236
sociology 115
Sonora, Mexico 32, 39, 45
Soule University 180
South America 173
South Plains--history 184
Southern Baptist Convention 22, 23
Southern University 75, 96, 212
Southwestern Baptist Theological Seminary 199, 200
Southwestern U.S. 7, 8, 15, 17, 20, 21, 26, 29, 31, 35-37, 39, 40, 42-44, 81, 112, 114, 116, 117, 120, 123, 124, 127, 130-133, 136, 166, 173, 174, 192, 199, 220, 231, 237, 239, 240 (see also "borderlands--U.S.-Mexico")
space exploration 211
space sciences 112, 130
Spanish American War 125
Spanish exploration 15
Spanish government--documents 125, 133

spas (see "bathing industry," "resorts--health")
Spiro Mounds, OK 157
Springer, NM 137
St. Edwards University 171
St. Joseph's Abbey 107
St. Joseph's Abbey and Seminary College 107
St. Mary's Parish, LA 87
St. Mary's University, San Antonio, TX 236
Stauffer, Thomas M. 212
steamboats 45, 99 (see also "shipping industry")
Stephen F. Austin State University 223
Sterne, Eva 224
Sterne-Hoya House, TX 224
Stilwell, Arthur 228
Strand, Paul 44
strawberry industry 79
Strecker Museum, Waco, TX 247
Sul Ross State University 164
Sun City, AZ 25
Superstition Mountains, AZ 1
Sydnor, John Seabrook 203
synagogues (see "Judaism")
Tamaulipas, Mexico 190
Taos, NM 138
Tarrant County, TX 198, 200
telegraph 228
television 55, 139, 162, 228
Tempe, AZ 37
Temple Houston 160
Temple Sanitarium 243
Temple, TX 243
Texana 185, 205, 216, 217, 225, 234, 237, 239
Texarkana 244, 245
Texas 40, 44, 162-166, 168-176, 178, 179, 181-183, 185-187, 189, 190, 192-194, 196, 198, 200-209, 211-231, 233-239, 241-245,247
Texas and Pacific Railroad 245
Texas Catholic Conference 168
Texas Christian University 200, 201
Texas Instruments Incorporated 187
Texas Memorial Museum 172, 173
Texas Panhandle 179, 227
Texas Regional Historical Resource Depository 194, 209, 219, 223
Texas, Republic of 170, 175, 204, 233
Texas, South 182, 183, 190, 235
Texas Tech University 220
Texas Woman's University 189
Texas--Colonial 233, 237
Texas--government 173
Texas--history 166, 174, 177, 182, 183, 185, 201, 211, 225, 227, 233-236, 238, 239, 242, 247
Texas--public lands 172
Texas--railroads 243
Texas--state agency records 173
Texas--Trans-Pecos region 164
textiles 48, 179

theater 83, 169, 170, 191, 201
Tombstone, AZ 38
Tonto National Monument, AZ 32
tourism 11, 46, 58
tourism--guest ranches 19, 46
Touro Hospital, LA 97
Tower, John Goodwin 205
trading posts 122
trail drives 198
trans-Mississippi 54, 61, 152
transportation 4, 109, 132, 145, 221
travel guides--Southwest 28
Travis County, TX 168
Truth or Consequences, NM 138, 139
Tubac, AZ 38
tuberculosis sanatoria 116
Tulane University 101
U.S. Air Force 233
U.S. Army 12, 195, 197, 220
U.S. Navy 201
U.S.-Mexico border 194, 236, 237
U.S.--Congress 174
U.S.--legal records 199
U.S.--presidents 171
U.S.--vice-presidents 171
U.S.--War Department 12
unidentified flying objects 241
United Church of Christ (Congregationalist) 98
United Methodist Church 53, 120, 154, 163, 216
University of Texas at Arlington 166
University of Central Oklahoma 145
University of Texas at Austin 169, 174
University of Dallas 214, 215
University of Texas Health Science Center 237
University of Houston 212, 213
University of Texas Medical Branch 204, 205
University of New Mexico 114, 116-118, 128, 138
University of North Texas 189, 190
University of Texas of the Permian Basin 225
University of Southwestern Louisiana 81, 82
Upper Gulf Coast 204
Upshur County, TX 206
urban life 100
Ursilines 103
utilities 30
Verde Valley 3
Vernon Parish, LA 83
Victoria, TX 246
Victorian era 246
Vietnam War--literature 160
Villa Raid 121
violence 55
visual literacy 37
Waller County, TX 230
War of 1812 77
Ward family 176
warships 201

Washington County, TX 56, 180
Waste Isolation Pilot Project (WIPP) 119
water 5, 11, 17, 18, 23, 28, 37, 41, 158, 218, 246
waterways 99 (see also "canals")
Wayland Baptist University 227
Wends 206
Westmoreland Farms, TX 177
Weston, Edward 44
Wharton County, TX 230
White, Amelia Elizabeth 134
White County, AR 67
Wickenburg, AZ 46
Wickenburg, Henry 46
Willcox, AZ 47
Williamson County, TX 170
windmills 179
Winogrand, Garry 44
Wisconsin--politics 151
Wise County, TX 187
Witte Museum 239
Wolcott, Marion Post 44
Wolfe, Thomas 162
women 53, 101, 189, 190, 208
women in medicine 101
women in military 189
Woodruff County, AR 63
Woodward, OK 160
World War I 160
World War II 201
WPA 76, 155
Xavier University of Louisiana 104
Yavapai County, AZ 31
York, Captain John 248
Yorktown, TX 248
Yuma County, AZ 45
Yuma Territorial Prison, AZ 46
Zavala, Adina De 234

NAME OF INSTITUTION: _____
STREET ADDRESS: _____
_____
MAILING ADDRESS: _____
_____
CITY, STATE, ZIP CODE: _____
TELEPHONE:_____ FAX:_____ E-MAIL:_____

NAME AND TITLE OF PERSON COMPLETING QUESTIONNAIRE
_____

PLEASE ANSWER ALL QUESTIONS THAT APPLY TO YOUR INSTITUTION

TYPE OF INSTITUTION

1. ___Archives   ___Historical Society   ___Library   ___Museum
   ___Other:_____

2. ___Federal   ___State   ___County/Local   ___City
   ___Academic ___Business ___Religious   ___Special
   ___Other:_____

DAYS/HOURS OF OPERATION: _____

ACCESS
___Open to the general public   ___Not open to the general public
___Public access by appointment only   ___Other:_____

PUBLIC SERVICE
___In-person reference   ___Mail reference   ___Phone reference   ___Fee for reference
___Photocopies   ___Other reproduction service:_____
Service restrictions:_____

COLLECTION INFORMATION
Primary collection focus: _____

Main topic(s) of holdings. Please use terms that will index well, preferably LC subject headings. Attach separate sheet if necessary.

_____   _____   _____
_____   _____   _____

Inclusive dates:_____   Total volume:_____

Collection format(s) (Please give approximate volume, indicating whether l.f., c.f., items, etc.)
_____Manuscript collections   _____Government Records
_____Institution's records   _____Photographs
_____Books/serials   _____Maps
_____Pamphlets/ephemera   _____Oral histories
_____Films/videotapes   _____Electronic records
Other:_____
Please list any of the above that circulate:_____

How are your holdings descr[ibed?]
___Card catalog   ___Database software
___OPAC (on-line public ac[cess catalog])   ___Repository guide
Other:_____

If database, name software u[sed:]
_____

If OPAC, name of system use[d:]

Computerized finding aids ar[e:]

Which of the following do yo[u use/receive?]
___NUCMC ___RLIN ___[...]   ___[Profession]al journal(s)
Other:_____

STAFF (Please give number [of staff])
Professional:
___Administrative   ___Map curator
___Photo curator   ___[Ot]her:_____

Non-professional
___Volunteer/docent   ___[Ot]her:_____

Professional development acti[vities]
___Tuition/registration reimbu[rsement]   [percenta]ge paid:___
___Payment of dues for professional organization memberships
___Reimbursement for professional meeting(s) registration___ and/or travel___
___In-house workshops on a regular basis
___Payment for mailings   ___Payment for telephone use
___Use of facilities and equipment permitted   ___Use of clerical staff permitted

SPECIAL SERVICES/PROGRAMS
___Classes   ___Exhibits   ___Fundraising/Endowment   ___Lectures/presentations
___Newsletter   ___Tours   Other:_____

FACILITIES/EQUIPMENT/PRESERVATION
___Disaster preparedness plan   ___Fire detection controls   ___Fire extinguishing system
___Humidity controls   ___Preservation lab   ___Temperature controls

PATRON USE INFORMATION (Number per fiscal year)
___In-house patrons   ___Telephone patrons   ___Mail reference requests
___Collections used   ___Reference photocopies   ___Microfilm/fiche copies
___User statistics not kept

IF YOU KNOW OF ANY INTERESTING ARCHIVAL COLLECTIONS THAT WE HAVE OMITTED BECAUSE OF THEIR SMALL SIZE, OUT OF THE WAY LOCATION, UNUSUAL HOLDINGS, ETC., PLEASE GIVE US THEIR NAMES AND ADDRESSES BELOW.